THE SUPPLY ORGANISATION OF THE GERMAN AIR FORCE, 1935 — 1945

I0270453

19/29 Woburn Place,
London, W.C.1.

7th November, 1946.

BCR/DO/408

Dear Butler

    I have received a copy of the publication on " The Supply Organisation of the German Air Force", which I have read with the greatest interest, and wish to congratulate you and thank you for the part you played in this work.

    I was most impressed throughout the work with the broad outlook displayed by those who wrote on all subjects and, frankly, I did not realise that so many people had so keen a grasp of the problems of production and provisioning in their broadest sense.

Yours sincerely,

[signature]

Squadron Leader R.L. Butland,
  C/o Headquarters, Air Division (Rear),
    B.A.F.O., Detmold, B.A.O.R.

DISARMAMENT
BRANCH OF THE
BRITISH AIR DIVISION

THE SUPPLY ORGANISATION OF THE GERMAN AIR FORCE 1935 — 1945

The Naval & Military Press Ltd

Published by
The Naval & Military Press Ltd
Unit 10 Ridgewood Industrial Park,
Uckfield, East Sussex,
TN22 5QE England
Tel: +44 (0) 1825 749494
Fax: +44 (0) 1825 765701
www.naval-military-press.com
www.military-genealogy.com
www.militarymaproom.com

*In reprinting in facsimile from the original, any imperfections are inevitably reproduced
and the quality may fall short of modern type and cartographic standards.*

THE SUPPLY ORGANISATION OF THE GERMAN AIR FORCE
TABLE OF CONTENTS

	Page
FOREWORD	VII
PREFACE	XIV
INTRODUCTION	XVI

PART 1

CHAPTER I:	The Supreme Command of the Armed Forces	1
CHAPTER II:	The Ministry of Armaments and War Production	13
CHAPTER III:	The Organisation of the German Air Force	29
CHAPTER IV:	The Air Ministry	37
CHAPTER V:	The Organisation of Supply in the Field	47
CHAPTER VI:	A Summarized Survey of the German Air Force Organisation: Its Merits and Defects, with Particular Reference to its Bearing on Supply	65

PART 2

CHAPTER I:	Details of Air Ministry Departments Connected with Supply	97
CHAPTER II:	Production and Provisioning	117
CHAPTER III:	Financial Control	151
CHAPTER IV:	Selection and Training of Personnel Employed in Supply and Technical Positions	161
CHAPTER V:	Movement	171
CHAPTER VI:	Motor Transport	187
CHAPTER VII:	Field Installations	195
CHAPTER VIII:	Repair and Salvage	227
CHAPTER IX:	Inspection	239
CHAPTER X:	Campaign in the Ukraine	247
CHAPTER XI:	Identification of Equipment	271

FOREWORD

AN ACCOUNT OF THE WORK INVOLVED IN COMPILING THIS STUDY OF THE G.A.F. SUPPLY ORGANISATION

AT first, the work of collecting information about the supply services of the G.A.F. was a subsidiary task of the Disarmament Branch of the Air Division, undertaken in response to a request from the Director General of Equipment for any interesting information on the G.A.F. system that might come to light during the general task of disarmament. This work was appropriately assigned to a section of the Disarmament Branch known as "Ministerial Control" because that section had already found it necessary to make a study of the ministerial organisation in the G.A.F., partly in order to keep all sections of the Disarmament Branch informed of equipment intelligence in the Luftwaffe, but, more particularly, to enable the section to discharge the task which, in theory, it would require to undertake when the Air Division reached Germany, viz., the control of such G.A.F. ministerial departments as remained intact at the time of the surrender. As events turned out, however, no ministerial departments were found intact and the Ministerial Control section found the only work it had left to do was to compile an authentic account of the supply system of the G.A.F. The first reaction to the sudden disappearance of the main task of the Ministerial Control section was an impulse to reduce staff drastically, leaving only the number which it was originally anticipated would be sufficient to carry out the subsidiary task of studying the supply system. On examining the means by which a proper study could be made, however, it became evident for several reasons that a complete reversal of this policy would be most likely to produce the best result. Chief amongst these reasons was the fact that most of the important prisoners of war and records, from which it was anticipated the necessary information could be extracted, were in the American Zone. The Americans were pushing ahead very rapidly with disbandment of personnel and the disposal of records, leaving the R.A.F. investigating staff working against time to exploit these sources of information. Furthermore, as the various Luftwaffe supply establishments had either been overrun in the fighting and destroyed, looted and wrecked by Displaced Persons, or suffered various degrees of disintegration from both causes, it became evident that the sooner an investigation of what remained was carried out the more complete would be the picture of these establishments. Moreover, unless this was done without delay there would be almost nothing left to examine but odd buildings converted to other uses. Consequently, it was decided that it would be better to increase temporarily the number of staff employed on the work and make an intensive effort and then decrease the staff rapidly when the main collection and write-up of material had been achieved. This was done and, for a time, as many as five officers were employed on various portions of the work.

2. The first phase therefore consisted in the rapid investigation of as wide a field as possible. Visits were paid to Denmark, Berchtesgaden and Frankfurt to interrogate the Germans and study records, and also to a number of places in the British Zone at which there had been Luftwaffe supply establishments. Each officer engaged on the work was assigned a

separate aspect to study and was attached, as circumstances dictated, to various Allied formations to further this work. One went to the Americans at Frankfurt to be alongside Field Intelligence Agency Technical in order to learn how the Luftwaffe supply system was connected to Speer's Ministry; one joined the British Army team of officers which was studying the organisation of O.K.W., his object being to see what part O.K.W. played in directing the activities of the Luftwaffe; and then, in September, another officer was attached to the Combined British and American Intelligence Party in England to continue investigations begun with the same party at Berchtesgarden.

3. Incidentally, during the time that this Party was located in Berchtesgarden the Americans were in charge of it; all the prisoners there undergoing interrogation were prisoners of the Americans and the records on which the Party were working were found in the American Zone. The tendency, therefore, was for the Americans, once they had extracted what they wanted, to agitate for the winding up of the interrogations and for the disbandment of personnel and disposal of records. However, as a concession to British needs they allowed certain selected P.O.W.s to be taken for a short time to England, together with the records, for exploitation.

4. Throughout the study, many difficulties and obstacles were encountered and some were such that they have seriously reduced the value of the study as a whole; for example, a negligible number of supply records have been found. The German ministerial departments, headquarters staffs, and supply establishments were so thorough in obeying orders to destroy records that it has been impossible to reconstruct the full detailed working of a single ministerial department or section, or other supply formation. Consequently, it has not been possible to make any comparisons whatever on some of the matters which would have been of particular interest to those for whom the study is written. For example, General Seibt, the Director of Supply, who was approximately equivalent to D.G.E. in the R.A.F., said that he himself destroyed all the most important data and statistics on the supply of equipment that were held, such as unserviceability of aircraft awaiting spares, percentages of non-availability over various ranges of spares, programmes for future supplies, and various supply plans to cater for future operational commitments. Similarly, no trace could be found of useful statistics about field formations such as depots and parks, e.g. tonnage outputs and numbers of issues and receipts per head, details of female substitution, and so on. Mention has already been made, in paragraph 3, of the difficulties which resulted from the fact that most of the important prisoners of war and such records as did exist were located in the American Zone, but it must also be mentioned that American hustling and pressing caused very much more than mere inconvenience. It also meant that the investigating party was forced to devote a disproportionate amount of time in the early stages of the work to a single aspect of the study at the expense of other aspects. By the time the important prisoners of war in American hands had been systematically interrogated it was found that, amongst the lesser personalities in both British and American Zones, practically all those in key positions in field formations had already been disbanded and could not be traced for interrogation.

5. Another rather surprising, but nevertheless real, difficulty encountered was that frequently German officers in important positions were distinctly less well-informed on their own job than are their counterparts in the Royal Air Force. (An opinion on the reasons for this is expressed in Part 1,

Chapter VI, paras. 62 to 65). In addition it was soon discovered that, even with those whose reputation for efficiency and knowledge stood high with their companions, their ability to make clear and straightforward appreciations of matters within their province was far lower than might reasonably be expected. With few exceptions they were addicted to many of the linguistic faults for which the Germans are notorious. Tedious long-winded vapourings, with sentences half-a-page long of inextricable complexity, couched in high flown language, and in some cases further obscured by entirely irrelevant poetical allusions, gave translators and interpreters an almost impossible task. So prevalent were these weaknesses that the impression was gained that many of these officers mistook a capacity for involved and extravagant language for real professional and literary ability. It seems probable that a natural national bias towards heavy, tortuous and also romantic thought and language was unconsciously strengthened and encouraged during their training by their tutors' failure to insist on simplicity, economy, and moderation of language.

6. It is of some interest in this connection to glance at the somewhat long extract of an extraordinary document produced by the 8th Department of the German Air Ministry on the qualities required of the General Staff officer. This extract is given at the end of this foreword. Quite apart from the fact that it would be a naive mentality that could seriously believe in the possibility of the existence of such a paragon as the ideal Staff officer depicted, the language used may fairly be described as romantic verbiage; scarcely a good pattern for the rarefied level of the German General staff.

7. But language difficulties were not confined to the Germans' inability to express themselves clearly. None of the investigating party had more than a schoolboy's knowledge of German and so complete reliance had to be placed on Service interpreters. These interpreters, though usually competent linguists, were of course unacquainted with the peculiarities of either German or British supply organisations and consequently were frequently unable to follow the drift of the interrogations. The result was that laborious explanations of the British system often had to be given to them to enable them to understand what it was that the interrogation sought to obtain from the Germans. It was inevitable therefore that misunderstandings should arise and wrong information be obtained which subsequently had to be corrected by further interrogations. They also had to acquire familiarity with specialised equipment terminology, both German and British. In consequence the work of collecting information was a slow and laborious process.

8. It may be of some interest to record the methods employed in dealing with the Germans and also the variety of conditions encountered in carrying out the investigations.

9. It was soon evident that the prescribed procedure for conducting interrogations of prisoners of war required considerable modification and intelligent application, to obtain the best results. It was useless to employ the interpreters to translate verbatim phrase by phrase. Not only did the conversation become extremely stilted but it also created a courtlike atmosphere of formality to which prisoners reacted unfavourably. Even at the expense of relevancy it was advisable to allow the interpreter and the German unhampered conversation until they became accustomed to each other's turn of phrase and until the German was at ease. With few exceptions the Germans talked freely, and often with obvious relief, once they were put at ease. The usual procedure adopted was for the

interrogating officer to make notes of the discussion and afterwards write up his understanding of the matter and also set the German the task of preparing a paper on the subject. The two accounts were then compared and differences between them settled by subsequent interrogations. Sometimes this was impossible, as, for instance, when two officers set out to obtain information in the Schleswig area about field formations. The German officer selected for interrogation was an Oberst (Group Captain) installed in ideal conditions at a former Luftwaffe Headquarters. He could give very little assistance but referred the interrogating officers to a German Beamte (official) at the same headquarters. He in turn referred them to another Beamte recently disbanded and living as a civilian on the outskirts of Hamburg. From there they were passed on to yet another Beamte, also a civilian, living on the other side of Hamburg. Each one added a little more information until at last they ended with a former subordinate of the last Beamte. This man had been a Depot foreman and he was able to supply all the information needed. The interrogation was conducted in a large house in which about 30 German families were living. It was midwinter and the long interrogation took place in great discomfort in an unheated attic bathroom converted into a miserable little living room.

10. By contrast other interrogating officers met with ideal conditions, as for example at Berchtesgarden, where they interviewed a group of German Staff officers in an American Intelligence centre. This centre had previously been one of Hitler's permanent war-time operational headquarters. Built before the war ostensibly as a girls' boarding school, it provided perfect working conditions. Installed there were not only a large number of German documents, valuable for reference purposes, but also many experienced secretaries from the German Air Ministry (several bilingual) who greatly assisted the German Staff officers to prepare papers and appreciations for the interrogating team in the shortest possible time.

11. Not all expeditions, however, met with such a smooth path as this one, nor were as successful, albeit accidentally, as the one to Hamburg. There were many which were entirely fruitless. Equipment which according to the latest intelligence should have been available for inspection at such and such a site in the American Zone was found on arrival to have been dismantled and sent away to America. Prisoners of war who, it was anticipated, would be able to supply missing links in the chain of information had been disbanded as civilians from the prisoner of war centre to which the interrogating officers were directed, and it was a commonplace experience to arrive at one-time Equipment depots, parks or holdings only to find they had suffered such destruction as to make them valueless for information purposes.

12. Added to these difficulties was the fact that a good deal of abortive work in connection with the translation of German documents and publications was unavoidable. Translators lacking in knowledge of what did and what did not constitute valuable information to the investigating team often spent much time on material which at first sight promised to be relevant but which finally yielded nothing of real value. On one occasion it was necessary to investigate the contents of a whole library of publications found at a German supply depot but the results were most disappointing.

13. Finally as an aid to the reader it is necessary to mention two facts about this publication. The first is that throughout it there is a certain amount of repetition of information. Whilst this is a disadvantage to anyone who intends to read the entire work, it is a distinct advantage to

those (no doubt the majority) who will only wish to read certain chapters. It enables each chapter to be read as a separate subject, more or less complete in itself, because sufficient background information is given in summarised form to show how the particular subject fits into the general scheme of the organisation of supply. The second fact is that certain comparisons have been drawn between the Royal Air Force and the German Air Force system of supply and opinions expressed as a result of these comparisons. It should be borne in mind that these opinions are based on the personal appreciation of the German system made by the staff responsible for the investigations. Their opportunities for forming their opinion were unique and the information on which they are based cannot be checked or verified, since it was gained by interrogation of many German officers and officials each of whose statements was used to cross-check the remainder. The cross-checking was done carefully and methodically, however, and it can therefore be taken that the bases on which the comparisons have been drawn are factual so far as can possibly be ascertained.

"The General Staff Officer"

A forthright personality with well defined qualities of leadership, who is a master of his calling and who is generally recognised as having proved his worth in action, is one bearing the stamp of the General Staff Officer.

His ability and bearing should call forth respect and recognition.

This respect and recognition will be all the greater if the officer shows that his innate vigour and elasticity can triumph with a minimum of rest over all the burdens of war. Highly developed powers of physical resistance and sound nerves are therefore essential conditions.

His knowledge of flying and his familiarity with it must remain at the required level.

The ability to tackle skilfully and with rapid and penetrating mental application the tasks which fall to an advisor of the command authorities, and to solve problems in advance by applying to them a sense of the essential, is one of the capabilities taken for granted in the General Staff Officer.

He must be capable of composing orders clearly and quickly in all situations, orders adapted to the aim in view and the details of the moment.

For this purpose it is just as necessary that the officer be well acquainted with military practice and routine as that he be inspired with enthusiasm for General Staff service, diligence and a degree of knowledge which cannot be too profound or all-embracing.

Only a few rules of land and naval war can be applied to air warfare. Constant and sustained care is therefore required to evolve the basic principles of successful air war, to digest them mentally and convert them into practical recommendations and to apply them.

Staff College training provides the mental basis for this purpose and broadens the view.

It is above all experience of life and of war itself which make the most valuable contribution to the education and training of the Staff Officer. The General Staff Officer will find in his period of service as a unit commander, and in the practical experience gained through General Staff service in front-line staffs, the strongest foundations on which to build his ability.

War reveals every inadequacy and fault. Thus it is frequently only in the heat of the struggle that the value of knowledge and ability is recognised.

This experience demonstrates what the aim of training should be. War measures with the standards of the enemy. Superior worth ensures victory over superior numbers.

Knowledge is therefore not an aim in itself on the one hand or a secondary matter which one can safely neglect on the other. Rather it is an indispensable weapon of war.

To forge this weapon for his own use and to strengthen others with it is therefore the duty of the General Staff Officer whatever post he may fill.

To understand sequences of cause and effect, to prognosticate consequences and to develop a just sense for the weighing of imponderabilia, to say nothing of the translation of such ability into practice, must prove impracticable without knowledge born of appropriate training.

That less appreciative evaluation of knowledge which one sometimes chances upon must be recognised and rejected by the General Staff Officer in the light of his experience as contrary to the requirements of war. He should appreciate clearly that lack of mental training today may mean the loss of a battle tomorrow.

Thus his life and service will be free from sterile and empty periods and will be filled with tireless striving for progress and betterment.

Intellects so strengthened and enlightened will be able to analyse the principles which great men have relied upon in fighting their battles and with the aid of which they have succeeded in overcoming the odds with which they were faced.

This requires the employment of all spiritual and physical powers. It is through this criterion that the best are selected. The choice is predetermined by the character in question which either has or has not this capacity.

The evenness of disposition which Clausewitz speaks of as the attribute of the military genius consists in achieving the correct relationship between the application of intellect and of feeling.

Action is motivated by the joy of creative work in the service of the whole.

The ambition of the General Staff Officer should be to make complete and comprehensive preparations with a view to success in action and to develop the art of recognising every possible hitch in advance and nullifying it.

This demands constant and concious practice on the small as on the large scale.

His watchword should be not the bureaucratic rut but fruitful and productive work.

As a natural consequence of his education he should be bold of thought, exact in his handling of details and capable of sure decisions even in completely unexpected situations.

For the final word in the prosecution of war still lies with the bold decision. Half measures and uncertainty and hesitancy in action ruin everything. The outcome of a struggle is often the result of a moment in which a stroke of genius brings about the decision and turns even the most unimportant action towards the goal.

Abundance of daily work should not be allowed to clip the wings of the spirit but should on the contrary send it soaring to new heights in the joyous consciousness of its sovereign mastery of the ever-changing sequence of events.

In all his work the tact and discretion of the General Staff Officer should spread the required influence about him.

He should derive new strength for this purpose from the close contact which he must maintain with the troops.

THE SUPPLY ORGANISATION IN THE GERMAN AIR FORCE

PREFACE

1. The aim of this Preface is to explain the design of the publication and to make some reference to the sources of information.

2. In Part 1 five chapters are devoted to a broad survey of the German organisation for supply. A sixth chapter sums up the advantages and weaknesses of the German system and makes certain recommendations that are derived from an examination of German experience. This chapter has been written so that it may be read, if necessary, without previous knowledge of the rest of the publication. In Part 2 there are eleven chapters which develop in greater detail certain subjects mentioned in Part 1. These subjects have been selected because of their particular importance in the organisation of supply.

3. Information has been obtained from the following sources: —
   - (i) Interrogation of officers of the German General Staff;*
   - (ii) Interrogation of German ministry officials and industrialists;*
   - (iii) Visits to German Headquarters and Units and interrogation of appropriate personnel;
   - (iv) Translations of German official publications and documents;
   - (v) Reports prepared by F.I.A.T., C.I.O.S., Air Ministry A.I. 12, and miscellaneous bodies and agencies.

* NOTE: For details of individuals interrogated see next page.

List of Persons Interrogated in the German Air Force Supply Organisation

Rank	Name	Main Subject of Equipment
Feldmarschal	Milch	Directorate General of Equipment
General	Dorstling	Supply in general
Generalleutnant	Von Criegern	The work of the Quartermaster General
Generalmajor	Christian	Relationship between the Operations Staff and Supply Staffs
Generalmajor	Schultz	Campaign in the Ukraine
Generalmajor	Seibt	The work of the Director of Supply
Generalmajor	Uebe	The work of a Luftflotte Quartermaster
Generalmajor	Buhle	The O.K.W. Armed Forces Armaments Department
General Oberstabsintendant	Plagemann	Administration
General Intendant	Winterhoff	The "Beampte" system
Diploma Ingenieur	Dorsch	Organisation of the Speer Ministry and the Production of Air Armaments
Diploma Ingenieur	Saur	
Diploma Ingenieur	Nobel	
Oberst	Christ	The War in Spain
Oberst	Von Dawans	Q.M.G. Department 4
Oberst	Eschenauer	Q.M.G. Department 6
Oberst	Prilipp	The Directorate of M/T
Oberst	Reichard	The Luftgau Quartermaster
Oberst	Ruhsert	Depot Organisation
Oberst	Engels	O.K.W. Quartermaster General
Oberst	Ehrhardt	Equipment Groups
Oberst Ingenieur	Seegebarth	Airfield Organisation
Ministerial Dirigent	Muller	Financial Control
Oberst Leutnant	Heubner	O.K.W. Organisation
Oberst Leutnant	Schraeder	
Oberst Leutnant	Riesterer	G.A.F. Liaison with O.K.W.
Major	Jacobi	Q.M.G. Department 6
Major	Platt	Repair and Salvage
Major	Stimpel	Equipment Groups
Hauptmann	Kamprat	Movement
Oberstabs Ingenieur	Kubler	Identification of Equipment
Oberstabs Ingenieur	Schink	Explosives
Oberstabs Ingenieur	Kiel	Identification of Equipment
Oberstabs Ingenieur	Otto	
Civilian Employee (Depot Foreman)	Baudach	Organisation of Air Parks

THE SUPPLY ORGANISATION OF THE GERMAN AIR FORCE.

INTRODUCTION.

1.   The object of this publication is to describe the supply organisation of the German Air Force and to examine the weaknesses and advantages of the system. In this way the Royal Air Force is presented with the opportunity to assess in retrospect the value of the supply organisation of its late enemy and may possibly be able to derive benefit from such knowledge.

2.   A supply system for a particular force is considerably influenced by the design of the operational side of that force and by the political motives that direct the use of the force. Throughout this publication, therefore, attention has been paid to these factors and they have been emphasised in Part 1, Chapter VI, which summarises critically the merits and defects of the German Air Force.

3.   The term "supply" in the present context is used to include the whole concept of matters concerned with making war material available to the users — war economy, procurement, distribution, storage, maintenance and repairs, accounting, and the training and employment of supply personnel.

4.   In equipping an air force, or any other military force, there are certain common factors which form the basic principles of supply and these principles, which are as follows, will be selected to form the framework of this publication:—

(i) The allocation to the Services of priorities in the nation's productive capacity and resources of raw materials;
(ii) The transformation of planned strategy into terms of war material;
(iii) The relationship of the individual service arms to industry;
(iv) The allocation of war materials within the individual services;
(v) The distribution, in accordance with the allocations, and the build-up and maintenance of reserves;
(vi) The care, repair, and salvage of war materials;
(vii) The financial control of funds allocated to the procurement of war materials.

5.   The application of these principles to a study of the German Air Force supply system determines a logical division of Part 1 of this publication into the following Chapters:

Chapter I   : The Supreme Command of the Armed Forces.
Chapter II   : The Ministry of Armaments and War Production.
Chapter III : The Organisation of the German Air Force.
Chapter IV   : The Air Ministry.
Chapter V   : The Organisation of Supply in the Field.

PART 1

CHAPTER I

THE SUPREME COMMAND OF THE ARMED FORCES

INTRODUCTION	Paragraphs	1—6
Development of the Supreme Command	,,	4—6
GERMAN WAR ECONOMY 1933—1942	,,	7—17
The Relationship between Service Development and German Economy	,,	8
The Directorate of Defence Economy and Armament	,,	9—10
The Armament Inspectorates and Commands	,,	11
The Ministry of Armaments and Ammunition	,,	12
The Effect of the Directorate of Defence Economy and Armaments on the German Air Force	,,	13
Summary	,,	14
Weaknesses in German Economy prior to 1942	,,	15—17
HANDLING OF COMMON SERVICE SUPPLY PROBLEMS	,,	18—30
Common User Items	,,	18
Clothing	,,	19
Motor Transport	,,	20
Movement	,,	21—24
Trends to Increase Central Control by the Supreme Command	,,	25—30
CONCLUSION	,,	31—33

PART I

CHAPTER I : THE SUPREME COMMAND OF THE ARMED FORCES

INTRODUCTION

THE Supreme Command of the Armed Forces (Oberkommando der Wehrmacht — OKW) was intended to be the supreme authority in all the military affairs of Germany. The Army, the Navy, and the Air Force, which existed independently of each other, were subordinate to this higher command.

2. The function of the Supreme Command in the sphere of supply was primarily to develop German economy in accordance with the needs of war, to co-ordinate service production programmes in the light of common strategy and to control the allocation to the services of raw materials. These tasks were undertaken by a department called the Directorate of Defence Economy and Armaments. In 1942, however, this Directorate was transferred to the Ministry of Armaments and Munitions and the Supreme Command lost all responsibility for these matters. The history of German war economy from 1933 to 1942 will, therefore, be dealt with in this Chapter and the period from 1942 to 1945 will be covered in Chapter II, entitled "The Ministry of Armaments and War Production".

3. The Supreme Command also acted as a central agency for the procurement of certain items for the three services. There were also departments, the Directorate of Armed Forces Transportation and the Home Staff for Overseas, which unified the direction of "Movements" for the services.

Development of the Supreme Command

4. The idea of a Supreme Command emanated from Hitler and, prior to 1934, no such organisation existed. From 1920 to 1934 the Minister of Defence was the arbitrator for the Army and Navy and during this period the Army, which was traditionally the Senior Service, was the dominating influence in the affairs of war and was responsible for the grand strategical planning of the nation.

5. In 1934 German militarism was resurrected by the reintroduction of conscription and by the formation of an organisation which emerged in February 1935 as the newly born Luftwaffe. These two developments naturally initiated a flood of military problems, and normally such matters would have been planned and co-ordinated at the highest level by the Army General Staff. This Staff was a corps d'elite of officers who had a background of magnificent military training and a heritage of great pride and superiority over all other classes and organisations within the German State. Such a body — though of course recognising and even welcoming the advent of National Socialism — would not easily be directed by the Party to adopt any measures other than those which they themselves had formulated. Hitler was sensitive to this power and so from the very beginning we find him suspicious of the Army General Staff — the "club of intellectuals" as he dubbed them.

6. Hitler, as author of the military renaissance in Germany, wished to institute a command which would direct and co-ordinate in general

terms, but to his orders, the efforts of the three services — and which would at the same time control the Army General Staff. His conception was theoretically sound. It gave to the individual services an independence which enabled them to expand and develop unshackled from the parochial influence of any overriding traditional military thought, and at the same time a common strategy was ensured and an arbitrator for the equitable allocation of material priorities installed. Finally, after considerable opposition — particularly from the Army — the principle of a unified command was upheld and the command was formed and entrusted to Blomberg. Prior to 1938 the title of the commander in chief of the unified command was the War Minister and Commander of the Armed Forces. In 1938 when Blomberg was dismissed the appointment of War Minister lapsed and Hitler installed himself as Supreme Commander of the Armed Forces, his control being exercised through the Supreme Command of the Armed Forces of which Keitiel was the head. However, though the Supreme Command was established it laboured under difficulties from the day of its inception — the Navy were aloof, the Air Force were encouraged by Göring to disassociate themselves from it, and the Army, stung with resentment, were mistrustful. A system of unified command demands mutual confidence and so it is not surprising to learn that the Supreme Command failed in its original mission and that by the end of the war it was little more than a second Army General Staff directing operations on all fronts other than the Eastern front, which was controlled in the main by the Army.

GERMAN WAR ECONOMY FROM 1933—1942

7. Shortly after the National Socialist Party came into power plans were made to build up a powerful military machine. The broad framework of the rearmament programmes required to support this intention was designed by Hitler himself. In conference with his military advisers he determined the extent and the phasing of these programmes and passed directives to the commanders in chief of the three Services, instructing them to prepare rearmament plans for their particular services in support of his policy. The plans thus prepared were submitted to Hitler for approval and the services were then instructed to proceed in the implementation of their programmes. The Ordnance Office of each service (the Ordnance Office of the Air Ministry was first known as the Technical Office; it was later renamed the Directorate General of Equipment and finally changed its name again to the Chief of Technical Armaments) then placed orders directly with industry.

The Relationship between Service Development and German Economy

8. To attain some relationship between service demands and general economic development, it was necessary to establish an authority which would co-ordinate individual service requirements and prepare long term plans that would ensure the availability of adequate raw materials and productive capacity. This task became the responsibility of the Directorate of Defence Economy and Armaments, which was established as a department of the Supreme Command. In all problems of economic mobilisation this directorate mediated between the Services and the two State authorities connected with war economy, the Ministry of Economy and the Plenipotentiary for the Four-Year Plan. Before examining further the role of the Directorate of Defence Economy and Armaments, it is

necessary to give the following brief description of the functions of the Ministry of Economy and the Plenipotentiary for the Four-Year Plan.
  (i) **Ministry of Economics.** This Ministry was charged with the control of imports, exports and domestic production. Although it exercised no direct influence on armament production it did, however, control the production and allocation of all raw materials and of machinery.
  (ii) **The Plenipotentiary for the Four-Year Plan.** Göring was the president of this organisation, which was designed to organise the production of raw materials which were anticipated as bottlenecks to a future war and to develop German autarchy.

The Directorate of Defence Economy and Armaments

9. This Directorate of the Supreme Command was established in 1934 with General Thomas at its head. The most important functions of the Directorate were: —
  (i) To co-ordinate service production programmes in the light of common strategy and to prevent inter-service competition for resources.
  (ii) To work out and control, in conjunction with the Ministry of Economics, the raw material and other requirements raised by service programmes.

10. The Directorate of Defence Economy and Armaments was subdivided into four deputy directorates which had the following responsibilities:—
  (i) **Deputy Directorate for Armaments.** Representation to the Ministry of Economics and the Plenipotentiary of the Four-Year Plan of the economic demands of the Armed Forces. The organisation of German armament production.
  (ii) **Deputy Directorate for Raw Materials.** Placing bulk demands on the Ministry of Economics for raw materials and allocating the quantities obtained to the three services in accordance with their requirements.
  (iii) **Deputy Directorate for Pricing.** Establishment and control of contract prices.
  (iv) **Deputy Directorate for Foreign Affairs.** Assessment of the economic strength of foreign nations and the recording and exploitation of strategic economic intelligence. The exploitation of occupied territories.

The Armament Inspectorates and Commands

11. The Directorate of Defence Economy and Armaments established and controlled an external organisation which was designed to supervise the armament industry in the field. This organisation was territorial and Germany was divided into areas known as Armament Inspectorates. These areas were sub-divided into Armament Commands. Each Armament Inspectorate had a Headquarters which comprised the following departments:
  (i) A Central Department for the execution of those tasks which concerned all three Services.
  (ii) A Technical Department for general technical affairs.
  (iii) A separate Department for each of the three Services.

The responsibilities of the Armament Inspectorates included:—
(a) In Peacetime:
   (i) The assistance and support of the service Ordnance Offices in placing peacetime orders with armament manufacturers.
   (ii) The supervision of the peacetime production.
   (iii) The investigation, recording and control of plant capacities suitable for armament production in the event of war.
   (iv) The implementation of reinforcement production programmes in preparation for war, including the planning of production means and labour.
   (v) The provision of A.R.P. measures in industry.
(b) In War.
   (i) The supervision of all orders given to armaments plants.
   (ii) The provision of production means and labour.
   (iii) The co-ordination of the separate demands placed by the three Services.
   (iv) The provision of protection for industry against aerial attack and against sabotage.

The Ministry of Armaments and Ammunition

12. One of the most powerful special Commissioners in Germany was Todt, who was head of the Organisation Todt, Inspector General of Roads, Water and Power, and Plenipotentiary for Building. In addition to these tasks Todt was appointed Minister of Armaments and Ammunition in 1940. This Ministry was formed to increase production for the Army and was charged with the supervision of all Army production arrangements. The powers of the Ministry did not extend to Air Force production.

The Effect of the Directorate of Defence Economy and Armaments on the German Air Force

13. The Directorate of Defence Economy and Armaments did not effectively control or influence the German Air Force armament programmes. As soon as the department attempted to restrict or reduce the Air Force allocation of war materials, Göring would use his political influence with Hitler and exert his authority as President of the Four-Year Plan to abrogate the decisions of General Thomas and ensure the satisfaction of the original Air Force proposals.

Summary

14. The administrative structure supporting war production up to 1942 may be summarised as follows:
(i) The armament programmes were drawn up, and the contracts were allocated to industry, by the individual Services, subject to the co-ordination of the Directorate of Defence Economy and Armaments which was in practice, insofar as the Air Force was concerned, largely nominal. The contracts were placed with the main armament firms — numbering about 5,000 individual concerns — which were nursed by the local Armament inspectors.
(ii) The main armament contractors were left to sub-contract and to obtain supplies of components on their own initiative from the smaller firms. These firms remained under the control of the Ministry of Economics.

(iii) The allocation of raw materials for armaments contracts was the responsibility of the Directorate of Defence Economy and Armaments, in consultation with the Ministry of Economies, which controlled the raw material producers.

(iv) The overall supply of labour was determined centrally by the Ministry of Labour, which met the demands of the Services by calling up on an age-group basis, and the demands of industry by reservations on the basis of age and occupation. It was the function of the Armament Inspectorates to ensure, by negotiation with the Regional Labour Offices, that the main Armament concerns retained sufficient labour. The interests in this connection of other firms were in the hands of the regional offices of the Ministry of Economics.

(v) In view of this organisation, the activities of the Minister of Armaments and Ammunition were in effect restricted to the supply of efficiency experts to tackle production engineering problems within the armaments industry, in order to make the best use of the raw materials and labour allocated by other authorities in the contracts placed by the Army. This limited task suited the personality of Todt, who is said to have been more interested in his building organisation than in his functions as Minister of Armaments and Munitions.

Weaknesses in German War Economy prior to 1942

15. Hitler prepared all his military and economic plans on the assumption that the political aims of the National Socialist Party would be achieved by a series of short wars that would be won without disrupting German war economy to the extent of a total mobilisation of industry. It was not until 1942 that he realised that his assumption was false. Before that date, therefore, he was unwilling to combine all the departments and Ministries handling economic matters and appoint a single Minister of War Production with the absolute powers that in a totalitarian state would be necessary to enable the full utilisation of all resources to be achieved efficiently. **Consequently, there were several authorities — the Ministry of Economics, the Four-Year Plan, the Ministry of Armaments and Ammunition, the Directorate of Defence Economy and Armaments, and the Service Ordnance Offices — all dealing in a separate and unco-ordinated fashion with matters of economy.** Furthermore, the organisation of armament production was almost entirely directed by military people instead of industrial experts. The result was that in the first two years of war very little more war materials were produced than in peacetime.

16. The defeat of the German armies at Stalingrad, coupled with the enormous losses of war materials and the general exhaustion of reserves, forced Hitler to realise that this would not be a short war and that at last German war economy would have to be mobilised to the fullest possible extent. At the same time, he began to appreciate that the control of war production by soldiers was inefficient and that only industrial experts could organise adequately such matters.

17. In 1942 Todt, the Minister of Armaments and Ammunition, was killed in an air crash and Hitler appointed Speer in his place, at the same time giving him the powers of a dictator in industry. Speer had the complete confidence of Hitler and also had an unusual talent for placating the

various temperaments of the high officials — both civilian and service — with whom he had dealings. With these advantages Speer began by slow stages to assert his authority, commencing in May 1942 by transferring to his Ministry the Directorate of Defence Economy and Armaments which, under Thomas, who was tired and nearly blind, had been steadily declining in power. Thus, the influence of the Supreme Command of the Armed Forces in war economy came to an end. This violent change in the economic structure of Germany heralded a period during which power became concentrated in the hands of industrialists. The consequent reorganisation of the control of industry and of industrial methods, which led ultimately to the total mobilisation of German resources, is described in Part 1, Chapter II, of this publication.

HANDLING OF COMMON SERVICE SUPPLY PROBLEMS

Common User Items

18. There was no central department in the Supreme Command charged with the responsibility of procuring all common user equipment for the three services. The system used by the German services was similar to that of the British in that the major service user was made responsible for provisioning for the other two — for example, the Air Force provisioned flak guns and ammunition for the Army and Navy; the Army provisioned small arms and small arms ammunition for the Navy and Air Force. Two exceptions were that the Supreme Command provisioned the raw materials required for clothing and accoutrements and, in addition, the complete Motor Transport vehicles for all three services.

Clothing

19. The General Armed Forces Directorate of the Supreme Command was responsible for receiving the demands for yarn from the Air Ministry and co-ordinating such requisitions with those from the other Services. The requirement was then passed to the Ministry of Armaments and War Production, which arranged the production of these desired quantities. The Armed Forces Procuring Directorate of the Supreme Command was notified of the total quantity produced and then arranged for the yarn to be made up into cloth; the finished cloth was allocated according to the requirements of the Services, either to Clothing Depots or uniform factories. This procedure applied to leather and other raw materials required for the manufacture of clothing and accoutrements.

Motor Transport

20. At the beginning of the war there was no control of Motor Transport by the Supreme Command. The Army was the main user and, as such, provisioned Motor Transport vehicles for all three Services. The increasing shortages of vehicles and petrol made it necessary to establish a central committee to consider the problems thus created. The committee was formed at the Supreme Command and it was the nucleus around which the Directorate of Armed Forces Motor Transport was formed in April 1944, when it was decided to divorce joint control of Motor Transport from the War Office. The responsibilities of the new Directorate included:

(i) The supply to the three Services and civilian concerns of Motor Transport vehicles, spare parts, etc., excepting P.O.L. and tyres.

(ii) Repair to all Service and civilian vehicles where repair was impossible under local arrangements.

Movement

21. Railway transport arrangements for the three services were centrally directed by the Director of Armed Forces Transport at the Supreme Command. This Director exercised control through the following organisations:

   (i) In Home Areas. Through two transport Directorates, one of which, the Central, was located in Berlin and the other, the South Eastern, in Vienna.

   (ii) In Operational Areas. Through the General Officers Commanding transport at the various Army Groups.

22. The Supreme Command maintained a very close liaison with the civil railway authorities, and the territory of the Transport Directorates and of the Army Groups was divided into Transport Commands which matched the railway's own district organisation.

23. The individual services calculated their requirements for railway space and submitted their commitments to the Director of Armed Forces Transport. This authority then allotted quotas of trains for the following 14 days.

24. All sea transport arrangements for the three services were also centrally controlled at the Supreme Command of the Armed Forces by a staff which was known as the Home Staff for Overseas, until the end of the African campaign, shortly after which it was renamed the Home Staff for Scandinavia. Under the latter title it performed the same duties as hitherto but in a more restricted area. The Headquarters of the Home Staff was near Berlin and it had branch offices to deal with local affairs in various appropriate areas such as Norway, Kurland, and Italy. The actual acquisition of shipping space was undertaken by a government office called the Commissioner for Shipping. This office was in Hamburg and was managed throughout the war by an individual known as Gauleiter Kaufmann. On instructions from the Home Staff Kaufmann would requisition ships from the merchant navy and private firms and put them at the disposal of the Armed Forces. For the African campaign Italian shipping was used and this was arranged by Kaufmann with the Italian government.

Trends to increase Central Control by the Supreme Command

25. In the last months of the war there was a definite trend to increase centralised control of certain supply matters. This is evident from an examination of the functions of two new departments which were formed in the Supreme Command:

   (i) Chief of Armed Forces Armaments.
   (ii) Quartermaster General of the Armed Forces.

26. The Chief of Armed Forces Armaments department was formed in February 1945, under General Buhle, and its function was to assess requirements and arrange production (through Speer) for the Army, and where common to the other Services of:—

   (i) Armaments equipment (not aircraft cannon).
   (ii) Munitions.
   (iii) Flak guns. These were allocated by the department to the three services by a special committee.
   (iv) All balloon barrage equipment.

27. The department was only in existence for a few months and never succeeded in assuming responsibility of supply to the Air Force even for

the weapons and ammunition of common usage. The Air Force was opposed to this centralisation, which was eventually intended to apply to all armaments, and Buhle remarked that the Chief of Technical Armaments in the Air Ministry usually applied direct to Speer for production and, if unsuccessful there, then approached Armed Forces Armaments. If this move failed to produce results and the matter was sufficiently important Göring would then go direct to the Führer.

28. The department of the Quartermaster General of the Armed Forces was formed in April 1945 under the command of Major General Topper, who was recalled from a post on the Eastern Front. Its institution was the result of several years' agitation in certain quarters for a centralised Quartermaster General's department. The reasons leading to its formation are said to be: —

(i) An argument put forward by the War Office Quartermaster General that since the Army provided 60 % to 70 % of the needs of Services in the Field (rations, M.T. fuel, barrack equipment, ammunition, etc.) a centralised organisation might as well cover 100 % of the supply. The inference here is that the Army Quartermaster General hoped for the new post, but this cannot be substantiated.

(ii) That Speer, in his capacity as Miniser for Armament Production, favoured the new department since he hoped it would lead to economies in production, for each Service would not then be able to overprovision, and surpluses of "common" items in one branch could be transferred to another.

(iii) The general realisation in the Supreme Command that the maintenance of separate Quartermaster General Staffs was leading to duplication of work.

(iv) That Allied bombing was gradually restricting production and it was essential to have equable distribution of stocks and restrict hoarding by one service at the expense of others.

29. Opposition to the scheme for introducing the department is said to have come from Keitel, who did not welcome the added high responsibility, which might lead to disputes with the Heads of the Navy and Air Force. In addition, these two services were not enthusiastic since they were satisfied with their present methods of obtaining supplies and did not favour losing any accumulations.

30. A major difficulty at the formation was that of finding a suitable personality to head the department; one who was capable enough to weld the three Services together and yet resist the enormous influence of Göring and Dönitz in the event of disputes on priority of supply allocation. It has been said that Major General Topper would not have been firm enough to retain the post.

CONCLUSION

31. Even while the Directorate of Defence Economy and Armaments existed as a part of the Supreme Command of the Armed Forces, it exercised little effective influence on the supply organisation of the German Air Force. Göring always encouraged his staff to remain aloof from the Supreme Command and he would always intercede with Hitler to obtain preferential treatment for the Air Force whenever obstruction was encountered.

32.   In matters of common user materials and common services the Supreme Command had more power — particularly in the spheres of Motor Transport and Movement. On the whole, unified control of these matters, while theoretically sound, was disadvantageous to the Air Force because the Staffs dealing with such matters were preponderantly manned by Army officers who gave preference to their own service. The tendency, in the last months of the war to increase unified control was opposed by the Air Force on the ground that they would have to suffer to the advantage of the Army. However, the war ended before the new departments of the Supreme Command concerned in these affairs assumed control.

33.   It may be said in conclusion, therefore, that the Supreme Command of the Armed Forces played but a small part in the system of supply to the Air Force and that the only influence it did exercise was usually to the disadvantage of that service.

PART 1

CHAPTER II

THE MINISTRY OF ARMAMENTS AND WAR PRODUCTION

INTRODUCTION	Paragraphs 1—8
HISTORY AND DEVELOPMENT OF THE SPEER MINISTRY	,, 9—30
Speer: His Appointment and Objects	,, 9—13
Speer: His Achievement of Autonomy in Industry	,, 14—19
Accession of Power: The Army and the Navy	,, 20—24
Accession of Power: The Air Force	,, 25—30
TRANSFER OF AIRCRAFT PRODUCTION TO SPEER	,, 31—42
General	,, 31—32
Production under the Air Force	,, 33—36
The "Fighter Staff"	,, 37—40
Final Transfer to Speer of Air Armaments	,, 41—42
ORGANISATION OF THE SPEER MINISTRY	,, 43—73
General	,, 43—46
The Technical Office	,, 47—49
The Main Committees and the Main Rings	,, 50—61
Purchasing Departments of the Services	,, 62
The Development Commissions	,, 63—72
The Programme Commissions	,, 73
CONCLUSION	,, 74—88
Comparison with British Organisation	,, 74—76
Criticism of the Speer Ministry	,, 77—87
Provisioning and Production: Reference	,, 88

PART I

CHAPTER II

THE MINISTRY OF ARMAMENTS AND WAR PRODUCTION

INTRODUCTION

1. This Chapter deals with the activities of the Ministry of Armaments and War Production under Albert Speer from 1942 until the end, during which phase of the war the control of German industry was reorganised and the production of armaments intensified and accelerated.

2. At the present time, now that it is possible to see the war in a different perspective, it is difficult to understand the complacency with which, until 1942, the German leaders regarded the admitted inefficiency of their industrial system. It is clear that although preparations for the war had begun early and were conducted methodically the extent of German economic mobilisation up to 1942 was entirely inadequate.

3. Two main factors contributed to this state of affairs: the first, and one which is woven into the whole fabric of the German war effort, is that of divided control in the economic and industrial sphere.

4. Hitler failed to realise the fact that in wartime the economic machine must be controlled by one authority, and he made no plans for a close co-ordination of armament production. As a result, the direction of German economy was placed in the hands of a number of authorities, both civil and military, none of which had power to correlate and control the general effort. The management of the armament industry was left to the divided and conflicting interests of the three Services.

5. Secondly, it is now well known that Germany envisaged a war of short duration. Mobilisation plans were, therefore, based on this assumption and her economic and industrial machine geared only for a comparatively low production over a short period of time.

6. The appointment of Todt as Minister for Armaments and Ammunition, in 1940, achieved little improvement in the industrial sphere generally since his jurisdiction was strictly limited, being confined as it was solely to intervention in the production of Army weapons. It required the reverses experienced at Stalingrad in 1942 to precipitate the violent and drastic change in the structure of economic and industrial direction which came about with the appointment of Speer.

7. Hitler, in appointing Speer to replace Todt in 1942, appeared at last to realise the importance of industry as an integral part of the German military machine and from this date, therefore, until the end of the war, the history of German economic and industrial effort is one of intensification and reconstruction, and of the transference of control of the production of armaments from the Armed Forces to industry.

8. This phase of the war, in addition to its interest on account of the fundamental change in the whole of German war economy, is also of importance to the present review of production for the Air Force, since

only in this period was the responsibility for the production of air armaments wrested from the control of the 'Air Force and treated as a general factor in the German war effort.

HISTORY AND DEVELOPMENT OF THE SPEER MINISTRY
Speer: His Appointment and Objects

9. The defects peculiar to the German organisation for armaments production have already been referred to, both in these present paragraphs and in Part 1, Chapter I, and Speer on his appointment as Reichsminister of Armaments and War Production, following the death of Todt, was aware of the difficulties to be faced in implementing his orders from Hitler to reorganise the Ministry and to provide for increased armaments programmes. He was by no means anxious to inherit a responsibility already the subject of displeasure by Hitler and was persuaded to accept office only on the promise that he would receive full support in the expansion of armaments production.

10. As will be seen, Speer, who was at least a realist in the industrial field, fully realised the defects of the economic and industrial machine, and the effect these shortcomings might have on the eventual outcome of the war.

11. Failure in achieving full industrial mobilisation in the period before 1942 is ascribed by Speer to a number of facts:—
- (i) Lack of central control and of co-ordination of economic and armament production.
- (ii) Failure of the economic war plans to envisage and prepare for a war of long duration.
- (iii) The fact that planning and execution were in the hands of officers of the Armed Forces without representation and guidance by industrial personnel.

12. Bearing in mind these facts, Speer applied himself to the reorganisation of German economy and industry with three main objectives in view:—
- (i) The creation of a central co-ordinating authority for all armament production.
- (ii) The expansion of the armaments industries and, in these and in civilian industries, the full utilisation of German resources.
- (iii) The transfer of responsibility for war production from the hands of the Armed Forces to industrial experts.

13. Offices taken over by Speer at this time were:—
- (i) Minister of Weapons and Ammunition (later Armaments and War Production).
- (ii) Head of the Organisation Todt.
- (iii) Inspector General for Roads.
- (IV) Inspector General for Water and Power.
- (V) Commissioner for Building in the Four-Year Plan.

Speer: His Achievement of Autonomy in Industry

14. At its inception the scope of the Ministry of Armaments and War Production was limited and its history under the control of Speer from 1942 is one of acquisition of powers from the three Services, from the

Ministry of Economic Warfare, and from the Four-Year Plan. As a preliminary to the transfer of responsibility from these bodies, Speer undertook the re-organisation of his own Ministry to prepare it for its future role of controlling a reconstituted industrial system.

15. The Ministry of Armaments and War Production, under Speer, was intended not to occupy itself in any of the executive responsibilities involved in development, production and distribution, but to delegate these functions to a self-governing industry, subject only to general guidance and co-ordination. Industry was designed to become self-administrative and to absorb the responsibilities for production previously in the hands of the Forces.

16. Two main principles were envisaged by Speer in this work. In the first instance, he was firmly convinced of the need for armament production to be in the hands of technical experts and to this end created the system of Main Committees (Hauptausschüsse), beginning with army weapons. As a complement to these Main Committees, Speer appreciated the paramount need for control of raw materials and semi-finished goods and, therefore, directed the formation of the Main Rings.

17. Each of these Main Committees was charged with the responsibility for production of a particular type of finished arament stores, e.g. ammunition, airframes. The Main Rings were designed to be responsible for the various classes of raw materials and semi-finished products.

18. In a comparatively short time, by June 1942, Speer had set up an extensive organisation of these Committees and Rings, all of which were composed entirely of industrialists and technicians and which were completely responsible, within the Ministerial organisation, for their own administration and planning.

19. The objects of Speer, and the extent to which he considered autonomy to have been achieved, at the end of two years, may be summarised in his speech to industrialists of the Ruhr at Essen on June 9th, 1944, an extract from which is appended:—

"Until 1942, Industry obtained its government contracts from official government agencies, ordnance departments of the armed forces, etc.

An Industrialist offered his plant capacity to the armed forces. He determined his own type of production. If he worked overwhelmingly for one branch of the armed forces, officers belonging to it, and especially the Technical Armaments Boards, would determine production.

Responsibility for the progress of armament production, for planning of schedules, for plant standardisation, for the exchange of experiences between plants, thus rested upon the officers whose ambitions and qualifications lay in an entirely different field . . . .

We (Dr. Todt and Speer) know from our own experience the energies inherent in the initiative of the private individual. We also knew the fanaticism which drives the engineer who is entrusted with a great technical task . . . .

Therefore, I resolved (in 1942) to draw the best leading engineers from all the industry at my disposal and to turn over to them the entire responsibility at first for the production of tanks, weapons and ammunition. Men like Rohland, Tix and Geilenberg were placed in charge of these most essential branches of the armament industry. Other industrial personnel were charged with the production of essential materials like steel, electrical products and parts.

We have to-day 21 Main Committees, responsible for final armaments production, and 12 Rings in charge of materials and parts essential for that production; by them, all the most important armament and war production is directed.

Apart from the Main Committees and Rings, a few agencies were created for the development of weapons in which plant engineers and representatives of the armed forces sit together on equal terms. These Commissions are usually presided over by outstanding industrial engineers. They have the last word regarding the development of weapons. Only the Supreme Commanders of the Armed Forces together with me, or the Führer himself, can reverse their decisions.

This unique organisation of the Autonomy of Industry is now composed of 6,000 unpaid technicians and engineers, put at our disposal by industry. These honorary collaborators from industry carry the detailed responsibility for what individual plants will manufacture and in what ways they will manufacture it. They have powers to issue all orders necessary to enforce their point of view, and to give the necessary directives to the plant managers.

The Autonomy of Industry thus practically directs, with its specialists, every last detail of industrial production. Among its main tasks are the distribution of contracts to industry; standardization of types; specialisation of industrial plants, possibly discontinuing lines of production of whole plants; standardisation from the point of view of raw materials, construction and production processes; and the unconditional exchange of industrial information regardless of patent rights."

Accession of Power: The Army and the Navy

20. After setting up the first of his Main Committees, dealing with Army weapons, Speer was anxious to transfer to his Ministry the responsibilities for armament production previously vested in the Supreme Command and in the Ordnance Offices of the Forces.

21. There was some opposition to Speer in this respect, but in May 1942 he was successful in divorcing from the Supreme Command the Directorate of Defence Economy and Armaments, hitherto under the control of Thomas, and in transferring its powers to his own Ministry and to industry. With this Directorate were transferred the Armament Inspectorates and Commands, both of which have been referred to in Part 1, Chapter I.

22. This was Speer's first step to restrict the power of the Supreme Command, at least in respect of army Weapons.

23. The allocation and control of orders on industry for army weapons were, even after this date, still in the hands of the Army Ordnance Office, but Speer very quickly transferred these powers to his Main Committees and Rings, thereby obtaining complete direction of production for the Army.

24. Control of production for the naval forces was transferred to Speer in October 1943, responsibility being placed in the hands of the Main Committees for Naval Construction.

Accession of Power: The Air Force

25. The independence of the Air Force was prolonged owing in part to the peculiar status of Göring, its chief, but Speer had always been interested in this phase of armament production and had, in fact, maintained friendly relationship with Field Marshal Milch, who had acted under Göring as Director General of Equipment.

26. Partial control of production for the Air Force was secured by Speer in February 1944 when, by reason of the heavy and sustained air attacks on the German aircraft plants by the Allies, it became necessary to re-organise the production of fighter aircraft. This re-organisation was achieved by the formation of a production control body known as the "Fighter Staff" (Jägerstab), having Speer as nominal head, Milch as Deputy and Saur as "Leader".

27. This change in the responsibility for aircraft production was quickly followed by a complete transfer to the Ministry of Armaments and War Production of all control in this field and, from August of 1944, Speer had therefore succeeded in acquiring direction of production for all three branches of the Forces.

28. Field Marshal Milch was transferred to the Speer Ministry, his office of Director General of Equipment being abolished except in respect of certain technical matters of supply, and until later replaced by Saur he acted as Speer's deputy in directing aircraft production.

29. The three Main Committees (airframe, aero engine, and accessories) concerned with aircraft production, which were previously under the control of Göring's "Industrial Council for Air Force Production", were incorporated in the Speer Ministry and re-organised to conform to the general pattern adopted for Main Committees.

30. The transfer of responsibility for the production of aircraft has been dealt with up to this point as a part of the process by which Speer achieved full control of armament production, but the subject of aircraft production generally under the Speer Ministry is dealt with separately in the following paragraphs.

TRANSFER OF AIRCRAFT PRODUCTION TO SPEER

General

31. The independence of all three Services of the Armed Forces, prior to the advent of Speer, has already been noted and, until the enforced formation of the "Fighter Staff", production of air armaments for the Air Force was entirely in the hands of that Service.

32. It is necessary, therefore, to distinguish three periods:—
   (i) Before the formation of the "Fighter Staff" in February 1944, when the Air Force was solely responsible for aircraft production.
   (ii) The interim period, between February 1944 and June of the same year, when partial responsibility had been assumed by the Speer Ministry in forming the "Fighter Staff".
   (iii) After June 1944, when full responsibility had been formally given to Speer.

Production under the Air Force

33. The first of these periods, until February 1944, is marked by the continued independence of the Air Force, until which time, at the direction of Göring, production remained in the hands of the Air Ministry.

34. This enforced isolation of the Air Force was negatived to a certain extent since Milch, as Director General of Equipment in the Air Ministry, maintained a close and friendly relationship with Speer and, in fact, utilised the organisation and resources of the Speer Ministry in re-organising the aircraft industry.

35. It was natural, in the re-organisation carried out by Milch during the years 1942 to 1944, that the aircraft industry should be modelled to a great extent on the pattern of Committees provided by Speer for the other two Services and, as will be seen in the following paragraphs, the eventual absorption by Speer of the responsibility for the production of air armaments did not necessitate any major change in organisation.

36. Although there were certain advantages gained by the co-operation of Milch and Speer, and although the former was successful in achieving increased production of aircraft, the failure of the Air Force in directing and controlling its own industry was clearly apparent by 1944. In February of that year the increased violence of the Allied air attacks precipitated a crisis, by threatening the whole of German industry, and Göring was forced to yield partial control of the aircraft industry.

The "Fighter Staff"

37. The failure of the aircraft industry to maintain its programme after the first phase of the Allied air attacks in February 1944, necessitated a re-organisation of responsibility for production by the creation of the "Fighter Staff" with Milch as Speer's deputy in this sphere.

38. The prime responsibility of the "Fighter Staff", with Saur as Leader, was the production of day and night fighters, since it was recognised that a strengthening of the defensive capabilities of the Air Force was indispensible to maintenance of war production in general.

39. In addition to restoring, protecting and stimulating production at fighter aircraft plants, although not within its original powers the "Fighter Staff" initiated a review of the Air Force programmes with the object of reduction in the number of types and sub-types and consequent increased rates of production of simplified and standardized types.

40. The "Fighter Staff" continued in existence until June 1944, and, during this time, its achievements were remarkable in re-organising the aircraft industry and increasing the quantities of fighter aircraft. Its main fields of activity in accelerating the production of fighter aircraft, and in revising the Air Force programmes are described below:—

   (i) The reconstruction or repair of the damaged aircraft factories. In this connection measures were taken for the protection against future air attacks by the special protection of machine tools, the provision of fireproof doors and the general strengthening of factory fire services.

   (ii) The organisation of labour and material facilities to ensure priority repair of damaged aircraft producing plants. These measures involved special action squads for the direction and organisation of repair after aerial attacks.

(iii) The revision of evacuation and dispersal plans. All schemes for the large-scale evacuation of major producing plants were suspended but energetic action was taken to protect the industry by the use of dispersed sites.

(iv) The review and revision of Air Force aircraft programmes to reduce the numbers of types and sub-types and the number of major modifications to types.

(v) General stimulation in all matters to do with factory management which had a bearing on production. e. g. priorities in labour and material supply, redeployment of technicians, exchange of technical information.

Final Transfer to Speer of Air Armaments

41. Formal transfer to Speer of full responsibility for all future aircraft production was not effected until later in the year when, by a Göring decree, the office of the Director General of Equipment was abolished. The same decree provided for future restriction of the activities of the Air Force in production matters (through the agency of the Chief of Technical Air Armaments) to:—

(i) The initiation of aircraft production programmes based on military needs.

(ii) The formulation of technical specifications in the performance of aircraft, etc.

42. The existing Main Committees responsible for aircraft production were brought under the direct control of the Speer Ministry, responsibility being centralised in the Technical Office under Saur.

ORGANISATION OF THE SPEER MINISTRY

General

43. Speer, in developing his Ministry, pursued the two complementary policies of centralised policy control and decentralised executive responsibility. With these principles in mind, Speer proceeded to set up:

(i) The administrative system of the Ministry which was to control and co-ordinate armament production.

(ii) The system of self-administrative Main Committees, whereby responsibility for production of finished products in classes was to be delegated to industrialists and technicians.

(iii) The organisation of Main Rings to deal with raw materials and intermediate products.

(iv) Development Commissions to act as complementary and parallel organisations to the Main Committees in providing for the future development of finished products.

44. It should be appreciated that Speer, in setting up this structure, was intent not on forming a large Ministry concerned with a multitude of executive functions, but a body responsible only for guiding and supervising a self-governing industry. It is clear, therefore, that the Speer Ministry, although wide in its scope and with many ramifications, is not comparable in its nature to the British Ministries.

45. The main departments of the Ministry, under functional headings, at the end of 1944, before the disorganisation caused by the impending total defeat of the German Forces, were:—

(i)   Planning Department
(ii) Central Department
(iii) Technical Department
(iv) Raw Materials Department
(v)   Consumer Goods Production Dept.
(vi) Building Dept. — Organisation Todt.
(vii) Power Dept

46.   The organisation of each of these Departments is adequately dealt with in other publications and it is intended in these paragraphs to refer only to the Technical Office which, since it dealt specifically with the production of armaments for the three Services, has a direct bearing on the system of supply for the Air Force.

The Technical Office

47.   In conformity with the general principles and policy of the Speer Ministry, the Technical Office was responsible only for policy control of the armaments industries, and not for the considerable executive functions involved in operating such a large part of the German economic machine.

48.   Saur, as head of the Technical Office, never had more than 200 officials working under his direction and, as will be seen in the Chapter devoted specially to Provisioning and Production, there is no analogy between this Department of the Speer Ministry and the British organisations concerned in manufacture for the Forces.

49.   From the details which follow, and from the chart which incorporates the Technical Office (Appendix A) it will be seen that the main functions of the Department were two-fold:—

(i) Control of Armament Production.
(ii) Direction of Design and Development.

The Main Committees and Main Rings

50.   As was made evident in the earlier part of this Chapter, the armaments industry, until the inception of the Main Committees of the Speer Ministry, had been directed by the three fighting Services, Army, Air Force and Navy.

51.   The General Staff of each Service presented to its military purchasing department the demands for weapons, and these demands, in the form of orders, were in turn transmitted to the appropriate armaments industries. Each Service, in its own sphere, was responsible for the issue of orders, supervision of manufacture, price fixing and payment and acceptance of deliveries.

52.   It was apparent, however, even before the appointment of Speer, that if maximum production of armaments in any particular sphere was to be achieved the firms concerned with that range of equipment would need to be related by a co-ordinating authority, in order that all manufacturers might adopt uniform methods of production and share patents and other technical information.

53.   The military departments, through lack of manufacturing knowledge, found it difficult to direct the firms concerned in armament production and so in 1942 the idea was conceived of self-government of industry, by means of Main Committees (Hauptausschusse) and the subordinate Special Committees (Sonderausschusse).

54. Each of the Main Committees was intended to deal with a particular range of equipment (finished products as compared with semi-finished items and raw materials) and the Subordinate Special Committees were designed to be responsible for individual items within the range. Of the Main Committees, each was composed of industrialists, appointed by Speer, the members in general being leaders of the subordinate Special Committees but, since the object was to concentrate production of armaments in the hands of industry, there was no representation by the Services or by the Supreme Command.

55. At the end of 1944, after a final re-organisation of the system of Main and Special Committees, by the elimination of those found to be unneccessary, the whole armaments industry was grouped into eight Main Committees:—

    (i) Main Committee for Weapons.
    (ii) Main Committee for Ammunition.
    (iii) Main Committee for Motor Vehicles.
    (iv) Main Committee for Electrotechnics.
    (v) Main Committee for Shipbuilding.
    (vi) Main Committee for Aircraft.
    (vii) Main Committee for Optics, Precision Instruments and General Services Equipment.
    (viii) Main Committee for Engines (including Aircraft).

56. Control over the Main Committees was effected directly by Speer, but routine supervision was vested in Saur as Head of the Technical Office, who was assisted in this work by Programme Commissioners.

57. Monthly production reports, showing actual production against programmes, were rendered to the Technical Office each month and, after collation and analysis, were sent to Hitler on the second day of the following month; in the case of important programmes, intermediate reports would be rendered every ten days. The completed reports were reviewed and discussed on the fourth of each month by Saur, as Head of the Technical Office, and the leaders of the Main Commissions.

58. Following the conception and establishment of the Main Committees, Speer realised the necessity of co-ordinating and controlling the production of the raw materials and intermediate products required by the plants producing finished armaments; for this purpose he originated the Main and Special Rings.

59. These organisation, as in the case of the Main and Special Committees, to which they were complementary, were composed of industrialists and were intended to be self-administering.

60. Four Main Rings existed after the 1944 re-organisation: —
    (i) Main Ring for Iron Production.
    (ii) Main Ring for Iron Processing.
    (iii) Main Ring for Steelmaking.
    (iv) Main Ring for Machinery.

61. The Rings were subordinate originally to the Armaments Delivery Office since, in the beginning, the Ministry was concerned only with production of raw materials and intermediate products for the Army, and could not assume direct responsibility for the supply of such items to the Navy and Air Force. The Armaments Delivery Office, created specially for the

control of supplies to the Technical Office (responsible for the Army), and to the Navy Ordnance Department and Air Force Ordnance Department, became redundant only when the Ministry assumed full responsibility for arming these two latter Services; on its dissolution in October 1944 the duties in this sphere for the supply of all raw and semi-finished products were transferred to the Technical Office.

Purchasing Departments of the Services

62. With the introduction of the Main Committees and Main Rings, and their subordinate organisations, the Purchasing Departments of the Services were of necessity regrouped in order that each Main Committee might have a military opposite number. The Purchasing Departments were intended in future to be concerned merely with eliciting military needs for armaments from their respective General Staffs and in passing the demands to the relevant Main Committees for action. Close collaboration between the Purchasing Departments and the Main Committees was maintained, but, except for responsibilities in the sphere of inspection and of price fixing, the Services had no part in the direction of industry or of actual manufacture.

The Development Commissions

63. Speer was firmly of the opinion that the right of deciding what particular weapons to develop belonged to those responsible for the eventual use of the arms i. e. the General Staff. At the same time, it was disconcerting for him to realise that the General Staff failed to appreciate the limitations of industry and that they were unable to effect any appreciable measure of co-ordination of related demands for similar items arising from the three Services.

64. The need arose, therefore, for an organisation capable of regulating development of armaments, and for this purpose the Development Commissions were formed, each of which was responsible, vis-à-vis its related Main Committee, for development of weapons in that particular field.

65. The main tasks of each Commission were:—
   (i) To co-ordinate, in each field of manufacture, the requirements for development of all three Services;
   (ii) To avoid over-elaborate or multiple designs leading to excessive consumption of labour and material;
   (iii) To ensure that all development projects were considered by technical experts and especially by series production specialists, before being approved for production.

66. The leaders of the Development Commission were drawn from industry and were appointed by Speer. The leader of the corresponding Main Commission was ex officio a member of the Development Commission for purposes of representing the production point of view, and included as members of each Commission were representatives of the Supreme Command, of the Army, Navy and Air Force, of technical institutes, of industry, and of the Ministry. In respect of certain equipment, such as weapons, all three Services were represented, since each had an interest in development.

67. Development projects had two sources. Where, as appears to have been the general rule, the development of a weapon arose from the formulation of a demand by one of the Services, the requirement was referred

to the appropriate Development Commission which, after consideration of the idea, proceeded to place development contracts with one or more private firms, depending on the importance of the project. The progress of the contracts was subjected to periodic review; trials of prototypes were carried out by the Service concerned in conjunction with the Development Commission, and the final decision as to whether the design should be put into service rested with the Service.

68. In the case of a development project originated by a private firm, it was transmitted by the appropriate Development Commission, through the Service representative concerned, to the appropriate Service for assessment of value and, at the same time, it was considered by the production expert of the Commission to determine its practicability in manufacture. The Development Commission, as a whole, then decided whether the project should proceed and placed development contracts accordingly. As in the case of demands originating with one of the Forces, the prototype was tested, and accepted or rejected, by the Service concerned.

69. The last of the Development Commissions to be formed was that for aircraft, late in 1944, and was never able to start work.

70. It is to be noted that as an exception to the general efficiency of the Speer Ministry there was a lack of overall co-ordination of armament development. The Development Branch of the Ministry, which controlled the Development Commissions, was itself signally weak in this sphere and the Commissions were efficient only in the limited range of the class of weapons with which they dealt.

71. The Services, by their intimate contact with industry and aided by the weakness of the Development Branch, were in a position to approach manufacturers direct but failed to secure any co-ordination of development.

72. No Government Armament Design Department existed in Germany and the possibility that such an organisation would yield any advantage was refuted by Speer on the ground that greater efficiency might be expected from private enterprise which, in the opinion of the Germans, worked more freely and faster than a Government Department, owing to its alleged freedom from the restrictions of bureaucratic administration.

The Programme Commissions

73. In order that liaison should be maintained between the Ministry and the Main Committees, and that Speer should have the advantage of advice on the progress of established programmes, Programme Commissions were established as part of the Technical Office. A Commission was appointed in repect of each range of equipment to facilitate work with its opposite Main Committee. The purpose of the Commissions is clear but it appears that, in practice, they were limited in scope.

CONCLUSION.

Comparison with British Organisations

74. In effecting a comparison of the British and German methods of directing armament production, it should be noted that a parallel may not be drawn between the Speer Ministry and the British Ministries of Supply and of Aircraft Production.

75. The German Ministry of Armaments and War Production did not assume any executive functions and was concerned only in the general

overall supervision and administration of the machinery of armament production. The organisations referred to, Commissions, Rings and Committees, were entirely extraneous to the Ministry and were in themselves only co-ordinating agencies.

76. Again, in considering a comparison of the British and German systems, it will be appreciated that while the structure of the Ministry of Supply and of the Ministry of Aircraft Production did not change fundamentally during the war, the German administration in this field was subject to violent changes even quite late in the war.

Criticism of the Speer Ministry

77. The fact that the Air Force maintained its independence in the industrial sphere for so long after its sister-services had surrendered theirs is a clear indication that Speer did not achieve full control of industry without considerable opposition.

78. Speer on his part has emphasised continually the failings of the Armed Forces in general but officials of the Air Ministry in their own defence have protested strongly that many of these deficiencies resulted from the domination of the Speer Ministry and from the subordination of military requirements to civil and industrial authorities. It is reasonable to bear in mind, therefore, despite Speer's constant plea for autonomy of the armament industry, that there were two sides to the picture.

79. Criticism of Speer by the German Air Ministry appears to be divided into two major parts. One is concerned with the subordination of the Air Force to civil and industrial directions, and the other is concerned with the gradual technical deterioration in aircraft and components.

80. In the first case, it is quite clear that resentment was felt against the Speer Ministry in its power-seeking activities. It is stated that the Air Force was of the opinion that planning and distribution of armament requirements was their own affair and that the task of industry should have been confined to securing rational planning of production and control. It was appreciated that some degree of co-ordination was necessary to achieve a common effort on the part of the Air Force and of industry, but it is maintained that this necessity had been recognised very early in the war by the German Air Force.

81. Göring, it is pointed out, did in fact seek to implement the need for some co-ordination body, by the creation of the Industrial Council for Air Force Production, with the prime object of assisting the Director General of Equipment in planning and production control, and it is maintained that this organisation served its purpose perfectly well until the creation of the "Fighter Staff" in 1944. It is also maintained that the Air Force received little assistance in its plan for control of production and this is ascribed to a diminishing faith on the part of the German leaders in the ability of the Services to conduct their own industrial affairs.

82. The forceful personalities of the Speer Ministry, such as Saur, are described as political climbers, and continual emphasis is placed by the Air Force on the damage done by these people in pressing for an extension of their influence both in the sphere of production and planning and in military affairs.

83. In the second place, the Air Force records that an unjustifiable and abnormal amount of attention had to be paid to the Speer Ministry's

deficiencies in the technical field which resulted in a clearly perceived deterioration in aircraft efficiency and the quality of component parts.

84. As the strength of the Speer Ministry increased, it is maintained, the Director General of Equipment was made to feel more and more dependent, particularly in respect of such matters as the allocation of raw materials, manpower, and factories; at the end, when full power over Air Force production was given to Speer, it was realised that legitimate Service interests had been subordinated to production requirements.

85. From the point of view of the Air Force, therefore, the history of production falls into a number of phases: —

(i) The control of industry by the Air Force, with admitted failings but without extensive or important technical faults.

(ii) The increase in quantitative efficiency of industry after 1942, with control still in the hands of the Air Force and again without loss of technical quality.

(iii) The continued increase in quantitative efficiency of industry, on transfer of control to Speer, but with a general and cumulative deterioration in the quality and performance.

(iv) The complete subjugation of technical efficiency to mere quantitative considerations, and the entire loss by the Air Force of any voice in deciding choice of weapons or of their relative efficiency.

This last phase is virtually one whereby the Speer Ministry dictated to the Air Force its policy in production of air armaments.

86. The opinion was held by the German Air Ministry that the lack of confidence in the Military Departments was shared by the industrial leaders and that this state of affairs led to the introduction of a number of so-called commissioners who replaced technical knowledge and skill with enthusiasm and optimism. Instances are put forward to demonstrate the bad provisioning which resulted from the exclusion of advice and assistance from the Service in devising and implementing aircraft and allied programmes.

87. Comment by the German Air Ministry is not entirely destructive and admits that from a number of points of view the Speer Ministry was successful. This was so particularly in respect of quantitative production of aircraft, but this superficial success by Speer in considerably discounted on a number of grounds, chief among which are:—

(i) The dangers and demerits attendant on the acceleration of series production of existing aircraft types; increase in the production of such aircraft, even with improved performance, was viewed with anxiety, since this meant the production of current or obsolescent types to the detriment of the introduction of new and improved models.

(ii) The alleged incompetence of the industry to produce high performance aircraft in adequate numbers; an example given is that of the Me. 262, for which the scheduled programme was never met, despite the curtailment of bomber and transport aircraft in favour of this type. Speer found certain mass production difficulties insuperable because he did not seek service advice which would have enabled him to compromise between prototype design and series production problems.

Provision and Production: Reference

88.   The administrative processes by which production of Air armaments for the German Air Force was directed and controlled are dealt with in Part 2 Chapter II, and that part of the publication should be read in conjunction with this present Chapter in forming a comprehensive picture of Provisioning and Production for the Air Force during the years 1942 to 1945. Similarly, Part 2 Chapter III, which deals with the subject of Finance in relation to the German Air Force, should be read in conjunction with these Chapters.

Appendix "A" do Part I, Chapter II

Chart Showing the Supply Organisation and Relationship of the G.A.F. and the Speer Ministry – late 1944.

Chief of General Staff of G.A.F.
- Chief of Technical Air Armaments.
  - Development Department.
  - Supply Department. → Orders to Industry thro' Committees.
- Quartermaster General
  - 6th Department.
  - 4th Department.

Statement of Requirements to Technical Office.

Speer: Ministry of Armaments and War Production.

Production Office. Technical Office. Raw Materials Office.
- Textiles.
- Clothing.
- Food.
- Packing.
- Oil
- Rubber

Department of Finished Products – Main Committees
- Munitions | Vehicles | General Service Equipment | Elec., Optical and Precision Equipment | Weapons | Motors | Aircraft

Department of Development – Development Commissions
- Munitions | Vehicles | Observer Equipment. | Elec., Optical and Precision Equipment | Weapons | Motors | Aircraft

Department of Programme Supervision – Programme Commissions.
- Munitions | Vehicles | General Service Equipment | Elec., Optical and Precision Equipment | Weapons | Motors | Aircraft

Department of Raw Materials and Semi-Finished Products – Main Rings.
- Iron Production | Iron Processing | Steel Making | Machinery

PART 1

CHAPTER III

THE ORGANISATION OF THE GERMAN AIR FORCE

INTRODUCTION	Paragraphs	1—8
The Regional Organisation of the German Air Force	,,	2—4
The Separation between Flying Units and Ground Units	,,	5—8
BRANCHES OF THE GERMAN AIR FORCE	,,	9
DEFINITION OF FUNCTIONS OF GERMAN AIR FORCE HEADQUARTER STAFFS	,,	10—13
Staffs Combining Operational and Supply Matters	,,	11
Headquarter Staffs for Operational Formations	,,	12
Headquarter Staffs for Ground Organisation	,,	13
ORGANISATION OF HEADQUARTER STAFFS	,,	14—16

PART 1

CHAPTER III

THE ORGANISATION OF THE GERMAN AIR FORCE

INTRODUCTION

1. In this Chapter the aim is to give an outline of the organisation of the German Air Force as an entity. Such a review will enable the reader to understand more easily the detailed organisation of the Supply services which is described in the succeeding Chapters.

The Regional Organisation of the German Air Force

2. The German Air Force was from its inception in 1935 an independent branch of the Armed Forces and as such it was able to develop an organisation free from the harness of preconceived military dogma. It must be remembered, however, that those responsible for designing the organisation of this new force were mostly senior Army officers and that their ideas were strongly influenced by established Army principles. Therefore, although the Air Force was both autonomous and a new weapon, full use was not made of these advantages because a complete severance from certain Army methods was not achieved.

3. One of the weaknesses that burdened the German Air Force in the later phases of the war was the regional system of organisation which was inherited from the Army. Instead of being separated into Bomber, Fighter, Coastal, Maintenance, etc., Commands, the German Air Force was divided into a number of territorial commands (Luftflotten — Air Fleets) each of which was virtually an independent Air Force commanding a composite range of aircraft types. The German Army was recruited and organised on a territorial basis and it is not surprising, therefore, that the Air Force was formed on similar principles. This is particularly logical when it is remembered that, in the early years of the development of the German Air Force, air strategical thought in Germany was concentrated largely on the use of the Air Force as an Army support weapon.

4. Towards the end of the war there was a tendency to concentrate aircraft into functional groups but this was done only to a small extent within the original design and did not cause any major organisational changes.

The Separation between Flying Units and Ground Units

5. The original staffs of the German Air Force observed immediately that mobility was the outstanding feature of their new weapon and, consequently, fashioned the basic organisation of the Air Force to enhance this valuable characteristic.

6. The advantage of a mobile Air Force was emphasised by the geographical situation of Germany, for the country was surrounded by potential battlefields. To build an air force in peace time which could be deployed in strength on all fronts at once would not be economical, and to spread an economical Air Force thinly on all sides would be contrary to the elementary principles of war. It was an obvious compromise, therefore, to develop many bases in all appropriate directions, to deploy air-

craft on a selected few, and to rely on the intrinsic mobility of the air weapon to concentrate rapidly in focal areas such force as circumstances might demand. To develop this principle it was necessary to provide "Hotel" facilities at all bases to maintain the incoming flying units. To ensure the utmost mobility of these flying units it was considered important to free them as far as possible from the encumbrances of long-term administrative and supply matters. This was done by establishing separate commands for flying units and divorcing them from the supply organisation. Thus, within each Luftflotte there were two separate commands: Fliegerkorps (Flying Corps) which was the Operational command and the Luftgau (Air Region) which was the Administration and Supply command.

7. This distinction between immediate operations and long-term administration and supply is the key to German Air Force organisation and is apparent in varying degrees from the Air Ministry to the front line Squadrons.

8. Before examining the detail of German Air Force organisation it may be said in summary that the Luftwaffe was built up of several small composite air forces (Luftflotte) and that within these commands there was a sharp distinction between the organisation of flying units and ground units.

BRANCHES OF THE GERMAN AIR FORCE

9. The German Air Force consisted of three main branches — the Fliegertruppe (units associated with flying), the Signals, and the Flak branches.

    (i) **The Fliegertruppe.** These consisted basically of the following:—
- (a) The flying units.
- (b) The units of the ground organisation which supported the flying units.

   The direction of both types of units was combined at command level — that is Luftflotte level — and each Luftflotte was directly subordinated to the Commander in Chief of the Air Force (Göring) in the Air Ministry. Within each Luftflotte there was a division of commands as follows: (For chain of command see Appendix 'A' to Chapter III).
- (c) Purely Operational Staffs. These were mainly, Fliegerkorps (Flying Corps), Fliegerdivision (Flying divisions), Geschwader (Wings — but more equivalent to R.A.F. Groups), Gruppe (Groups — but more equivalent to R.A.F. Wings). (For explanation of function see paragraph 10).
- (d) Ground Staffs. These were the staffs concerned with supply, accomodation, defence and construction of bases for flying units. Such staffs were Luftgau, Flughafenbereich (Airfield Regional Command — A.R.C.), and Fliegerhorst (Station Command). (For explanation of function see paragraph 10).

    (ii) **The Signals Branch.** In the German Air Force the Signals personnel formed a special branch. This branch was responsible for:—
- (a) The system of communications.
- (b) All navigational aids such as W/T, D/F, radio and visual beacons.
- (c) Observer corps and R.D.F.
- (d) Control of traffic, air safety, and rescue service.

(e) Interception of enemy signals ("Y" service).
Signals units were allocated to the Headquarters Staffs quoted in paragraph 9 (i) and they were commanded through the same channels (see Appendix "A" to Chapter III).

(iii) **The Flak Branch.** Anti-Aircraft Defence (Flak) was in all respects incorporated in the German Air Force. Flak forces were organised as follows:—

(a) For the air defence of the Reich into Flak Divisions (static) or Flak Brigades (static) which were subordinated to the various Luftgaus.

(b) Within the sphere of Army operations into Flak Corps, Flak Divisions, and Flak Brigades, all of which were motorised. These formations were subordinated to the Luftflotten or the Luftwaffen Commands.

(The supply of Flak units was in principle similar to that of Flying troops but this is the subject of a British Army study and will not be developed in this publication).

DEFINITION OF FUNCTIONS OF GERMAN AIR FORCE HEADQUARTER STAFFS

10. The following are brief definitions of the functions of the German Air Force Headquarter formations that will figure in this publication.

Staffs Combining Operational and Supply Matters

11.
(i) **The Air Ministry.** The Air Ministry was divided into two staffs — the Command of the German Air Force and the Minister for Air.

(a) The Supreme Command of the German Air Force (Oberkommando der Luftwaffe — O.K.L.). This staff was responsible for the direction of air operations, planning the supply of war material and personnel, general directions for employment of material and personnel, for the ground organisation and for all staffs, formations and units.

(b) The Minister for Air (Reichsminister der Luftfahrt — R.d.L.). The ministerial departments were charged with Administration, Finance, Legal Matters, Personnel and, until 1944, Aircraft Production.

(ii) **The Air Fleet Commands (Luftflottenkommando).** These were directly subordinated to the Commander in Chief of the German Air Force and were supreme within their own territory. They were responsible for the employment of subordinated units belonging to the Fliegertruppe, Flak and Signals branches in accordance with Air Ministry instructions. They were also responsible for supply and ground organisation throughout their Luftgaus.

(iii) **German Air Force Commands (Luftwaffenkommando).** These formations ranked between a Luftflotte and a Luftgau. Such a command was normally set up only when a theatre had become of secondary importance — in practice the staff was composed of the operational elements of a Luftflotte and the Quartermaster and Administrative elements of a Luftgau.

(iv) **German Air Force General in ...... (Kommandierender General in .....).** This was a similar staff to a German Air Force Command but of less importance. For example, the German Air Force General in Denmark.

Headquarter Staffs for Operational Formations

12.
- (i) **Fliegerkorps. (Flying Corps).** These were the largest formations of the purely operational commands and consisted of a variable number of flying units of several different types — the strength would vary from about 300 to 750 aircraft.
- (ii) **Fliegerdivisions. (Flying Division).** These were similar to Fliegerkorps but were smaller. They were usually subordinated directly to a Luftflotte but could come under a Fliegerkorps.
- (iii) **Geschwader (Wing).** Subordinated to either a Fliegerkorps or Fliegerdivision. Strength normally from 100 to 250 aircraft or 3 to 4 groups.
- (iv) **Gruppe (Group).** Subordinated to a Geschwader. Strength normally 36 to 64 aircraft or 3 to 4 staffel (squadrons). A Gruppe was the standard flying unit and usually its staffel would be based on the same or adjacent airfields.

Headquarter Staffs for Ground Organisation

13.
- (i) **Luftgau (Air Region).** This was a territorial authority carrying out supply and administration for all Air Force units within its area in accordance with the direction of its superior Luftflotte. It was responsible for the employment of subordinated Flak and Signals Units and supply establishments, for the development of the ground organisation and administration of personnel and Air Force property. The Luftgau was normally divided into about five Airfield Regional Commands.
- (ii) **Flughafenbereich (Airfield Regional Command).** Each Luftgau delegated part of its administrative responsibilities to the Airfield Regional Commands. These were normally located at the most important Air Force stations. Their main functions were the distribution of equipment, maintenance, airfield development, and defence. An A.R.C. would be responsible for about 5 airfields, 15 satellites and a number of signals and construction units, issuing stations, and supply columns.
- (iii) **Fliegerhorstkommandantur (Airfield Command).** These were static staffs installed at airfields to provide "hotel" facilities for flying units. They had to ensure the serviceablity and defence of the airfield, the installations, barracks and storehouses, and to look after the men and aircraft of the flying units based on the station. They also acted as agents for the flying units in procuring supplies and equipment from the Luftgau and Airfield Regional Command organisation.

ORGANISATION OF HEADQUARTER STAFFS

14. The Commander in Chief, the Air Officer Commanding or the Officer Commanding a Luftflotte, a Luftgau, or a Fliegerkorps, was alone in personal authority over all Headquarter Staffs and units under him. He was personally responsible for everything that was ordered to take place and which took place in his sphere of command. To assist him in his work he was provided with a staff under a Chief of Staff. The Chief of Staff, or, in the case of the Air Ministry, Luftflotte, Luftgau, and Fliegerkorps, the Chief of General Staff, was the adviser and principal aid of the commander.

15. In regard to their work, all departments of a Staff (of a Luftflotte for example) were subordinated to the Chief of General Staff — with the following four exceptions:—
  (i) Judge Advocate.
  (ii) The Intendant — except in matters of administration which directly affected the fighting spirit of the troops. The Intendant even had power of veto on orders of the Commander relating to expenditure if these orders ran counter to regulations.
  (iii) The Medical Officer, and —
  (iv) The Chief Signals Officer — only in their capacities as disciplinary authorities over their particular units.

In a disciplinary sense all members of the Staff were also subordinated to the Chief of General Staff with the four exceptions shown above. Any additional member of the Staff who ranked higher than the Chief of General Staff — for example the Chief Quartermaster was a General where as the Chief of General Staff was usually a Colonel — also became directly subordinated to the Commander in desciplinary matters.

16. All staffs were put together on similar lines so that each special part of a staff had its counterpart in the next higher command or lower staff — the strength of these staffs of course varied with the importance of their duties. A chart showing the organisation of German Air Force staffs at various levels is at Appendix "B" to Chapter III — only the main sections of the staff are shown. It will be noticed that the chart is so arranged that the departments at the various levels appear vertically above each other. These departments were, however, not in theory subordinated directly to the corresponding departments at higher formations. They were responsible only to their own Commander or Chief of Staff.

Appendix "A" to Part I, Chapter III

Chain of Command between the Higher G.A.F. Staffs.

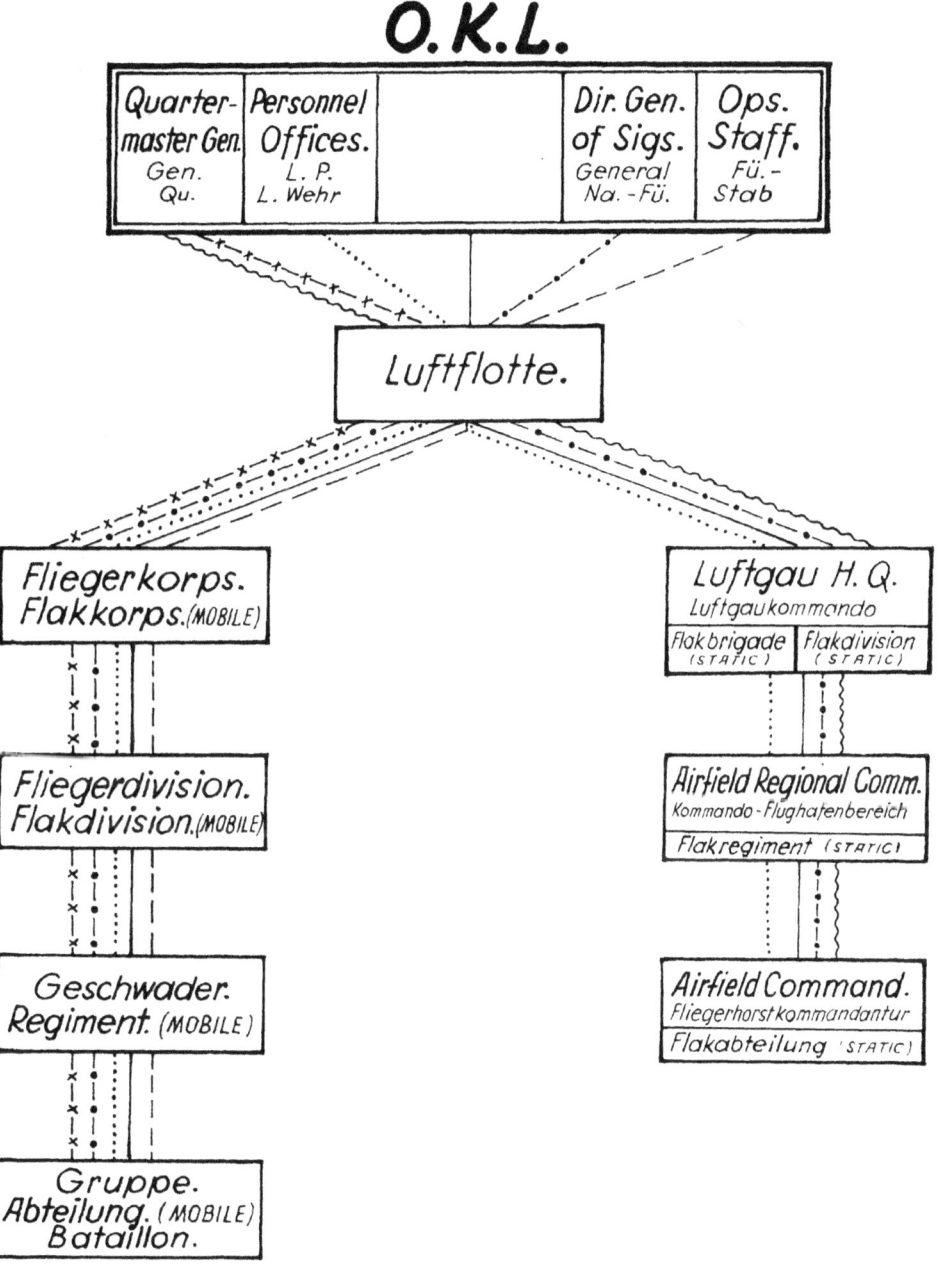

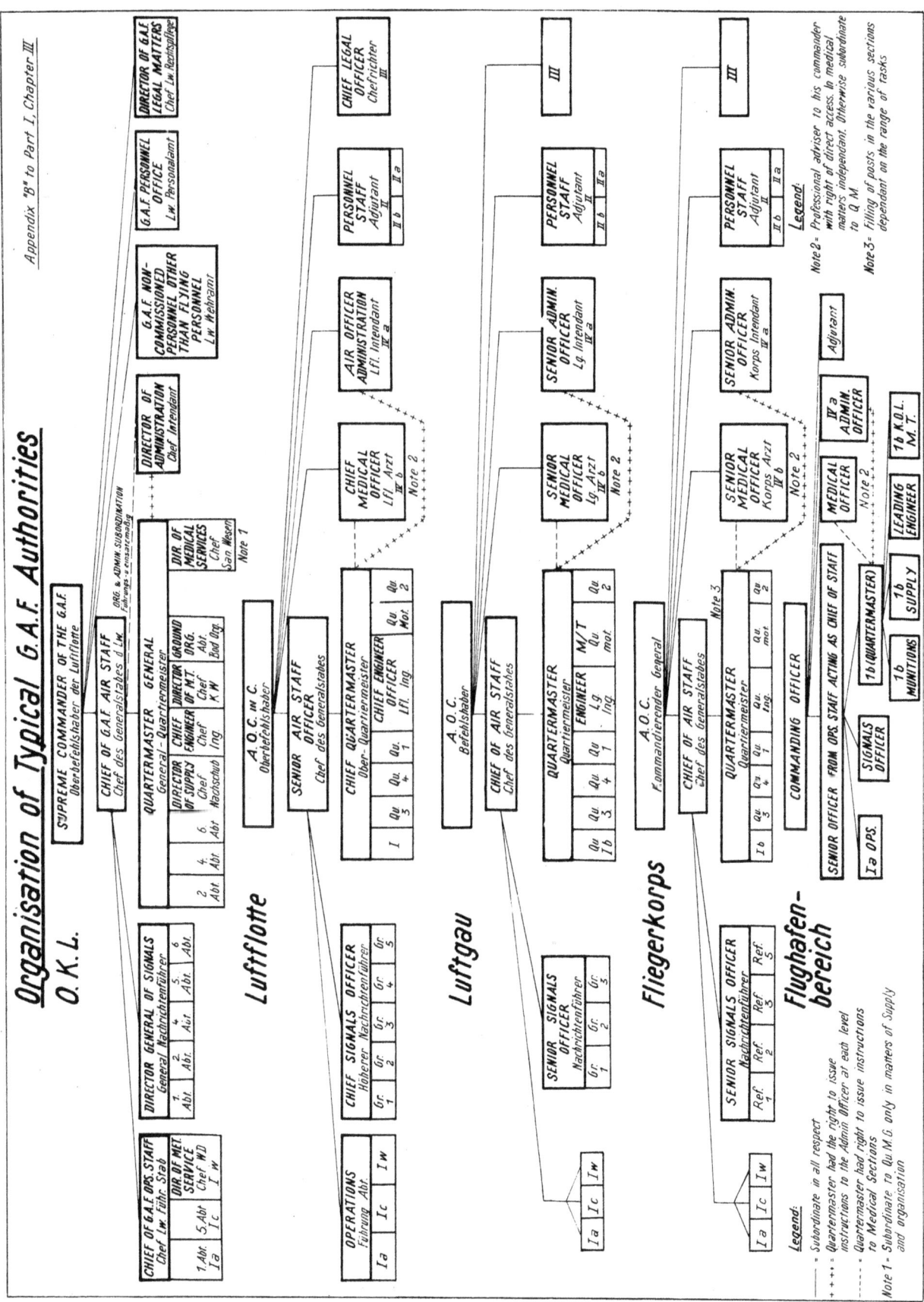

PART 1

CHAPTER IV

THE GERMAN AIR MINISTRY

INTRODUCTION Paragraphs	1—2
Dual Nature of the Air Ministry ,,	2
THE HIGH COMMAND OF THE GERMAN AIR FORCE ,,	3—12
Wartime Division of the High Command of the German Air Force ,,	8—12
THE STATE MINISTER FOR AIR ,,	13—14
THE RELATION OF AIR POLICY TO SUPPLY ,,	15—17
THE IMPLEMENTATION OF THE SUPPLY POLICY ,,	18—22
ALLOCATION AND DISTRIBUTION OF MATERIAL ,,	23—28
Movement ,,	28
MAINTENANCE, REPAIR AND SALVAGE ,,	29
FINANCIAL CONTROL ,,	30—31
CONCLUSION ,,	32—33

PART 1

CHAPTER IV

THE GERMAN AIR MINISTRY

INTRODUCTION.

1. It is the aim of this Chapter to show the part played by the German Air Ministry in organising supply for the Air Force. For the sake of simplicity the Chapter will be limited to a brief description of certain departments with particular emphasis on the relationship that existed between them. A detailed description of the Air Ministry departments connected with supply is given in Part 2, Chapter I.

Dual Nature of the Air Ministry

2. The German Air Force was directed by the Air Ministry (Reichsluftfahrt Ministerium — R.L.M.) which was a dual organisation:—

   (i) The High Command of the German Air Force (Oberkommando der Luftwaffe — O.K.L.). This section of the Air Ministry was concerned with the purely military direction of the Air Force.

   (ii) The State Minister for Air (Reichsminister der Luftfahrt — R.d.L.). This section of the Air Ministry was concerned with ministerial problems, long-term administration, financial control, civil aviation and, until 1944, Aircraft production.

Göring was head of both sections and held the title of Commander in Chief of the German Air Force and State Minister for Aviation.

THE HIGH COMMAND OF THE GERMAN AIR FORCE

3. All the departments of the High Command that are of interest to the student of supply were included in the Chief of General Staff's organisation. The core of this General Staff was formed from nine numbered departments (Abteilungen): —

   Department 1: Operations.
   Department 2: Organisation.
   Department 3: Training.
   Department 4: Preparation of Supply Directives. Allocation of operationally important supplies. Transport.
   Department 5: Intelligence.
   Department 6: Provisioning of operationally important equipment and supplies and of all initial equipment. Allocation of operationally important equipment.
   Department 7: Meteorology and mapping.
   Department 8: Historical.
   Department 9: Personnel.

4. Of these departments, numbers, 1, 3, 5, and 7 were co-ordinated by and subordinated to the Chief of the Operations Staff. This staff was responsible not only for operations but also for all basic decisions referring to the implementation of the general plan of air strategy laid down by the Chief of General Staff. The 8th Department was subordinated directly to the Chief of General Staff.

5. The other departments — numbers 2, 4, 6 and 9 — were co-ordinated by and subordinated to the Quartermaster General (General-Quartiermeister), and from this it is clear that the Quartermaster General was in fact part of the General Staff. Departments 2 and 9 together with another department called 'Strength and Establishment' (responsible for personnel establishments and for the preparation of unit equipment schedules) formed the Quartermaster General's Organisation staff. Departments 4 and 6 existed independently of each other. There were also eight other departments under the Quartermaster General but of these only three need to be considered at this stage.

(i) The Director of Supply (Chef des Nachschubwesens). Responsible for delivering all equipment except Motor Transport and Intendant supplies. He controlled the Main Equipment Depots (Signals Equipment, Ammunition, Fuel and Flak Equipment). He was also responsible for maintaining stock levels of all equipment other than aircraft, aircraft equipment, fuel, ammunition, flak equipment, Intendant supplies, and Motor Transport. Responsible for inspection of all storage installations.

(ii) The Director of Motor Transport (Chef des Kraftfahrwesens). Responsible for all matters connected with G.A.F. Motor Transport — training, procurement, allocation, storage, distribution and maintenance. Also responsible, in conjunction with Department 4, for the allocation of Motor Transport fuel. (For details see Part 2, Chapter VI.)

(iii) Chief Engineer (Luftwaffe Chef Ingenieur). Responsible for the serviceability of all aircraft and for all technical services other than Motor Transport. Controller in technical matters of all G.A.F. Engineers.

6. In addition to the numbered departments, the majority of the Inspectorates and "Air Officers" (Waffengenerale) also came under the direction of the Chief of General Staff. The object of these departments was to co-ordinate and standardise the work of the Luftflottes. The detail of their functions and their influence on supply is dealt with in Part 2, Chapter X.

7. The Chief Intendant, although subordinated for disciplinary purposes to Göring, was operationally controlled by the Chief of General Staff. His responsibility was to act as a link between the military commands and the Administration Office. The Administration Office, as is explained below, was responsible for accomodation, real estate, auditing and accounting, clothing, barrack equipment, rations, construction materials, and solid fuel. The Chief Intendant would be informed by the Quartermaster General of future plans — such as the formation of new units. He would ascertain unit requirements and receive reports on experience gained by commands and units in all administrative spheres. Such information he would collate and forward to the Administration Office to form a basis for its ministerial work and its activity in the acquisition of supplies.

Wartime Division of the High Command of the German Air Force

8. Throughout the major part of the war the High Command of the German Air Force was divided into two parts — an advanced echelon and a rear echelon. The advanced echelon comprised the Chief of General Staff, the Operations Staff, the Director General of Signals and the heads of his

Department, the Director of Training and a section of the Intelligence Department. This echelon was known by the code name "Robinson" and was located at various places throughout the war including Winniza, Goldap, Rosengarten, Insterburg and Berchtesgarden. The Quartermaster General and the other departments of the High Command made up the rear echelon which was located in and around Berlin and was known by the code name "Kurfürst".

9. Contact was maintained between "Robinson" and "Kurfürst" by an excellent Signals communications service, by a command train which ran between the two Headquarters and by a liaison officer of the Quartermaster General, with a small staff, who was permanently stationed at "Robinson". Operational orders were sent out from "Robinson" direct to the Commanders in Chief of the Luftflotten and administrative orders to "Kurfürst" for elaboration and execution.

10. "Robinson" was in the immediate neighbourhood of Hitler's Headquarters and it was here that the direction of the war was decided. There were two conferences daily at which the affairs of the German Air Force were discussed:

    (i) The afternoon conference at which Hitler presided, and at which the Air Force was represented by the Chief of the General Staff or the Chief of the Operations Staff only. At this meeting conduct and progress of the war as a whole was considered and decisions of the highest importance taken.

    (ii) The morning conference of Air Force chiefs, presided over by the Chief of the General Staff, at which the operations of the Luftwaffe on the various fronts and the decisions of the conference on the previous afternoon were discussed, and the necessary orders issued.

11. While it is true that the Chief of the General Staff in "Robinson" was in daily touch on the telephone with the Chief of the General Staffs of the Luftflotten and that Signals communications from "Robinson" were excellent, all reports from the units and commands went to "Kurfürst" for evaluation and were then available by teletype, W/T and telephone for "Robinson".

12. The liaison officer of the Quartermaster General at "Robinson" attended the morning conferences regularly. All material at "Kurfürst" was at his disposal. Unless, therefore, the Quartermaster General or any of his Departmental Chiefs were in "Robinson", it was he who provided information required by the Chief of the General Staff or took orders for the Quartermaster General departments. Examples of the day-to-day information which he had to supply were specific questions on the supply of personnel, of weapons and munitions, aircraft fuel, motor vehicles and on the production, delivery and state of equipment of aircraft. Immediately after the conference the liaison officer spoke on the telephone to the Quartermaster General and confirmed his instructions by teletype.

THE STATE MINISTER FOR AIR

13. The main ministerial departments connected with supply matters were the Director General of Equipment, the Administration Office, and the Economics Office.

    (i) Director General of Equipment (General-Luftzeugmeister). This department was responsible for the development, testing, and production of all Air Force equipment. In 1944 Speer took over all production from the Air Force and the D.G.E. was dissolved. Certain departments connected with development, testing and procurement, were retained and were reorganised to form the Chief of Technical Armaments (Chef der Technisches Luftrüstung), a department which was placed under the Chief of General Staff and acted as his link with Speer's Ministry. For further details see Part 1, Chapter II, and Part 2, Chapter II.

(ii) The Administration Office (Verwaltungsamt). This office formed all the laws and regulations that governed Air Force administration. It was responsible for auditing, accounting, accommodation and real estate, and the management of war expenditure. It was also responsible for obtaining rations, clothing, furniture, construction materials and solid fuel, and for distributing and storing these items. For further information read Part 2, Chapter VII.

(iii) Economic Office (Wirtschaftsamt). This office was responsible for preparing all contracts for the purchase of Air Force equipment, for financial and economic control of the aircraft industry, and for all patent and license matters. This subject is further discussed in Part 2, Chapter III.

14. Now that a brief analysis of the German Air Ministry has been made it is possible to give an explanation of how the various departments worked together to bring supplies to the Air Force units.

THE RELATION OF AIR POLICY TO SUPPLY

15. The future strategy of the Services was deliberated at the Supreme Command of the Armed Forces (O.K.W.), where it would receive the influence and authority of Hitler. Broad directives would then be issued by that Command to each of the three services. The Commander in Chief of the Air Force would pass on such instructions to his Chief of General Staff for detailed implementation. Within the terms of the original directive the Chief of General Staff would then indicate on what lines he wished the Air Plan to be formed and he would instruct the Chief of the Operations Staff to prepare in detail the necessary plans.

16. In long term matters the Operations Staff would issue guiding principles of policy to all the other departments of the Chief of General Staff. In short term matters — such as the planning of a particular operation — there was usually great secrecy and only a very limited number of departments were informed. To prepare for such operations the Operations Staff would issue operational orders to the Luftflotte and Department 4 of the Quartermaster General's branch would issue the complementary supply orders — special supply directives. (For further details see Part 2, Chapter I, paragraph 17.) According to Generalmajor Christian — one time Chief of the Operations Staff — the only Air Force officers informed during the planning stages of the Ardennes offensive were the Chief of Operations Staff, the heads of Ia (Ops) and Ia (Flak) of his Staff, the head of Department 4, and in the later stages, the Director General of Signals.

17. The section of the Operations Staff responsible for the Air Plan was Ia (Ops) and in order that his policy might be supported by an adequate supply he would, in all long term planning, pass appropriate orders to the Quartermaster General and to the Director General of Signals.

On paper there was a special section in the Operations Staff for signals matters — Ia (Ln.) — Luftnachrichten — Signals — but in practice these affairs were handled by Ia (Ops). There was also a Ia (Flak) section which acted in the same way as Ia (Ops) but dealt with Flak matters.

THE IMPLEMENTATION OF THE SUPPLY POLICY

18.   From the information supplied by the Operations Staff the Director General of Signals calculated his future requirements of signals and radar equipment and passed his commitments on to the Quartermaster General. The Quartermaster General then had all the data required to formulate his provisioning programmes. This information was fed into the 6th Department, whose first action was to assess the total amounts of raw material that would be necessary to implement the air policy. The results of these calculations would be passed to the Technical Office of the Director General of Equipment — and after 1944 to the Procurement Department of the Chief of Technical Armaments — the Director General of Equipment then passed on the requirements to O.K.W. who approved or reduced the figures. After the dissolution of the Defence Economy Department of O.K.W., in 1942, allocation of raw materials to the three Services was made by a special committee under the Presidency of Hitler. After July 1944 the 6th Department submitted their figures through the Chief of Technical Armaments who passed them to the Speer Ministry which, in turn, submitted them to Hitler's committee. The final quantities approved by the higher authority were notified to the 6th Department which would then apportion the raw materials to the various types of equipment required and would place orders for appropriate production through the Director General of Equipment or, later, through the Chief of Technical Armaments. The subject of provisioning is developed in Part 2, Chapter II.

19.   In accordance with the agreed policy the Quartermaster General's organisation staff would arrange to set up and man new units or dissolve existing ones. The Establishment Department of the Organisation Staff would then prepare equipment schedules for the new units and the total amount of initial equipment required would be notified to the 6th Department for inclusion in the assessment of raw materials — the Director of Supply would also be notified so that he could anticipate heavy issues from his stocks.

20.   Motor Transport vehicles and Motor Transport petrol fuel were obtained from Army sources and it was, therefore, necessary to advise also the Director of Motor Transport of future policy so that he could place his bids with the Director of Motor Transport at the Supreme Command.

21.   The Quartermaster General also warned the Chief Intendant of his future intentions so that all Administrative facilities would be ensured. The Chief Intendant correlated these commitments with those which he received from other Intendants at lower levels and passed the programme thus formed to the Administration Office for execution.

22.   The only part played by the Chief Engineer at this stage was to calculate the requirements of material and personnel for the technical ground services in the light of the present and future total strength of the Fliegertruppe units, operational conditions and anticipated concentration of effort in this or that direction. The results of these calculations he would forward to the 6th Department and to the Organisation Staff to assist them in the preparation of their programmes.

ALLOCATION AND DISTRIBUTION OF MATERIAL

23. War material produced by industry for the Air Force passed into the Director of Supply's Main Depots and the quantities were notified to the 6th Department. The first action taken by this Department was to create special reserves of equipment that was in short supply. These reserves were frozen in the Main Depots, or, in the case of aircraft, on specially selected airfields. Such reserves were classified in four categories: —

- (i) Quartermaster General's Reserves. These could be released on the authority of the Quartermaster General. They included such items as Aviation Fuel, Ammunition, Heavy Flak Guns, certain types of aircraft, and other equipment in short supply.
- (ii) O.K.L. Reserves. These could be released only on the authority of the Chief of General Staff. They included similar items to those in the Quartermaster General's reserves.
- (iii) O.K.W. Reserves. These could be released only on the authority of the Chief of the Supreme Command — Keitel. They included normally certain quantities of aviation fuel and flak equipment.
- (iv) Mobile Quartermaster Reserves. In the early years of the war, the Quartermaster General had part of his reserves of aviation fuel and explosives in trains parked in railway sidings ready for immediate despatch to any front which might suddenly become a focal point.

24. On receipt of the appropriate authority quantities of these special reserves would be released and allocated to the various Luftflotten. Department 4 would allocate all fuel and munitions, and Department 6 all other special reserve equipment. These departments would inform the Director of Supply of the allocations made and instruct him to release and deliver the materials to the consumers indicated. All operationally important equipment (aircraft, aircraft equipment, Flak equipment, and bottleneck items) and all operationally important supplies (munitions and aviation fuel) regardless of whether they formed special reserves were allocated by Departments 6 and 4 respectively in the manner described. ('Operationally important' may be defined as "equipment or supplies of which the production was limited by the amount of raw material available, by plant capacity or by any other reason").

25. Main Equipment Depots, under the direct control of the Director of Supply, maintained their stock levels of all materials other than operationally important equipment — but including aircraft spares — by direct contact with industry. Each depot specialised in certain ranges of equipment and could place running orders — based on consumption figures — for its future requirements with the particular industrial establishments which manufactured its special lines of equipment. In this way industry became automatically geared up to the supply organisation. (See also Part 2, Chapter II). Each Main Equipment Depot acted as a warehouse to its particular branches of industry, kept stock records, forecasted requirements and gave industry its orders. Equipment in this category was released by the Director of Supply on receipt of proper demands from the lower formations. (For further information on Main Depots see Part 2, Chapter VII).

26. Stocks of motor transport vehicles were held in Motor Transport stock depots under the control of the Director of Motor Transport. This

director was responsible for the allocation and distribution to all formations. (For further information read Part 2, Chapter VI).

27. Clothing depots, furniture depots, ration dumps and coal dumps were controlled by the Administration Office and that office was responsible for allocation and delivery to all formations. (For further information read Part 2, Chapter VII).

Movement

28. All arrangements for the movement of Equipment and Personnel were directed by the 4th Department. This responsibility originally involved the control of rail, sea, air and road transport. Towards the end of the war, however, — in February 1945 — the responsibility for air transport was removed from the 4th Department and a new department, the Director of Air Transport, was established to handle these affairs. Applications for rail and sea transport had to be negotiated with the Director of Transportation and the Home Staff for Overseas, in the Supreme Command of the Armed Forces, who controlled these forms of movement for the three Services. Further details of the system for Movements are given in Part 2, Chapter V.

MAINTENANCE, REPAIR AND SALVAGE

29. The Chief Engineer was responsible for all maintenance, repair and salvage of equipment, (with the exception of Motor Transport which was handled by the Director of Motor Transport). He directed the employment and equipment of all workshop sections, field workshop units, salvage units and other technical units. He was also responsible for the training of technical personnel and the inspection of technical units. In the execution of his duties the Chief Engineer worked in close collaboration with the 6th Department, the Organisation Staff, the Director General of Signals and the Director General of Equipment (later the Chief of Technical Armaments). Further information on the organisation of maintenance, repair and salvage services is given in Part 2, Chapter VIII.

FINANCIAL CONTROL

30. In peacetime the German Air Force budget was prepared by Milch who submitted it to Göring, who, in turn, took it personally to Hitler for approval. Göring has stated that Hitler always approved the budget without any discussion and, furthermore, that he raised no objections when it was exceeded. After 1939 the method was still more simplified as Göring did not even bother to see Hitler but submitted the budget to him in writing and received automatic approval.

31. Although the German Air Force was at all times free from the financial restriction of "votes" it was, of course, necessary to control expenditure within the Service. Such control was exercised by the Air Ministry department known as the Administration Office, which drew up laws and regulations covering expenditure and arranged the necessary audits to ensure that such regulations were enforced. The placing of contracts and the economical control of industry were exercised by the Economic Office of the Air Ministry. Details of the Financial Control system are given in Part 2, Chapter III.

CONCLUSION

32. At this stage — having described the Supreme Command of the Armed Forces, the Ministry of War Production and Armaments, and the

Air Ministry — it is interesting to consider again the seven basic principles of supply mentioned in the Introduction to this publication. It is now possible to show the various authorities governing the execution of these principles insofar as the German Air Force supply system was concerned.

(i) "The allocation to the Services of priorities — the nation's productive capacity and resources of raw materials." Until 1942 the Supreme Command of the Armed Forces (Directorate of Defence Economy and Armaments) was the controlling power. From 1942 a committee, under the presidency of Hitler, took over this work and in 1944, although this committee still existed, Speer's influence became very considerable.

(ii) "The transformation of planned strategy into terms of war materials." This was effected by the close collaboration between the Operations Staff and the 6th Department of the Air Ministry.

(iii) "The relationship between the individual service arms and Industry." Until 1944 the Director General of Equipment and the head of the Economics Office of the Air Ministry controlled the aircraft industry and represented the requirements of the Air Force to Industry. For the rest of the war Industry was controlled by Speer and the Chief of Technical Armaments represented the interests and requirements of the Air Force.

(iv) "The allocation of war materials within the service arms." This task was executed by Departments 4 and 6 of the Air Ministry Quartermaster General.

(v) "The distribution in accordance with the allocation and the build up and maintenance of reserves." This function was the responsibility of the Air Ministry Director of Supply, who was assisted by the 4th Department which provided the necessary transportation.

(vi) "The care, repair and salvage of war materials." The care of materials in storage was the responsibility of the Director of Supply. Repair and salvage was organised by the Chief Engineer.

(vii) "The financial control of funds allocated to the procurement of war materials." This function was undertaken by the Administration Office of the Air Ministry. The financial relationship of the Air Force to industry was the responsibility of the Economic Office.

33. In this conclusion it would be interesting to compare the departments of the German Air Ministry with the appropriate supply authorities in the Royal Air Force. An exact comparison is, however, impossible, but the following approximation may be of value:

German Departments.	**British Equivalent.**
(i) Operations Staff.	Air Ministry — Air Staff.
(ii) Quartermaster General.	Air Member for Supply and Organisation.
(iii) Department 6.	Director General of Equipment.
(iv) Department 4.	Director of Movements.
(v) Director of Supply.	Maintenance Command.
(vi) Chief Engineer.	Director General of Servicing and Maintenance.
(vii) Director General of Equipment.	Ministry of Aircraft Production.
(viii) Administration Office.	Director of Accounts.
(ix) Economics Office.	Director of Contracts.

CHART SHOWING AIR MINISTRY DEPARTMENTS.

Appendix "A" to Part I Chapter IV

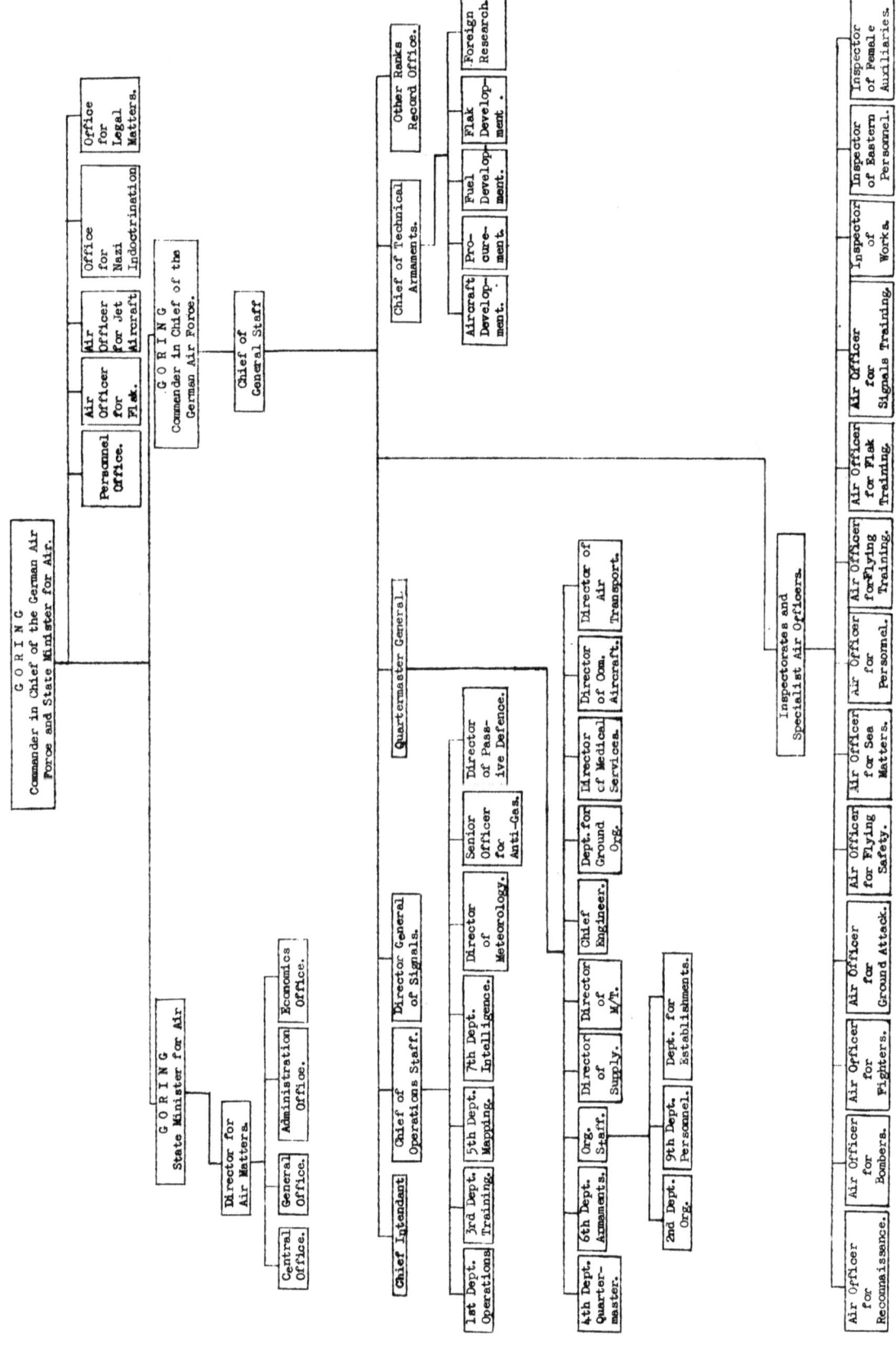

PART 1

CHAPTER V

THE ORGANISATION OF SUPPLY IN THE FIELD

INTRODUCTION	Paragraphs	1
LUFTFLOTTE	,,	2—10
Luftflotte Staff Organisation	,,	4
Operations Department	,,	5
Chief Signals Officer	,,	6
Chief Quartermaster	,,	7
Intendant	,,	8—9
Summary of Luftflotte Organisation	,,	10
LUFTGAU	,,	11—21
Luftgau Staff Organisation	,,	14—15
Luftgau Installations	,,	16
Intendant Installations	,,	17
Other Aspects of Supply (Movement, Repair, Salvage)	,,	18—21
EQUIPMENT GROUP	,,	22—34
Organisation	,,	26
Personnel	,,	27—28
Function	,,	29—31
Abolition of Equipment Groups	,,	32—34
AIRFIELD REGIONAL COMMAND	,,	35—37
AIRFIELD COMMAND	,,	38—45
Airfield Command Organisation	,,	39
Signals Section	,,	40
Workshop Section	,,	41
Motor Transport Section	,,	42
Munitions Section	,,	43
Administration Section	,,	44
Summary of Airfield Command Organisation	,,	45
CONCLUSION	,,	46—49

PART 1

CHAPTER V

THE ORGANISATION OF SUPPLY IN THE FIELD

INTRODUCTION

1. It has been explained in Part 1, Chapter III, that in the German Air Force there was a definite distinction between the flying and the ground organisation and that the two aspects were co-ordinated at Luftflotte level. The execution of supply was handled entirely by the Luftgau organisation and the system used will be further examined in the following paragraphs. In addition to the Luftflotte and Luftgau supply staffs there were, in each of the flying commands and staffs (Fliegerkorps, Geschwader, Gruppe and Staffel), very small sections — manned by a maximum of six and a minimum of one officer — detailed to supervise the supply system. These sections, however, took no part in the mechanics of supply but watched the results of the Luftgau system in relation to operational requirements. It should be explained that the officers who manned these sections were General Duties officers who did this work in addition to their own flying duties. They were given very short specialised courses to fit them for the work, (vide Part 2 Chapter IV — Personnel). When necessary, these sections brought pressure to bear on any weaknesses and represented suggestions and complaints to the Luftgau staffs or to the higher operational formations to ensure that they received adequate allocations of operationally important materials on time and in proper quantities, and that the necessary standard of aircraft serviceability was maintained. It will be observed, therefore, that, although below Luftflotte level there was complete separation of flying and supply organisations, adequate liaison was theoretically established. In practice, however, the satisfactory working of this arrangement depended to a considerable degree on the personalities of the individuals concerned.

LUFTFLOTTE

2. Each Luftflotte was virtually a small composite air force under the direct subordination of the Air Minister and Commander in Chief of the Luftwaffe (Göring). It was these commands, therefore, that executed the air plan in accordance with Air Ministry directives. In order to effect their plans the Commands passed operational orders to the flying staffs and supply orders to the Luftgau staffs and in reverse from these two channels difficulties, suggestions, reports and future requirements flowed to the Luftflotte where they were arbitrated, co-ordinated, and, if necessary, submitted to the Air Ministry. Originally it was intended that the Luftflotte staffs should only intervene in supply matters of high level importance and give general directives. However, as shortages became more severe the Luftflotte became more and more concerned in the detailed allocation of equipment — particularly of aircraft, aviation fuel and Flak ammunition.

3. As they were practically individual, independent air forces, the Luftflottes tended to become very autonomous and in many cases a Commander in Chief with a strong personality would introduce

organisational innovations that were contrary to Air Ministry rulings. It is not possible in the following paragraphs to account for all local alterations and, therefore, only the approved system will be described.

Luftflotte Staff Organisation

4. The Headquarters Staffs of German Air Force commands were all similarly constructed and each similarly organised into departments and sections which corresponded with each other from command to command (see Part 1 Chapter III). The departments of major importance in the sphere of supply were the Operations Department, the Chief Signals Officer's Department, the Chief Quartermaster, and the Intendant.

Operations Department

5. The Operations Department of the Luftflotte corresponded to the Air Ministry Operations Staff and planned current and future operations and gave general directions to **all** staffs within the Luftflotte on future policy. The orders and information issued by the Operations Department formed the basis of the supply orders which were elaborated by the Chief Quartermaster.

Chief Signals Officer

6. Operational orders to Signals regiments were issued by the Chief Signals Officer and formed the basis of corresponding Signals supply orders which were prepared by the Chief Quartermaster. The Chief Signals Officer also allocated major items of ground signals equipment to the appropriate formations and on his instructions such equipment would be released and delivered by arrangements initiated by the Chief Quartermaster.

Chief Quartermaster

7. The Operations Department was enjoined to keep the Chief Quartermaster constantly advised of their operational intentions. The Chief Quartermaster, therefore, was the only supply authority in the Luftflotte area who knew the operational plans, which were usually most secret and closely guarded by security. With this knowledge he was enabled to issue instructions and direct the Luftgau Quartermasters who executed the detail work. The Chief Quartermaster was not concerned with details of execution and this will be more clearly understood if it is pointed out that the location of a Luftflotte Headquarters was usually hundreds of miles nearer the battle front than that of the Luftgau Headquarters and was considerably smaller and more mobile. In addition to giving orders and directions, the Chief Quartermaster kept himself constantly advised of the supply situation in his area by studying the reports of his Luftgau Quartermasters and was, therefore, able to offer accurate information and advice when so requested by his Chief of Staff. The Chief Quartermaster was instructed to reveal any difficulties being experienced or expected and to ensure that operations were not hindered or delayed by any negligence on his part or on the part of the organisations below him. The Chief Quartermaster performed his task through the following organisations:—

(i) O.Qu./1b. This section corresponded to the Quartermaster General's Organisation Staff at the Air Ministry. Its tasks included the formation, transfer, establishment, reorganisation and disbandment of units. Mobilisation records of personnel and materials. Supervision of establishments and strength for personnel and war materials. Supervision of quartering.

(ii) O.Qu/Qu. 1. This section was responsible for the allocation and control of aircraft, aircraft equipment, aircraft armament, explosives, aviation spirit, special fuels, oxygen, smoke, ground equipment and General Army Equipment. General Army Equipment included such common user items as bicycles, field kitchens, tents, entrenching tools, signalling equipment and anti-gas equipment. — it did not include common user armament and ammunition.

(iii) O.Qu/Qu 2. This section was responsible for planning the development and construction of the ground installations and for liaison with the Todt organisation.

(iv) O.Qu./Qu 3. This was the transport section that corresponded to the 4th Abteilung of the Quartermaster General's Department in the Air Ministry. It directed the railroad and water transport within the Luftflotte Ministry. It did not control movements by M/T columns (see Qu. Mot.).

(v) O.Qu/Qu 4. This section was responsible for the allocation, control and supervision of all Flak equipment and common user ammunition.

(vi) O.Qu/Qu. Mot. This section was responsible for the operational readiness and allocation of Motor Transport within the Luftflotte area, for the training of M/T personnel, for organisation of M/T units, for the allocation and control of M/T columns and for liaison with the Army M/T authorities at Army Group level.

(vii) O.Qu/Qu. Chief Engineer. The authority of the Chief Engineer varied according to the personality of the individual and his relationship with the C. in C. Luftflotte and the Chief Quartermaster. Normally he was responsible only for repair, maintenance and employment of technical personnel. Occasionally — in Luftflotte Reich for example — he would assume in addition to his usual duties part of the responsibilities of Qu. 1. That is, the Chief Engineer became responsible for the allocation and control of aircraft, aircraft equipment and ground equipment.

Intendant

8. Insofar as equipment is concerned, the Intendant's office was responsible for the supply of clothing, barrack equipment, solid fuel, rations, and construction materials. All Intendant duties were performed by beamte (uniformed civil servants), Truppensonderdienst (literally — special duties officers — actually beamte raised to officer status but with certain limitations) and civilians. This type of work was handled by officials because it was considered to be too detailed and too non-military in character to be delegated to regular officers. For many years in the past of German military history the administrative or Intendant's duties were undertaken by beamte and the air force automatically adopted this tradition.

9. The Luftflotte Intendant, although a separate department, worked very closely with the Chief Quartermaster from whom he obtained advice

as to future policy. The Intendant supervised and directed the Luftgau Intendants, who executed the detailed work, co-ordinated their requirements and represented difficulties and future commitments to the Air Ministry. The Luftflotte Intendant performed his duties through a staff which was divided into two sections as follows:—

(i) **Section I.** This Section was responsible for Administrative organisation, accounting, rations and catering, canteen, and personnel matters for officials.

(ii) **Section II.** This section handled clothing, accommodation, works matters, real estate, and personnel affairs for civilian employees.

Summary of Luftflotte Organisation.

10. The Luftflotte Headquarters was a small staff near the battle front in close touch with operational requirements and with the daily battle movements. In collaboration with the Operations Department, the Chief Signals Officer, the Chief Quartermaster, and the Intendant were able to determine the future supply policy and to settle important points arising from the day to day situation. The policy thus formed was passed on to the Luftgau for execution. In the later stages of the war the Luftflotte Headquarters took an interest in detail to the extent of determining allocation of operationally important equipment.

LUFTGAU

11. The importance of the Luftgau has already become apparent from the survey of the Luftflotte organisation and in the following paragraphs a study will be made of the machinery available within the Luftgau for the execution of the supply policy.

12. The Luftflotte area was usually divided into two or three Luftgau (Air Administrative Areas) whose responsibilities included the control of the whole ground organisation, the operation of supply and repair installations and the construction and maintenance of airfields. It should be noted that the operation of supply was subject to a dual control. Directions on the deployment of supply installations, stock movements and general administrative policy emanated from the Luftgau (Quartermaster Staff), while technical control and Equipment Administration were directed by the Air Ministry (Director of Supply). The two channels of command were united in an organisation known as an Equipment Group, which was responsible for putting the two policies into effect. (For details of the Equipment Group's function and organisation, see paras. 22.—34).

13. As the theatre of war expanded outwards from Germany the home Luftgaus would send forward a Field Headquarters to be conveniently placed for undertaking its responsibilities for supervising administration and supply. Projected still further forward, almost to the front line, were Special Luftgau Staffs (Luftgau Stabe z b. V.) whose duties were to reconnoitre and to establish forward airfields and to organise the new forward supply lines and set up supply installations. Each Special Luftgau Staff was normally responsible for the area occupied by a Fliegerkorps. If the area of operations was limited, then a Special Airfield Regional Command might assume the duties of the Special Luftgau Staff. When, however, the conditions in the forward areas became more stable and the Airfield Regional Commands and the Airfield Commands had been set up at their new bases the Special Luftgau Staffs were withdrawn and their

work was taken over by the organisation that they had established. The whole organisation of installations, Airfield Regional Commands, and Airfield Commands, was then controlled by a permanent "field" Luftgau which usually adopted the name of the country or area it administered — for example: Luftgau Holland, Luftgau Sicily and Luftgau Kiev.

Luftgau Staff Organisation

14.   The Luftflotte has been described as a small directing authority and the Luftgau as an executive authority and it is now appropriate to examine the machinery available for this work.

15.   The staff organisation at a Luftgau Headquarters was to the same design as that of the Luftflotte and again it was the operational department, the Signals Officer, the Quartermaster and the Intendant who worked together to control supply matters. The main differences in the functions of these departments were as follows:—

   (i)   **Operations Department.** In the general direction of Luftgau affairs this department played a comparatively less important role than the corresponding staff at the Luftflotte. In actual operational affairs its main concern was with Flak units.

   (ii) **Signals Officer.** The Signals Officer's Staff played a similar role to that of the Chief Signals Officer at Luftflotte though his work was more detailed and in nearer relationship to the operational signals units. He worked closely with the Quartermaster in supply of ground signals equipment.

   (iii) **The Quartermaster.** The Quartermaster's staff was organised into sections on similar lines which had similar functions to those under the Chief Quartermaster. The main difference was, of course, that the sections were larger and dealt with more detailed work. A further difference was that the Luftgau engineer's tasks were restricted to repair, maintenance and salvage, though he worked very closely with Qu.1.

   (iv) **The Intendant.** The Intendant's staff was also larger than that of the Luftflotte Intendant and it dealt with more detailed work. The organisation of his staff was somewhat different and instead of consisting of two sections it was divided into three sections as follows:—

   (a) **Section A.** This section was responsible for administrative organisation, accounting and economic management, clothing, messing, rations, canteens, and pay and personnel matters relating to officials and civilian employees.

   (b) **Section L.** This section was responsible for accommodation, furniture, solid fuel, etc., property and estate matters, agriculture, forestry and fire precautions.

   (c) **Section T.** This section was responsible for all Works matters — that is, control and maintenance of all permanent machines and technical installations (e.g. power plants), provision of electric current and contracting for gas and water supply.

Luftgau Installations

16.   The Luftgau Headquarters controlled certain storage installations, within the Luftgau area, which handled the physical aspects of supply. The deployment and general administrative policy of such installations

was controlled by the Quartermaster and the Intendant. After 1943 the technical and detailed control of the Quartermaster installations was also handled by the Quartermaster staff. Prior to 1943, however, technical and detailed control of the Quartermaster installations was exercised through organisations called Equipment Groups (see paragraphs 22 to 34). Storage installations existed for the following types of equipment. (For details of those installations see Part 2 Chapter VII).

Quartermasters Installations

(i) **Aircraft Equipment and Ground Technical Equipment.** To handle these materials there were usually one or two Air Parks (Luftpark) per Luftgau, each holding a 3 months' stock of a universal range. These parks were replenished from Main Equipment Depots which were operationally and technically controlled by the Director of Supply in the Air Ministry and for administrative and disciplinary matters by the Luftgau. In addition to the Air Parks there were usually 4 or 5 Equipment Issuing Stations (Geräteausgabestelle — GAST) or Enlarged Equipment Issuing Stations holding a 3 months' supply of an appropriate range controlled either directly by the Luftgau H.Q. or the A.R.C. H.Q., and small station stocks held under the control of the Airfield Commands.

(ii) **Flak Equipment.** In each Luftgau there were from 5—10 Flak Equipment Issuing Stations, which were replenished from Flak Equipment Depots, controlled operationally and technically by the Air Ministry Director of Supply and for administrative and disciplinary matters by the appropriate Luftgau.

(iii) **Signals Equipment.** In the German Air Force, signals equipment was handled by separate specialist installations. In each Luftgau there were about 2 Air Parks, whose universal holding included signals equipment, and 4 or 5 Air Signals Equipment Issuing Stations. These units were replenished from Main Air Signals Equipment Depots, controlled operationally and technically by controlled by the Air Ministry (Director of Supply in conjunction with Director General of Signals) and only for administrative and disciplinary matters by the Luftgau. Small stocks were also held on stations and units.

(iv) **Aviation Spirit.** The Luftgau allocations of aviation spirit were stored in Air Tank Depots of which there were 2 to 4 in each area. These were replenished from Bulk Tank Depots which were operationally and technically controlled by the Air Ministry (Director of Supply) and for administrative and disciplinary matters by the Luftgau. In addition, there were a number of Aviation Fuel Issuing Stations and, of course, airfield storage tanks.

(vi) **Explosives.** Explosives were made up and to a small degree stored at Main Ammunition Depots — the majority of stocks were stored in Ammunition Depots. Both types of depot were operationally and technically controlled by the Air Ministry (Director of Supply) and for administrative and disciplinary matters by the Luftgau. Explosives allocated to the Luftgau were stored:—

    (a) **Air Explosives:**   On G.A.F. station bomb dumps;
    (b) **Flak Ammunition:** In Flak Ammunition Issuing Stations.

Intendant Installations

17.
- (i) **Clothing.** In each Luftgau there were 2 to 5 Clothing Stores which held stocks on the basis of 20% per strength of the units within the area. These clothing stores were replenished from the Main Clothing Depots which were operationally and technically controlled by the Air Ministry (Administrative Office) and for administrative and disciplinary matters by the Luftgau. There were also small clothing stores at stations known as Clothing Rooms.
- (ii) **Barrack Equipment.** This type of equipment was procured by the Luftgau Intendant's office and stored in warehouses under his control. Small quantities were stored on stations.
- (iii) **Construction Materials.** Several large works depots were subordinated to the Luftgau Intendant. These depots held all types of constructional machines and materials.

Other Aspects of Supply

18. In addition to the storage of war materials, there are three other aspects of supply that are important and require consideration at this stage. These subjects will be covered only briefly in the following paragraphs and the detailed study is made in the appropriate Chapter of Part 2.

Movement

19. Each Luftgau had an allocation of Transport Columns, some of which it retained for its own use and some which it attached to the A.R.C.s. For movement by rail it could apply either directly to the G.A.F. liaison officer with the Army Transport Commands or to the Air Ministry (4th Abteilung) via Luftflotte H.Q. (For further details see Part 2, Chapter V).

Repairs

20. Each Luftgau was responsible for repairing damaged equipment or returning such equipment to be repaired by the appropriate industry. Generally, the Luftgau organisations repaired equipment which showed up to 30% damage, provided such damage, did not include main component parts — other repairs would be undertaken by industry. Overhauls and repairs to engines were not normally done by the Luftgau. Repair units available to the Luftgau were static workshops on airfields and mobile repair columns. (For further details see Part 2, Chapter VIII).

Salvage

21. In each Luftgau there was a small section of the Qu.Engineer's staff which directed the salvage organisation throughout the area. Under his control there was usually a salvage battalion — consisting of a Headquarters and 4 companies, a booty park and dismantling establishment. (For further details see Part 2, Chapter VIII.)

EQUIPMENT GROUPS

22. Until 1943, there were located with each Luftgau Headquarters offices known as "Equipment Groups". These offices were subordinated to the Luftgau Headquarters for operational and disciplinary matters, but received technical instructions (viz. methods of storage, care of equipment, safety precautions, stock-taking procedures, equipment regulations, etc.) from either the Luftgau Quartermaster or the Air Ministry Supply Office — later Director of Supply.

23. The Equipment Groups were virtually separate organisations to which all the **Luftgau** supply installations were subordinated. Luftgau supply installations included such units as Air Parks and Issuing Stations. Main Equipment Depots, Main Ammunition Depots, Ammunition Depots and Petrol Depots were technically controlled directly by the Director of Supply, administered and disciplined by Luftgau, and were therefore outside the province of the Equipment Groups.

24. It should be noted that Equipment Groups controlled no Intendant materials other than those stored in Air Parks and Issuing Stations. This range included office materials, forms, etc. The main range of Intendant material, such as clothing, barrack equipment, solid fuel, etc., was controlled through Intendant channels, i. e. Air Ministry Administration Office — Luftflotte Intendant — Luftgau Intendant.

25. It was the responsibility of the Equipment Groups to send Inspectors to Airfield Storeholding Sections to ensure that all Equipment regulations were enforced. These "Inspectors" were found from the ordinary Equipment Group staff, and were not specially established as Inspectors. The installations controlled by the Equipment Groups (Air Parks and Issuing Stations) on the other hand, were periodically visited by Inspectors from the Air Ministry Supply Office. These Inspectors, however, were engaged on ful-time duties of Equipment Inspection.

Organisation

26. The Equipment Group was divided into five sections, as follow:—
- (i) **Section I:** This section was responsible for Administration, Organisation and Personnel. It was headed by an officer of the rank of Lieutenant Colonel or Major, whose duties included those of Second in Command of the Equipment Group.
- (ii) **Section II:** This section was responsible for aircraft and aircraft spares. It comprised four subsections which were:
  - (a) II/1. Complete aircraft.
  - (b) II/2. Airborne equipment.
  - (c) II/3. Airframe spares.
  - (d) II/4. Aero engines, engine spares, propellers, and propellor spares.
- (iii) **Section III:** This section was responsible for miscellaneous equipment, P.O.L., and signals equipment. It comprised six sub-sections which were:—
  - (a) III/1. Ground equipment.
  - (b) III/2. Tools and working materials.
  - (c) III/3. Photographic equipment.
  - (d) III/4. Signals equipment.
  - (e) III/5. P.O.L.
  - (f) III/6. Compressed gases and associated apparatus.
- (iv) **Section IV:** This section was responsible for all armament and explosives. It comprised five sub-sections which were:—
  - (a) IV/1. Anti-aircraft guns and predictors.
  - (b) IV/2. Machine guns and small arms.
  - (c) IV/3. S.A.A.
  - (d) IV/4. Bombs and pyrotechnics.
  - (e) IV/5. Torpedos, mines and special weapons.

(v) **Section "K"** This Section was responsible for Motor Transport. It comprised three sub-sections which were:—
    (a) K/1. Complete vehicles.
    (b) K/2. Motor Transport spares.
    (c) K/3. Motor Transport fuel and tyres.

Personnel

27. The Equipment Group was commanded by an officer, usually of the rank of Colonel. Each section was also commanded by an officer of the rank of Major, with the exception of Section I where the rank was usually that of Lieutenant Colonel. As has already been mentioned, this officer was Second in Command of the Equipment Group. None of the Officer appointments, including that of the Commanding Officer, was established as posts for General Staff Officers and, consequently, no General Staff Officer had any real understanding of the problems in connection with the work undertaken by an Equipment Group. The majority of the remaining posts requiring personnel of Officer status were filled by Officials, who had specialised experience in appropriate technical subjects. The total number of Officers and Officials amounted to 25 to 30 people, who were spread fairly evenly over the five sections.

28. The Staff supporting the Officers and Officials consisted of up to 200 "other ranks", lower grade officials and civilian employees. Of this number, approximately 100 were female workers who were stated to have been particularly suited to duties of this nature.

29. The function of the Equipment Groups was to control issues from the Luftgau Equipment Installations to the Consumer Units. To enable this to be done the Equipment Group maintained a record of stocks held in all installations. A quarterly or half-yearly stock return of all items was compiled by Air Parks and Issuing Stations and forwarded to the Equipment Groups, whilst items in short supply and Main Items of equipment (the issue of which was rigidly controlled by the Luftgau Quartermaster) were the subject of a monthly return. All demands for Equipment raised by consumer units were routed through the Equipment Group, and that office, with its knowledge of stock positions at the various installations, was able to allocate the demand to whichever Air Park or Issuing Station could satisfy it from available stocks. The number of demands handled daily by the Equipment Groups has not been positively ascertained, but it can be stated that it would not compare with the vast number of transcriptions handled daily by a Master Provision Office in the Royal Air Force. The individual airfields were encouraged to maintain stocks at a comparatively high level, and except for "short supply" items (which in any case would have been forwarded direct to the Luftgau Quartermaster as explained in paragraph 30) the demands would normally represent bulk replenishments of items in fairly sound supply. The fact that the Equipment Group handled all demands enabled them to keep accurate and up-to-date stock records of equipment holdings within the area without the necessity of more frequent stock reports being supplied by Air Parks and Issuing Stations. The accuracy of Stock Returns submitted by the Installations was ensured by a system of periodical checks of physical stocks by the Equipment Group Staffs. These checks were sometimes of a cursory nature ("snap" checks of certain important items) and sometimes in extreme detail, covering all items and engaging the attention of the appropriate section of the Equipment Group Staff for three or four weeks.

30. It is interesting to observe that, before the war, the average time taken to satisfy a demand from a consumer unit was 7 to 8 days. In wartime, somewhat naturally, the time taken to satisfy a demand depended to a large extent on the degree of priority accorded to it. Demands of a low priority continued to take eight days or probably a little longer, but important demands would be satisfied in three to four days. Demands for operationally important (short supply and main items) or "bottleneck" items were forwarded direct to the Luftgau Quartermaster, in many instances being transmitted telephonically in advance. The Luftgau Quartermaster would authorise an Air Park or Issuing Station (also telephonically) to meet the demand, and would subsequently advise the Equipment Group of the action taken.

31. Provisioning data in the form of past consumption figures and current stocks, was forwarded to the Director of Supply by the Equipment Groups in respect of all items other than "Operationally Important" equipment (short supply and main items) and "Supplies". The Director of Supply incorporated this information with similar reports received from the Main Depots, and with other relevant information received from the Quartermaster General (i. e. the proposed formation of new units, the establishments of such units as laid down by the Organisation Department, and the anticipated intensity and duration of future operations) would prepare instructions to be passed to Industry. For "Operationally Important" equipment (as defined above) and "Supplies", however, the Luftgau Quartermaster, with the assistance of the Equipment Group, would forward appropriate returns to the 6th Department who took the necessary provisioning action. (See also Part 2, Chapter II).

Abolition of Equipment Groups

32. The system of "Equipment Groups" proved cumbersome and finally, in 1943, they were abolished — part of their work being taken over by the Main Equipment Depots and part by the Luftgau Quartermaster Staff. The division of responsibilities between these two formations could be described as follows:

(i) Luftgau Quartermaster. The major responsibilities were assumed by the Luftgau Quartermaster and to enable him to perform his new duties efficiently a proportion of the Equipment Group specialists were transferred to his staff. From all points of view, this must be considered a progressive step, as all demands now came under the control of one office. That is to say, both normal "stock" demands, and demands for Operationally Important and Short Supply items came directly under the Quartermaster.

(ii) Main Equipment Depots. Shortly before the abolition of the Equipment Groups, the Aircraft Industry in Germany was re-organised and, at the same time, the Main Equipment Depots were authorised to place orders directly on Industry (instead of through the Director of Supply) through the new "Committee Leaders". The Main Equipment Depots now received periodical returns of current stocks and past consumption data from the Air Parks and Issuing Stations, via the Luftgau Quartermaster. This information, combined with appropriate details, provided by the Director of Supply, enabled the Main Equipment Depots to place considered orders with Industry. (See also Part 2, Chapter II).

33. The dissolution of the Equipment Groups formed the centre of a controversy in the German Air Force, and although it is interesting to examine in the following paragraph some of the reasons that led up to their abolition, it must be realised that it has been almost impossible to obtain a disinterested and unprejudiced opinion upon the subject. Although many German officers, including those of General rank, have expressed opinions, such views have been necessarily biased because of the appointments held by these officers and the consequent addition to or reduction of personal prestige and responsibilities engendered by the revision of policy.

34. At the Luftgau Headquarters, supply matters were handled through a threefold division of Staff — the Operational Staff, the Quartermaster Staff (Operational supply) and the Equipment Group (Executive supply). This system, however, did not prove to be an unqualified success. The three staff divisions, which should have maintained a close liaison, were each restricted by security regulations and, furthermore, these staffs were often separated by considerable distances. For example, Luftflotte 1 had one of its Luftgau Headquarters at Königsberg while the complementary Equipment Group was at Riga, 400 miles away. Luftflotte 2 had a Luftgau Headquarters at Posen with its Equipment Group at Minsk, a distance of 500 miles away. These factors combined with insufficient transport, and a low priority of signals communications, to make the supply system cumbersome. Such circumstances tended to create a "self-rule" and "self-sufficiency" in the Equipment Groups, which drew them apart from their own Luftgau Headquarters, and still further separated them from the Luftflotte, so that gradually they lost contact with the immediate operational picture. Difficulties were further increased by shortages of equipment and by the loss of initiative to the Allies, and it became more and more necessary to centralise control, and reduce the stages between the Luftflotte Headquarters and the supply installations. Finally, the arguments of the Luftflotte Commanders won the day and the Equipment Groups were dissolved.

AIRFIELD REGIONAL COMMAND

35. The Luftgau could not carry out the tasks and supervision of the whole ground organisation through the Luftgau central control channels only. Hence the whole Luftgau area was sub-divided into a number (varying from 3 to 5) of subordinate administrative commands called Airfield Regional Commands (A.R.C.). The staff of the A.R.C. was made up of sections that corresponded to those of a Luftgau, although they were very much smaller and had a more limited scope. The Staffs directing and handling supply were 1a. (equivalent to Operations Department), Senior Signals Officer, 1b. (equivalent to Quartermaster Staff) and the Administrative official (equivalent to Intendant).

36. Subordinated in every respect to the Commanding Officer of the A.R.C. were all airfield commands, airfields, landing grounds, ranges, dummy sites, wireless transmission control stations, and ground defence companies. G.A.F. Works Units, State Labour Service Units and landing ground destruction units were subordinated to him for operational purposes. In addition, various transport columns, supply columns and issuing stations were subordinated to the A.R.C. from time to time on the orders of the Luftgau. At one time all issuing stations — except those for Flak — were subordinated in every respect to the A.R.C. and these issuing stations were stocked according to the units in their region. This was not

very economical, as it meant that three months' reserve of equipment was being held in each A.R.C. and thus equipment in short supply was being frozen in many places. The result was that the stocks of neighbouring issuing stations had to be adjusted so that they could help each other and reduce the total number of reserves — to do this effectively necessitated the transfer of control from the A.R.C. to Luftgau. In particular circumstances, however, the A.R.C. retained control.

37. The duties of the A.R.C. commander included the following tasks:—
   (i) The supply of the flying and signals units situated within the region in accordance with the orders of the Luftgau Headquarters. Such supply tasks included the supervision of airfield stocks, the representation of difficulties and special requirements to the Luftgau and occasionally the control of issuing stations.
   (ii) The supervision of repair facilities in the region. Field workshop platoons, each specialising in the repair of a particular type of aircraft and one or more M/T repair platoons, were attached to the A.R.C.
   (iii) The air and ground defence of all G.A.F. installations in the region but only air defence insofar as Flak had not taken over protection.
   (iv) The administration, maintenance, development, reconstruction and repairs of G.A.F. airfields and installations.
   (v) Camouflage, A.R.P., firefighting and anti-gas measures for all G.A.F. units in the region.
   (vi) The development and operation of signals communications.
   (vii) The supervision of M/T, the execution of M/T regulations and the maintenance of the operational readiness of the transport and fuel columns.

AIRFIELD COMMAND

38. The division between flying and ground organisation is clearly illustrated by the system adopted for running the German Air Force airfields. On the one hand there were the flying units in occupation, the commander of which took precedence over all other officers so long as the units were based there: on the other hand there was the airfield commander who organised the supply and administrative matters and commanded the station in the absence of any flying units. In addition to the airfield on which it was based, the airfield command normally controlled a small number of reserve airfields and landing grounds. Flying units frequently moved from one station to another but the Airfield Command generally remained on the same station. In a war of movement the Airfield Command would advance to newly organised or newly constructed bases and make the necessary arrangements for the incoming flying units.

Airfield Command Organisation

39. Throughout the war there were many organisational alterations in the set up of German Airfield Commands but these were mainly questions of subordination and the guiding principles remained comparatively unchanged. A typical illustration of the various sections of an Airfield Command is shown at Appendix "A" to this Chapter. This organisation may be compared roughly with that of a Luftgau Headquarters, etc. — the offices for Special Duties corresponding to the Operations Department; the Signals Section to the Chief Signals Officer; the Workshop Section, the

M/T Section and the Ammunition Section to the Quartermaster; and the Administration Section to the Intendant. These sections were each independently responsible for their own stores and for demanding replenishments, which they did in the manner described in the following paragraphs.

Signals Section

40. This section handled equipment for the ground signals organisation only. The channels of supply and demand have to be considered in two categories:

(i) Main Equipment. This included such items as transmitters, receivers, telephone exchanges and teleprinter sets. The channels of demand and supply were: —

(a) Demand. Signals Section to A.R.C. to Luftgau to Luftflotte to Air Ministry (Director General of Supply).

(b) Supply. Director General of Signals would instruct the Director of Supply to release the equipment from the depots under his control.

(ii) Accessory Equipment and Expendable Materials. These types of equipment were demanded by the Signals Section directly from the Air Signals Issuing Stations or the Air Signals Stores Parks.

Workshop Section

41. This section was headed by a Technical Superintendant, an engineer official of the equivalent rank of Squadron Leader. The section handled the repair of aircraft, armament and ground equipment, and was responsible for demanding and storing aircraft equipment, ground equipment, armament equipment and petrol. It was divided into three sections as follows: —

(i) Workshops Section. This section was headed by an engineer official of the equivalent rank of Flight Lieutenant. The section was divided into five-sub-sections responsible for the repair of Airframes, Engines, Instruments, Armament and Ground Equipment.

(ii) Testing Section. Headed by an engineer official of the equivalent rank of Flight Lieutenant. There were three sub-sections — Airframes, Engines, Ground Equipment (including Instruments and Armament) — which were responsible for testing the repairs done in the appropriate workshops.

(iii) Aircraft Technical Administration Section. This section was headed by a Technical Official usually of a rank equivalent to a Flight Lieutenant. The section was divided into four sub-sections for supervision of stores, preparation of demands, stock recording, and petrol. The channels of supply and demand for aircraft equipment, spares, armament equipment and ground equipment were as follows: —

(a) Main Equipment. All main equipment — engines, engine starters, bomb trollies, etc. — special equipment, and items in short supply were demanded through Quartermaster channels — i.e. A.R.C., Luftgau, Luftflotte, Air Ministry (Quartermaster General Abteilung 6). When authority for release was given by Abteilung 6 the material would be delivered through Supply channels — Main Depots, Parks, Issuing Stations — on arrangements made by the Director of Supply.

(b) **Accessory Equipment, Spares, and General Army Equipment.** Components and spares for main equipment, General Army Equipment (bicycles, field kitchens, anti-gas equipment, etc.) and working materials (wood, metal, tubes, leather, nuts and washers, etc.) were demanded directly from supply installations.

(c) **Fuel.** Aviation Fuel was issued on a quota basis — the Airfield Command reported its stocks daily to the Luftgau and automatically received replenishments if this was possible from the amount allocated by the Luftflotten to the Luftgau. Replenishments were delivered through supply channels — Tank Depots and Issuing Stations.

Motor Transport Section

42. The M/T section received allocations of vehicles in accordance with the unit establishments from Quartermaster channels. Demands for replacements were made through such channels and stocks would then be released from M/T Stocks depots. Small repairs were done within the Airfield Command by the M/T section, who demanded spares from Army Central Spares Depots. (For further details see Part 2, Chapter VI.)

Munitions Section

43. The bomb dumps and ammunition stores were under the control of a Munition official. Daily consumption reports were rendered through the Technical Administration Section to the Luftgau Quartermaster, who arranged automatic replenishments from his quota. Special demands had to be submitted through Quartermaster channels to the Air Ministry (Abteilung 4) who authorised supply through the Director of Supply.

Administration Section

44. The Administration Section controlled the Airfield Command clothing rooms, ration stores, and barrack equipment.

(i) **Clothing.** The clothing rooms demanded replenishments directly from the Luftgau clothing stores.

(ii) **Rations.** On arrangements made by the Luftgau Intendant each Airfield Command drew its ration daily from the designated Army Issuing store.

(iii) **Barrack Equipment.** The Administration Section was empowered by the Luftgau to procure locally small amounts of barrack equipment. The bulk of equipment had to be demanded from the Luftgau Intendant who would release stocks from the warehouses under his control.

Summary of Airfield Command Organisation

45. The function of the Airfield Command was to provide "hotel" facilities for the flying units and to free them as far as possible from all ground responsibilities. The Airfield Command would be warned by the Luftgau that a certain flying unit was to be accommodated for a certain period and it would then ensure that all preparations were made to support, house and maintain both the aircraft and the personnel. Equipment and supplies were not controlled centrally by one authority but independently by the Signals Section, the M/T Section, the Technical Administration Section and the Administration Section. The Technical

officers of the flying units would maintain a very close liaison with these authorities to ensure that their wishes were executed.

CONCLUSION

46. From the above examination of the supply organisation in the field it is possible to see a clear example of the German military principle that distinguishes "operational direction" from "execution". Supply in the German Air Force was considered in two phases — "Operational direction of supply" (Versorgungsführung) and the "Execution and Administration of Supply" (Versorgungsdurchführung und Verwaltung). The first phase was the control of supplies — that is the issue of orders for the procurement of war materials and the allocation of them to units in accordance with the plans of the operational staffs. The staffs controlling the operational direction of supply were the Quartermaster General at the Air Ministry (through his organisation staff and the 4th and 6th Abteilungs), the Chief Quartermasters at the Luftflotten and the Quartermasters at the Luftgaus and Fliegerkorps. The second phase — the execution and administration of supply — was the provision of war materials and the transportation of them to units in accordance with the orders of the operational directors of Supply and the organisation, safeguarding and repair of the items supplied — insofar as this last function was not effected by the units themselves. The staffs concerned with this phase were the Supply Office (later transferred to the Quartermaster General, where it was renamed the Directorate of Supply) and the Air Equipment Groups (later absorbed into the Luftgau Quartermaster Staffs), and these staffs acted through the various storage installations, workshops and repair columns.

47. Another German Air Force principle — that of separating supply from flying — also emerges. The organisation of supply in the field was designed to free the operational formations as far as possible from the day-to-day labours of supply responsibilities and thus to preserve the intrinsic mobility of the air force. There was, however, a tendency for the two spheres — supply and flying — to draw so far apart as to prejudice efficiency, especially in a theatre where the battle was constantly mobile. This fact was appreciated by the more able and broad minded commanders, who were constantly striving to achieve a compromise that would blend operational activities more intimately with the supply machinery without hampering the mobility of the flying staffs. Examples of such experiments in organisation are given in Part 2, Chapter X, which illustrates the working of the Air Force supply organisation in the field under battle conditions in the Ukraine.

48. A critical appreciation of the German Air Forces Ground organisation, prepared in December 1944 by the German Air Ministry Historical Staff, contends that the separation of flying units from the ground organisation is appropriate only for a force based on a homeland in a war that assumes negligible territorial expansion. In a war of movement, the appreciation continues, repair and supply installations should be attached to the operational commands so that constant harmony is maintained between operational activities and the system which provides the materials and services necessary to the success of such operations. From a psychological angle the Luftgau failed, for its main offices were usually very far away from the front and had no visible connection with any successes and, therefore, remained unlauded and unappreciated — in consequence of

which the Luftgau tended to become autonomous and lacked interest in co-operating with the operational commands.

49.   The organisation of supply in the field for the German Air Force was designed originally for the conditions of the blitz warefare that was the popular German military strategy of the period. This form of strategy was frustrated by events in Russia which deprived the German forces of initiative, but no efforts were made to alter basically the ground organisation to suit the new military situation. The German Air Force was bound to a system that was fast becoming out-dated, and, consequently, the field commanders were forced to make local improvisations, some of which in time might have become generally adopted throughout the air force if it had been decided to reconstruct completely the theoretical system of ground organisation.

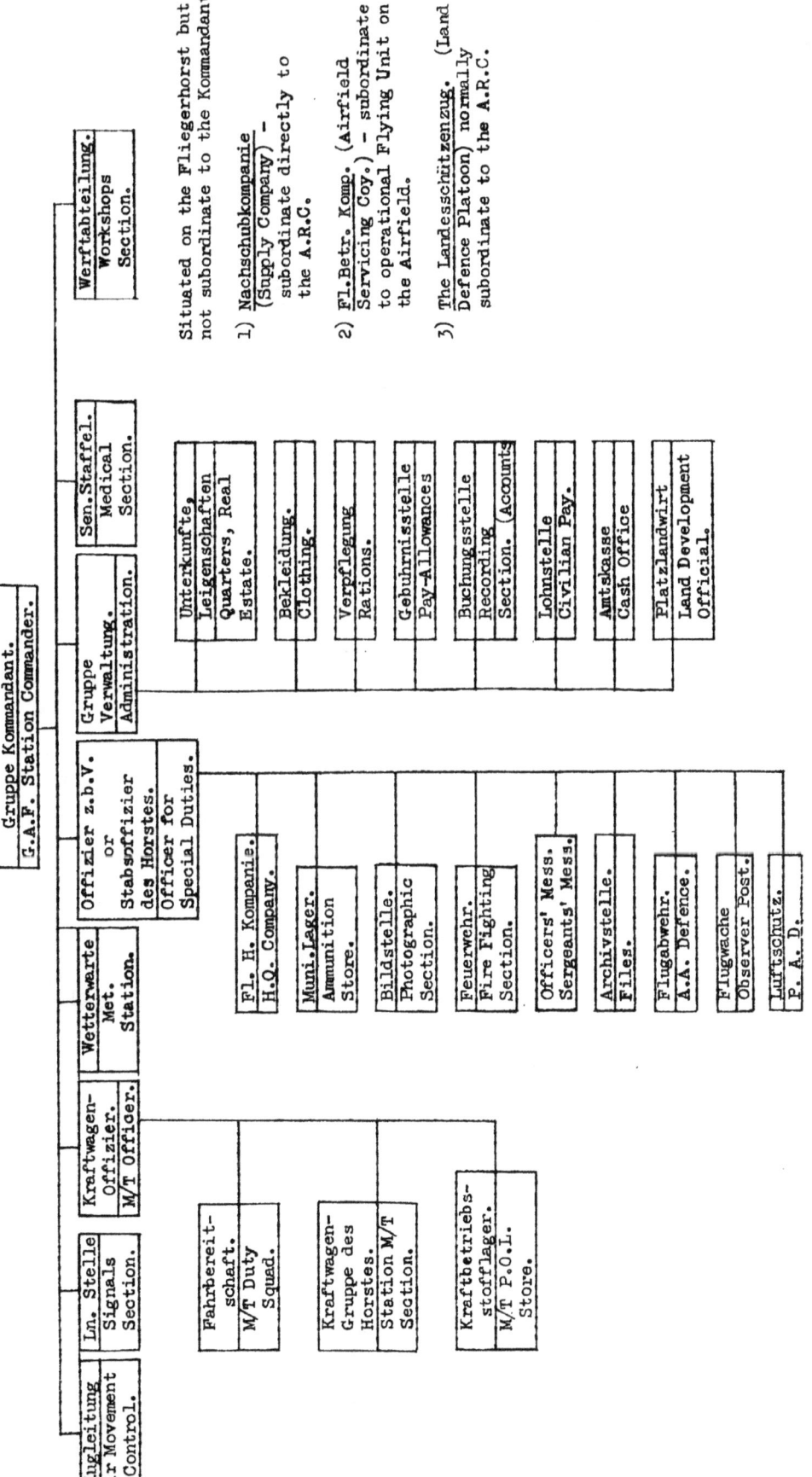

PART 1

CHAPTER VI

A SUMMARISED SURVEY OF GERMAN AIR FORCE ORGANISATION. ITS MERITS AND DEFECTS WITH PARTICULAR REFERENCE TO ITS BEARING ON SUPPLY.

INTRODUCTION	Paragraphs 1—33
The Development of the German Air Force — Historical Background	,, 3—6
The Development of the German Air Force as influenced by the Relationship between Milch and Göring	,, 7—15
The Strategy of the German Air Force	,, 16—21
The Formation of the Supply Organisation	,, 22—24
Commentary on the Supply Organisation	,, 25—30
The Failure of the Luftwaffe	,, 31—33
THE SUPREME COMMAND OF THE ARMED FORCES	,, 34—45
Commentary	,, 34—41
The Defence Economy and Armaments Directorate	,, 42
The Directorate of Transportation	,, 43
The Directorate of Motor Transport	,, 44
Conclusion	,, 45
BASIC ORGANISATION	,, 46—49
Commentary	,, 46—47
Conclusion	,, 48—49
PERSONNEL	,, 50—83
Officers	,, 50—51
Officials	,, 52—53
Civilians	,, 54
German opinion on the question of Officials and Officers	,, 55—56
Conclusion	,, 57—83
ADMINISTRATION	,, 84—87
Commentary	,, 84—85
Conclusion	,, 86—87
INSPECTION	,, 88—95
Commentary	,, 88—92
Conclusion	,, 93—95
SUPPLY IN THE FIELD	,, 96—110
Commentary	,, 96—99
Conclusion	,, 100—101
FINANCIAL CONTROL	,, 102—110
PROVISIONING AND PRODUCTION	,, 111—140
Commentary	,, 111—117
Conclusion	,, 118—140

PART I

CHAPTER VI

A SUMMARISED SURVEY OF THE GERMAN AIR FORCE ORGANISATION — ITS MERITS AND DEFECTS, WITH PARTICULAR REFERENCE TO ITS BEARING ON SUPPLY

INTRODUCTION

THE German Air Force, in its history and its structure, was so unlike the Royal Air Force that a general comparison between the supply organisation of the two services is impracticable. Certain outstanding features of common importance, however, were treated in such a different way from the methods of the Royal Air Force that useful comment may be made. These features will be examined under the following headings:

- (i) The Supreme Command of the Armed Forces (paras. 34—45).
- (ii) Basic Organisation (paras. 46—49).
- (iii) Personnel (paras. 50—83).
- (iv) Administration (paras. 84—87).
- (v) Inspection (paras. 88—95).
- (vi) Supply in the Field (paras. 96—101).
- (vii) Financial Control (paras. 102—110).
- (viii) Provisioning & Production (paras. 111—140).

2. Before considering the above subjects in detail, it is perhaps advisable to give very briefly an outline of the development of the German Air Force and make some reference to the political and strategical factors that influenced the fundamental design of the Luftwaffe.

Development of the German Air Force — Historical Background

3. The Treaty of Versailles forbade the use of military aircraft in Germany, and until Hitler's accession to power, in 1933, there was no German air force. To implement his intended programme, Hitler required the early emergence of an air force — not necessarily as a military force, but rather as a political weapon with which he could bluff the world into accepting his ideals. Furthermore he wished to have this powerful weapon as an independent force which would be entirely in the hands of the Nazi party, for at that time he was mistrustful of both the Army and the Navy. In this connection it is interesting to note that at a later date Hitler said: "I have a National Socialist Air Force, a Conservative Army and an Imperial Navy".

4. Hitler demanded the development of a large air force in the shortest possible time and he charged Göring with the creation of such a force. Göring knew little of strategy and still less of production, and immediately called in Milch of the Lufthansa Air Line Company to assist him in his tremendous task. Göring and Milch therefore were the master architects of the Luftwaffe and a sketch of the characters of these two individuals will help one to understand the ideas behind the composition of the Luftwaffe.

5. Göring came from a military family and was a renowned fighter pilot in the First World War. After the war he tried his hand at many

jobs, including civil flying and selling parachutes. In 1922 he met Hitler and became a staunch Nazi — at this time he was drinking heavily and taking morphine. He married well, soon becoming extremely wealthy and at the same time developed an oriental love of extravagance. When Hitler came to power, Göring was appointed Air Minister — probably more on account of his fidelity to the Nazi party than on his past reputation as an airman. He was a popular figure, but he was not a man who loved the study of military history, he had no patience for technical detail and he had not even an elementary understanding of aircraft production. His character was reflected in his direction of the Luftwaffe. He blustered his way through every obstacle, would abide no criticism, and regardless of reality pursued relentlessly Hitler's policy of producing large numbers of aircraft. His whole attitude, is summed up in a remark made to Milch: "Don't flatter yourself that I read the rubbish you send me".

6. Milch was a very different character — he was a hard worker, ignorant of military affairs it is true, but far more of a realist than his master, Göring. He was the son of a Jewish chemist who had a Gentile wife — theoretically, therefore, he was a Jew, which makes it all the more remarkable that he achieved such a high position in the Nazi hierarchy. He was, however, so valuable to Göring that he was allowed to become an honorary Aryan by the humiliating trick of forcing his old mother to declare that he was the illegitimate offspring of an affair that she had enjoyed with a Gentile lover. Milch, as may be seen from this last example, was a man who was determined to achieve his ambitions at any cost, but, according to the opinion of several officers of the General Staff, when he reached the highest level he was content to take second place and had no desire to usurp Göring's position. After the first World War he worked with the Junkers aircraft company until 1925 when he left that firm to become a director of Lufthansa. In this position he first met Göring and Hitler, who made note of his ability, and shortly after the accession of Hitler to the German Chancellery, Milch was approached and invited to become second in command to Göring — an appointment which he accepted after, so he says, some hesitation. In 1933 Milch became Secretary of State for Air and shortly after this appointment he was given the military rank of Oberst (Group Captain) and rose swiftly to Field Marshal. This rapid promotion annoyed the regular army officers. One of them is known to have said: "Milch may be an able general manager, but he will never be a general".

The Development of the G.A.F. as Influenced by the Relationship Between Milch and Göring

7. Milch's work before the war and his relationship with Göring, are described in the following paragraphs — the information being obtained from interrogation of Milch himself.

8. The G.A.F. suffered at the very beginning from an over-hasty and ill-considered development. Milch considered that eight or ten years were needed in order to train flying men to assume leadership in the new arm, which over this period of time could have been built up into a strategic Air Force. In the first eighteen months or two years after the Nazis came to power, little more than preparatory work could be achieved. The Government was careful not to proceed too openly against the Treaty of Versailles and was afraid that France in particular might intervene. Not until the end of 1934 or beginning of 1935 was large scale production of military aircraft begun. Until then the only aircraft under construction

were JU. 52's, a very few fighters, and a number of Do. 11's, a type which had resulted from the experiments of the Army Staff. This body did not aim in 1933 and 1934 at a higher total than 200 aircraft, including 144 fighters, 12 bombers and the rest reconnaissance. Milch had in mind the building up over a number of years of six bomber and six fighter Geschwader (roughly equivalent to R.A.F. Groups). He intended at first to set up only instructional units and to concentrate upon the training of thousands of flying and ground personnel. This plan was worked upon in 1934 and put on paper in 1935. No exact time could be fixed for its accomplishment as there was still at that time no definite knowledge of the ability of industry to carry out even the preliminary training programme.

9. Milch stated that he did not know in advance the official policy of the Government and that it was made known only through Hitler's speeches, from which all that emerged clearly was that Germany had to escape from her very weak international position by leaving the League of Nations and denouncing the Treaty of Versailles. Consequently, as a result of Hitler's influence, a bomber force was thought to be necessary to prevent Germany's enemies from beginning a war against her.

10. Göring always allowed himself to be carried away by grandiose ideas, and he saw in the G.A.F. an organisation with which he could accomplish literally anything. He was almost sorry for the Army as being a poor, old-fashioned arm of the Service and the Navy he considered to be completely out of date. At the same time he had no understanding of technical matters and expected to get results simply by issuing orders such as "Everything must be trebled in three month". In the early years Milch conferred with Göring about four times a year, and on each occasion Göring laughed to scorn his long term plans and demanded that a five-years' programme should be accomplished in one year or less. He then boasted in other quarters of his success in bullying Milch into action. Milch tried to form a defensive front with his colleagues in an attempt to prevent planning from exceeding what was possible of achievment, but when Hitler supported Göring's demand for immediate results, Milch found himself alone.

11. Göring declared himself incapable of withstanding Hitler's hypnotic, fascinating influence, and readily promised anything. Hitler spoke not of waging war but of his anxiety that other countries might intervene. Hitler was as ignorant as Göring of the technical and tactical aspects of the Air Force — he was more interested in the Army — but he did realise the value of organisation, and as long as he had confidence in Göring and Milch he left them a free hand. (Later, however, in 1942 when his confidence in Göring began to wane he constantly interfered with the Luftwaffe and in so doing showed such a lamentable ignorance of Air Force affairs that in one interrogation Göring stated: "You had a great ally in your aerial warfare — The Fuhrer").

12. In contrast to Raeder and later Dönitz, who pressed the claims of the Navy and succeeded in obtaining preferential treatment, Göring always told Hitler that everything was going splendidly and that he could manage perfectly well on his own without any support.

13. Relations between Milch and Göring gradually became strained, until in 1937 mutual confidence was completely lacking. According to Milch, this distrust was brought about by enemies of Göring within the Party, who carried on a whispering campaign that "The C.-in-C. of the G.A.F. is not really Göring, but Milch", and by enemies of Milch, Army officers

who, jealous of his rank, declared that he was assuming powers and inspecting troops like a C.in-C. Then came the occasion when Hitler turned down some proposals of Göring, saying "Let Milch attend to that, he's quite capable. Why do you constantly concern yourself with details?". Göring bothered himself very little about anything until the end of 1937: in the early years he had consulted Milch four or five times a year and had seen nobody else. Later he summoned others and Milch knew nothing of what was discussed.

14. The result of Göring's jealousy was that in 1937 and 1938 Milch was gradually deprived of certain powers, and lost control in turn of the Air Staff, the Personnel Office and the Technical Department. Doubting Görings ability to be more successful than himself, Milch feared that he would continue to be held responsible when things went wrong. Göring had never been capable of keeping for a single day to the programme of conferences which he drew up every year during his Christmas holiday at Karinhall. Milch reminded Göring of this weakness and requested that he should be relieved of responsibility as well as of power. He claimed the right to go back to the Lufthansa, but was flatly refused; it was for the higher authority to say when Milch might go. Göring even warned him not to feign illness, but agreed that he was free to commit suicide.

15. From the above account it is possible now to appreciate the political influence behind the development of the Luftwaffe and to see the emergence of the major intrigues and conflict of personality that characterised the Air Ministry throughout the war. This first major error of judgement is also revealed — the decision to concentrate on the bombers that were to be Hitler's mailed fist in the face of the world, but light bombers for speed in production. Galland — the German fighter ace — claimed this to be one of the greatest mistakes of the German Air Force. The basic tenet of air strategy was ignored — that is that victory over the enemy's air force is the first prerequisite of total victory. Such victory, he added, can only be achieved with superior fighters.

The Strategy of the German Air Force

16. Hitler and the heads of the German Air Force have been shown as ignorant of any real appreciation of the strategical use of air forces. The military staff of the Air Ministry were little better informed.

17. From 1918 to 1933 no cadre of air force personnel remained from the first world war, and therefore, when the Luftwaffe was formed in 1935, the highest military appointments were filled by old Army generals. Such people had no understanding of pure air force strategy, their minds were fogged with reminiscences of past Army doctrines and their only aim was to develop an air force that would be able to co-operate with the Army and extend its role. Furthermore, the Supreme Command of the Army recognised the Luftwaffe as a Party weapon and were therefore determined to draw it more under their own influence by insisting that it should co-operate very closely with them.

18. As Hitler's political aims became defined and it was generally realised that he intended to pursue a programme of gradual annexation of territory, so the Army was moulded to a form of strategy that would enable it to support by force the execution of this policy. The Army was designed for short campaigns into which it would concentrate its maximum power — recuperating and re-equipping in the intervals between such assaults. Incidentally, the success of these operations was always taken as granted and a long war of attrition was never considered.

19. The Luftwaffe also adopted these principles and relied on suitable pauses between campaigns during which time it would be able to gather fresh strength. The result was a light, extremely mobile air force unhampered by large reserve of equipment. It was also numerically large in comparison with other air forces. Its strength, however, was superficial for its period of development was too short to enable accumulation of the experience and the reserves required to sustain a continuous battle. Like many young things, the Luftwaffe was aggressive, precocious and lacking in experience. Consequently it took to flight before it was fully fledged.

20. The early successes of the Luftwaffe may be attributed to the fact that it was operating in the precise role for which it had been designed. It was mobile, experienced in army co-operation, superior in numbers, the morale of the pilots was high and it took part in a series of campaigns between which there were intervals for recuperation. The Nazi party and the air force commanders were intoxicated with these early achievements of the Luftwaffe and became careless of future planning and critical assessment. Their attitude was reflected in production figures. At the beginning of the war the total strength of the German Air Force was 4331 aircraft — of which it is interesting to note that 771 were fighters, 1180 bombers and 366 dive bombers — and production at the time was approximately 750 per month. From 1939 to 1941 production averaged about 800 per month and it was not until 1942 that the masters of the Luftwaffe realised the error of complacency. Milch, assisted by advice from Speer, then re-organised the aircraft industry to such an extent that in the late summer of 1944 a peak production of over 4000 aircraft per month was achieved.

The Formation of the Supply Organisation

21. In the following paragraphs 22 to 32 the term "Supply Organisation" refers to the system within the Air Force whereby supplies already delivered from Industry are fed to the forces in the field. It is not used in the wide sense that the title of this publication suggests i.e. as embracing Provisioning and Production as well as the mechanics of supply within the service. Thus although in these paragraphs brief mention is made of Production, this complex subject is fully discussed in paras. 111—140.

22. The leading pioneers of the German Air Force concerned themselves entirely with aircraft production, the training of pilots and the dissemination of propaganda. They had little time for consideration of supply problems and were still less interested in matters connected with repairs and salvage. An example of this attitude was given by Milch in an answer to Udet in January 1938, when the subject of repairs was being deliberated. "The movement of squadrons must not be hampered by administrative work. Officers will not be dependant on engineers — such a situation would prejudice the whole morale of the Luftwaffe. All campaigns will be short and German aircraft production will be so tremendous that during such periods of operation no major repairs will be necessary. Damaged planes will be repaired and salvaged at home after the campaigns are won." Udet questioned the advisability of such methods and asked whether such a system would be expected to work in a war of attrition, to which Milch replied that Hitler's plans were for blitz campaigns and that Udet's remarks were outrageous. The problem was solved!

23. The organisation of supply and repairs was left therefore in the hands of the old gentlemen of the first world war — supply they knew a

little about, but repair of aircraft was beyond their capabilities. Consequently the supply system of the German Air Force was a great deal more adequate than the repair organisation.

24. In planning the supply system the first factor which had to be taken into consideration was the general organisation of the Luftwaffe — this was, of course, on a territorial basis, and not on a functional one as was the Royal Air Force at home. Each Air Command (Luftflotte) was in fact a composite air force and each command therefore had to have its own self-contained supply system. The second factor was the necessity of keeping the operational side of the air force free from administrative problems. This led to the formation of separate Administrative Commands (Luftgaus) within the command area. The advantages and disadvantages of this system will be discussed later under the heading "Basic Organisation" (Paragraphs 46—49).

Commentary on the Supply Organisation

25. The basic manual governing supply in the German Air Force summarises the functions of the supply services as follows: "The function of supply is to equip the troops in the field with everything they require to carry out the operational and tactical orders issued by the higher commands. This principle illustrates the high importance of supply in the prosecution of a successful war. The extent and timing of a military operation can be decisively affected by the precious supply factors. Everyone concerned in supply must be thoroughly conversant with his role and duties. He must strive constantly to serve his command and must never be a drag on it in difficult situations."

26. On this high and admirable principle, the German Air Force Supply system was designed. The main handicap encountered in the implementation of this principle was the poor quality of officers, who were appointed to supply posts. Almost the whole effort of the recruiting system was devoted to encouraging young men to enlist for flying duties, and the supply and repair services were manned by the remnants. In the opinion of all German officers interrogated on supply, the system was sufficiently adaptable to meet the conditions it encountered and very little basic re-organisation was required during the course of the war. The only major controversies that arose were in reference to the Equipment Groups and the Basic Organisation (See: for Equipment Groups Part 1, Chapter V, paras. 22—34 and for Basic Organisation paras. 46—49 of this Chapter). Furthermore, the Luftflotte commanders in chief were allowed considerable latitude in adapting the supply organisation to meet local conditions.

27. To the Germans, therefore, their supply system did not appear to be inherently faulty. Considered objectively, the supply machinery was undoubtedly handicapped by the adherence to the regional supply organisation, particularly in mobile theatres. Other factors, however, must also be taken into account when assessing the system critically. Towards the end of the war the deteriorating military situation and the disruption of road and rail facilities placed an almost intolerable strain on supply. This strain was accompanied by the general decay of all German military and civil organisations, which led to the utter collapse of the Reich. In such conditions no deficiency of any particular supply system could be argued.

28. In the war in the East the vast area of the operational theatre, the climate and the condition of the lines of communication all militated

against supply. Pressure by the enemy caused long and difficult retreats, in which vast quantities of equipment were lost, and supply problems became more and more difficult as reserves dwindled. It may be argued that the supply authorities should have built up greater reserves and anticipated such tremendous losses of materials. But the provisioning of equipment depends largely on the directions given by the operational staffs which plan the extent of future operations. If military appreciations of the future situations are erroneous the supply programmes based upon them will fail. Therefore it may be said that supply to the German Air Force in the campaign against the Red Army was inadequate not necessarily through any fault of the system but through the ambitious nature of the whole operation, which was undertaken on a false conception of the enemy's will and power to resist.

29. In the West, from the invasion period to the final defeat of Germany, the situation differed considerably from that on the Eastern front. The theatre of operations was more compact and the German forces were served by a good railway system and good roads. In the East the vast size of the area of operations was a primary cause of German plight and by ironic contrast in the West it was the limited battle field that brought disaster. Allied aircraft were able to range over the whole area and the good railways and roads were either destroyed or became so dangerous that movement, and therefore supply, was paralysed. The supply services again failed, but not necessarily through any inherent defect in the system.

30. From the moment the Nazis lost the initiative in Russia the tide of battle turned and slowly came in and flooded the Reich with chaos and final destruction. As war material was lost and expended in enormous quantities, so tremendous efforts were made to increase production to the scale demanded by total war. As these efforts grew, however, so commitments increased and furthermore the allied strategic bombardment of industry from the air began to assume effective proportions. Shortages became acute and even the production achieved was lost in the West by harassing attacks on communication and in the East by the ever advancing Soviet forces. To these problems there was no purely supply answer. Industry finally reached its production peak and no changes in supply organisation or supply establishments could replace the essential shortages of raw materials and labour or provide protection against bombardment from the air.

The Failure of the Luftwaffe

31. The failure of the Luftwaffe may be summed up briefly in the following way. The development of the force was hasty and based on a political adventure rather than sound military conceptions. Its organisation was designed to support an Army operating in a series of short, violent, but successful campaigns. This organisation was neither efficient nor economical in a long war, but no attempt was made to revise it in the face of actuality. The confidence of the Nazi leaders in the success of their original plans was so great that they made no attempt to mobilise totally German war industry until 1942, after most of their reserves had been consumed an the battle for Russia.

32. The organisation of supply services is determined largely by the design of the operational force to which they are attached and the

industry which feeds them. In themselves they may be efficient, but if harnessed to an incompetent machine they are bound to fail by association alone.

33. An outline of the general development of the German Air Force has now been presented and a stage in the narrative of this Chapter has been reached where the theme may turn to a detailed examination of the subjects suggested in paragraph 1.

THE SUPREME COMMAND OF THE ARMED FORCES

Commentary

34. One of the outstanding differences that existed between the German and British Armed Forces was the fact that whereas in Germany the three arms of the services — the Army, the Navy and the Air Force — were theoretically subordinated to a higher command (the Supreme Command of the Armed Forces: Oberkommando der Wehrmacht), for the British Armed Forces there is no such authority. Before examining the effect of this organisation on Air Force supply it is necessary to understand the background of the system and to examine the major defects of the machine.

35. Hitler dominated the whole German military organisation. In the early stages of the Nazi regime he was accepted by the militarists as a leader who was likely to further service interests. Later some of his rash moves, dictated more by intuition than military appreciation, began to worry the service leaders but their protests were disproved by his obvious successes. Such successes gave Hitler a steadily increasing confidence in his powers as a military genius and he came to discard the carefully considered plans that were submitted by his military staffs. As the situation deteriorated so Hitler took a more and more personal interest in military affairs and finally took hold of every control himself in the vain hope of saving Germany from defeat.

36. The German Army was traditionally the senior service and also had the responsibility for the general conduct of war and all important planning. The Army General Staff consisted of a small band of very highly-trained and experienced officers, a corps d'elite, and was an institution of ancient heritage, revered and respected by the German people as a symbol of military strength. Early in his era of power Hitler learned to mistrust, and perhaps even fear, this exclusive staff and wished to institute a superior organisation which, under his direction, would serve to execute his aims without opposition or criticism. This was the reason behind the formation of the Supreme Command which was to direct in general terms and co-ordinate the efforts of the three services and the nation for total war. The aim was that the Supreme Commander should issue broad directives to the services and the appropriate civil authorities, that the service staffs should prepare the detailed plans for the specified projects, and, finally, submit their reports to the Supreme Command for co-ordination and approval. In theory this conception was admirable but it failed in practice for the following reasons.

37. A system of Supreme Command demanded mutual confidence from the three subordinated services but, in fact, there was no such confidence. Hitler mistrusted the Army General Staff and favoured the Air Force which he knew was in the staunch National Socialist care of Göring. The General Staff resented the new command which usurped their powers and was

also mistrustful of the Air Force. Göring received his orders directly from Hitler. He refused to be influenced by the Supreme Command and encouraged his staff to remain aloof. The High Command of the Navy, until 1943, pursued a policy of isolationism and endeavoured to keep the Navy self-contained in every respect.

38. Another reason which contributed to the failure of the Supreme Command was the fact that it was not content to remain limited to the role of director. Hitler encouraged the Supreme Command to engage in detailed planning and conduct of operations that should have been the prerogative of the Service Staffs, particularly the Army General Staff. Consequently, the Supreme Command became so engrossed in the details of day-to-day policy that it was unable to view the general situation with the detachment required for the proper development of grand strategy.

39. Yet another reason for failure must be recorded. A Supreme Command directing independent services must be manned by a representative staff drawn proportionately from the three arms. The German Supreme Command was dominated by Army officers and the Naval and Air Force representation was extremely small. Furthermore, the system demands close liaison between the planning section of the Supreme Command and the staffs of the service ministries. In the British system the planners and the heads of Intelligence, for example, held appointments in their resepective service ministries and were, consequently, in the closest touch with the development of events. In the German system the planners and heads of Intelligence held appointments in the Supreme Command but not in their own ministries and were therefore isolated from their respective services. Therefore, through lack of adequate liaison and also through antagonism of their ministries, they were frequently out of touch with reality.

40. Finally, the effect of Hitler's character in relation to the failure of the Supreme Command cannot be disregarded. He should have ordered, in broad outline, the political direction and grand strategy of the war. These orders should have been transmitted in somewhat greater detail by the Supreme Command to the Services whose staffs should have developed the absolute details. This method of approach did not appeal to Hitler. He was obsessed with the idea of imposing his will on the Army General Staff and devised and used the Supreme Command as an instrument for this purpose. His methods at first brought him success and he was tempted to interfere still further. As success faded and was superseded by disaster he could not refrain from even closer personal direction. He had achieved great things before and was convinced that he could again succeed where others failed. In the final stages of the war he was so deep in detail that bridges could not be demolished except on his orders, brigades on the Russian front could not be switched from one place to another without his consent and even small tank reinforcements could not be sent forward without his approval.

41. The Supreme Command is revealed, therefore, as an organisation which failed. Its general influence on the supply system of the German Air Force was consequently not of very much importance. Three departments of the Supreme Command, however, warrant consideration: —

    (i)   Defence Economy and Armaments Directorate.
    (ii)   Directorate of Transportation.
    (iii) Directorate of Motor Transport.

Defence Economy and Armaments Directorate

42. The function of this directorate was to develope German economy in accordance with the needs of war, to co-ordinate service production programmes in the light of common strategy and to control raw materials. General Thomas, who was head of this directorate, asserted in a postwar document that the main control of armament production was in the hands of the Service Ministries and that his function was limited in practice to the negotiation for and the allocation of raw materials. Even in this matter the Service chiefs — particularly Göring — paid little regard to their allocations and would often go to Hitler for revised figures. Finally, in 1942, shortly after the Stalingrad disaster, the whole department was transferred to Speer's Ministry as it was considered that the Army were not qualified to handle such a complex subject as war economy.

Directorate of Transportation

43. This department controlled the allocation of railway space to the three services in much the same way as the British War Office "Q Movements" functions for the British services. Shipping was handled by a separate department of the Supreme Command which was called the Home Staff for Overseas. The system is said to have been efficient.

Directorate of Motor Transport

44. The allocation of the whole production of motor transport vehicles was effected by this directorate to both military and civil organisations. Repair of vehicles was also controlled centrally by the Director of Motor Transport. This system of unified control of all motor transport was economical and efficient in design but in practice it was not advantageous to the Air Force. The department was staffed mainly by Army officers and there was only a very small German Air Force liaison staff. Consequently, the Directorate gave priority to Army requests and did not really appreciate the importance of the Air Force demands.

CONCLUSION

45. The nearest British equivalent to the Supreme Command would be a combination of the War Cabinet and the Chiefs of Staff's Committees. Although the idea of a Supreme Command may appear more logical and more efficient than the British system in that it unifies all departments dealing with joint service problems into one command, there are also considerable disadvantages. The greatest disadvantage — exemplified by German experience — is that the planning staffs of an autonomous Supreme Command become isolated from their service ministries and, consequently, get out of touch with current military developments. There is also a tendency for the preponderant service — the Army in Germany — to override the other services and to prejudice impartial direction. Yet another weakness appears from the fact that a Supreme Command may strive to undertake greater responsibilities in the direction of war economy than it is able to handle efficiently. This was certainly true of the German Supreme Command up to 1942. There are many problems of war economy that are beyond the scope of military decision. The mobilisation of industry to support a modern war so gravely burdens the national life of the country that only experts in economy and production should plan such affairs. This was appreciated by Great Britain but the Germans did not learn the lesson until the war had passed through half its course. Advantages of a Supreme Command are that it provides a machinery

through which the Services can exploit their experiences for a mutual benefit and it forms a central agency through which common user items may be procured and common services (Movement for example) may be directed. The German Supreme Command made use of these facilities only to the extent of common procurement of Motor Transport and unified direction of Movement. To achieve these advantages there is, however, no need to establish a supreme command, for such matters could be handled by joint service committees attached to one or more of the existing service ministries. The formation of such committees is recommended, for in this way certain equipment could be developed and procured by a single agency, certain services could be centrally directed and individual methods could be exploited for the common good without suffering the disadvantages of a Supreme Command.

BASIC ORGANISATION

Commentary

46. The essential difference between the organisation of the German Air Force and the Royal Air Force was that the former force was organised regionally and the latter both functionally and regionally. The German planners decided in favour of regional control because their military plans were aggressive and they desired their air force to comprise a number of tactical air forces (Luftflottes) which would work closely with the army in "lightning" campaigns. The need for an elaborate fighter defence of the Reich and a home based heavy bomber force was not warranted by their military and political intentions. They expected wars to be won quickly and easily; but "war is the last of all things to go according to programme". The whole German military machine was geared to blitz warfare and this form of strategy was frustrated in the battle for Russia. The Germans were deprived of the initiative in early 1942 but, in spite of this, no efforts were made to alter radically the organisation of the Luftwaffe to accord with the requirements of the new military situation.

47. The pioneers of the German Air Force were impressed with the mobility of aircraft, and their conception of organisation was considerably influenced by the desire to preserve this quality. Each Air Fleet (Luftflotte) consisted of operational commands (Fliegerkorps, etc.) and separate supply and administration commands (Luftgau, etc.), the aim being to free the operational formations as far as possible from long term supply responsibilities and thus to preserve the essential mobility of the fighting force. There was, however, a tendency in practice for the two spheres — flying and supply — to draw so far apart as to prejudice efficiency, especially in a theatre away from the homeland where the battle was constantly fluid. This fact was appreciated by certain commanders who were striving ceaselessly to achieve a compromise that would blend operational activities more closely with the supply machine without hampering the mobility of the flying staffs. However, no general direction was given by the Air Ministry in this connection and separation remained in force.

CONCLUSION

48. The main factor of importance that emerges from the German Air Force organisation for supply is the need to distinguish between the home based air force and the tactical air forces working abroad with mobile armies. In the former case the operational air force should be functional

in character and be supplied by a separate supply command which should be divided into functional groups each operating a regional supply system. This method reduces the number of supply installations required and, consequently, reduces also the amount of material frozen in pipelines and local reserves. Furthermore, strict centralised control over all supply stations can be exercised. In the latter case, i.e. supply to tactical air forces, policy varies from day to day according to the movement of the battle, which is an imponderable factor. Supply matters, therefore, must be directed from the Operational Headquarters and supply and operational staffs must work side by side. In addition, the Operational Headquarters, through its supply staff, should have direct control of its own supply installations, which can then be located and replenished in direct relation to tactical developments. The German fear that control of supply installations by an Operational Headquarters would prejudice the mobility of that formation was disproved by the practical example of Nos. 83 and 84 R.A.F. Groups which supported the British armies in the battle which brought final defeat to the Third Reich.

49. The Royal Air Force unquestionably adopted the logical system of supply and made the proper differentiation between home based and tactical air forces. A similar system, in spite of the different geographical situation, would also have served the German Air Force more efficiently and more economically than their own organisation. The German mistake may again be attributed to the failure of their original military intentions in 1942 and the subsequent obstinate adherence to an organisation that with the change of strategy became immediately outdated.

PERSONNEL

Officers

50. In the German Air Force there were no officers equivalent to the Equipment and Technical Officers of the Royal Air Force. There were three main specialist branches of the German Air Force — Flying, Flak and Signals — but within those branches there was no further officer specialisation. All Air Force officers were given military operational training which during their careers was supplemented by short courses in technical and supply subjects. All officers were encouraged, therefore, to have a general rather than a particular outlook. Furthermore, it was a German principle that all officers should keep in very close touch with operational activity and consequently officers were not kept in base appointments for more than a maximum two years at a time. Thus, Quartermaster, Technical and Supply appointments were filled by officers who had only a very superficial knowledge of their duties.

51. The system, therefore, demanded some backing of workers who could undertake the detailed work and provide an element of continuity. This was found in the corps of German officials (Beamte) and civilians.

Officials

52. The officials were a branch of the German Civil Service that had for three centuries provided the Army and Navy with administrative, professional and technical experts. The German Air Force on its formation naturally adopted this traditional institution. Officials were neither civilians nor yet entirely soldiers. They were classified into four broad categories:

(i) Higher Grade, equivalent approximately to Senior Officers.
(ii) Medium Higher Grade, equivalent approximately to Junior Officers.
(iii) Middle Grade, equivalent approximately to Senior Non-Commissioned Officers.
(iv) Simple Grade, equivalent approximately to Junior Non-Commissioned Officers.

The four grades were subdivided into ranks which were equivalent to military ranks and were also descriptive of the appointment held — for example Oberstingenieur, Group Captain Engineer; Oberstabsintendant, Squadron Leader Administration; Ministerialamtsgehilf, Flight Sergeant Administration Assistant. Officials wore German Air Force uniform appropriate to their rank but without the insignia of military rank. They were classified as combatants according to the Geneva convention and they were expected to, and often did, take part in front-line defensive action. Officials possessed administrative authority over all those subordinated for duty, but their military authority was limited to subordinate officials and civilian employees. Those officials who held ranks equivalent to officer status were accorded the privilege of salute from other ranks, they received the precedence of their rank at social but not at military ceremonies and they were members of officers' messes.

53. An advantage of the "official" system was that it enabled the German Air Force to recruit professional and technical experts who might otherwise have lacked the military qualifications required by the officer class. It had, however, the great disadvantage of introducing a large degree of confusion and friction as to what constituted a purely military command reserved for officers and what was an administration sphere and, therefore, within the scope of officials. Officers had a higher rate of pay and an improved rate of promotion which caused a certain amount of resentment amongst the officials. Another handicap which was apparently of great importance was that the officials felt a definite social inferiority in comparison with officers. These faults were realised by the German authorities and they endeavoured to counter them by instituting in 1944, a branch of the German Air Force called the Special Duties Service (Truppensonderdienst) to which all officials were to be transferred. Those of officer status were to have been known not as officials but as officers of the Special Duties Service. By the end of the war very few officials had been transferred. The new system made improvements in pay and promotion but did not really eliminate the feeling of inferiority, because the officials, or officers of the Special Duties Service, were still without military training or command.

Civilians

54. Civilians employed in the German Air Force were classified in two categories. The first category was the salaried workers (Angestellte) who acted as assistants to the officials, and the second was the wage earners (Lohnempfänger) who performed manual tasks. All civilians were sworn in with the German oath of loyalty for soldiers and they also carried certain identifications of their combatant status.

German Opinion on the Question of Officials and Officers

55. Dr. Winterhoff, a Generalintendant at the German Air Ministry who was head of the personnel branch dealing with officials, admitted during interrogation that officials would probably not have been introduced into the Air Force if it had been possible to foresee the estrangement that

came to exist between officials and officers. This feeling developed, so he claimed, largely because the officials felt that they were constantly at a disadvantage when compared with the professional soldiers. Winterhoff agreed that specialisation was essential in order to meet the technical requirements of an air force, but added that it should be undertaken by the officers themselves.

56. Various General Staff officers interrogated on this subject agreed that the very general training encouraged in the German Air Force developed a type of officer who had a very superficial knowledge and believed, therefore, that he was able to give judgment on all things whereas, in fact, he was not qualified to judge at all. In the higher and more important positions there were extremely few officers who had sufficient grip of their subject to direct vigorously the supply and technical services. The consequence was that those at the top accepted the opinion of the mass without critical appreciation, and direction suffered accordingly. Although it was agreed that a degree of specialisation was desirable it was stressed that overspecialisation was dangerous, at it meant a limitation of career prospects and tended to produce autonomous sects of narrow minded people who were out of touch with broad operational principles.

Conclusion

57. From the foregoing paragraphs it seems clear that German policy for the selection, training and employment of personnel, produced two very serious weaknesses in the organisation of the Supply Services, which undoubtedly affected the efficiency of those Services. They were as follows:—

(i) By reason of the inadequacy of their training, the officers operating the supply organisation were not sufficiently knowledgeable to do their work efficiently.

(ii) The members of the supply organisation who did possess intimate knowledge of both "supply mechanics" and equipment — i.e. the Beamte — were separated by a class barrier from the officers directing operations, and also, due to their confinement to relatively subordinate positions, never had the opportunities of learning the wider problems of supply. In consequence they could not bring to bear in the very quarters of the organisation where it was most lacking, the knowledge indispensible to the proper planning of operations.

58. Before attempting to suggest what lessons may be learned from these observations, it is necessary to determine what basic principles should have been observed in formulating policy, and what mistake in policy led to their weaknesses.

59. In the first place it may be said that there are three main aspects to be considered in the employment of a military force:

(i) the conduct of operations,
(ii) the means to support the operations, i.e. supply, and
(iii) the special services necessary to maintain the means to be employed.

60. In explanation of the above division it should be said that such apparently separate activities of a service as Signals, Intelligence, Technical Maintenance, Training and Personnel control, are to be regarded as coming under heading (iii) as factors determining the **conditions** in which (i) and (ii) are related to each other.

construction materials and solid fuel. The branch was manned by officials and was completely separated from the Quartermaster staff.

85. This system of separating non-technical from technical supplies was traditional in the German Army and was adopted automatically by the Air Force. The reason advanced for this rather peculiar arrangement was that German officers were only interested in military affairs and that such routine and commercial subjects as clothing, rations and barrack equipment were best handled by the officials. German officers interrogated on the question of whether or not the Quartermaster should have handled these matters seemed to be little interested in the problem and ventured that it might have simplified control if all supply matters were the responsibility of the Quartermaster, but that it worked very well as it was. Officials, of course, had nothing but praise for the efficiency of the system and stated that officers would have neglected such matters and would have been constantly striving to be posted away to more military work. The attitude of the German officers is understandable particularly when it is remembered that they were primarily General Duties officers and did not specialise in supply.

Conclusion

86. The complete separation of technical and non-technical equipment is not economical. Such an organisation requires separate administration, separate storage installations and separate channels of demand. It also encourages competition for transport and manpower, and false priorities may be determined from branch jealousy instead of true appreciation of military necessity. Furthermore, such autonomous systems have a tendency to assume an importance totally unrelated to their real value.

87. There appears to be no advantages in the German system — except that officers are freed from somewhat tedious employment — and the complete separation of non-technical and technical equipment is not recommended.

INSPECTION

Commentary

88. The Commanders in Chief of the Luftflottes carried out the duty of inspection themselves, inasmuch as they, or the officers on their staffs, were ultimately responsible for the efficiency of all units and staffs within their sphere of authority. Consequently, they had to pay visits from time to time to convince themselves that their orders were being carried out efficiently and accurately. Inspection was, therefore, a function of the command.

89. The German Air Ministry authorities realised, however, that the basic system of regional, rather than functional, control created a lack of uniformity in training, methods of command, operational execution, etc., in the various theatres of war. To counteract this tendency authorities were established on the staff of the Chief of General Staff at the Air Ministry. These authorities were known as G.A.F. Inspectorates (later some were called "Waffengenerale") and each one was concerned with the units of a particular aspect of the German Air Force — for example, Bomber Units, Flak Units, Medical Units — no matter to which command (Luftflotte) such units were allocated. These Inspectorates had powers of inspection over all the units within their sphere of influence, but inspection was only one of their many duties, which included:—

(i) Co-ordination in planning and equipping units.
(ii) Technical development and introduction of new types of equipment.
(iii) Training.
(iv) Supervision of personnel.

90. These inspectorates could make recommendations to the Chief of General Staff and directly to the Quartermaster General on supply subjects as they affected the particular types of units for which they were responsible.

91. In addition to the Inspectorates, whose duties only included inspection among other tasks, there were also certain inspectors (inspizient as opposed to inspekteur) who carried out inspection as a full time occupation. The "Inspizienten" were mostly employed by Air Ministry authorities who had powers of inspection vested in their departments, but in view of their other duties were not able to perform physical inspection themselves. Those of particular interest to supply were:
  (i) Inspection of Supply (Nachschubinspizient), who was under the Director of Supply.
  (ii) Inspector of Clothing (Bekleidungsinspizient), who was in the Administration Office.
Each inspector had a small staff consisting, usually, of six people.

92. These inspectors were entitled to visit and inspect all storage installations including station stores and workshops in the German Air Force. It was usual, however, to notify the appropriate command of intended visits. The purpose of the visits was to ensure that materials were being properly stored, that returns were accurate and that equipment was not being hoarded, that orders were being executed and that manpower was being utilised economically. The effect of local conditions on organisation and methods would also be studied.

Conclusions

93. Powers of inspection were vested in the German Air Ministry departments because there was no other way of ensuring standardisation throughout an air force that was regionally organised. Regardless of this primary reason, the system was particularly useful to the supply authorities as it gave them right of access to every German Air Force unit where stores were held. In the Royal Air Force there is no Equipment Agency with such wide powers of inspection. The Inspectors General may, of course, visit any unit in the service and may comment on supply subjects, but there is no Equipment representative on their staffs and, consequently, important points may be disregarded. A supply inspectorate within the Director General of Equipment's department would have the following advantages:—
  (i) Uniformity in all Commands would be ensured.
  (ii) The value of inspection would increase because a central staff would investigate matters with a completely detached interest. Criticism would, therefore, be unprejudiced and objective.
  (iii) Useful innovations in organisation and methods developed locally could be studied and made available generally to the Service. Progress to efficiency would, therefore, be hastened.
  (iv) Control of economy in methods and materials would be exercised.
  (v) Criticism from units, which is often valuable, would be passed swiftly to Air Ministry authorities without undergoing the almost inevitable modifications consequent upon the particular outlook of individual commands.

94. The formation of such an organisation as is proposed above suggests that it should include in its scope all those duties undertaken during the war by the Controller General of Economy and that Section of A.M.S.O.'s department known as Organisation and Methods. These two departments studied such matters as the application of Commercial equipment and methods to service organisation and the relation of economic problems to service requirements and also provided a means of communication with the other two services on similar matters.

95. If the service is to keep abreast of modern developments in supply organisation and maintain economy in the employment of its resources, it is considered that study of these subjects should be continued.

SUPPLY IN THE FIELD

Commentary

96. The German system of Supply in the Field provides a clear example of their principle of segregating the "Operational" from the "Administrative" side of their Air Force. The flying units were freed completely from the normal day-to-day responsibilities of Supply, and it is almost undeniable that for the conditions of "blitz" warfare, (for which the German Air Force was undoubtedly designed), such a system is practicable and efficient. For a home based force, in a war involving little or no territorial expansion, the close link which exists between the Operational and Administrative sides of the R.A.F. may be desirable but is not, as far as can be seen, a necessity.

97. On the other hand, as soon as the character of a war changes to one of rapid movement, it is essential that the closest possible link should be forged between the units conducting the operations, and the units bound up with those supplies rendering the operations practical. In the German Air Force, the Luftgau Headquarters was usually very many miles behind the fighting forces. It had no visible connection with the early success of the "Operational" Air Force, and the psychological effect on the members of its staff was unfortunate. They considered themselves overlooked and unappreciated, and developed a tendency to lose interest in operational commands.

98. The Main Depots of the German Air Force (described in detail in Part 2, Chapter VII) are worthy of special consideration, playing as they did an important role in the provisioning scheme in addition to their normal use as bulk storage installations. The system whereby Main Depots may deal direct with Industry to a limited extent with advantage is dicussed in this Chapter, para. 128. The Main Depots provide a further example of the Air Force being bound to a system which became out-of-date immediately the original concept of "blitz" warfare was proved at fault. They supplied on a "technical" rather than "territorial" basis — that is, they specialised in specific ranges of equipment, of which they held the total stocks delivered to the order of the Director of Supply prior to its issue to the German Air Force. The advantage of such a system when producing stock figures and consumption data is apparent, but it was a system based on the entirely false premise that the danger of attack by air or land forces was negligible. With the intensification of Allied air attacks, it became necessary to disperse the Main Depot holdings over a fantastically wide area, and in due course the over-running by land forces of certain depots deprived the German Air Force of its total reserve stocks of whole ranges of equipment.

99. The Air Parks — next in the chain supply — had the advantage of carrying a three-months' stock of the "universal" range. Towards the end of the war, however, when Allied air attacks were concentrated on rail and road transport, they were virtually isolated from the Main Depots, from whom they were expected to obtain replenishments. Due to the "specialisation" of the Main Depots the Air Parks were required to maintain contact with Depots as widely separated as Erding (for Messerschmitt spares) and Küpper (for Heinkel spares) — a distance of over 300 miles. The efficiency of the smaller installations — the Equipment Issuing Stations — was naturally affected by the difficulties besetting the Air Parks from whom they — the Equipment Issuing Stations — drew their supplies.

Conclusions.

100. It is difficult to draw any positive conclusions regarding the German System of Supply in the Field beyond the fact that the basic organisation of the German Air Force rendered it unsatisfactory. The "Operational" and "Administrative" sides of any fighting force cannot remain effective if divorced either by distance geographically or by distinctive psychological treatment.

101. The outstanding defect of the system was that, when called upon to play a role for which it was not originally designed, it lacked the elasticity to adapt itself to changed conditions.

FINANCIAL CONTROL

102. The financial system employed by the German Air Force in developing and directing the aircraft industry was peculiar to that Branch of the Armed Forces. This was due to the unusual status of the Air Force and to its long-continued independence under Göring.

103. From the early days of the Nazi regime, the Air Force had been regarded as the child and instrument of the Party, quite apart from its potential use as a war weapon, and it had been permitted to pursue its own course in building and expanding industry without financial limitation. Financial agencies owned and directed exclusively by the Air Force were set up, and at no time, either before or during the war, were there any restrictions in the allocation of its funds.

104. True, a system for the preparation and submission of budgets existed before the war, but in the case of the Air Force such means of control were purely nominal. At the beginning of the war all effort at budgetary control was discontinued, and except for the exercise of general discretionary powers by the Supreme Command, the Air Force assumed full power in assessing and controlling its expenditure.

105. The arbitrary powers given to the Air Force in managing its own financial affairs, and the fact that Germany had no free economic system of prices and wages, make it impossible to assess the real cost of development, or of the efficiency of the Air Force in utilising its funds to the best advantage. It would appear, however, that the Air Force, in comparison with the Army and with the Navy, was reasonably experienced in the management of its finances, and that of the three Services it was the most successful in guiding and aiding industry.

106. In directing and managing the aircraft industry, the Air Force effected control of its financial operations through the agency of the Aviation Bank. All the shares of this concern were held by the Air Ministry.

Before the advent of Speer in 1942 there was a tendency on the part of the Air Ministry to acquire direction of industrial concerns through the medium of capital participation and of actual ownership of factories and plants. This policy accorded well with the structure of the German Air Force at this time, as being complementary to its independence and isolation from the other Services and from German econmoy generally.

107. The identity and working of the Aviation Bank was continued after Speer came into power and, in fact, until the end of the war. The policy of the Air Force in acquiring owneship of industry was, however, reversed to a very considerable extent by Speer for, in pursuing his ambition of creating an autonomous industry, he desired as far as possible private ownership of manufacturing plants.

108. The working of the Aviation Bank, although unusual in comparison with the British system of financial control, was quite successful and under the reasonably expert guidance of the Economics and Finance Office of the Air Ministry it did much to facilitate the development of industry.

109. Some mention must be made of the German system of price fixing, since this had a great bearing on the desire of Speer to rationalise industry in 1942. In the early days of the war Germany, in company with England and America, was forced to rely on the unhappy system of a "cost-plus" basis. The defects of this system in failing to restrict the inefficient plants and in permitting excess profits on the part of normal or highly efficient producers, were recognised very clearly by the German industrialists and financial experts, particularly Speer, and early steps were taken to set up an organisation capable of devising and using fixed prices.

110. A workable system of grouped and graduated fixed prices for all industrial war products was introduced by Germany before America and Britain and materially assisted Speer in his re-organisation of industry from 1942 onwards.

PROVISIONING AND PRODUCTION
Commentary

111. In reviewing the systems of provisioning and production employed in the German Air Force, it is necessary to consider two separate and distinct periods of the war — the first phase, up to 1944 being marked by the complete independence of the Air Force in controlling its own production, and the second, from 1944 until the end of the war, when responsibility for production was assumed by the Ministry of Armaments and War Production.

112. Notwithstanding Speer's remarkable achievements in the re-organisation of German Industry and Economy since his appointment to the Ministry of Armaments and War Production in 1942, it was not until 1944 that he was given control of Air Force production. The responsibility for this two year delay must rest entirely with the German Air Force, whose reluctance to relinquish control was marked. It may be assumed, however, that Hitler, whose confidence in Speer had already been amply justified, would most certainly have intervened had the possibility of a long war been apparent in 1942.

113. The German Air Force was designed for, and was remarkably successful in, a series of short and sharp campaigns. Throughout the period of its operation as the sole arbiter of its own production, the quality

of its materials was of the highest order, and had the various campaigns terminated in the successful manner envisaged by Göring and Hitler, the quantities produced would conceivably have been adequate.

114.   Although 1944 marks the period from which Speer assumed complete control of Air Force production, a considerable amount of preliminary work was done between 1942 and 1944 by Milch who was (or claims to have been) forsighted enough to have realised the extremely unsatisfactory manner in which Air Force requirements were being produced, but by the time the strategic situation had deteriorated to such an extent that Speer's intervention was essential, the time when such an intervention could have succeeded in saving the situation was past. Speer was faced with programmes involving such a multiplicity of types and sub-types that an instantaneous turn over to mass production was well nigh impossible. In spite of this, production under Speer achieved remarkable results, although his ruthless cuts in programmes to permit of mass production of standard items was the subject of heated criticism by Air Force officers, who claimed that quality was being sacrificed, without realising (or admitting) that quantity was, at that stage, the chief consideration.

First Period (up to 1944) — Merits and Defects

115.   The first period, (i.e. the period during which the German Air Force was responsible for both production and provisioning), was marked by the high standard of quality of items being produced in sufficient quantities to satisfy the needs of a comparatively small Air Force. It is scarcely possible, however, to accept this as a merit, when the system was so lacking in elasticity that it was incapable of the required degree of expansion when quantity became a primary consideration. An obvious defect, on the other hand, was the fact that by its insistent isolation the German Air Force denied itself the benefits of skilled industrial and economic organisation. Its insistence, moreover, in the sphere of raw materials and manpower, on adherence to provisioning programmes unrelated to the total war capacity of the State cannot but have contributed materially to the low output of production for all three Services during the first half of the war.

Second Period (1944 onwards)
Merits

116.   The over-riding authority of the Speer Ministry in co-ordinating all production, including that for the German Air Force, resulted in a greatly increased output of armaments, and the outstanding merits of the system as compared with that existing prior to 1942 (or, where the Air Force was concerned, 1944) may be summarised as follows:—

  (i)   The co-relation of all Economic and Industrial resources resulted in an improved utilisation of raw materials and ensured a proper degree of allocation between the different Services. It ensured a more economical use of production capacities by eliminating inefficient plants and by preventing the erection of identical or similar plants designed to produce for competing consumers. It resulted in a better use of available manpower by the more specialised employment of technicians and by the opportunities available for the rapid deployment of labour from one plant or area to another.

  (ii)   It eliminated any atmosphere of competition which may have existed between the three fighting services.

Defects

117.　The creation of an autocratic authority with powers to act without relying upon advice or direction from the fighting services presents obvious opportunities for misuse of power. Although it is not suggested (except by certain German Air Force officers) that Speer did misuse his powers to the positive detriment of the strategic situation, it is evident that

- (i) no one person or body is competent to deal adequately with all the aspects and ramifications of provisioning and production from both the industrial **and** military points of view, and
- (ii) considerations of expediency in factories may be allowed to overrule strategic necessities, and military requirements may be subordinated to industrial and technical considerations.

CONCLUSIONS

118.　In order to resolve the difficulties inherent in the British system of provisioning and production, which are well known, and those in the German system which have been described in this Chapter, it is suggested that it is necessary to impose a different division of responsibility between the Air Force and Industry than existed under either system. The following paragraphs suggest how this might be achieved.

AIR FORCE RESPONSIBILITIES

119. (i) Responsibility for specifications of type of equipment to be produced, subject to advice of industrial technicians on elimination of sub-types, and restriction of number of prototypes to an economical number from a production point of view. Thus tactical and strategical considerations are safeguarded.
- (ii) Responsibility for providing figures of past consumption and for stating **ranges** of equipment required (based on foreknowledge of strategic committments). This statement not to include rigid enumeration of precise items nor actual quantities, (excepting for initial equipment to meet definite programmes), but to be expressed as so many weeks' or months' stocks of certain ranges for delivery at certain points by fixed dates. This would be accompanied by forecast factors to cover future strategic committments.
- (iii) Responsibility for agreeing with Industry the detail of parts for each range of spares for new type equipment.
- (iv) Responsibility for quality control.

RESPONSIBILITIES OF INDUSTRY

120.　Responsibility for deciding and stating, by means of Rings and Committees of technicians specialising in particular kinds of equipment,
- (i) the precise items to be produced,
- (ii) the quantities necessary to maintain stocks for the prescribed periods, and
- (iii) the methods of production to be adopted.

(i) and (ii) above to be in agreement with the Air Force.

121.　By such a division of responsibility the following advantages are assured:—
- (i) The service obtains the kind of weapons it considers necessary from a tactical and strategic point of view.

(ii) It obtains the required quality of equipment.
(iii) It allows industry the opportunity to standardise common user equipment to the fullest possible extent.
(iv) It achieves the most accurate estimation of future requirements that can reasonably be expected because full advantage is taken of the experience of technical experts in each range of equipment.
(v) It achieves maximum and most economical production possible with the means available.
(vi) It permits the timely planning of expansion of industrial resources to meet increasing consumption, the trend of which can best be anticipated if full responsibility for estimating future requirements is in the hands of technical experts.
(vii) The service does not become involved in a struggle with manufacturers (as was the case in Britain, notwithstanding the latters' acceptance of contracts), in order to obtain, for the maintenance of the Air Force, spares which are also required by the same manufacturers for assembly in major components to meet programmes.

122. Regarding (vii) above. If one authority is responsible for estimating requirements of parts, both for the assembly line and for maintenance in the field, and is also responsible for providing them, any failure to supply adequate quantities for either purpose lies at the door of that authority alone. There can be no shifting or confusion of responsibility such as was experienced in the United Kingdom, where it too often happened that in their zeal to increase their output of complete assemblies (for which bonuses were paid and which incidentally raised the morale of the workers) manufacturers neglected to maintain an adequate flow of spares for maintenance purposes.

123. In fairness to British contractors it must be said that the case was by no means a clear cut one. Contracts were subject to such a complexity of alterations in the form of supplementary orders, additions to quantities, deletion, superceding items, modifications and alternative items that even if manufacturers did not use these factors as excuses for falling behind in their supply of spares (which they undoubtedly did on occasions) it was exceedingly difficult for them to keep pace with the demands made on them.

124. At first sight it may seem that there is really no essential difference between the British system whereby the Air Force decides exact quantities of equipment required, leaving industry, often at too short notice, to manage as best it can to meet the demand, and the German system whereby industry estimated requirements and planned its resources to meet them. It may seem that as in either case it is the same manufacture who is producing both for the assembly line and for maintenance stocks, it is on him that ultimate responsibility must rest.

125. In principle this is true, but in reality, under the British system, in contrast to the German system, manufacturers laboured under a feeling of divided allegiance: "Our requirements" and "The Air Force requirements". It is natural that their own requirements loomed larger than those of the Air Force and it was therefore understandable that they saw, in the complexities of Air Force contracts, justification for their disinclination to sacrifice their own target figures of complete assemblies for the sake of meeting Air Force needs. In a nutshell, the British manufacturers felt little real responsibility for the committments placed on them by the Air Force. It was not their plan.

126. In the case of the German system, Industry, in calculating in detail the future requirements of the Air Force to meet strategic committments and weighing these against the industrial resources available, was able to make the necessary dispositions of its resources at the earliest forseeable moment in order to meet the situation adequately. In doing so it pledged itself to the task of carrying out the plan in its entirety without conceiving any artificial distinction between its own requirements and those of the Air Force. In fact, the plan as a whole was the responsibility of Industry, who did not seek to disclaim any part of it.

127. It is true that Saur, who was responsible for aircraft production, was accused by the German Air Force of seeking to curry favour with Hitler by producing spectacular output figures of complete aircraft at the expense of maintenance spares, but it was not difficult for the Air Force to confront him on the spot with their shortages of equipment for which he was also directly responsible. In such circumstances it was not possible for him to confuse the issue by introducing complicated arguments to show that the blame could be attributed to others, since he was solely responsible for all production.

128. In order to relieve industry of unnecessary administrative burdens, the system proposed above could in time be modified to some extent by allowing Air Force Depots to assume responsibility for the provisioning and ordering in detail of a very limited range of equipment, e.g. barrack, domestic and general utility equipment. The reason for this suggestion is that with the great majority of non-technical items, once a suitable design has been selected, the article need undergo very little development and change in design and it is therefore not necessary from this point of view to employ industrial experts on the provisioning of future requirements. Moreover, as the issue of such items is to a fixed scale, future requirements can be perfectly well calculated with a high degree of accuracy by non-technical people. It would be advisable, however, to defer this relaxation of the system until industry had had adequate time to do all it could to standardise common user equipment.

129. Finally it is appreciated that if this general scheme for Provisioning and Production were to be adopted it would necessitate some adjustment of the existing financial procedure whereby funds are voted to a Service against Budget estimates prepared by that Service. It is not considered that any change in responsibility for estimating service requirements should create any difficulties from a financial point of view. In view of the fact that the money allotted for the provision of maintenance spares follows an agreed percentage of the cost of the main programme it appears to be of little importance which particular administrative channels are used for assessing the percentage, and administering the Budget. Moreover, in time of war the necessity is such that nothing should be allowed to hamper maximum efficiency and thus the system would appear to be justified and finance would have to adjust itself to practical needs.

130. This, then, is suggested as the most desirable system to be adopted for Provisioning and Production in wartime, viz., a shifting of responsibility from the service to Industry with the service retaining both control over type and design of equipment (through specifiications) and broad control over quantity (through forecast factors) leaving Industry to chose, subject to service agreement, the particular items to be produced for

maintenance purposes and the rate and scale of production to meet future consumption.

131. That such a shifting of responsibility would have benefited Britain's wartime production appears to be borne out by consideration of the weaknesses from which it suffered.

132. Not only is it true, as already described, that the Royal Air Force found itself constantly in conflict with manufacturers in order to obtain maintenance spares off contract owing to the latters' bias towards their own requirements, but it is equally undeniable that the Royal Air Force system of provisioning is open to criticism on the grounds that it was staffed by officers and civil servants who were almost wholly lacking in the technical knowledge necessary to do the work efficiently and economically. From lack of real technical knowledge of the equipment for which they were provisioning their work often amounted to little more than a matter of applying elementary mathematics to consumption data. The work became too mechanical and the results were constantly criticised by manufacturers, who claimed that intelligent anticipation of modifying factors was absent from the calculations.

133. But in defence of the provisioning branches it must be said that efforts were made to maintain contact with manufacturers and with M.A.P. technical branches in an endeavour to keep up to date with current developments affecting future production, e.g. modifications, superceding items, and alternative items. It is contended, however, that they were not sufficiently successful and that the manufacturers themselves, by reason of their expert knowledge of technical developments, were in a far better position than the provisioning branches to anticipate the trend of future requirements and so make intelligent amendments to the purely theoretical calculations thrown up by consumption data. This appears to be convincing because even though the provisioning branches were able, whenever they thought necessary, to consult M.A.P. Technical branches in case of doubt, this is not at all the same thing as a system which provides, as a matter of course, for the systematic compilation of all estimates by a body of technical experts working with the aid of all necessary figures of past consumption.

134. Now that an outline has been given of a new division of responsibility between Service and Industry for Provisioning and Production, and some comparisons have been drawn between the British and German systems during wartime, it remains to be seen whether the suggested scheme could be made to work in peacetime conditions.

135. In the first place it is certain that it would be impossible for the service to allow manufacturers, working in an unco-ordinated and uncontrolled fashion, scope to assess service requirements. Contractors' commercial ambitions would at once operate to the disadvantage of the service. The temptation to exploit the service for commercial gain would be too great. Moreover, the system as envisaged presupposes an industry already organised as a whole under the control of some central authority. If therefore it may not be possible to perpetuate some authority comparable to the Ministry of Aircraft Production, it can be said at once that the scheme is impracticable and that there would be no other alternative but complete reversion to the previous peacetime practice whereby the service is entirely responsible for provisioning and production of its armaments by direct negotiation with separate manufacturers.

136. But providing that the requisite conditions are created it is considered that the system would still work efficiently and to the advantage of the service in peacetime. These conditions would be as follows:

(i) There must exist a Ministry or organised governing body (comparable to the wartime M.A.P.) with powers to co-ordinate and control that portion of the aircraft industry engaged on the production of service equipment. This body's main concern would be with industrial production problems to ensure that raw materials, manpower and production capacity are economically employed. It would need to create committees of industrial experts to deal with these subjects, and these committees' duties would also include the estimation of service requirements of maintenance spares.

(ii) Within or attached to this authority there must be serving officers whose knowledge of service conditions throughout the world would enable them to supervise the development of air armaments by industry so that practical operational needs are fully satisfied. These officers could well be drawn from the existing Technical branches of the Royal Air Force.

(iii) There would also have to be serving officers attached to this body whose duties would include: (a) agreement of the committees' estimates of maintenance spares and the resolving of differences of opinion between the service and industry on the subject; (b) action between the service and manufacturers to ensure that the rate of supply is maintained or adjusted to changing requirements; (c) the working out of prepackaging problems. With suitable training, Equipment officers would be best qualified to do this work.

(iv) The Service must continue to control quality of armaments through its network of A.I.D. inspectors at all concerns producing Air armaments.

137. It will be noted that the essence of this scheme is that whilst Industry, working under the control of a central authority, is entrusted with the formulation and production of service requirements, the service interests are safeguarded by placing Air Force officers within the industrial organisation in key supervisory positions.

138. But the success of this scheme would depend on the availability of a plentiful supply of suitably qualified officers to fill these supervisory posts. As far as Technical officers are concerned, the service already has in its Technical Branches suitable officers, but in its Equipment officers it would not find more than a sprinkling capable of discharging these duties adequately. They are deficient of sufficient technical knowledge to deal on an equal footing with members of industry, with whom they would have to agree such matters as spares programmes and rates of supply.

139. The scheme therefore argues that Equipment officers would have to receive much better technical training than is accorded to them at present. They would naturally not have to be trained to the same degree as the officers of the Technical Branches but they would have to specialise to some extent. It would probably be necessary to give them basic training in either of the two main branches of engineering affecting Service equipment viz., Mechanical Engineering and Electrical Engineering.

140. Before ending this review of Provisioning and Production, it is necessary to consider whether the advantages claimed for the proposed scheme in wartime apply equally to peacetime conditions. One of the

important advantages claimed was that a shifting of responsibility to Industry would eliminate friction between the service and Industry. In peacetime such friction does not exist. Industry is only too anxious to supply the service with what it requires. Industry has no personal interests to compete with service requirements and it is therefore not a factor to be taken into consideration in peacetime. But the other advantages enumerated in paragraph 111 remain and therefore on balance the arguments appear to favour the placing of the main responsibility for Provisioning and Production in the hands of Industry.

PART 2

CHAPTER 1

DETAILS OF AIR MINISTRY DEPARTMENTS CONNECTED WITH SUPPLY MATTERS

INTRODUCTION	Paragraphs 1—3
OPERATIONS STAFF	,, 4—5
1st DEPARTMENT	,, 6
QUARTERMASTER GENERAL	,, 7—8
ORGANISATION STAFF	,, 9—10
2nd DEPARTMENT	,, 11
9th DEPARTMENT	,, 12
DEPARTMENT FOR PERSONNEL AND EQUIPMENT ESTABLISHMENTS ,,	13
4th DEPARTMENT	,, 14—24
Preparation of Supply Directives	,, 17
Allocation of Aviation and Motor Transport Fuel	,, 18—19
Allocation of Explosives and Ammunition	,, 20
The Director of Airfield Servicing Companies	,, 21
The Deployment of Supply Installations and Supply Services	,, 22—24
6th DEPARTMENT	,, 25—35
Section I: Raw Materials and Production Programmes	,, 29
Section II: Manpower	,, 30
Section III: Allocation of Operationally Important Equipment	,, 31—32
Section IV: Standards	,, 33
Section V: Munition Programmes	,, 34
Section VI: Operational Forecasting	,, 35
DIRECTOR OF SUPPLY	,, 36—39
DIRECTOR OF MOTOR TRANSPORT	,, 40—45
DIRECTOR OF ARMED FORCES AIR TRANSPORT	,, 46
CHIEF OF THE GROUND ORGANISATION DEPARTMENT	,, 47—49
CHIEF ENGINEER OF THE GERMAN AIR FORCE	,, 50—53
CHIEF OF TECHNICAL ARMAMENTS	,, 54—59
THE ADMINISTRATION OFFICE	,, 60—61
THE ECONOMICS OFFICE	,, 62

PART 2

CHAPTER I

DETAILS OF AIR MINISTRY DEPARTMENTS CONNECTED WITH SUPPLY MATTERS

INTRODUCTION.

1   An outline of the functions of the various departments of the German Air Ministry connected with supply matters has been given in Part 1 Chapter IV of this paper. This present chapter is intended to give in greater detail the exact responsibilities of the departments concerned.

2.   When a department was formed in the German Air Ministry its duties were defined in a directive known as a "General Definition of Status and Duties". The information in this Chapter is based on the terms of reference extracted from such directives.

3.   The departments described are:—
- (i) **The High Command of the Luftwaffe.**
  - (a) Operations Staff — 1st Department.
  - (b) The Quartermaster General — Organisation Staff, 2nd and 9th Departments, Equipment Establishments Staff, 4th and 6th Departments, Director of Supply, Director of Motor Transport, Director of Transport Aircraft, Chief of Ground Organisation, and the Luftwaffe Engineer.
  - (c) The Chief of Technical Armaments.
  - (d) The Chief Intendant.
- (ii) **The State Minister for Air.**
  - (a) The Administration Office.
  - (b) The Economics Office.

OPERATIONS STAFF

4.   The Chief of the Operations Staff was subordinate to the Chief of General Staff and was his permanent deputy. On behalf of the Chief of General Staff he prepared orders for the employment of all forces subordinate to the Commander in Chief of the German Air Force including allied forces. He made recommendations for the conduct of the air war and planned air operations including those for active and passive air defence. He was also responsible for co-operation with the other services.

5.   After personal conferences with the Chief of General Staff he submitted directives to the other departments of the General Staff and to the Specialist Air Officers and Inspectorates. These directives embraced tactical and technical requirements and such organisational, training and supply requirements as were considered necessary for the support of future operational policy. Such directives also included the commitments of the Signals branch. The following staffs were subordinated to the Chief of Operations Staff:—
- (i) 1st Department: Operations.
- (ii) 3rd Department: Training.
- (iii) 7th Department: Cartography.

(iv) Director of Meteorology.
(v) Senior Officer for Anti-Gas.
(vi) The Passive Air Defence Planning Staff.

1ST DEPARTMENT

6. The Chief of the 1st Department made recommendations to the Chief of Operations Staff on all subjects concerned with the prosecution of the air war. He was responsible for implementing the policy of the Commander in Chief and the Chief of the General Staff and in this connection would prepare orders and instructions governing the employment of all units subordinated to the Commander in Chief. He formulated and submitted to the Chief of Operations Staff his assessment of the operational requirements in respect of organisation, supply, armament, training, intelligence, meteorological services, anti-gas and cartography. In all current operational affairs he collaborated directly with the other departments of the General Staff, the Director General of Equipment (later Chief of Technical Armaments), the Director General of Signals, the Specialist Air Officers and Inspectorates, and with the other services and allies.

QUARTERMASTER GENERAL

7. The Quartermaster General was subordinate to the Chief of the General Staff but he had the right of direct audience with Göring. He directed and superintended the entire supply system of the Air Force in respect of material and of personnel in accordance with the instructions of the Chief of the General Staff. He had to make long term plans that would ensure the maintenance of the striking power of the Air Force, including formations subordinate for tactical purposes to the Army and Navy, in terms of both men and material. He was also responsible for arranging all transport matters. In addition, he had to strike the necessary balance in the direction of current supplies of personnel and material to the front, to schools, depot units, and newly formed units, after taking into account the emphasis being placed on any given aspect of supply at the moment in question and subject to the instructions of the Chief of the General Staff. He was responsible for putting mobilisation into effect and for handling all questions relating to the wartime organisation of the Air Force in accordance with the instructions of the Chief of the General Staff. Furthermore, he kept check on the state of ground organisation and handled its further development.

.8 On behalf of the Chief of the General Staff he issued appropriate instructions and orders to the corresponding higher command authorities, the Director for Air Administrative Matters and Personnel and the Director General of Equipment. The Quartermaster General also maintained contact with the Army Quartermaster General with regard to the use of services afforded to the Air Force by the Army and, where necessary, with the Chief of Staff of the Navy.

ORGANISATION STAFF

9. The Chief of the Organisational Staff was responsible to the Quartermaster General for:—
 (i) The wartime organisation of the Supreme Command and Reich Minister for Air at the highest levels. Battle order and organisation, including planning for the formation of new units.
 (ii) Armed forces affairs (welfare, pensions and P.O.Ws).

(iii) Planning in respect of personnel.
(iv) Personnel establishments and equipment establishments.

10. To assist him in the execution of the above task the Chief of the Organisational Staff had subordinated to him the following staffs:—
(i) The 2nd Department of the General Staff.
(ii) The 9th Department of the General Staff.
(iii) The Establishments and Equipment Establishments Department.

2ND DEPARTMENT

11. The responsibilities of the 2nd Department of the General Staff included:—
(i) Wartime organisation of the Air Force at the highest level (other than the organisation of the Air Ministry and its branches).
(ii) Battle order of the Air Force.
(iii) Planning the setting up of new units.
(iv) Ground organisation and fixing locations for stations.
(v) General Armed Forces affairs (welfare, pensions, P.O.W.s insofar as they affected the Air Force.
(vi) Matters concerned with Reich defence, collaborating in drafting laws relating to Reich Defence (war laws) and to the war.
(vii) Mobilisation.

9TH DEPARTMENT

12. The Chief of the 9th Department of the General Staff was responsible to the Chief of the Organisational Staff for:—
(i) Planning all personnel matters resulting from the armament programme.
(ii) Supervising the standard of readiness for action of Air Force Personnel.
(iii) Guaranteeing the supply of replacement personnel.
(iv) Supplying information as to the personnel position and high level direction of the entire personnel of the Air Force.

The Chief of the 9th Department was directed to collaborate closely with the Operations Staff and the Chief of the 6th Department of the General Staff in matters concerning flying personnel.

DEPARTMENT FOR PERSONNEL AND EQUIPMENT ESTABLISHMENTS

13. The Chief of the Department for Personnel and Equipment Establishments was subordinate to the Chief of the Organisational Staff and his responsibilities included: —
(i) Determining the internal organisation and establishments (establishment lists) for the staffs and units of the Air Force.
(ii) Composing the equipment establishments (equipment establishment lists).
(iii) Analysis of reports on experience gained and of recommendations submitted by the specialist departments and units for the redrafting or modification of establishment and equipment establishment lists.
(iv) Determining the Pay Groups to which the various establishment posts figuring on establishment lists of Air Force units belonged.
(v) Drawing up and keeping the list of units in the light of the orders setting up new units and the mobilisation decrees.

(vi) Collaborating in the introduction of new trades for N.C.O.s and men.
(vii) Collaborating in introducing new items of equipment for units (orders for the introduction of new equipment); drawing up the key on the basis of which such equipment was allocated.
(viii) Making arrangements for the drawing up and distribution in good time to the appropriate authorities and units of establishment and equipment establishment lists and of the orders which went with them.
(ix) Checking of establishment lists with a view to economy of manpower.

4TH DEPARTMENT

14. The 4th Department was responsible for the preparation of Supply Directives, the allocation of operationally important supplies (aviation fuel, explosives, etc.) to the Luftflotte, "Movements", the deployment of supply installations and units and the direction of Airfield Servicing Companies.

15. The Department was divided into five sections as follows:—
 (i) Section I. The main functions of this section were:—
  (a) The preparation of "Special Supply Directives" to the Luftflottes, relating to the manner in which their supplies and equipment (including their aircraft) would reach them. These Directives formed the counterpart to the Operational Orders issued by the Operations Department of the General Staff, and they were prepared by the Quartermaster General on the instructions of the Operations Staff.
  (b) The allocation of aircraft fuel to Luftflottes, and the issue of instructions to the Director of Supply to deliver the fuel allocated.
  (c) The allocation of bombs and aircraft ammunition to Luftflottes and the issue of instructions to the Director of Supply to deliver the munitions allocated. The allocation of Flak munition to the whole of the armed forces.
  (d) The direction of the Airfield Servicing Companies.
 (ii) Section II. The main functions of this section were:—
  (a) The deployment of supply installations.
  (b) The deployment of supply units.
 (iii) Section III. The main functions of this section were:—
  (a) Provision of rail transport.
  (b) Allocation of Transport Columns.
  (c) Provision of transport by sea and inland waterways.
 (iv) Section IV. This section provided the Air Force liaison officer to the Director of Armed Forces Transport (O.K.W.).
 (v) Section V. This section was dissolved in February 1945 but, before that date, it handled Air Transport matters.

16. The functions of Sections III, IV and V are amplified in Part 2, Chapter V. The functions of Sections I and II are examined in some detail in the following paragraphs.

Preparation of Supply Directives

17. The Operations Staff of the General Staff issued Operational Orders to the Luftflotte, and at the same time to the Quartermaster General. The complementary orders for the supply of aircraft fuel, munitions and

equipment for the support of these operations were then prepared by the 4th Department and issued likewise to the Luftflotte as a "Special Supply Directive" and signed by the Quartermaster General. The 4th Department alone issued such directives. Each Operational Order to the Luftflotte from the Operations Staff required a corresponding "Special Supply Directive" from the Quartermaster General. Orders and regulations relating to the supply of materials other than those which the 4th Department allocated were also included in the "Special Directive". Thus, orders which the 6th Department, the Director of Motor Transport, or the Director of Supply wished to issue were included, so that only one such directive would be issued. It is true that for the sake of speed the other Departments mentioned might issue their orders separately through the Quartermaster General; they would then be supplements to the "Special Directive" and sent out as such. Special Supply Directives contained the following information:—

(i) A battle order of the operational units, transport units, training and other units to be supplied with aircraft fuel, oil, and lubricants.
(ii) A statement of the source from which Flak units both of the Army and the Air Force were to obtain their flak ammunition, and from which Luftflotte quota is was to be drawn.
(iii) Ditto for motor transport fuel.
(iv) Statement of the channels for obtaining aircraft and the route they would follow.
(v) Ditto for flak guns and heavy flak guns.
(vi) Supply routes for aircraft engines, etc.
(vii) Supply routes for ordinary equipment (coming from the Director of Supply).
(viii) Measures relating to provision of clothing, rations and pay.

Allocation of Aviation and Motor Transport Spirit

18. Each Luftflotte had to submit a daily report of the consumption and stocks of aircraft fuel to the 4th Department by teleprinter or in code by telephone. This information, interpreted in the light of forthcoming operations, formed the basis for estimating the requirements of the Luftflottes. The quantity becoming available from industry for distribution was made known to the 4th Department by the Chief of Technical Armaments who was responsible for production. Proposals for the monthly allocation to the Luftflottes were then prepared and submitted to the Chief of the General Staff through the Quartermaster General. The fuel was held in the various Bulk Fuel Depots, and after approval of the proposed allocations a plan was drawn up showing which depots were to supply which Luftflottes. The 4th Department would then issue orders to the Director of Supply to draw the aircraft fuel and lubricants from the depots.

19. In the home defence area the allocation of fuel for motor vehicles was done by the 4th Department. In the operational areas outside Germany motor transport fuel was supplied by the Army.

The Allocation of Explosives and Ammunition

20. The 4th Department allocated bombs, aircraft ammunition and special missiles to the Luftflotte on the same principle as aviation fuel was allocated. Flak ammunition was allocated by the 4th Department to the whole of the Armed Forces. The needs of the Army for Flak munition were presented to the Luftflottes, and the Luftflottes included the Army figures

in the weekly reports to the 4th Department. The weekly reports gave data on stocks, consumption and the numbers of guns. From these reports the requirements of the Armed Forces in each area were calculated. The quantity available for distribution was notified to the Department by the Chief of Technical Armaments who was responsible for production. As the 6th Department had the allocation of heavy flak guns in its keeping, the 4th Department would work closely with the 6th in the matters of allocation of munitions. The 6th Department, the 4th Department and the Director of Supply kept themselves currently informed about the state of production and the location of the flak ammunition produced. After the allocation to Commands, the 4th Department gave orders to the Director of Supply to despatch the quantities indicated from particular Ammunition Depots to each Command.

The Direction of Airfield Servicing Companies

21. In 1943 a pool of Airfield Servicing Companies was established to assist those attached to Long Range Bomber, Dive Bomber units and other similar flying units in maintaining their aircraft, wherever such additional help was necessary. These companies formed a Quartermaster General Reserve and were allocated by the 4th Department in agreement with the Operations Staff, usually to Airfield Regional Commands. Such Airfield Servicing Companies differed from those attached to flying units in that they were capable of attending to several types of aircraft. It was in some ways an anomaly that the 4th Department, which was mainly concerned with the allocation of transport and supplies, should be charged with the duty of allocating Airfield Servicing Companies, and when the Chief Engineer was set up at the end of 1944, they passed to his charge. By that time the Air Force consisted very largely of Fighter units. The Servicing Companies were renamed Aircraft Maintenance Companies and were employed almost exclusively on servicing fighter aircraft.

The Deployment of Supply Installations and Supply Services

22. Section II kept records of the number and location of the various supply installations of the Air Force, viz. Air Equipment Depots, Flak and Signals Equipment Depots, Aircraft Fuel Depots and Issuing Stations of various kinds. In the light of these records the 4th Department controlled the allocation of the Issuing Stations to the Luftflottes according to tactical needs. In the case of evacuation the stationary establishments, for example Air Parks, would be withdrawn to new locations on the orders of the 4th Department to the Director of Supply and to the Luftflotte concerned.

23. Supply services in this context included Air Regional Command Headquarters, Station Command Headquarters, Supply Companies, Land Defence Units, Works Battalions, Rapid Construction Companies, Hangar Construction Companies, and so on. The 4th Department also directed these units to their commands in accordance with tactical requirements and kept records of their location and subordination. When the Ground Organisation Department was established these units passed under the control of that authority.

24. The 4th Department was also responsible for controlling the development of ground installations. In the first place, the execution of these duties involved keeping records of the boundaries of the Luftgaus and Airfield Regional Commands and submitting proposals to the Chief of the General Staff and to the 2nd Department for any changes in these boundaries which were desirable. At that time the development of the

ground organisation within the A.R.C. was supervised by this Department, i. e. location and the state of airfields, ammunition depots, aviation fuel depots, etc. With regard to further development, the 4th Department was the competent authority to issue orders for the construction of airfields in accordance with the requirements of the Operations Staff. Originally these orders were passed to the Luftflottes for action by the Luftgau Works Section. In June 1944 the Directorate of Works was established (subordinated to the Quartermaster General) to whom such orders were also passed. Later the Department for Ground Organisation was formed (Abteilung Bodenorganisation) to take over from the 4th Department the whole subject of ground services, which had long been too much for this Department.

6TH DEPARTMENT

25.   The Chief of the 6th Department of the General Staff was responsible to the Quartermaster General for:—
   (i) Supervising the standard of serviceability and readiness of the Air Force both from the material and the personnel point of view.
   (ii) Equipping the Air Force with operationally important material.
   (iii) Ensuring supply, including accumulation of the Command reserves in all spheres of prime importance.
   (iv) Supplying information with regard to the personnel situation in general and direction of personnel reported as ready and suitable for front line employment.
   (v) Supplying information as to the overall raw materials and production situation.

26.   For this purpose the Chief of the 6th Department of the General Staff had to analyse the serviceability and readiness reports submitted by Command authorities and units, both from the standpoint of personnel and of material.

27.   In the light of the documents submitted by the various interested Departments of the Air Ministry, and by Command authorities, he had to draw up and analyse equipment statistics and make recommendations to the Quartermaster General on the requirements revealed by these statistics. In accordance with the instructions of the Quartermaster General he prepared the programmes pertaining to the acquisition of operationally important equipment and carried out the allocation of this equipment. He was also responsible for preparing programmes for the production of operationally important supplies (munitions, and aviation spirit) although the allocation of such items was the responsibility of the 4th Department. In the case of deliveries of equipment to foreign countries, he made the necessary investigations to see that the serviceability and readiness of the Air Force were not affected by such deliveries.

28.   The functions of the 6th Department were performed through five Sections whose responsibilities were briefly as follows:—

Section I — Raw Materials and Production Programmes

29.   This section was informed by the Director General of Equipment (later the Chief of Technical Armaments) of the quantities of raw material available to the Air Force. From this information the section calculated what operationally important war materials should be produced from the available raw materials. The following are examples of operationally important equipment: Aircraft, airframes, aero engines, power units,

airborne equipment (instruments, air signals equipment, oxygen apparatus etc.) aircraft armaments, ground technical equipment (engine starters, and heaters, bomb trollies and airfield petrol tanks, etc.). In conjunction with Section III, Section I would inform the Director General of Equipment (later the C.T.L.R.) of the numbers and types of operationally important equipment required. In the last years of the war the 6th Department had little real influence in the numbers manufactured as this was entirely determined by the raw materials available and the capacities of factories. The Department did, however, retain its influence in the proportionate use of the raw materials allocation to the Air Force and in the types of aircraft and equipment that were produced. It should be noted that the Air Force suffered greatly from the fact that more and more substitute materials had to be employed in the manufacture of aircraft and aircraft equipment and it became, therefore, more and more difficult to relate the consumption of raw materials to final products. Section I also controlled the allocation of raw materials, within the Air Force, for production of operationally important supplies (aviation fuel and explosives).

(i) Aviation fuel. Section I received from Section III a forecast of the future strength of the Air Force in aircraft and this forecast was based on present strength, probable losses and production estimates. On the basis of this information Section I prepared a forecast of the fuel requirements for operations and added to this the requirements for training, ferrying, testing and for civil flying and in this way computed the total aircraft fuel requirements which were passed to the Director General of Equipment (later C.T.L.R.) for production.

(ii) Explosives. Section I informed Section IV of the raw materials available for the production of explosives, chemical weapons and ammunition and the latter Section prepared the actual programmes of requirements within this quota.

Section II. — Manpower

30. This Section dealt with the Air Force manpower situation. With effect from January 1945, however, this Section ceased to be an integral part of the 6th Department and was given independent status as the 9th Department.

Section III — Allocation of Operationally Important Equipment

31. The most important function of this Section was the allocation of aircraft and other operationally important equipment. To illustrate this function an example will be given of the method used for the allocation of aircraft — other operationally important equipment was allocated in a similar fashion. A "Forecast of Production" was forwarded, at one time by the Director General of Equipment, and later by the Speer Ministry through the Director of Technical Armaments, at the beginning of each month. This forecast covered the coming month. Section III then drew up a schedule for the distribution of aircraft to the Luftflotten in the light of the aircraft situation in the flying units, and submitted this schedule to Hitler, Göring, and the Operations Staff for approval. If any changes were regarded as necessary these would then be indicated, or otherwise the schedule as submitted would receive approval. The schedule, with any necessary amendments, was received back in Section III through the Operations Staff and the aircraft were allocated accordingly during the month. The schedule as approved was telephoned with certain reservations to the Chief Quartermasters of the Luftflottes. The distribution of aircraft was managed in

such a way that the Director of Supply received orders from Section III, based on the daily reports of finished aircraft by the Air Factory Inspectors, as to how, within the framework of the month's planning, the individual aircraft should be allocated to Luftflottes, independent flying units or units in the course of re-equipping. The Director of Supply then passed on the destination of the aircraft to the Factory Inspectors and to the Aircraft Ferrying Geschwader. The latter ferried the aircraft to the distributing airfields of the Luftflottes or the stations of the flying units. (It will be noted that there was a radical difference between the German Air Force and the Royal Air Force in that there was no German equivalent to Aircraft Storage Units. Such reserves as were available were either dispersed throughout the Luftflotte in small numbers on various airfields or else went straight to the formation of new squadrons). At the end of each month a so-called aircraft balance sheet was drawn up. In this table a comparison was made between the number of aircraft advised by industry to the Quartermaster General during the month and the number distributed to commands, etc. The number taken over during the month by the Quartermaster General excluded aircraft sent, after manufacture, to workshops for modifications or to conversion workshops. A modification workshop was a unit which carried out such alterations as proved necessary on tactical or technical ground but which could not be introduced during production in the factory without great loss of time. These workshops formerly belonged to the Air Force but were transferred to the aircraft industry in November 1944 so as to force the manufacturers to embody modifications as quickly as possible into serial production. A conversion workshop was an industrial workshop or factory which converted finished fighter aircraft into reconnaissance aircraft, or bombers into torpedo-carriers, etc.

32. All modifications to aircraft, fitment of new installations in aircraft and re-armament had to be approved by Section III. After the Section had agreed to any such innovations it would make arrangements for the provision of the appropriate equipment or materials required. After 1944 all such modifications had to receive the additional approval of Göring himself. The new procedure was introduced as the result of a grave incident — the Air Force was commissioned to undertake a very important reconnaissance near Rostov and failed since the reconnaissance squadron detailed no longer had the required tactical range because of additional machine guns which had been fitted without authority.

Section III T — Standards

33. Until August 1943 a Section of the Operations Staff, Section I T, worked out the requirements which future new flying equipment would have to satisfy, as well as improvements that were called for in existing front-line equipment, on the basis of operational experience. On account of personal differences, between the then head of Operations Staff, Section I T and the Director General of Equipment, as well as through difficulties which existed in co-operation between the then Chief of the General Staff (Jeschonnek) and the Director General of Equipment (Milch), Section I T was dissolved and in its place a Technical Office, under Göring's Adjutant, was set up instead. This Office had to bring into line all demands made by the Waffengenerale (Air Officers for the various arms of service) and of the Operations Staff with regard to future equipment and to pass them out to the Director General of Equipment as orders from Göring. The Waffengenerale received the right to discuss all these matters directly with

the Director General of Equipment. But as it turned out, the Technical Office was never in a position to be able to bring these various demands into line, so that in practice each Waffengeneral made whatever demands on the Director General of Equipment seemed to him to be right and necessary. The result of this was that the Director General of Equipment, partly in ignorance of tactical needs (for he had scarcely any contact with the Operations Staff and had no idea of its views) and partly in an endeavour to produce the largest possible number of aircraft, interpreted the demands in such a way as would be simplest for him to manufacture. Apart from this, special difficulties arose when there were aircraft in which more than one Waffengeneral was interested. Me 109, for instance, was used as a fighter or as a reconnaissance machine. But frequently these two Waffengenerale would make completely opposite demands for the same pattern of machine. This state of things went on till March 1944. In order to overcome the difficulties inherent therein and to permit the Operations Staff to obtain more influence in the development of new flying equipment, but most important of all to cancel the exercise of individual powers by the Waffengenerale, Section III T of the 6th Department was set up. This section had the task of examining and co-ordinating the various requests which came up through operational experience, that is via the Waffengenerale, as well as from the Operations Staff about new development of equipment, going into the question of the possibility of satisfying them with the Director General of Equipment and then taking them by way of the Operations Staff to Göring for a decision. After the Reichsmarschall had approved them they were returned to the Director General of Equipment for execution.

Section IV — Munitions Programmes

34.   This section handled the programmes for Flak equipment and ammunition and aircraft bombs, war gases, ammunition, etc. Section I informed Section IV of the raw materials available and within this quota the Section prepared a programme based on information of consumption and stocks from units and on instructions relating to the future air policy from the Operations Staff. Programmes for production were passed by Section IV to the Director General of Equipment who made arrangements with industry for manufacture — except in the case of munitions common to the Army and the Air Force and 50, 250, 500 and 1000 kilo bombs which were passed to the war office for manufacture under their auspices. Finished products were allocated to the service by the 4th Department.

Section V — Operational Forecasting

35.   This Section was approximately similar in its function to the British Air Ministry Operational Forecasting department. It handled all Air Force statistics and evaluated all operational readiness reports and in this way provided the numerical data for all Air Ministry departments. All reports of losses were rendered to Section V and from these reports average wastage rates for various conditions were calculated and were passed to Sections I and IV of the 6th Department for use in calculating programmes of requirements. This Section also prepared a monthly report on the state of armament of the Luftwaffe for Hitler, Göring and the Supreme Command of the Armed Forces.

DIRECTOR OF SUPPLY

36.   The Director of Supply was responsible for supplying (receiving, storing and delivering) the entire Air Force with war materials of all kinds

except Motor Transport and Intendant materials (clothing, rations, barrack equipment and solid fuel). All the Main Depots were under the control of the Director of Supply and all goods ordered for industry flowed into this storage from which the supply establishments of the Luftgaus were replenished. The Director's responsibility for supply ended when the materials in question were taken over by the units or by supply establishments subordinate to the Command authorities concerned.

37. The Director of Supply kept the Director General of Equipment informed with regard to basic supply matters insofar as they affected the acquisition of supplies. He was empowered to communicate directly with the Chief Quartermasters of Luftflottes and the Quartermasters of Luftgaus in matters concerning the supply of operational areas within their spheres.

38. In addition, the Director of Supply's responsibilities included:
  (i) The taking over of war materials of all kinds after manufacture or repair and rendering them available for the making of initial equipment pack-ups for units, and for current supply. The transfer of aircraft to their future holders in accordance with the special directions of the Quartermaster General. To assist in the movement of aircraft the Director of Supply had subordinated to him a pool of ferry pilots.
  (ii) The Director of Supply was responsible for assessing the future requirements of the Air Force for all equipment other than Motor Transport, Intendant materials and such equipment and supplies as were included in the special programmes of the 6th Department. In this connection he had to take into account the formation of new units, the scales given in Equipment Establishment Lists, special directions given by the Quartermaster General or the Director General of Signals and his own experience of past consumption. The orders resulting from these calculations were forwarded either by the Director of Supply to the Director General of Equipment or to the Army Supreme Command or by the Main Equipment Depots directly to industry. (For full description of provisioning procedure see Part 2, Chapter II.)
  (iii) The Director of Supply had to ensure adequate and prompt production of Flak ammunition (other than 2 cm) in Main Ammunition depots. He was also responsible for taking over from industry all other types of ammunition and ammunition components, storage in Ammunition Depots, and the issue of these types and components in accordance with the directions of the Quartermaster General.
  (iv) Taking over aviation fuels and lubricants, special petrol, oils, and lubricants, oxygen, smoke acid, and their containers (railway tank waggons, petrol, oil and lubricant drums, tins) and servicing equipment, and issuing these items in accordance with the instructions of the Quartermaster General.
  (v) Issuing official instructional publications, decrees and orders relating to the taking over of all supply goods from the manufacturers; storage of these goods in supply establishments; regulation of the system of supply; administration, storage, handling and maintenance of equipment while in the hands of supply authorities.

(vi) Working on recommendations concerning formation of new units, regroupings, reinforcement, strength and equipping of units, filling of establishment posts and trade training for personnel of all supply establishments and installations.

(vii) Establishing repair workshops other than aircraft repair workshops, aero-engine repair workshops, power unit assembly lines, M/T workshops and repair workshops for aviation ground equipment; arranging the despatch of damaged equipment for repair; and supervision of the repair of equipment (other than those detailed above); in the case of equipment belonging to these categories but not capable of repair in Air Force workshops, he issued instructions for its despatch to industrial concerns or if necessary to Army repair establishments.

39. The Director of Supply was empowered to issue instructions in supply matters to the Officers Commanding Equipment Groups. Main Equipment Depots, Field Equipment Depots, Flak Equipment Depots, Signals Equipment Depots, Field Signals Equipment Depots, Main Ammunition Depots and Gas Plants were directly subordinate to him as far as their regular functioning was concerned. The Director of Supply had powers of inspection over all supply installations. He was entitled to inspect stores and workshops in all Air Force Stations by agreement with the appropriate command authority so as to assure himself that spare parts, petrol, oil, lubricants and works materials were properly stored and he was empowered to issue orders to the formation inspected.

DIRECTOR OF MOTOR TRANSPORT

40. The Director of Motor Transport was directly subordinate to the Quartermaster General and his responsibilities included:—

(i) The supervision of the standard of training and employment of Motor Transport personnel and of the serviceability and replacement of Motor Transport equipment.

(ii) The direction of primary and subsequent training, selection and assessment of all Motor Transport personnel, including those employed as drivers in Motor Transport Columns and for transport purposes.

(For further information see Part 2, Chapter VI.)

41. Within the scope of the Operations planned by the Chief of the Operations Staff the Director of Motor Transport submitted recommendations concerning the organisation of Motor Transport services, Motor Transport repair services and stocks of Motor Transport held on hand. He directed the employment of Motor Transport repair units in collaboration with the 4th Department and issued instructions covering the employment of Motor Transport stocks units. In addition, the work of the Director of Motor Transport included:—

(i) Planning and allocation of Motor Transport. Air Force requests to the Director of Armed Forces Motor Transport (Supreme Command of the Armed Forces).

(ii) Registration, taking over, and administration of all available stocks accumulated from manufacture and repair.

(iii) Supply, allocation and equitable distribution of Motor Transport equipment.

(iv) Collecting technical information on Motor Transport culled from experience and making use of it. Inventions and recommendations for improvements in the Motor Transport technical sphere and the issue of Motor Transport technical publications and instructional matter.

(v) Special equipment for vehicles and conversion to gas generator power units.

(vi) Carrying out of laws and decrees on traffic, approving the marking of vehicles.

(vii) Regulations for the administration of Motor Transport equipment and use of vehicles, supervision of traffic, analysis of accidents, losses and damage to Motor Transport equipment.

42. The Director of Motor Transport was responsible for the development of Motor Transport equipment. He carried out technical tests and gave orders for the introduction of approved equipment. He issued directives for the development of special super-structures and fittings in collaboration with the Air Officer for Flak, Director General of Signals, Air Inspectorate 13 and Director General of Equipment. He also gave orders for construction modifications.

43. The Director of Motor Transport was further responsible for all Motor Transport repair services. He issued instuctions putting into effect the organisation of repair services ordered by the General Staff and for the setting up and equipping of these services. He arranged collaboration with the Motor Transport repair installations of the Supreme Command of the Armed Forces and of the other services. He issued directives for the rejection and sale on salvage of sub-standard Motor Transport equipment and for the hiring of vehicles and application of the Reich Requisition Law.

44. He ordered Motor Transport petrol, oil and lubricants, drums and tanks for petrol, oil and lubricants, tyres, tyres for flak equipment and for mobile aircraft servicing equipment (the latter in co-operation with the Director of Supply). Distribution was carried out in collaboration with the 4th Department.

45. The Director of Motor Transport co-operated:—

(i) In the formation of units involving Motor Transport personnel, equipment and equipment outfits (with 2nd and 6th Departments).

(ii) In the drawing-up and modification of War Establishment Lists, War Equipment Establishment Lists and Training Equipment Establishments (with Establishment and Equipment Establishment Department).

(iii) In filling establishment posts with Motor Transport personnel (with the Personnel Office, the Director General of Equipment, the Administrative Office and the G.A.F. other ranks records office).

(iv) In Motor Transport technical constructional projects (with 2nd Department and with the Administrative Office).

(v) In the affairs of state employees and workers employed on Motor Transport services, pay questions, clothing, insurance, etc., (in conjunction with the Administrative Office).

(vi) In the testing and introduction of special Motor Transport clothing (with the Administrative Office).

DIRECTOR OF ARMED FORCES AIR TRANSPORT

46. The Director of Armed Forces Air Transport was the specialist department of the Armed Forces Supreme Command for all matters relating to air supply and was an operational authority of the Air Force

Supreme Command. He was directly subordinate to the Air Force Quartermaster General and his responsibilities included:—

(i) Within the framework of the responsibilities and powers of Inspectors in wartime the Director of Armed Forces Air Transport exercised powers of inspection over all flying units earmarked for air transport purposes.

(ii) The Director of Armed Forces Air Transport paid visits to units employed in air supply and satisfied himself as to:—
   (a) The suitability of their employment.
   (b) Their serviceability both technically and in respect of their personnel.
   (c) The possibilities of stepping up performance.

(iii) The Director of Armed Forces Air Transport collaborated in the planning of new units and in the organisation and equipment of air transport units. He was directed to collaborate closely with the Director of Technical Armaments, the Air Officer for Training and the Chief Engineer and had to be consulted by these departments in all matters touching on his sphere of work.

(iv) The Director of Armed Forces Air Transport formulated requirements in respect of armament and the development of aircraft and submitted them to the Quartermaster General (6th Department). He maintained close contact with the Director of Technical Armaments and with the Air Force Testing Stations in respect of the development of new types of aircraft for air transport purposes.

(v) The Director of Armed Forces Air Transport was responsible for giving orders for and carrying out trials in units, where such trials were concerned with the air transport system.

(vi) The Director of Armed Forces Air Transport kept check on the standardisation of training and issued for this purpose manuals, directives and pamphlets.

(vii) The Director of Armed Forces Air Transport was responsible for the full use of all available transport space in every aircraft by agreement with the appropriate Specialist Air Officers and for making recommendations with regard to the employment of this space.

(viii) The Director of Armed Forces Air Transport was responsible for the collection, analysis and application of operational experience gained within the sphere of his authority.

(ix) The Director of Armed Forces Air Transport collaborated in accordance with the instructions of the Personnel Office in making recommendations for the filling of the principal establishment vacancies in the air transport units.

CHIEF OF THE GROUND ORGANISATION DEPARTMENT

47. The Chief of the Department for Ground Organisation was directly subordinate to the Quartermaster General. He represented the tactical requirements of the Operations Staff when constructional projects were being planned and carried out and he formulated requirements in respect of the construction of airfields in agreement with the Specialist Air Officers and Commands. In conjunction with the Director of Works he checked the airfields or sites recommended for development by the Luftflotte H.Q.s to ascertain their general suitability for the proposed development. He

co-operated in fixing the volume of construction and determined the priority of the various constructional projects in accordance with the directions of the Operations Staff. He also superintended the carrying out of constructional projects taken over from the Director of Works and kept the Operations Staff and the Quartermaster General currently informed with regard to the state of development attained by the ground organisation.

48.   The Chief of the Ground Organisation handled orders, instructions and directives with regard to:—
  (i)   Employment of Airfield Regional Commands and Airfield Commands.
  (ii) Distribution of airfields.
  (iii) Suitability of airfields and their capacity in terms of aircraft, etc.
  (iv) The carrying out of defence measures on airfields.
  (v)   Preparations for winter and distribution of snow clearing apparatus.
  (vi) Distribution of dummy aircraft.
  (vii) Small engineer services (temporary measures of a constructional nature carried out by units on their own account).

49.   The Chief of the Ground Organisation Department arranged the allocation of hangars, permanent buildings, barrack huts, and temporary billets on airfields. He obtained and distributed as a central agency camouflage material for the entire Air Force including industrial plant on service stations. He was also responsible for collecting, analysing and applying operational experience gained within his sphere.

CHIEF ENGINEER OF THE GERMAN AIR FORCE.

50.   The Chief Engineer was the advisor to the Chief of the General Staff in aeronautical technical matters. He was subordinated to the Quartermaster General and was responsible for:—
  (i)   Directing the employment of the personnel and material for the ground aeronautical-technical services.
  (ii) Recording trials of aircraft equipment carried out in units and co-operating in the analysis of the results.
  (iii) Imparting introductory instruction to the Fliegertruppe with regard to new equipment. In agreement with the Director of Technical Armaments he arranged the employment of industrial technical services attached to the Fliegerkorps.

51.   The details of the responsibilities of the Chief Engineer were as follows:—
  (i)   He advised the Quartermaster General in regard to the employment of all aeronautical technical ground services including Airfield Servicing Companies and he made the necessary adjustments in their employment throughout the Air Force so as to match his policy with the distribution of forces. For this purpose the Operation Staff/Ia (1st Department — Operations) were consulted.
  (ii) He supervised the aeronautical technical ground services including those in flying units, flying training schools, supply units for aircraft equipment and other Fliegertruppe units.
  (iii) He made recommendations with regard to the organisation of aeronautical technical services and co-operated in planning the establishment of new units.
  (iv) He collaborated in the organisation and planning of new units for the aeronautical technical services of flying units, flying training schools, and other Fliegertruppe units in agreement with the

appropriate Specialist Air Officer (Waffengenerale) and the Air Officer for Training.
- (v) He analysed the Fliegertruppe serviceability reports from a technical standpoint.
- (vi) He collaborated in the recording of technical faults and inadequacies in aircraft equipment discovered by units and in dealing with the technical aspect of Defect Reports.
- (vii) He calculated the requirements of material and personnel of the aeronautical technical ground services in the light of the present and future total strength of the Fliegertruppe units, operational conditions, and anticipated concentration of effort in this or that direction. The results of these calculations he forwarded to the 6th Department.
- (viii) He collaborated in examining requests submitted by units for the modification of aircraft equipment.
- (ix) He collaborated in the publication of technical directives and other equipment manuals for the attention of the Fliegertruppe.
- (x) He collaborated in the introduction of new aircraft equipment.
- (xi) He collaborated in dealing with shortages in the supply of aircraft equipment likely to endanger the prosecution of operations.
- (xii) He published general directives governing Fliegertruppe technical services.
- (xiii) He collaborated in the planning of constructional projects for the aeronautical technical ground services.

52. The Chief Engineer was commander for technical purposes of the members of the Engineer Corps and of the officials of the aircraft technical and armament services. He collaborated in agreement with the Specialist Air Officers, Director General of Signals, Director of Motor Transport, etc., in determining the type and number of establishment vacancies, and in drawing up trade regulations and training directives for these trades and for ground aeronautical technical personnel.

53. The Chief Engineer was entitled to obtain information from all establishments in respect of matters touching on his sphere of responsibility and to establish direct contact with all research, development and testing authorities and with the armament industry authorities of the Minister for Armament and War Production by agreement with the Director of Technical Armaments.

CHIEF OF TECHNICAL ARMAMENTS (C.T.L.R.)

54. The Chief of Technical Armaments was directly subordinate to the Chief of the General Staff and his responsibilities included:—
- (i) Research, development, testing, and acceptance for quality (equivalent to R.A.F. A.I.D.) of all Air Force equipment including fuels.
- (ii) Handling and analysing requirements in connection with development of armaments which had been formulated and submitted by the Operations Staff, Specialist Air Officers (Waffengenerale), etc., through the 6th Department.
- (iii) Dealing with the overall requirements of armaments submitted by the 6th Department and the Director of Supply in respect of quantity, type and quality. Representing these departments, when submitting their requirements to the Minister for Armaments and War Production.
- (iv) Declaring newly completed requirements ready for introduction.

(v) Suggestions for long-term measures when introducing new equipment in conjunction with the Operations Staff, Quartermaster General, Air Officer for Training and the Specialist Air Officers.
(vi) Provision of technical manuals, directions for use, spare parts lists, and instructional material for the equipment supplied.
(vii) Collection and analysis of complaints and unfavourable reports for the guidance of units in the use of technical equipment.
(viii) Issue of technical directives to units.

55. The Chief of Technical Armaments kept watch on all tasks being handled for the Air Force in the sphere of responsibility of the Army and Navy with regard to research on, or development and testing of technical equipment. He represented the interests of the Air Ministry in all questions relating to the arming of the Air Force when dealing with the Minister for Armaments and War Production. He collaborated in the drawing up of Establishment and Equipment Lists and in the introduction of new equipment. The Chief of Technical Armaments was also directed to collaborate closely with the other appropriate departments of the Air Ministry and, in particular, with the Specialist Air Officers in all matters relating to his sphere of work.

56. Subordinated to the Chief of Technical Armaments were:—
(i) **Operationally:** All Air Force Testing Stations.
(ii) **For the carrying out of experiments:** The Air Force Technical Academy.

THE CHIEF INTENDANT

57. The Chief Intendant of the G.A.F. was the advisor to the Commander in Chief of the Air Force and Reich Minister for Air (Göring), in all administrative matters and was subordinated to him directly in respect of his own person. For technical and operational purposes he was subordinated to the Chief of the General Staff. His responsibilities included:—
(i) The direction and execution of administrative tasks in all Commands and units (from Luftflotte and Luftgau level downwards) in pursuance of the laws, instructions and regulations for military administration.
(ii) The direction and distribution of supply for all goods which it was incumbent upon the administration to provide, (clothing, rations, furniture, solid fuel, etc.).
(iii) Ascertaining unit requirements and exploiting experience gained by Commands and units in all administrative spheres. Determining the requirements resulting from this information and forwarding them to the Administration Office as a basis for its ministerial work and its activity in the sphere of training and the acquisition of supplies.
(iv) Direction of the acquisition of such administrative goods as were procured independently by units rather than through the Air Ministry.

58. In matters relating to his sphere of responsibility the Chief Intendant had the right to issue directives and instructions to Commands and units subordinated to the Commander in Chief of the Air Force and Reich Minister for Air.

59. Within the framework of the powers exercised in wartime by Inspectors in general, the Chief Intendant exercised powers of inspection

over all administrators such as Luftflotte, Luftgau, Korps and Divisional Intendants with their subordinate administrative establishments in staffs and units of sufficient standing to possess administrative sections. These powers covered canteens and baker and butcher companies and coal stores maintained from the Eastern Coal Quota. The Chief Intendant was also the senior specialist (i.e. commander for purposes of their administration work) of all Special Service officers (administrative branch) and administrative officials of the above-mentioned administrations.

ADMINISTRATION OFFICE

60. The Chief of the Administration was subordinated to the Director for Air Matters (Chef der Luftfahrt), and his duties included:—
  (i) Providing the basis for the administrative work of all Air Force establishments in the form of laws, instructions and regulations, including the negotiations necessary for this purpose with all authorities, whether Air Force or otherwise.
  (ii) Obtaining and disposing for use all supply goods (clothing, rations, furniture, etc.) which had to be provided by the administrative authorities.
  (iii) Carrying out training in all branches of administration.
  (iv) Preparation, care and maintenance of all real estate, including the management of agriculture, forestry, fire precautionary measures and technical administration.

61. The Chief of the Administration Office had the right to issue directives and orders to commands and units subordinated to the Commander in Chief of the Air Force and Minister for Air in matters which related to his sphere of responsibility. The Chief of the Administration Office also had powers of inspection over all independent administrative authorities.

ECONOMICS OFFICE

62. The Chief of the Economics Office was directly subordinated to the Director for Air Matters (Chef der Luftfahrt) and his responsibilities included:—
  (i) Financing and making economic provision for aircraft industry and allied raw material and semi-finished product industries.
  (ii) Working on all general, economic, financial and legal questions, economics of management, price control and statistics. Keeping check on expenditure for technical purposes.
  (iii) Acting as the principal authority for correspondence in export matters.
  (iv) Patent and license questions.
  (v) Economic and financial direction of companies in which shares were held by the Reich, of research and of research institutes. Financial and legal questions arising out of discoveries by members of the Armed Forces Gefelgschaft (i.e. civilian employees and paramilitary personnel).
  (vi) Drawing up programmes for visits by foreign military and civilian personalities to aircraft industry subject to the prior approval of the 6th Department (Intelligence) of the Operations Staff. Negotiations for treaties with foreign governments and firms.

(For further details see Part 2, Chapter III.)

PART 2

CHAPTER II

PROVISIONING AND PRODUCTION

SECTION I. INTRODUCTION
Paragraphs 1—5

SECTION II. PROVISIONING AND PRODUCTION
BEFORE AUGUST, 1944
Paragraphs 6—125

GENERAL	Paragraphs 6—7
THE SUPPLY ORGANISATIONS	,, 8—27
The German Air Ministry	,, 8—12
The Quartermaster General	,, 13—17
The Director of Supply	,, 18
The Director of Motor Transport	,, 19
The Director General of Equipment	,, 20
The Chief Intendant	,, 21
The Aircraft Industry	,, 22—25
The Main Depots of the German Air Force	,, 26
Summary	,, 27
THE PROVISIONING AND PRODUCTION CYCLE	,, 28—29
Presentation	,, 28—29
THE ALLOCATION AND UTILISATION OF RAW MATERIALS	,, 30—37
General	,, 30—36
Summary	,, 37
THE TRANSLATION OF SERVICE REQUIREMENTS INTO TERMS OF SUPPLY	,, 38—80
General	,, 38—39
Operationally Important Equipment	,, 40—51
Operationally Important Supplies	,, 52—54
General Technical Equipment	,, 55—65
Motor Transport	,, 66—72
Signals and Radar Equipment	. 73
Intendant Materials	,, 74—79
Summary	,, 80
THE MANUFACTURE AND ACQUISITION OF EQUIPMENT AND SUPPLIES	,, 81—104
General	,, 81—86
Orders on Industry	,, 87—91
Inspection and Specification	,, 92—95
Contracts	,, 96—101
Finance	,, 102—103
Summary	,, 104

THE RECEIPT, STORAGE AND ALLOCATION OF EQUIPMENT AND SUPPLIES	,,	105—125
General	,,	105—108
Acceptance on Manufacture	,,	109
Delivery into Air Force Storage	,,	110—112
General Allocation of Operationally Important Supplies	,,	113—116
Allocation of Operationally Important Supplies	,,	117
Allocation of Operationally Important Equipment	,,	118
The Issue of Supply Directives	,,	119
Motor Transport and Intendant Materials	,,	120—124
Summary	,,	125

SECTION III. TRANSITION PERIOD
1942—1944
Paragraphs 126—133

GENERAL	Paragraphs	126—127
RECONSTITUTION OF THE AIRCRAFT INDUSTRY	,,	128
THE "FIGHTER STAFF"	,,	129—133

SECTION IV. PROVISIONING AND PRODUCTION
AFTER AUGUST, 1944
Paragraphs 134—191

GENERAL	Paragraphs	134—136
PRESENTATION	,,	137
ORGANISATION OF THE SPEER MINISTRY	,,	138—144
PROGRESSION OF DEMANDS BY THE SPEER MINISTRY	,,	145—184
General	,,	145
Aircraft	,,	146—152
Components	,,	153—154
Spares	,,	155—160
Embodiment and Standardization	,,	161—162
Ground Technical Equipment	,,	163—164
Motor Transport	,,	165—168
Non-Technical Equipment	,,	169—174
Flak Equipment	,,	175—177
Petrol, Oils and Lubricants	,,	178—180
Rations	,,	181—182
Medical Supplies	,,	183—184
MANUFACTURE AND DELIVERY	,,	185—191

SECTION V. CONCLUSION
Paragraphs 192—196

PART 2

CHAPTER II

PROVISIONING AND PRODUCTION

SECTION I. INTRODUCTION

1.   This chapter deals specifically with the methods employed by the German Air Force in provisioning equipment and supplies, and with the general administrative processes by which air armaments were produced.

2.   It is necessary, in describing these methods of provisioning, and in presenting an estimate of their success or failure, to distinguish between two periods, the first of which covers the major part of the war until 1944, and the second the later years from 1944 to the end. This distinction is rendered necessary not by a mere change in the routine method of provisioning, but by reason of complete and fundamental reversal of policy in controlling and regulating the production of equipment for the Air Force.

3.   The first phase, until 1944, is marked by complete independence of the German Air Force in controlling production of its equipment. From the first statement of requirements and the compilation of production programmes, to the last stage of manufacture and distribution, direction was vested entirely in the hands of officers of the Air Force, with a complete subordination of the aircraft industry to their requirements. Co-ordination of the requirements of the Air Force with the needs of the other two Services was not intended, nor were the activities of the Air Force in the industrial field related to German war economy as a whole.

4.   The second period beginning in 1944, is distinguished by the Air Force losing control of production of air armaments, and thereafter being limited to expressing its needs in the shape of programmes. In this late stage of the war, the policy pursued in the early years was completely reversed. Control of production was entirely divorced from the Service chiefs and given to the industrial leaders. At the same time, a great effort was made to relate the aircraft industry to the general war economy and to achieve some degree of unified effort in armament production.

5.   Each of these two periods will be dealt with separately. In addition comment will be made on the period of transition between 1942—44, during which time the ground work was prepared for the separation of provisioning proper and of control of industry.

SECTION II. PROVISIONING AND PRODUCTION BEFORE AUGUST 1944

GENERAL

6.   It is intended to describe the system of provisioning and production in force before 1944 under two main headings. First, as an essential preliminary in dealing with the routine methods of provisioning it is necessary to describe briefly the sections of the German Ar Ministry and the units of the Air Force concerned in supply matters, and to show the nature and position of the aircraft industry in this period.

7. Secondly, with a clear understanding of the nature and functions of those organisations concerned in the supply of equipment for the German Air Force, it will be possible to describe the routine administrative methods involved in the provisioning and production cycle, from the first statement of requirements by the Operations Staff to the final stage of manufacture and delivery.

THE SUPPLY ORGANISATIONS

The German Air Ministry

8. The German Air Ministry was of a dual nature, consisting of the High Command of the German Air Force and the State Minister for Air.

9. The High Command was concerned primarily with the military direction of the Air Force but included in its organisation, under the Chief of General Staff, were those departments comparable in their function to the British Air Member for Supply and Organisation and the British Directorate General of Equipment.

10. The State Minister for Air was concerned mainly with ministerial problems and with administration but also dealt with aircraft production in a manner comparable to that of the British Minister for Aircraft Production.

11. These three departments of the German Air Ministry, approximating to their British equivalents were:—

German:	**British:**
The Quartermaster General.	The Air Member for Supply and Organisation.
The Director of Supply.	The Directorate-General of Equipment.
The Director General of Equipment.	The Minister for Aircraft Production.

12. Each of these three important sections, together with other specialised organisations, notably that of the Chief Intendant, are described more fully in the following paragraphs.

The Quartermaster General

13. The Quartermaster General was subordinate to the Chief of the General Staff. In connection with supply matters, he was responsible for directing the following departments:—

    (i) **Departments of the Chief of Staff.**

        Department 2. : : Organisation.
        Department 4. : : Preparation of Supply Directives. Allocation of Operationally Important Supplies. Transport.
        Department 6. : : Provisioning of Operationally Important Equipment and Supplies and of all initial equipment. Allocation of all Operationally Important Equipment.
        Department 9. : : Personnel.

    (ii) **Other Departments.**

        Of the other departments under the Quartermaster General, two only, concerned with supply, need be considered: —
            The Director of Supply.
            The Director of Motor Transport.

14. The responsibilities of the Director of Supply and of the Director of Motor Transport are dealt with separately below, and it is intended here to describe only the general responsibilities of the Quartermaster General, and the particular part played by Departments 4 and 6.

15. The Quartermaster General, acting in a manner comparable to the British Air Member for Supply and Organisation, was responsible for the direction and supervision of the entire supply system of the German Air Force in accordance with the instructions of the Chief of General Staff.

16. In the light of commitments advised to him by the Chief of General Staff, the Quartermaster General was required to formulate long-term plans for the production and supply of equipment and for its allocation to the units of the German Air Force. Of his Departments, the 4th and 6th are the most important in relation to the system of provisioning. These two Departments existed independently of each other, the first being responsible for:—

(i) The preparation of supply directives. These directives addressed to the Luftflotte of the German Air Force dealt with the manner in which their supplies and equipment would reach them.

(ii) The allocation of "operationally important" supplies, viz. aviation fuel, and explosives.

17. The 6th Department was responsible for:—

(i) Provisioning "operationally important" equipment and supplies, including aircraft, airframes, aero engines, power units, airborne equipment, aircraft, armaments and ground technical equipment.

(ii) The allocation, as distinct from provisioning, of "operationally important" equipment.

The Director of Supply

18. The Director of Supply, subordinate to the Quartermaster General, was responsible for supplying (receiving, storing, and delivering) to the Air Force war materials of all kinds, other than motor transport, and those materials dealt with by the Chief Intendant (clothing, furniture, solid fuels and rations). The Main Depots, into which flowed all manufactured equipment for the Air Force, were controlled by the Director of Supply. His responsibility began at the point where equipment was received by officials of the Air Force at the factory (Aeronautical Inspection Service) and ended when the materials were delivered from the Main Depots to units or supply establishments subordinate to command authorities.

The Director of Motor Transport

19. Directly subordinated to the Quartermaster General, the Director of Motor Transport was responsible for all matters connected with the procurement, storage, distribution and maintenance of mechanical transport.

The Director General of Equipment

20. This Department was responsible, by control of the aircraft industry, for the development and production of all German Air Force equipment.

The Chief Intendant

21. Acquisition and issue for use of all supply goods, (clothing, furniture, solid fuels and rations) were the responsibilities of the Administration Office in the Air Ministry but direction on policy in these matters and in

maintaining contact with the other Services regarding the supply of common items devolved upon the Chief Intendant.

The Aircraft Industry

22. The aircraft industry, until drawn within the organisation of the Speer Ministry in 1944, was controlled and directed entirely by the German Air Ministry. This was not an abnormality in the scheme of German war economy for, until 1942, the whole range of armament producing plants was without any central control, and each industrialist was able to act independently in working for one or more of the Armed Forces.

23. Of the three Services, the German Air Force was the most active, and by far the most independent, in developing and managing its manufacturing plants. This was due, in a large measure, to the peculiar status of the Air Force, long regarded by the Nazi party as its own political weapon, and to the fact that Göring was its head.

24. Control of the aircraft industry was not limited to a mere administrative link. The Air Force had unrestricted financial resources and through the agency of its own Aviation Bank was enabled, by long-term loans, capital participation or actual ownership, to acquire controlling interests in a great many of the major plants.

25. The Directorate of Defence Economy and Armaments, intended to exercise some degree of co-ordinating influence over German war industry, did little to influence the working of the aircraft industry, and the Director General of Equipment, already referred to, was in a position, virtually, of dictating to industry the requirements of the German Air Force.

The Main Depots of the German Air Force

26. As the result of a reorganisation during 1943, Main Depots became important agents in the provisioning scheme as from that time they were empowered to demand direct on industry for the range of equipment previously dealt with by the Director of Supply.

Summary of the Supply Organisations

27. It is desirable, before describing the provisioning cycle, to summarise the organisations concerned. These were:
- (i) The Quartermaster General.
- (ii) The Director of Supply.
- (iii) The Director of Motor Transport.
- (iv) The Director General of Equipment.
- (v) The Chief Intendant.
- (vi) The Aircraft Industry.
- (vii) The Main Depots of the Air Force.

THE PROVISIONING AND PRODUCTION CYCLE

Presentation

28. It is intended to show consecutively the steps in the provisioning and production cycle, and the next part of the Chapter is divided therefore into a number of phases:—
- (i) The allocation to the Air Force of raw materials and production capacities, expressed in the form of priorities by Hitler and the Supreme Command, and the administrative organisation involved in the utilisation of these materials.

(ii) The translation of Service requirements into terms of equipment and supplies, with distinction between the different classes of equipment, and between equipment and supplies.

(iii) The issue of orders to the aircraft industry, and the administrative processes involved in controlling production, in exercising financial and contractual control and in accepting delivery of manufactured equipment.

(iv) The receipt and storage of manufactured equipment and its allocation to the Service.

29. Distinction will be made necessarily between equipment and supplies, and between classes of equipment. Broadly they may be distinguished in the following categories:—

(i) Operationally important equipment, including the following major items: aircraft, airframes, engines, power plants, airborne equipment, aircraft armaments, ground technical equipment, and Flak Weapons.

(ii) Operationally important supplies, consisting of aviation fuel and explosives.

(iii) Equipment other than that described as operationally important, including spares.

(iv) Supplies generally, including clothing, furniture, solid fuels and rations.

THE ALLOCATION AND UTILISATION OF RAW MATERIALS

General

30. Originally, and until 1942, responsibility for the allocation of raw materials to the Services was that of the Defence Economy and Armaments Department of the Supreme Command but, after the dissolution of this Department in 1942, the work was carried out by a Special Committee under the presidency of Hitler.

31. Advice on the availability of raw materials for use by the Air Force was received by the Director General of Equipment. The Departments concerned in the discussion of the use of available materials, and in planning their programmes of production accordingly, were:—

(i) The 6th Department of the Quartermaster General, responsible for all operationally important equipment and supplies.

(ii) The Director of Supply, responsible for classes of equipment other than "operationally important".

(iii) The Director of Signals.

(iv) The Director of Motor Transport, responsible for mechanical transport and fuels.

(v) The Chief Intendant and the Administration Office, responsible for domestic supplies, (clothing, furniture, solid fuel and rations).

32. Normally, the supply of raw materials governed provisioning, in that the framing of programmes of future production necessarily depended on the quantities of raw materials available in any given period. The Director General of Equipment, informed on one side of the raw materials available, and on the other side of the aggregate demands for equipment, was responsible for the preparation of data on which production programmes might be based.

33. To the Director of Supply, and to the Chief Intendant, the quota of raw materials allocated was usually conclusive in determining their

future action in provisioning. The Director of Supply, concerned only in maintaining stocks of equipment other than operationally important, would not usually seek to question the quantities of materials allocated and, in the same manner, the Chief Intendant, responsible only for domestic supplies, would frame his directions to the Administration Office on the basis of available raw materials.

34. The action pursued by the 6th Department of the Quartermaster General did not, however, always follow a rigid routine. This Department was responsible for the preparation of programmes for all major items (including aircraft), and essential supplies (aviation fuels and explosives). Generally, of course, these programmes were compelled to follow the available raw materials, but occasions arose which demanded review of allocations as between the services. This was particularly so where choice of aircraft types had to be taken into account in determining future production programmes. Similarly, where strategic requirements necessitated heavy or varied commitments, discussion on the allocation of raw materials would take place before preparation of production data.

35. Deliveries and stocks of raw materials, having once been allocated to the Air Force, were controlled by the Director General of Equipment. This responsibility was a logical one since the direction of the whole of the aircraft industry at this time was in his hands. Allocations to the factories were controlled by the Director General of Equipment, in relation to existing and anticipated programmes; at the factories he supervised stocks and use of the materials mainly through the agency of the Aeronautical Inspection Service, which organisation worked under his jurisdiction.

36. It will be seen, in the second part of this Chapter, that after control of the aircraft industry had been assumed by Reichsminister Speer in 1944, the allocation to the services of raw materials was very largely in his hands. As between the two periods (prior to and after 1944) there was little difference, from the point of view of the Air Force, in the manner in which the requirements for manufactured items was reconciled with available raw materials except that in the first phase the Director General of Equipment was responsible and in the second period responsibility was with the Chief of Technical Air Armaments.

Summary of Allocation and Utilisation of Raw Materials

37. Before proceeding to discuss the next phase in the provisioning system, it is useful to list the authorities concerned in the allocation and use of raw materials:—

  (i)   The authority for determining quotas and priorities of raw materials — the Department of Defence Economy and Armaments until 1942, and after that a Committee under the direction of Hitler.

  (ii) The department of the Air Ministry responsible for receiving advice of raw material quotas, for circulating this information to the other departments of the Air Ministry and for reconciling requirements with available materials — The Director General of Equipment.

  (iii) The department of the Air Ministry responsible for furnishing to the Director General of Equipment details of requirements of operationally important equipment and supplies, in the light of raw materials available — the 6th Department of the Quartermaster General.

(iv) The department of the Air Ministry responsible for determining requirements of all equipment other than operationally important items based on available raw materials, and for advising the Director General of Equipment of such needs — the Director of Supply.

(v) The department of the Air Ministry responsible for assessing production of domestic supplies, on the basis of available raw materials — the Chief Intendant.

(vi) The department of the Air Ministry responsible for the receipt and storage of raw materials, within the Air Force or factories, and for regulating the use of these materials — the Director General of Equipment.

THE TRANSLATION OF SERVICE REQUIREMENTS INTO TERMS OF SUPPLY

General

38. To describe adequately the methods employed by the German Air Ministry in translating the needs of the Air Force into terms of material it is essential to differentiate between equipment and supplies, and to distinguish equipment in the categories dealt with by various departments. Each of the following classes of material will, therefore, be considered separately:—

(i) Operationally important equipment.
(ii) Operationally important supplies.
(iii) Equipment other than that described as operationally important.
(iv) Supplies generally, including those of a domestic nature.

39. At the same time, special mention will be made of signals and radar equipment and of motor transport. The first of these is important owing to the special action pursued by the Director of Signals in computing his requirements and his powers in allocating such equipment for use. Motor transport, since it was provisioned separately and independently by the Director of Motor Transport, is also of special importance.

Operationally Important Equipment

40. This class of equipment, although not necessarily the largest in aggregate compared with equipment not classified as being operationally important, was by far the most vital. It included all major items: aircraft, airframes, engines and power plants, air armaments, airborne equipment generally (instruments, etc.), and ground technical equipment. Since this term "Operationally Important Equipment" is referred to continually throughout the following paragraphs, it is necessary to provide a definition of the term:— "Equipment of which the production was limited by the amount of raw material available, by plant capacity, or by any other reason." It will be appreciated that, by virtue of the shortage of raw materials in Germany, or at least in the competition for their alternative uses, most major items fell within the terms of this definition.

41. The list of equipment included under the heading "operationally important" was not rigid and items, although not of a major nature, were capable of being drawn into this class by reason of short supply.

42. Responsibility for both the provisioning and allocation of this range of equipment rested with the 6th Department of the Quartermaster General. The task of planning future production of equipment consisted, as in the case of all provisioning, British and German, of reconciling the material needs arising from policy and strategy with available raw materials and factory capacities.

43. The Chief of the Operations Staff was responsible, to his Chief of General Staff, for the preparation and issue of air plans. Guiding principles of the policy to be followed in implementing the plans were, except in the case of short-term operational matters, issued by the Chief of the Operations Staff to all the departments of the Chief of General Staff, including the 6th Department of the Quartermaster General. Thus, in all normal long-term matters the 6th Department was advised of future commitments, and was required to translate the needs into terms of equipment.

44. Imformation indicating the allocation, in quotas, of raw materials to the Air Force, was received by the 6th Department of the Quartermaster General from the Director General of Equipment. In addition, the Director General of Equipment, by virtue of his position in controlling and directing the aircraft industry, was able to provide data on factory capacity and labour forces.

45. Combining these two essential factors, of strategic commitments on the one hand and available resources on the other, the 6th Department was responsible for deciding what types and quantities of operationally important equipment should be produced, and for formulating provisional programmes of production.

46. In addition to these two major factors, the 6th Department was required, as a matter of course, to consider:—
   (i) Current stocks of manufactured items, and previous consumption rates.
   (ii) Statistics and estimates relating to losses — actual and anticipated.

47. Details of current stocks and past consumption were furnished to the 6th Department in the form of monthly returns by each of the Luftgau Quartermasters who were assisted in this work by the staffs of the Equipment Groups.

48. All Air Force operational statistics were dealt with by Section V of the 6th Department. Losses of aircraft and other main components were reported to this Section and from these reports average wastage factors were calculated under various conditions of operations. From this Section, therefore, it was possible to derive information necessary in the preparation of production programmes.

49. Programmes, on completion by the 6th Department, were passed to the Director General of Equipment who, in control of the aircraft industry, was responsible for the issue of orders for production. All programmes compiled by the 6th Department followed this routine procedure but it is necessary to remark specially on two points concerned with programmes for major items:—
   (i) In the case of programmes which included major items affecting the major strategy of the German Air Force (e.g. aircraft), the 6th Department before passing the programmes into production was required to refer them to higher authority for discussion. The procedure was that the 6th Department first established the possibilities of production and then passed the programmes to the Chief of Operations through its own Quartermaster General. The Operations Staff, in reviewing such proposed programmes, was in a position whereby it might bring to bear factors outside the knowledge and responsibility of the 6th Department. The overriding factor influencing these discussions however was still that

of the availability of raw materials and, excepting in cases where strategic requirements made an additional allocation of raw materials an unavoidable necessity, such variations as were introduced into the programmes concerned either the type or design of equipment rather than the quantity.

(ii) Changing strategy did at times however call for greater allocations of raw materials than were budgeted for in existing quotas and in such circumstances it was necessary for the 6th Department to consult the Department of Defence Economy and Armaments whose task was then to determine how to provide the extra quantities. Sometimes re-adjustments to the quotas of the other services had to be made, and sometimes the amounts were found by reducing civilian quotas.

50. Normally, issues of equipment to consumer units were controlled by the Equipment Groups but, in the case of operationally important items, demands were dealt with and release authorised by the Luftgau Quartermaster.

51. Details of the operation of the Luftgau Quartermasters, of the Equipment Groups, and of their place in the scheme of supply in the field are contained in Part 1, Chapter V, "Organisation of Supply in the Field".

Operationally Important Supplies

52. The German Air Ministry, in its scheme of provisioning, included aviation fuel and explosives as being of "operational importance" and dealt with the production and distribution of these supplies specially through the departments of the Quartermaster General.

53. The 6th Department was responsible for the preparation of all production programmes of aviation fuel and explosives. The allocation of raw materials within the Air Force for the production of these two classes of supplies was advised by the Director General of Equipment to Section 1 of the 6th Department, and programmes were then compiled in the following manner:—

(i) Aviation Fuel. Data on aircraft strength, on operational policy, on training and transport, was received by Section 1 of the 6th Department from other Sections of that Department and from other Departments of the Quartermaster General. Using these forecasts, and bearing in mind the limitations imposed by the supply of raw materials and the necessity of using synthetic products, Section 1 prepared programmes of production. These programmes were passed to the Director General of Equipment for translation into orders on industry.

(ii) Explosives. Section IV of the 6th Department was responsible for the preparation of programmes providing for the production of bombs and explosives generally, of ammunition (including Flak), and of chemical weapons. The quantities of raw materials available for this purpose were advised by Section 1. Current stocks and figures of past consumption were advised by the Luftgau Quartermasters, and information on future policy and strategic commitments was furnished by the Chief of Operations Staff. Completed programmes were passed to the Director General of Equipment for manufacture by industry or, in the case of certain items common in use to the Air Force and the Army, for transmission to the Army provisioning authorities.

54. The 4th Department of the Quartermaster General was responsible for the allocation within the Air Force of both aviation fuel and explosives; this matter is dealt with in later paragraphs under the heading "Receipt, Storage and Allocation".

General Technical Equipment

55. The class of equipment designated "operationally important", and dealt with by the 6th Department of the Quartermaster General, has already been referred to. Outside this special range of major and short-supply items lies the general category of technical equipment, including aircraft spares and other spares.

56. The provision of this general category of technical equipment was the special responsibility of the Director of Supply. The responsibilities of his Department, working under the direction of the Quartermaster General, were wide, for in this general range of equipment were included all war materials for the Air Force other than motor transport, "Intendant" materials and the operationally important equipment and supplies already referred to. In addition to his responsibilities in provisioning, the Director of Supply was charged with receiving, storing and delivering all these materials, other than motor transport and "Intendant" materials. His responsibilities in accepting equipment from the manufacturers, and in directing and controlling the Main Storage Depots will be referred to in greater detail later in this Chapter.

57. In discharging his responsibility for provisioning this general range of equipment the Director of Supply was required to take into account the following factors:—
- (i) General directives issued by the Quartermaster General on future policy and its effect on supply. In this connection the Director of Supply was concerned particularly in:—
  - (a) The formation of new units, the reconstituting or regrouping of existing units and the disbandment of units.
  - (b) The increased, or varied, load on consumption necessitated by operational measures.
  - (c) The issue of new scales of initial and replacement equipment.
- (ii) The available quantities of raw materials and manufacturing capacities. Information on these two matters was communicated by the Director General of Equipment, who was responsible for the direction of industry and for all negotiations with higher authority on the subject of raw material quotas.
- (iii) The current stocks of equipment manufactured and accepted from industry, and held in the Main Depots awaiting issue to equipment installations of the Air Force. These Main Depots were subordinated directly to the Director of Supply and information on stock positions was, therefore, readily available.
- (iv) Past consumption of equipment in the Air Force, and the current stocks held in the hands of the equipment installations of the Air Force. All issues of equipment of the class dealt with by the Director of Supply were regulated by Equipment Groups, and it was from these organisations that provisioning data in the form of past consumption and current stocks was received by the Director of Supply. These Equipment Groups were dissolved in 1943, and their responsibilities in recording issues and stock data assumed by the Main Depots. This major change in policy, which

had a considerable effect on the provisioning cycle, is referred to in greater detail below.

58. Programmes of production, and routine requisitions for the replenishment of stocks were passed by the Director of Supply to the Director General of Equipment, for issue to industry in the form of orders. This routine method of translating the requirements of the Air Force into demands on industry lasted until 1943, but mention must now be made of the change in organisation which occurred at that time.

59. The Equipment Groups, previously responsible for controlling all issues of equipment other than those classed as operationally important, and for supplying to the Director of Supply data on which he was able to base his provisioning, were disbanded in 1943. The major responsibilities previously borne by the Equipment Groups in regulating issues were transferred to the Luftgau Quartermasters but the task of maintaining provisioning records became that of the Main Depots.

60. This re-organisation, although a controversial one from the point of view of the German Air Force, appears not unreasonable for, by its means, the Luftgau Quartermasters became responsible for regulating the issue of all technical equipment, both that designated operationally important and that regarded as of a normal nature. At the same time the Main Depots were enabled to relate the whole of stock figures and consumption data required for provisioning: stocks of manufactured equipment awaiting issue to equipment installations were held by them, and data on the past consumption and current stocks in the hands of the Air Parks and Issuing Stations were furnished by these units as returns through the Luftgau Quartermasters.

61. The Main Depots were all of a specialised nature, each dealing in certain ranges of equipment and each related to a particular part of the aircraft industry. It was considered expedient, therefore, with the dissolution of the Equipment Groups, to arrange for all provisioning action to be undertaken by the Main Depots, by direct contact with industry.

62. From 1943, each Main Depot, under the control of the Director of Supply, became a provisioning authority. In respect of the special ranges of equipment held at the Depot, it maintained provisioning records, forecasted requirements and gave industry its orders. The Director of Supply, responsible for the working of the Main Depots, furnished information on matters of policy and on the allocation of raw materials.

63. Special mention must be made, however, of aircraft and engine spares behind the major programmes for aircraft and engines. Until 1942, the Director of Supply in the Air Ministry was responsible for advising industry of the range and quantity of spares required for each type and mark of aircraft and engine but in that year it was decided, on a high level, that the Air Ministry had failed in this particular sphere of provisioning.

64. It was decided, therefore, that provisioning of spares behind airframe and engine programmes should be undertaken by the Special Committees set up at this time. (see Part 1, Chapter II and also the fourth section of this Chapter.)

65. This major revision in the general provisioning system was facilitated by the formation in 1942 of the Main Committees for Aircraft Production, when, under the direction of Milch (and indirectly of Speer),

the aircraft industry was partly remodelled to conform to Speer's general plan of industrial autonomy.

Motor Transport

66.   Motor transport in the German Armed Forces was regarded as a common user item and its procurement from industry was dealt with by the Army during the first part of the war and later by a specially constituted authority — the Director of Armed Forces Motor Transport.

67.   On behalf of the Air Force, the Director of Motor Transport in the Air Ministry (subordinate to the Quartermaster General) was responsible for representing to the Director of Armed Forces Motor Transport, requirements of vehicles and associated equipment.

68.   In framing his estimates of requirements preparatory to representing the needs of the Air Force, the Director of Motor Transport in the Air Ministry considered the following factors:—
  (i)   Current establishments and strength.
  (ii)   Data on losses, and on ratios of unserviceability.
  (iii) Estimates of future wastage from normal running.
  (iv)   Estimates of future losses arising from operations.
  (v)   Needs of newly formed or projected units.

69.   In considering these factors, and in assessing aggregate requirements, the Director of Motor Transport worked in conjunction with the Chief of Operations Staff, in discussing future strategic commitments, and with the 4th and 6th Departments of the Quartermaster General. In addition, liaison was maintained with the Headquarters of each Luftflotte.

70.   On completion of his estimates, the Director of Motor Transport presented to the Army authorities (or the Director of Armed Forces Motor Transport) the aggregate needs of the German Air Force, to be obtained from current manufactured stocks or from future production.

71.   Motor Transport spare parts, required for use by the repair organisations of the Air Force, were not obtained by any independent provisioning action but by issue from Army Central Repair Depots.

72.   When the Air Force required special purpose vehicles such as flak wagons and signals trucks, the Director of Motor Transport would order only the chassis from the Army authorities or the Director of Armed Forces Motor Transport. In conjunction with the appropriate Air Ministry specialist branch he would then contact the Director General of Equipment who would arrange the development of suitable designs and pass the chassis to industry with instructions to embody coachwork to Air Ministry specifications.

Signals and Radar Equipment

73.   The provision of signals and radar equipment was undertaken, as with all other technical equipment (less Motor Transport) by the Director of Supply and the 6th Department, according to its classification. It is necessary here to note that although the Director of Signals was not strictly concerned with the provisioning of signals and radar equipment he had a very great deal to do with this type of equipment in that he entirely controlled its movement and disposition. This fact is not important at this point but will be referred to again when discussing the receipt, storage and allocation of manufactured equipment.

Intendant Materials

74. Responsibility for the supply to the Air Force of clothing, barrack equipment, rations and solid fuels, referred to generally as "Intendant Materials", rested with the Chief Intendant of the Air Force and the Administration Office of the Air Ministry.

75. The Chief Intendant was subordinated for technical and operational purposes to the Chief of General Staff. His responsibilities included the issue of directions to the Administration Office on the acquisition and distribution of all these materials. A full explanation of the status and responsibilities of the Chief Intendant is given in Part 2, Chapter I.

76. In maintaining adequate stocks and in acquiring supplies of "Intendant materials", the Chief Intendant was guided by the Quartermaster General. The Chief Intendant, warned by the Quartermaster General of supply commitments generally, including the formation, disbandment or regrouping of units, and on future long-term operational plans, was able to combine this data with the information obtained from the lower levels of his own organisation in formulating his programmes.

77. The programmes completed by the Chief Intendant were transmitted to the Administration Office of the Air Ministry where arrangements were made for the acquisition of the necessary supplies. Of the "Intendant materials", the greater part were of a common-user nature. The materials required for making clothing were of common use to all three Services, a considerable proportion of barrack equipment was in general use, and few items of foodstuff (other than flying rations) were peculiar to the Air Force.

78. The nature of these materials made it necessary, therefore, for the Administration Office to work in conjunction with the Headquarters of the Supreme Command of the Armed Forces where supply was co-ordinated by departments of that body and with the Army where, as in the case of rations, this branch of the Armed Forces was responsible for general supply.

79. The acquisition of Intendant materials is dealt with in paras. 120 to 124.

Summary of the Translation of Service Requirements into Terms of Supply

80. To facilitate reference to this phase, and to assist in the understanding of the following sections of the Chapter, it is considered desirable to provide a summary of the provisioning authorities and procedure already discussed.

   (i) Operationally important equipment. Provisioned by the 6th Department of the Quartermaster General. Programmes passed from the 6th Department to the Director General of Equipment for orders on industry. The most important class of technical equipment in the German Air Force.

   (ii) Opertionally important supplies. Provisioned by the 6th Department of the Quartermaster General. Programmes passed from the 6th Department to the Director General of Equipment for orders on industry, or, in the case of common user items of explosives, for transmission of requirements to Army.

   (iii) Technical equipment other than that classed as operationally important. Provisioned, until 1943, by the Director of Supply and after that date by the Main Depots. Programmes and requisitions passed by the Director of Supply to the Director General of Equipment for orders on industry until, after 1943, the Main Depots dealt direct with industry without an intermediary.

(iv) Motor Transport. Provisioned by the Director of Motor Transport. Requirements for motor transport submitted by the Director of Motor Transport to the Army provisioning authorities or, after 1944, to the Director of Armed Forces Motor Transport.

(v) Signals and radar equipment. Provisioned by the 6th Department of the Quartermaster General and by the Director of Supply (or the Main Depots). Of special importance owing to the powers vested in the Director of Signal of directing its allocation in the Air Force and its movement.

(vi) Intendant Materials. Provisioned by the Administration Office of the Air Ministry at the direction of the Chief Intendant of the Air Force. Acquisition of the materials arranged according to their nature from industry, from organisations of the Supreme Command, or from the Army provisioning authorities.

MANUFACTURE AND ACQUISITION OF EQUIPMENT AND SUPPLIES

General

81. This part of the Chapter deals with the issue to the aircraft industry of orders for manufacture, the administrative processes involved in controlling production, and the means employed in exercising financial and contractual control. The following paragraphs refer generally to technical equipment for the Air Force; special reference has already been made to the supplies provided by the Chief Intendant and the Director of Motor Transport.

82. The organisations and authorities concerned in the acquisition of equipment and supplies for the Air Force were:—
   (i) The Aircraft Industry.
   (ii) The Director General of Equipment.
   (iii) The Main Depots of the Air Force.
   (iv) The Administration Office of the Air Ministry.
   (v) The Economics and Finance Office of the Air Ministry.

83. Before describing the routine methods involved in placing orders on industry, it is necessary to remark briefly on the nature and position of the aircraft industry during the years of the war until 1944.

84. Until 1944, the aircraft industry was controlled and directed entirely by Air Force Offices. Production plants were enlarged or built within the policy formulated by the Air Force and plants were, in many cases, owned and controlled in the financial sense through the agency of the Aviation Bank.

85. The isolation and independence of the Air Force, in directing its own industry, was intentional and, until the later events of the war forced a change of policy, industry was left to operate under the control of the Air Force. It should be stated, however, that although this control was not diminished in any great sense, the reconstitution of the aircraft industry in 1942 under the direction of Milch assisted in the later separaton of provisioning proper from production control.

86. The separate matters which require to be discussed in relation to the manufacture and acquisition of equipment and supplies are:—

(i) The placing of orders on industry.
(ii) Specifications and their issue.
(iii) Contracts.
(iv) Finance.

Orders on Industry

87. Until 1943, all orders for the production of equipment and supplies, other than Motor Transport and Intendant materials, were issued by the Director General of Equipment. With the two exceptions named, this Department, subordinate to the State Minister for Air, was responsible for the development, testing and production of all Air Force equipment and supplies.

88. The Director General of Equipment received programmes and requisitions in respect of three main classes of equipment and supplies:—

(i) Operationally important equipment. Programmes in respect of all equipment in this range, consisting of major items and items in short supply, were received from the 6th Department of the Quartermaster General.

(ii) Operationally important supplies. Programmes in respect of these supplies, comprising all aviation fuels and explosives, were also received from the 6th Department.

(iii) Equipment other than operationally important. Programmes and requisitions for this range of equipment, comprising the bulk of the technical items including spares, were received from the Director of Supply.

89. The general responsibility for placing orders, as described in para. 88, was modified after 1943. From this date, and until the reorganisation brought about by the transfer to Speer of control of the aircraft industry, the Director General of Equipment was concerned only with orders for operationally important equipment and supplies. All other orders, for the bulk of the technical equipment required by the Air Force, were issued direct to industry by the Main Depots.

90. It is necessary to emphasise the fact that the Director General of Equipment, during this period, was more than an agency responsible for the procurement of equipment. He was, in fact, the controller of the aircraft industry. All aircraft plants were directed by him, and he was responsible for their design and working, for the allocation of the necessary machine tools, for the recruitment and use of the labour forces, and for the allocation and utilisation of raw materials. The issue of formal contracts by the Economics and Finance Office, and the financial matters dealt with by the same Office, were both subject to the general supervision of the Director General of Equipment. In addition, he was responsible, through an inspectorate organisation, for the quality control of production.

91. Control of industry by the Director General of Equipment did not end until 1944, when direction of production was assumed by Speer. Some mention must be made at this point, however, on the formation in 1942 of the Main and Special Committees in the aircraft industry. Speer, who came into power at this time, was anxious above all to place responsibility for production in the hands of the industrial leaders. Although unable to secure control of Air Force production for two years he was successful in re-organising industry in the Main and Special Committees, chiefly by his personal relationship with Milch, the Director General of Equipment. It is true, therefore, that during the years 1942—1944 the leaders of the

aircraft producing plants played a large part in the management and direction of industry, even though nominal control remained in the hands of the Director General of Equipment.

Inspection and Specification

92. This matter is one which, being in the main of a technical nature, is more fully and more adequately dealt with in the reports of the Directorate of Aeronautical Inspection and the Royal Aircraft Establishment representatives, and the principal object of the following paragraphs is to provide only such an outline as will show generally the German system of inspection of materials and manufacture as a link in the process of production for the Air Force.

93. Responsibility for inspection was separately controlled by each of the three Services in their respective spheres of production and, although an effort was made to provide a system of general inspection for items manufactured for more than one Service, independent inspectorates were maintained until a very late stage in the war.

94. In the Air Force the central authority governing the inspection of air armament manufacture was the Aeronautical Inspection Service (Bauaufsicht der Luftwaffe), known generally by the initials B.A.L., subordinate as a branch to the Director General of Equipment. The headquarters of the B.A.L. was quite small, being concerned mainly with matters of administration and training and appointing staff for resident posts in the organisation.

95. The main function of the B.A.L. was the verification of quality and performance during manufacture and repair but it was also responsible for studying and eliminating production difficulties. The organisation of the inspectorate provided senior officers, each of whom was responsible in an area for the inspection of a specific class of equipment, and subordinate to them were inspectors resident at factories, similarly responsible for a specific range of equipment.

The responsibilities of the inspectorate included:—
(i) Checking and supervision of specifications laid down in orders.
(ii) Acceptance and inspection, on behalf of the Air Force, of finished goods prior to issue into storage units or to assembly units.
(iii) Direction of delivery to order of the Director of Supply of finished products, and responsibility for advising Air Ministry and recipients of despatch.
(iv) Supervision of use of Air Force raw materials to ensure that they were used economically and that none was directed to improper use.
(v) Assistance in solving production problems.
(vi) Ensuring the fulfilment of monthly production quotas against programmes.

Contracts

96. The Director General of Equipment in the Ministry was responsible for the issue of orders to industry against programmes. Production programmes specified the contractors involved, with the details of quantities and delivery dates, and in the majority of cases the Director General of Equipment informed the firms directly of the commitments involved, thereby providing information which was accepted as being in the nature of a preliminary contract.

97.   Details of these preliminary commitments were then forwarded by the Director General of Equipment to the Economics and Finance Office of the Air Ministry in order that that Office might prepare and issue formal contracts in accordance with a uniform scheme.

98.   The special arrangements to which resort was sometimes made in financing orders have been described in Part 2, Chapter III (Finance), but generally, payment was made against contracts in the normal commercial manner.

99.   After delivery of equipment by the manufacturer to the Air Force, the relevant account was rendered to the authority which had issued the contract, either the Economics and Finance Office or, in the case of replacement spares, the Air Equipment Depots. The account was then forwarded either to the official Pay Office of the Air Ministry, in the case of orders of the Economics and Finance Office, or, in the case of orders of the Air Equipment Depots, to the appropriate subordinate official Pay Office for payment. These latter Pay Offices, specially constituted for dealing with Air Force accounts, existed at various levels of the Air Force Command and were subordinate units of the Administration Office.

100.   Payment by the Pay Office was effected only subject to the following conditions being fulfilled:—

   (i) The account being checked for arithmetical accuracy, and certified as correct, by a specially appointed official.

   (ii) The account being checked for agreement of quantities, prices, etc., and certified as correct in this respect by the official responsible for the administration of the appropriate funds from which payment was going to be made. This certificate was required to be accompanied by a copy of the contract.

   (iii) A certificate of technical acceptance (A.I.D.) being given by either the inspector at the factory or at the consignee unit.

   (iv) The receipt of the equipment being certified by the authority responsible for its custody and record; the time lag involved in the payment of accounts by the inability to submit these certificates sufficiently quickly was countered by the substitution of a declaration on the part of the manufacturer to the effect that the equipment in question had either been dispatched or stored by the contractor as trustee for the purchasing authority.

101.   After payment, the receipted accounts and their accompanying certificates were held by the official Pay Officers, in whose hands they remained in support of subsequent audit. Auditing of accounts was carried out by the Preliminary Auditing Office and by the Court of Reich Account; checking by these bodies was very thorough and proved of value in revealing mistakes made by industry and errors of the German Air Force authorities.

Finance

102.   The system whereby funds were made available to defray the cost of production for the German Air Force, and the means employed in regulating such expenditure, are pertinent to the present discussion on provisioning and production, but in view of the scope and complexity of this subject it has been considered expedient to treat the matter separately in Part 2, Chapter III.

103. Reference should be made, therefore, to that Chapter, which deals with:—
  (i) The nature, position and function of the Departments of the Air Force concerned with financial matters.
  (ii) The financing of the aircraft industry.
  (iii) The financing of orders.
  (iv) The system of budgetary control for the Air Force.

Summary of Manufacture and Acquisition of Equipment and Supplies

104. To provide easy reference to this phase in the provisioning cycle, the following summary is appended:—
  (i) **Orders on Industry.** Responsibility for the issue of orders to industry for production were given by:
    (a) Operationally important equipment — the Director General of Equipment.
    (b) Operationally important supplies — the Director General of Equipment.
    (c) Other technical equipment — the Director General of Equipment (after 1943, the Main Depots).
    (d) Motor transport — the Director of Motor Transport.
    (e) Intendant materials — the Administration Office, under the the direction of the Chief Intendant.
  (ii) **Quality Inspection.** The organisation for regulating quality inspection was a service one, and was controlled by the Director General of Equipment.
  (iii) **Contracts.** Orders on industry were issued by the Director General of Equipment but formal contracts were regulated by the Economics and Finance Office of the Air Ministry.
  (iv) **Finance.** Matters dealing with the financing of industry and of orders, of price control and budgetary allocations, are dealt with in Part 2, Chapter III.

THE RECEIPT, STORAGE AND ALLOCATION OF EQUIPMENT AND SUPPLIES

General

105. This part of the Chapter describes the last link in the chain of provisioning, in which manufactured equipment and supplies were delivered to the Air Force from industry and allocated for storage and use within the Service.

106. The Directorates and Departments of the Air Ministry responsible for regulating the receipt, storage and allocation were: —
  (i) The Aeronautical Inspection Service, under the orders of the Director General of Equipment.
  (ii) The Director of Supply.
  (iii) The Director of Signals.
  (iv) The Director of Motor Transport.
  (v) The 4th Department of the Quartermaster General.
  (vi) The 6th Department of the Quartermaster General.
  (vii) The Chief Intendant of the Air Force.

107. Distinction must be made between classes of material which require to be dealt with separately. The remarks in paragraphs 108—119 relate to the general range of equipment and supplies for the Air Force,

while the receipt, storage and allocation of Motor Transport and Intendant materials are dealt with separately in paragraphs 120—124.

108. The following matters will be discussed in relation to the acceptance, receipt, storage, allocation and issue for use of equipment and supplies:—
   (i) Responsibility for acceptance by the Air Force on manufacture.
   (ii) Delivery from contractors to Air Force storage.
   (iii) The general allocation and distribution of equipment and supplies, and the creation of reserves.
   (iv) The special methods used in allocating operationally important supplies.
   (v) The special methods used in allocating operationally important equipment.
   (vi) The supply installations of the Air Force to which allocation and issue were made.
   (vii) The means of co-ordinating storage, allocation and use by supply directives.

Acceptance on manufacture

109. Responsibility for the acceptance of manufactured goods at the factory, and for directing delivery, was that of the Air Force. This work was carried out, under the control of the Director General of Equipment, by the officials of the Aeronautical Inspection Service, who were responsible for the inspection and acceptance of all finished goods. Arrangements for dispatch and delivery were undertaken by these same officials, at the orders of the Director of Supply.

Delivery into Air Force Storage

110. With the exception of motor transport and Intendant materials, which will be dealt with separately below, the Director of Supply, subordinate to the Quartermaster General, was responsible for the whole range of equipment and supplies for the Air Force in its passage from the manufacturers into storage and use.

111. Each of the Main Depots, under the control of the Director of Supply, dealt with a specialised range of materials, and, therefore, with a certain section of industry. All war materials received from industry flowed into these storage units, from which the supply establishments of the Air Force were replenished.

112. The powers and responsibilities of the Director of Supply were wide, and they are discussed in some detail in Part 2, Chapter I. For the sake of continuity however, in describing the delivery of equipment into Air Force storage, the broad responsibilities of the Director of Supply in this connection are recapilutated below:—
   (i) The issue of official instructions, publications and orders relating to the acquisition of all equipment and supplies from the manufacturers.
   (ii) The issue of directions to the Director General of Equipment on delivery from manufacturers to the Air Force.
   (iii) The bulk storage of all equipment and supplies ready for issue to the equipment installations of the Air Force.
   (iv) The storage of all aviation fuels and ammunition.
   (v) The transfer of aircraft to units, in accordance with the directions of the Quartermaster General.
   (vi) The preparation of all initial equipment pack-ups.

General Allocation and Distribution of Equipment

113.   It has been seen that all war materials produced for the Air Force passed into the Main Depots of the Director of Supply. All operationally important equipment and supplies and items in short supply that were taken into storage were notified to the 6th Department of the Quartermaster General.

114.   The first action taken by this Department was to create special reserves of equipment that was in short supply. The reserves were frozen in the Main Depots, or, in the case of aircraft, on specially selected airfields. Such reserves were classified in four categories:—

  (i)   **Quartermaster General's reserves.** These could be released on the authority of the Quartermaster General. They included such items as Aviation Fuel, Ammunition, Heavy Flak Guns, certain types of aircraft, and other equipment in short supply.

  (ii) **O.K.L. Reserves.** These could be released only on the authority of the Chief of General Staff. They included similar items to those in the Quartermaster General's reserves.

  (iii) **O.K.W. Reserves.** These could be released only on the authority of the Chief of the Supreme Command. They included normally certain quantities of aviation fuel and flak equipment.

  (iv) **Mobile Quartermaster Reserves.** In the early years of the war, the Quartermaster General had part of his reserves of aviation fuel and explosives in trains parked in railway sidings ready for immediate despatch to any front which might suddenly become a focal point.

115.   On receipt of the appropriate authority quantities of these special reserves would be released and allocated to the various Luftflotten. Department 4 would allocate all fuel and munitions, and Department 6 all other special reserve equipment. These departments would inform the Director of Supply of the allocations made and instruct him to release and deliver the materials to the consumers indicated.

116.   The special procedures adopted in the allocation of operationally important equipment and supplies are referred to in detail below.

Allocation of Operationally Important Supplies

117.   The allocation of aviation fuels and of explosives and ammunition was carried out specially by the 4th Department of the Quartermaster General. Each class of supply is dealt with separately below:—

  (i) **Aviation fuels.** Each Luftflotte had to submit a daily report of its consumption and stocks of aircraft fuel to the 4th Department by teleprinter or in code by telephone. This information, interpreted in the light of forthcoming operations, formed the basis for estimating the requirements of the Luftflotten. The quantity becoming available from Industry for distribution was made known to the 4th Department by the Director General of Equipment who was responsible for production. Proposals for the monthly allocation to the Luftflotten were then prepared and submitted to the Chief of the General Staff through the Quartermaster General. The fuel was held in the various Bulk Fuel Depots, and after approval of the proposed allocations a plan was drawn up showing which depots were to supply which Luftflotten. The 4th Department would then issue orders to the Director of Supply to draw the aircraft fuel and lubricants from the depots.

(ii) **Explosives and Ammunition.** The 4th Department allocated bombs. aircraft ammunition and special missiles to the Luftflotten on the same principle as aviation fuel was allocated. Flak ammunition was allocated by the 4th Department to the whole of the Armed Forces. The needs of the Army for Flak munition were presented to the Luftflotten and the Luftflotten included the Army figures in the weekly reports to the 4th Department. The weekly reports gave data on stocks, consumption and the numbers of guns. From these reports the requirements of the Armed Forces in each area were calculated. The quantity available for distribution was notified to the Department by the Director General of Equipment who was responsible for production. As the 6th Department had the allocation, of heavy flak guns in its keeping, the 4th Department would work closely with the 6th in the matters of allocation of munitions. The 6th Department, the 4th Department and the Director of Supply kept themselves currently informed about the state of production and the location of the flak ammunition produced. After the allocation to Commands, the 4th Department gave orders to the Director of Supply to despatch the quatities indicated from particular Ammunition Depots to each Command.

Allocation of Operationally Important Equipment

118. The allocation of all major items of equipment regarded as of primary importance or being in short supply, was dealt with by the 6th Department of the Quartermaster General.

The Issue of Supply Directives

119. The Operations Staff of the General Staff issued Operational Orders to the Luftflotten, and at the same time to the Quartermaster General. The complementary orders for the supply of aircraft fuel, munitions and equipment for the support of these operations were then prepared by the 4th Department and issued likewise to the Luftflotten as a "Special Supply Directive" and signed by the Quartermaster General. The 4th Department alone issued such directives. Each Operational Order to the Luftflotten from the Operations Staff required a corresponding "Special Directive". Thus, orders which the 6th Department, the Director of Motor Transport, or the Director of Supply wished to issue were included, so that only one such directive would be issued. It is true that for the sake of speed the other Departments mentioned might issue their orders separately through the Quartermaster General: they would then be supplements to the "Special Directive" and sent out as such. Special Supply Directives contained the following information:—

(i) A battle order of the operational units, transport units, training and other units to be supplied with aircraft fuel, oil and lubricants.

(ii) The source from which Flak units both of the Army and the Air Force were to obtain their flak ammunition, and the Luftflotte quota from which it was to be drawn.

(iii) The source from which motor transport fuel was to be drawn.

(iv) The channels for obtaining aircraft and the route they would follow.

(v) The source of supply of flak guns and heavy flak guns.

(vi) Supply routes for aircraft engines.

(vii) Supply routes for ordinary equipment (coming from the Director of Supply).

(viii) Measures relating to provision of clothing, rations and pay.

Motor Transport and Intendant Materials

120. These two classes of supply for the Air Force were excluded from the general description of the receipt, storage and allocation of equipment and supplies.

121. All stocks of motor transport vehicles were received and held by Motor Transport Stock Depots under the control of the Director of Motor Transport. This Director was responsible for the allocation and distribution of motor transport to all formations of the Air Force.

122. Details of the responsibilities generally of the Director of Motor Transport, in controlling storage and allocation of vehicles, are contained in a special chapter on the subject of Motor Transport (Part 2, Chapter VI).

123. The supplies described as Intendant materials, comprising clothing, furniture, rations and fuel, provisioned by the Administration Office at the direction of the Chief Intendant, were received and stored by the Air Force in special installations.

124. Clothing and accoutrements, including manufactured cloth and other fabricated materials, were received into Clothing Depots. Barrack equipment was received by Billet and Office Furniture Depots. Rations, except for special items, were not held in major Air Force Depots, but in Army installations. Installations holding major stocks of clothing and furniture (and of fuels) were controlled by the Administration Office, and that Office was responsible for the allocation and delivery to all formations of the Air Force. (See Part 1, Chapter V.)

Summary of Receipt, Storage and Allocation of Equipment and Supplies

125. (i) Acceptance at factories was the responsibility of the Aeronautial Inspection Service, working at the direction of the Director General of Equipment.

   (ii) Delivery of manufactured items into storage was controlled, except in the case of motor transport and Intendant materials, by the Director of Supply.

   (iii) The Main Depots responsible for specialised bulk storage of equipment and supplies were controlled by the Director of Supply.

   (iv) Normal issues of equipment and supplies to replenish Air Force installations were made from the Main Depots. Operationally important supplies, comprising aviation fuels and explosives, were controlled by the 4th Department of the Quartermaster General. Allocation of operationally important equipment was directed by the 6th Department of the Quartermaster General.

   (v) Supply directives, governing supply in relation to operations, were prepared and issued by the 4th Department of the Quartermaster General.

   (vi) Motor Transport. Receipt, storage and allocation of motor transport and the control of Depots dealing with this class of equipment were the responsibility of the Director of Motor Transport.

   (vii) The receipt and storage of Intendant materials, including clothing, furniture, rations, and fuels, were the responsibility of the Administration Office.

SECTION III. TRANSITION PERIOD 1942—44

GENERAL

126. August 1st 1944 marks the point at which responsibility for the production, as distinct from the provisioning, of all war materials required for the Air Force passed to Speer as Minister of Armaments and War Production, and in this Chapter the date has been regarded as marking the dividing line in distinguishing the periods in which the general system of provisioning and production differed.

127. There was, however, a transitional period in which preparations were made for the later transfer of control of industry to Speer and in which, later, part control of production was transferred from the Air Force to the Speer Ministry.

RECONSTITUTION OF THE AIRCRAFT INDUSTRY

128. From 1942 to 1944 Milch acted as Director General of Equipment in the Air Force and from his close and friendly relationship with Speer it was possible for the latter to arrange the reconstruction of the aircraft industry on the same pattern as the industries responsible for Army and Navy war production. No transfer of responsibility took place but it is important to bear in mind that, during these two years, the aircraft industry was formed into Main and Special Committees and that, consequently, responsibility for the direction of production tended to move from Air Force officers to industrialists and technicians.

THE "FIGHTER STAFF"

129. Partial control of production for the Air Force was secured by Speer in February 1944 when, by reason of the heavy and sustained air attacks on the German aircraft plants by the Allies, it became necessary to re-organise the production of fighter aircraft. This re-organisation was achieved by the formation of a production control body known as the "Fighter Staff" (Jägerstab), having Speer as nominal head, Milch as Deputy and Saur as "Leader".

130. The prime responsibility of the "Fighter Staff" was the production of day and night fighters, since it was recognised that a strengthening of the defensive capabilities of the Air Force was indispensable to maintenance of war production in general.

131. The main measures adopted by Speer in stepping up production were:—

    (i) the formation of special mobile "action squads", which were to restore production at aircraft plants immediately after damage by Allied air attacks,

    (ii) the increased protection of plants by dispersal of important and essential machine tools and by the introduction of special walls, bunkers, etc., and

    (iii) the general stimulation of production at all aircraft plants, especially at fighter producing factories.

In addition to these measures, Speer initiated a review of all current programmes with the object of reducing the number of types and sub-types of aircraft planned. By this means, and along with the measures described above, Speer was successful in achieving increased rates of production of simplified and standardised types of fighter aircraft.

132. Action in this respect did not involve a complete change in the existing control of production by the Air Force since the original terms of reference of the "Fighter Staff" were limited to organisational measures in protecting the aircraft industry and, although Speer went beyond these powers in revising the aircraft programmes current at that time, the major change in responsibility, involving a division of labour between provisioning and production, did not become effective until July 1944.

133. The "Fighter Staff" continued in existence until July 1944, during which time its achievements were remarkable in re-organising the aircraft industry and increasing the production rates of fighter aircraft.

SECTION IV. PROVISIONING AND PRODUCTION AFTER AUGUST, 1944

GENERAL

134. For all practical purposes, from the beginning of July 1944, but with official effect from the 1st August of that year, the Speer Ministry assumed full responsibility for all air armament production, deriving its authority from a Göring decree of June 20th 1944, (Appendix A). Control of production was then vested in the Technical Office, under Saur, and the "Fighter Staff" dissolved.

135. From that date, the system by which equipment and supplies were provided for the German Air Force underwent a radical change. Provisioning proper, i.e. the assessment of requirements of war materials and the formulation of programmes, remained a responsibility of the Air Ministry, but control and direction of industry passed into the hands of Speer and the industrialists.

136. The department of the Director General of Equipment was abolished and replaced by a Chief of Technical Air Armaments (Chef der Technischen Luftrüstung), General Milch moving from the Air Ministry to become Speer's deputy for aircraft production. Until this re-organisation took place the Director General of Equipment had been responsible for regulating the whole process of production from the issue of programmes to the final delivery of manufactured items into service depots. The responsibilities of his successor, the Chief of Technical Air Armaments, were very much less, being restricted to expressing the needs of the Air Force. He played no part in production.

PRESENTATION

137. It should be noted that in describing the methods of provisioning and production in the period after August 1944 to the end of the war the presentation of the facts is influenced by the following considerations: —

(i) it is necessary to deal in some detail with the administrative processes by which the Speer Ministry directed and controlled production, since the assumption of power by Speer is the essential new factor in the subject, but

(ii) it is unnecessary to decribe the routine methods of provisioning in force in the German Air Force since they are materially the same as described in Section II of this Chapter, the only difference being that responsibility for the issue of programmes was transferred from the Director General of Equipment to the Chief of Technical Air Armaments.

THE ORGANISATION OF THE SPEER MINISTRY

138. The organisation of the Speer Ministry of Armaments and War Production is dealt with fully in Part 1, Chapter II, to which reference should be made to obtain a basis and a background for the following discussion of the production responsibilities of the Ministry.

139. The Main Committees concerned with aircraft production, of which there were three, already existed before August 1st, 1944, under the direction of Milch, with only nominal control by Speer. These Committees, responsible for the production of airframes, engines, and ancillary equipment, each had its subordinate Special Committees dealing with a certain type of aircraft, a certain type of engine, or a certain range of ancillary equipment.

140. This arrangement had been made by the mutual consent of the Air Force and Speer to ensure as far as possible uniformity of organisation in armament manufacture. The Main Rings responsible for the production of raw materials and semi-finished products required by the aircraft industry also found it preferable to deal with these Main Committees, composed like themselves of industrialists, rather than with a multiplicity of Service departments.

141. On the assumption by Speer of full responsibility for aircraft production it was necessary, therefore, only to incorporate the existing Main Committees within his general organisation.

142. Although it never became effective, at this late point of time, a Special Development Commission was formed to deal with aircraft development for the Air Force. It is probable that, had this Commission been more active, or instituted in 1942 when the Aircraft Committees were formed, some of the defects in qualitiy and performance alleged by the Air Force against Speer might have been reduced or eliminated.

143. With the incorporation of the existing Main Committees and the formation of this Development Commission, Speer was at last able to exercise control over the entire range of armament production.

144. At the date of the transfer, there was no change in the principles of administration of the Committees, but later in the year both the Main Committee for Aero Engines and the Main Committee for Ancillary Equipment lost their separate identity. The responsibility for engine production generally, of all types including aero engines, was transferred to the Main Committee for Motors. Responsibility for aero-engine production, under the general control of this Main Committee was vested in a Subordinate Special Committee. At the same time, responsibility for ancillary equipment (instruments, electrical and hydraulic) was divided among a number of Main Committees, each range of equipment being the responsibility of a Subordinate Special Committee of a Main Committee.

PROGRESSION OF DEMANDS BY THE SPEER MINISTRY

General

145. It is expedient, in describing the work of the Speer Ministry, to differentiate between the following classes of equipment:—
    (i) Aircraft, Airframes, Engines, and Airframe and Engine Components and Spares.
    (ii) Ground Technical Equipment.
    (iii) Motor Transport.

(iv) General Non-Technical Equipment.
(v) Flak Equipment.
(vi) Supplies, including P.O.L., Medical Stores, etc.

Aircraft

146. The manufacture and provision of airframes and of engines, and the supply of components are, of course, directly related to aircraft programmes and it is necessary, therefore, to deal first, and in some detail, with the production of aircraft proper.

147. It has been seen that in the Air Force itself requirements for the development of aircraft types, and for quantity production against programmes, were initiated by the Operations Staff in collaboration with the 6th Department of the Quartermaster General. Normally, the Chief of Technical Air Armaments of the Air Force was responsible for translating the General Staff requirements into detailed orders and for transmitting them to the Speer Ministry. This routine was short circuited to a considerable extent, however, by personal discussion between the Head of the Main Committee for Aircraft and the officers in charge of the 6th Department.

148. Such discussion on the setting up of aircraft programmes resolved itself mainly into reconciliation of aircraft requirements and aircraft factory capacity. The Main Committee for Aircraft, under Speer, was in complete control of the airframe industry and in discussions of this kind no attempt was made on the part of the Air Force to disagree on the question of factory capacity; in respect, however, of other factors, including the time involved in reaching programme peaks, the use of alternative types of machines, and the introduction of new types, the Air Force usually had its way. Before responsibility was transferred to Speer, during the operation of the Main Committee for Aircraft under Milch, no appeal could be made against a decision of the Air Force to introduce new types of aircraft. Even after August 1944, there was little Speer could do in such cases against Göring, when the latter chose to exercise his influence. When not faced with direct intervention from Göring there is little doubt that Speer did tend to allow considerations of expediency in production to override military requirements.

149. On the basis of each proposed programme, the Main Committee for Aircraft would consult the members of the Main Comittees for engines and engine accessories and for ancillary airborne equipment, to determine whether the programme could be covered in respect of these classes of equipment, plus spares. Normally, there were no difficulties in the provision of engines or of ancillary equipment, the main bottleneck being in the airframe range.

150. The programme in its final form, showing anticipated production month by month, would then be presented through either the 6th Department or, more correctly, the Chief of Technical Air Armaments, to the Operations Staff. In the earlier part of the war, programmes were devised to provide contracts for periods of 18 months, but 12 months was the normal period; programmes were revised and re-issued in much the same way as in England, each main programme being followed, where necessary, by amendments or by complete re-issue when amendments were too numerous to be incorporated.

151. In conformity with general practice, the responsibility for placing orders with industry against agreed programmes lay with the

appropriate Service, and preliminary contracts against each programme were placed with manufacturers by the Chief of Technical Air Armaments.

152. Each programme, in its completed form, became the basis not only of contracts for airframes but also of planning by the other Main Committees for engines and for ancillary equipment. The translation of an aircraft programme into terms of requirements for engines, engine accessories, and airborne accessories occupied at least one month and was calculated by use of Hollerith machines.

Components

153. Ancillary airborne equipment was divided into three main classes: (a) instruments; (b) electrical equipment; (c) hydraulic equipment. Each of these classes of equipment was a very broad one and was intended to cover a wider range of equipment than is perhaps understood in the Royal Air Force when using these terms.

154. In the production of aircraft components there appears to have been no co-ordinating authority. Responsibility rested entirely with the Special Committees in formulating forecast programmes for major components, which were designed to show anticipated output over a period of 6 or 8 months. Firms manufacturing the same component under the guidance of the responsible Special Committee each received a copy of the component programme, but only insofar as their own individual production was concerned.

Spares

155. In respect of spares generally, it was considered expedient, after 1942, to place responsibility in the hands of the various Special Committees. Each of these was constituted as a subordinate body controlling a group of firms engaged in the manufacture of the same type of aircraft, engine, or aircraft or engine main component or class of ancillary equipment.

156. For each new type of aircraft engine, component or item of ancillary equipment, the appropriate Special Committee planned, on a theoretical basis, for the production of spares. Manufacture was then allocated to the firms operating under the control of the Special Committee.

157. On manufacture the spares were despatched from the factories into Air Force Main Depots. Complete and accurate records were maintained of issues from these Depots and each month the summarised issues in the form of tabulations were transmitted to the Special Committees. From these summaries the Special Committees were enabled to compare consumption with theoretical provisioning and to adjust production accordingly.

158. Thus, after initial provisioning, and as each range of spares passed into general use, replenishment of stocks became a matter of routine between the storage units of the Air Force and the aircraft firms, through the agency of the Special Committees.

159. There was no system comparable to the British "A.O.G." procedure but it is certain that in some of the formations of the German Air Force irregularities occurred whereby squadrons were able to short circuit the normal supply system.

160. Reference has been made already to the time relationship of airframes and engine programmes, and of the general method of provisioning engine spares. Spare engine production at the beginning of the war

was planned on the basis of 20 per cent spare engines behind aircraft production but, in the light of experience, efforts were made to increase provision to 30 per cent.

Embodiment and Standardisation

161. Items issued on embodiment loan were engines and power plants, propeller gear, guns, turrets and other armament equipment, radio and radar equipment, all automatic pilot equipment and the majority of specialised instruments; all other items were contractors' supplies.

162. According to the Head of the Main Committee for Aircraft, German industry was successful in standardizing aero-engines, hydraulic equipment, wheels, tyres and instruments. Development of these proceeded independently of airframe development and always in conformity with a limited number of standard specifications but, except in the case of these items, standardization of components was not carried very far.

Ground Technical Equipment

163. Initially, responsibility for the production of the various classes of ground technical equipment lay with the Main Committee for Equipment; this general committee was later dissolved and its functions were distributed between other Main Committees, such as the Electrical Apparatus Committee, the Precision and Optical Instruments Committee, the Committee for General Forces Equipment, etc. Development of the various classes of equipment in the ground technical range was delegated to Development Commissions, of which there was one for each Main Committee, each responsible for a particular range of equipment.

164. Initiation of demands of ground technical equipment, and the preparation of programmes, was carried out within the system already described for other technical equipment, the Air Force itself being responsible ultimately for the issue of orders to industry.

Motor Transport

165. A separate Main Committee existed, with its complementary Development Commission, to supervise and guide industry in the production of motor transport for the Armed Forces, and although these two organisations were constituted and governed in the same way as were other bodies in the Speer Ministry, certain differences of procedure became necessary since the equipment concerned was of "common user" nature.

166. The Army was the major user of motor transport and at the beginning of the war was responsible for satisfying the needs of the German Air Force and Navy. Towards the end of the war, however, in 1944, the difficulties of maintaining production necessitated the formation of a Directorate of Armed Forces Motor Transport which was charged, under the Supreme Command, with problems of motor transport, and reconciling the competing requirements of the three Services.

167. After this date, therefore, the German Air Force was required to present its demands to this Directorate for motor transport vehicles and spares.

168. The Directorate of Armed Forces Motor Transport, in providing vehicles and spares for the three Services, was linked directly with the Technical Office of the Speer Ministry, and through that Department with the Main Committee and Development Commission directing this part of industry.

Non-Technical Equipment

169.   Items of non-technical equipment, including all textiles and furniture, were obtained through the Production Office of the Speer Ministry. This office was responsible for the production of general economic goods after September 1943, when this function was taken over by Speer from the Ministry of Economics. The Production Office operated in much the same way as the Technical Office, in that Production Committees were formed dealing with the various classes of equipment.

170.   It has been pointed out in Part 1, Chapter I (The Supreme Command of the Armed Forces) that in respect of common user items the major user was made responsible for the supply to the other two Services. The supply of material for making clothing and accoutrements was an exception, and responsibility for its supply to all three Services was undertaken by the Supreme Command.

171.   The Air Ministry presented its demands to the General Armed Forces Directorate, for co-ordination with the requirements of the other two Services, and for transmission through that body to the Speer Ministry. The Ministry received the aggregate demands of the Services expressed in the form of yarn and other unfabricated or unprocessed materials.

172.   On receipt of these demands the Provision Office of the Speer Ministry was responsible for the provision of the materials required. Authority for their disposal to the Armed Forces, however, was vested in the Armed Forces Procuring Directorate of the Supreme Command. This Directorate then arranged for the manufacture of the materials into cloth and other textiles.

173.   After manufacture, the cloth and other textiles allocated to the Services were issued either to storage depots, for use in their finished state, or to factories, for turning into uniforms.

174.   A proportion of barrack equipment was regarded as being of a common-user nature, and the Army as the major user was responsible for its provision. The Air Ministry was responsible for advising its requirements to the High Command of the Army, but a distinction was observed between equipment for Air Force units with the Army and those which were independent of Army formations.

   (i)   **German Air Force Units with the Army.** Demands were submitted by the Air Ministry to the Quartermaster General of the Army High Command, by whom yearly estimates of requirements for all three Services were prepared and passed to the Chief of Army Armaments. The requirements were then translated into aggregate demands for the necessary raw materials, and referred by the Chief of Army Armaments to the Speer Ministry. The Ministry was responsible, through the Production Office, for the allocation and delivery of the necessary materials and for manufacture where the Army had no facilities. After manufacture, either by the Army or by industrial concerns, the equipment was delivered to Army storage units and from these to units of the Air Force.

   (ii)   **German Air Force Units Independent of the Army.** In the case of demands for equipment required by the Air Force independent of the Army, the Air Ministry was itself responsible for preparing and submitting direct to the Chief of Army Armaments estimates of raw materials needed. The Chief of Army Armaments was responsible for including in the general demands to the Speer Ministry the requirements of the Air Force, and thereafter the same procedure was followed as in (i) above, except that for manufacture or after manufacture the equipment was issued direct to the Air Force depots.

Flak Equipment

175. The development and testing of Flak Equipment lay with the respective Development Commissions, while responsibility for production rested with the complementary Main Committees, as under:—

Guns:	Main Committee for Weapons.
Observation and Fire Control Apparatus: Searchlights and Radar:	Main Committee for Electrical Apparatus.

176. Provision of this range of equipment followed the same course as that for aircraft and airborne equipment generally, demands being formulated by the Air Ministry in agreement with the Technical Office of the Speer Ministry and orders made on industry in conjunction with the Main and Special Committees.

177. In conformity with the usual German practice in respect of common user equipment, the Air Force, being the major Flak user, was made responsible for the supply of all such items to the Army and the Navy. The Air Ministry, therefore, was responsible for the co-ordination of the requirements of these Services, and for including their requirements when demanding on industry.

Petrols, Oils & Lubricants

178. General responsibility for the bulk production of fuel lay with the Raw Materials Office of the Speer Ministry which made use of its subordinate organisations (Reichsstelle) for mineral oil, for rubber, and for chemicals.

179. The Air Force played a very considerable part on its own initiative in furthering development of fuel, in conjunction with the Reichsstelle for Mineral Oil but its programmes involving long-term bulk commitments were required to be transmitted from the Air Ministry to the Supreme Command. As early as 1942 the increasing shortage of fuels had necessitated a degree of central planning to co-ordinate and control bulk demands of all three Services and to determine policy in the utilisation of raw and synthetic materials.

180. The organisation of the Supreme Command charged with the responsibility of co-ordinating the bulk requirements of all three Services maintained liaison with the Speer Ministry, advising this organisation of commitments and directing the flow of finished materials into bulk storage and ultimately into Service supply channels.

Rations

181. Responsibility for the production of foodstuffs rested with the Production Office of the Speer Ministry, working in conjunction with the Ministry of Food, the former responsible for special products, preservation, and packing, and the latter for foodstuffs proper.

182. The Air Force was itself responsible for certain products, notably special flying rations, but generally the same principle as that of the British Forces was followed, in that the Army was made responsible for the day-to-day requirements of both Forces.

Medical Supplies

183. In respect of requirements of the Air Force for medical stores, distinction was made between supplies of medicines, textiles, etc., for which the Raw Materials Office was responsible, and for apparatus and instruments, which were dealt with by the Main Committees, particularly those concerned with Electrical Apparatus and Optical and Precision Instruments.

184. The Chief of Armed Forces Medical Services was intended to co-ordinate the medical organisations of the three Services and to ensure the most effective distribution of equipment but this applied only very generally and the Air Force maintained a great deal of independence in this field, particularly in those problems peculiar to air matters.

MANUFACTURE AND DELIVERY

185. The acceptance of manufactured equipment by the Air Force and its delivery into Service custody have been described already in the earlier part of this Chapter, but the matter is dealt with here to show the part played by the Speer Ministry in this sphere after responsibility for production had been divorced from the Service heads.

186. Before 1944 the supervision and checking of production plans was confined to the German Air Force. After this date, when control of the aircraft industry was assumed by Speer, each manufacturer was required to work under the sole direction of the Main and Special Committees responsible for its products. The German Air Force, however, retained a small measure of responsibility, through the Chief of Technical Air Armaments, in that it exercised control over quality production by means of the Aeronautical Inspection Service (B.A.L.).

187. One of the most important benefits derived from the work of the Main and Special Committees was the pooling of knowledge and technical processes to the advantage of those firms engaged in the same field of production. This experience was applied in examining the proposals put forward in each programme.

188. Responsibility for maintaining production against programmes and contracts devolved on the Special Committees, each regulating manufacture of a specific range of equipment.

189. Production Reports, showing production against programmes, were rendered to the Technical Office of Speer's Ministry at the end of each month and, after collation and analysis, were sent to Hitler on the second day of the following month; in the case of important programmes, intermediate reports would be rendered every ten days. The completed reports were reviewed and discussed on the fourth of each month by Saur, as Head of the Technical Office, and the leaders of the Main Committees.

190. In order that liaison should be maintained between the Ministry and the Main Committees, and that Speer should have the advantage of advice on the progress of established programmes, Programme Commissions were established as part of the Technical Office. A Commission was

appointed for each range of equipment to facilitate work with its opposite Main Committee. The purpose of the Commissions is clear but it appears that, in practice, they were limited in scope.

191. The Air Force was itself responsible for the acceptance of finished products at the factory, and for directing their delivery. These tasks were carried out through the agency of the Aeronautical Inspection Service (B.A.L.), the inspectors of this organisation being responsible for the acceptance and inspection of finished goods, and for ensuring their despatch and delivery to the order of the Director of Supply.

SECTION V
CONCLUSION

192. Special mention must be made of the comparative efficiency and success of the system, under Speer, in providing for the needs of the Air Force. Considerable criticism has been levelled at the Ministry of Armaments and War Production by the German Air Force, and its members, including Speer, have been accused of power-seeking and political proclivities, but if only in the light of quantity of air armaments there is little doubt that industry, in accelerating and intensifying production, succeeded where the Service had failed.

193. Absolute control by Speer of the production of air armaments lasted only a short time — between 1944 and the end of the war — but in reality his influence dates from 1942 when, under the guidance of Milch, the Main Committees for aircraft were set up. Bearing this fact in mind, it is possible to compare the production of aircraft in the period 1942—1945 with that of the preceding years 1939—1941; during these later years of the war the monthly rate of production was 4,000 aircraft compared with the average monthly production of 800 in the first two years of the war.

194. It is dangerous to draw general conclusions from the mere quantitative achievements of Speer, and of course the system had its faults. Quite serious difficulties were encountered by the Air Force on the question of quality and efficiency of its equipment but, had the war continued, it is probable that these matters would have been rectified.

195. In comparing the British and German systems of provisioning and production during the period after 1944, the most notable fact is the degree of responsibility devolving upon industry. It was intended, in principle at least, that the Air Force should be restricted to making known its broad strategic commitments and that all control of production (including assessment of quantities to meet the commitments) should be in the hands of the Speer Ministry and of industry. This principle is a contradiction to that embodied in the British organisation where the Air Ministry is intended to play a dominant and active part in deciding what quantities of air armaments will be necessary.

196. Speer's action in seeking and achieving autonomy in industry had one particular result worthy of note. In any system where entire responsibility is given to one organisation, there can be no doubt who must take the blame for any failure or fault that may occur. Thus, the German Air Force, having lost control of production of its equipment, could clearly point to industry as being responsible for whatever degree of failure there may have been to compete with British and American industry in mass production, quality and design of air armaments.

APPENDIX "A"
to Part 2, Chap. II.

BERLIN, 20. June 44.

It will be necessary to mobilise the whole German armament industry for the purpose of increasing the strength of the Luftwaffe.

In order to create the necessary conditions, I order that the arming of the Luftwaffe is to be executed in accordance with the strategic requirements and technical principles, decreed by the C.-in-C. This programme will be the responsibility of the Minister for Armaments and Production. The appropriate executive orders are to be submitted to me not later than the 1st August 1944.

(Signed) Hermann Goering,
Reichsminister of Aviation,
and
C.-in-C. of the Luftwaffe.

PART 2

CHAPTER III

FINANCE

INTRODUCTION	Paragraphs 1—2
FINANCING OF THE AIRCRAFT INDUSTRY	,, 3—11
General	,, 3—7
Bank Credits	,, 8—9
Participation in Capital Ownership	,, 10—11
State Ownership	,, 12—14
FINANCING OF ORDERS	,, 15—18
BUDGETARY CONTROL	,, 19—24
General	,, 19
Procedure in Peace	,, 20—23
Procédure in War	,, 24
PRICE FIXING AND CONTROL	,, 25—36
General	,, 25—27
Policy and Procedure during the War	,, 28—36
FINANCE: DEPARTMENTS OF THE AIR MINISTRY	,, 37
CONCLUSION	,, 38—40

PART 2

CHAPTER III

FINANCE

INTRODUCTION

1. This Chapter does not provide a comprehensive picture of German finance in war time, and is intended only to describe shortly those aspects of the financial system concerned with the production of air armaments. The paragraphs which follow are limited, therefore, to:—
   (i) The financing of the aircraft industry.
   (ii) The financing of orders.
   (iii) The system of budgetary control for the German Air Force.
   (iv) The methods of price fixing and control.
   (v) The nature and function of the Departments of the Air Ministry concerned with financial matters.

2. Since the subject of finance, in relation to the German Air Force, is a wide and complex one, it has been considered preferable to deal with the matter separately in this Chapter, but reference should be made to the related subject of Provisioning and Production in Part 2, Chapter II, particularly in connection with the routine methods employed in the issue of contracts and in payment on manufacture.

FINANCING OF THE AIRCRAFT INDUSTRY

General

3. The main role of the War Economic and Armaments Board, in preparing German industry for war (i.e. the search for self-sufficiency in raw materials) has already been referred to in Part 1, Chapters I & II. A subsidiary task was that of formulating broad policy for financing industrial enterprises engaged in war production, but as the Board was concerned only very generally in industrial development the narrow work of producing specialised armaments became the task of the individual branches of the Armed Forces.

4. The methods employed by the Forces in financing armament production, however, differed between the Services, and no standard method had been devised even at the end of the war.

5. The German armaments industry obtained the funds required for expansion from both private investors and from the State. As a principle, it was intended that, in the first instance, industry should secure additional capital by private means, and in fact a large part of the capital requirements for new plants, and extensions and alterations of existing plants, was obtained in the normal commercial manner.

6. The full application of this principle was, however, impossible in the case of the aircraft industry and expansion was aided to a very considerable extent by the State.

7. State financial aid, which took various forms in the three Services, developed so far as the German Air Force was concerned mainly by means

of credits. Of the three Services, the Air Force had the greatest comprehension of commercial and financial questions involved in setting up and developing a war industry. The Army High Command maintained its conservative Prussian fiscal policy, and the Navy was simply inexperienced in commercial matters. To a certain extent, therefore, the financial organisations described below were peculiar to the Air Force.

Bank Credits

8. The most common form of financial aid given by the Reich was that of credits to complete war plants, without ownership by the State. The Aviation Bank (Bank der Deutscher Luftfahrt A.G.) received block credits from the State, based on estimates submitted by the Air Ministry in its budgets. From the funds thus provided by the State, the Bank issued to industrial concerns the credits they required. The Bank was aided in this task of financing industry by a specially constituted Reich Credit Board (Reichskreditausschuss).

9. The whole of the shares of the Aviation Bank were in the hands of the Air Ministry and although nominally the Bank was independent in the granting of credits and had no responsibility to anyone beyond its own organisation, in actual fact it was controlled and instructed by the Air Ministry, and was the agent in financial matters of the Air Ministry.

Participation in Capital Ownership

10. As an alternative to the long-term credits provided through the agency of the Aviation Bank, the aircraft industry was assisted by the participation of the Reich as a share or stock holder. Purchase of stocks and shares was carried out by the Aviation Bank, from funds made available by the State; and the Air Ministry, by its control of the Bank, thus acquired partial or full control of a number of enterprises.

11. Provision was made for the aircraft concerns to convert the larger credits given to them into the stock or shares of the individual companies. Industry as a whole preferred this procedure, and the policy was also favoured by the Air Force in that it assured a more lasting influence on the policy of manufacture. There was therefore a greater degree of Service ownership and direction in this sphere than in the industries concerned with the other two Services.

State Ownership

12. In addition to long-term credits and to part or full ownership of capital by the Air Ministry Bank, the aircraft industry was, in certain cases, assisted by the Reich assuming direct responsibility for the construction of factories. This practice was increasingly favoured from 1936, the Luftfahrtanlagen G.m.b.H., which belonged to the Reich, being charged with the construction and administration of factories and with the leasing of them to private firms. Tenants enjoying these facilities were such works as Messerschmitt, Heinkel, Focke-Wulf, Vereinigte Deutsche Flugmotorenwerke (VDM), etc.

13. The effort of Speer in seeking autonomy of industry is reflected in the financial sphere, for in 1943 and 1944 he insisted that factories belonging to the Reich should be transferred to private firms. Although this policy was not generally pursued in the aircraft industry, there were a few cases in which leased properties belonging to the State were turned over to the aircraft companies.

14. In the Air Ministry itself the Economics and Finance Office was responsible for all those problems arising from the needs of the aircraft industry, and although it was found impossible in developing aircraft production to retain entirely the independence of private enterprise, this Office by its control of the Aviation Bank and its understanding of the financial requirements of the aircraft firms played a large part in preserving the industry from a greater degree of nationalisation.

FINANCING OF ORDERS

15. Military orders frequently involved very large sums of money, and the provision of the working capital required in accepting these orders was frequently beyond the resources of the many companies drawn into the armaments industry. These firms were quite unable to meet the expense of providing labour and materials during the long periods before completion and payment of the long-term contracts. It became necessary therefore to find ways of financing companies by advances against the total cost of contracts.

16. Up to 1943 a system was operated whereby very considerable relief was offered in financing military orders, advances at the time of the orders being as much as 50 to 60 per cent of the total purchase price, but Speer in 1943 prepared and issued the "Instructions for the Financing of Armaments Orders" which changed entirely the basis of payments. The practice of paying a first instalment at the time the order was placed was forbidden on principle, except in cases where the transaction had already been settled as a part-payment contract.

17. In the first instance, the banks were intended to provide credit to manufacturers, but where such sources failed owing to lack of private security, it was arranged that facilities should be given by credit institutions. It was arranged that these credit institutions should provide funds to the manufacturer in return for the legal transference to them of full rights to the monies paid on completion of the contract.

18. For some of the important ranges of armaments special Reich corporations were set up, charged with assistance in financing orders. In the case of spare parts and components for the Air Force the Gesellschaft für Luftfahrtbedarf was formed as a subsidiary of the Aviation Bank.

BUDGETARY CONTROL

General

19. Expenditure for the Air Force was assessed and controlled by means of formal budgets. The importance attached by the Nazi heirarchy to the development of an Air Force has already been commented on in earlier Chapters; and in peacetime, applications for funds by means of budgets were normally granted automatically. This purely nominal regulation of expenditure for the Air Force was later relaxed even further for after 1939 the Ministry of Finance delegated to the Supreme Command of the Forces authority to approve any expenditure necessary for the prosecution of the war.

Procedure in Peace

20. Under normal peace conditions the Budget of the Reich Minister for Air and Commander in Chief of the German Air Force formed the basis of Air Force expenditure. Preparation of the Budget in the form of

an estimate for the ensuing fiscal period April 1st to March 31st took place at the end of each calendar year. For the compilation of the estimate all the Departments of the Air Ministry dealing with budget funds rendered supplements to the Administration Office and then, after the assembled budget estimate had been checked, from both the administrative and military points of view, it was submitted for the approval of the Chief of the General Staff. From this point, after approval, the estimate was laid before the Reich Minister for Air and Commander in Chief German Air Force by the Secretary of State for Air and then passed to the Headquarters of the Supreme Command.

21. The Supreme Command was responsible for examining the budget estimate submitted by the Air Force together with those of the other two Services and for forwarding all three budgets and its own to the Reich Minister of Finance. The collected budget estimates, forming the total Budget of the Armed Forces, were then subject to the approval of the State and to the wishes of Hitler. It is worthy of note that this formal procedure was sometimes varied and the Air Force budget estimate was taken by Göring direct to Hitler, the former exercising his political powers and friendship with Hitler for this purpose.

22. After the Budget had been approved, the funds granted to the German Air Force were dealt with by the Budget Department of the Administration Office in the Air Ministry. This Department, with the approval of the Air Force General Staff, assigned the funds to the separate departments of the Administration Office in conformity with the proposals on expenditure set out in the original estimates.

23. The funds provided by the Budget were administered in the departments of the Administration Office to which they had been allocated. These departments sometimes delegated power of expenditure to subordinate units, particularly the Luftgau Headquarters. In turn the Luftgau Headquarters had authority to effect some measure of delegation to their subordinate units, for such purposes as local purchase.

Procedure in War

24. During the war financial control was relaxed to a very great extent. Only an abbreviated and simplified budget was required to be submitted, without details of departmental estimates. General authorisation was given for the appropriation of any funds needed for the prosecution of the war in the air, and the Supreme Command was empowered to act without the use of the financial formalities imposed in peace-time.

PRICE FIXING AND CONTROL

General

25. The imposition of a state system of price control was not a wartime measure in Germany, a Price Commissioner being instituted as early as 1936 and vested with considerable powers in regulating price levels.

26. At first the main function of the Price Commissioner was the regulation of prices of consumer goods but later his chief task changed to that of evolving the guiding principles for price fixing.

27. The principles provided by the work of this Office, especially in the range of consumer goods, met with some success and were carried on without major change into the early period of the war.

Policy and Procedure in War

28. At the beginning of the war emphasis naturally shifted from the sphere of consumer goods to war production, and the difficulties of applying the principles of a peace-time system of price fixing to a war economy soon became apparent. The prices for armament products had to be re-established completely, and an organisation created to deal with price-fixing in a rapidly expanding industry.

29. The advantage of a fixed price system for armament products was clearly understood, but the difficulties of the early war years prevented its adoption. No experience had been accumulated in forming a reliable basis of comparison between plants of varying capacity, but it was imperative that some system should be formed which would not impede industry. Any arbitrary system of fixed prices involved risks: prices fixed at low level would restrict the output of the inefficient producer and, almost equally detrimental, inflated prices would result in large and unjustified profits.

30. Under these circumstances, therefore, there was no alternative to the adoption of a system based on factory costs. This method of price fixing involved two factors:—

(i) The establishment of principles and procedure in determining the factory costs which were to form the bases of prices. It was intended that to the total cost of each product (materials, wages, overhead charges, etc.) a scale of permitted profits should be added, forming thereby an agreed price. This work was embodied in "Guiding Principles for Settling Prime Costs in Public Contracts" (Leitsätze für die Selbstkostenabrechnung bei öffentlichen Aufträgen), known shortly as "L.S.O.".

(ii) The recruitment and training of a staff of price examiners whose responsibility was to be the checking of costing methods of all plants engaged in war production.

31. Despite the inherent defects of any "cost plus" system the L.S.O code, although complex, proved both equitable and workable; in addition, the work of the examining organisation was quite successful in regulating basic prices to a point where excess profits were eliminated.

32. Between 1937 and 1942 the machinery of price fixing and contract examination was controlled by the Supreme Command of the Forces, under the direction of Thomas as Head of the Directorate of Defence Economy and Armaments. When, in 1942, Speer took over the functions previously exercised by Thomas, responsibility for the control of prices was transferred to the Ministry of Armaments and War Production, a Price Control Branch being separately instituted to deal with matters of contract prices. This Branch was eventually absorbed into the Central Office of the Ministry.

33. Speer's main object, after 1942, was to increase German war production, and he considered it essential, in aiding general expansion, to discard the "cost plus" system. A new method of price fixing was, therefore, introduced, consisting of fixed prices arranged in graduated groups.

34. In respect of each general range of products, a committee formed of staff drawn from the Office of the Price Commissioner, the Ministry of Armaments and War Production, and the service concerned was responsible for the calculation of fixed group prices. Three, or even four, price Groups were designed, in each of which a price was fixed for the manufacture

of the same product. Price Group I was the lowest, and succeeding Groups arranged in ascending order, the last, III or IV, being roughly equivalent to the old price calculated on the "cost plus" basis. Each contractor, on his own responsibility and according to the efficiency and capacity of his plant, chose a price group for his products. To make this system attractive to the manufacturer, it was arranged that all profits arising from contracts based on the lowest group price should be tax free, and a similar but graduated relief given for prices lower than those of the highest group. The system was equally attractive to the State because the effect of it was to induce manufacturers to produce their products at the lowest possible cost, thereby ensuring that in the aggregate the State paid the least amount for its armaments.

35. Competition between the different firms in seeking the lowest Group prices was assured by adequate publication of choice of grades, and the established prices were checked every three months with the object of further reduction.

36. It is estimated that by the middle of 1944 the committees had fixed group prices for more than 20,000 products, and in the opinion of Germans closely concerned with production and finance the fixed price system proved eminently satisfactory and speedy in operation.

FINANCE: DEPARTMENTS OF THE LUFTWAFFE

37. Financial administration in the German Air Force was the responsibility of the Air Ministry, two separate Departments being constituted:—
   (i) The Administration Office. The main responsibilities of the Department were:—
      (a) the administration of German Air Force accounts.
      (b) the compilation and administration of the budget.
      (c) the payment of accounts.
      (d) the disbursement of pay to Air Force personnel.
   (ii) The Economics and Finance Office. This office was concerned primarily in dealing with the economic problems arising in the aircraft industry, but its responsibilities also included the general administration of contracts. Concentration of the economic problems of production for the Air Force in this Office was intended, before the Speer organisation became fully operative, to relieve the technical authorities of such tasks and to ensure a fully uniform treatment of difficult economic questions. Even though it was not possible, under the pressure of war, to defer always to economic considerations the Economics and Finance Office was able to make useful contributions to increased production by a study of the various industrial complexes.

CONCLUSION

38. From the foregoing paragraphs two facts of some general importance are worthy of note.

39. First, the emphasis placed by Hitler on the need for air power and the subordination of monetary and financial questions to this end. The National Socialist Government in the early days of the Third Reich was quick to appreciate the importance of air power, not only as a military force, but also as a political weapon, and considerable attention was devoted to the creation of an Air Force. In order to implement the foreign

policy of the Reich such a force was required quickly and in numbers sufficiently imposing to constitute a threat that could not be ignored. To enable rapid development of the Air Force ample funds were allocated, and from its inception the German Air Force was able to expand its striking power without any real financial difficulty.

40. Secondly, the virtual isolation of the Air Force in financial matters. The lack of any co-ordinating authority in controlling and directing German industry has already been commented on at some length, and the Air Force was even further removed from control and restriction than the other two services. This was due, as has already been explained, to the fact that the air was a new weapon and one which was particularly exploited for its political value.

PART 2

CHAPTER IV

SELECTION AND TRAINING OF GERMAN AIR FORCE PERSONNEL EMPLOYED IN SUPPLY AND TECHNICAL POSITIONS

INTRODUCTION	Paragraphs	1—5
SELECTION AND TRAINING OF OFFICERS	,,	6—10
SELECTION OF OFFICERS FOR STAFF COLLEGE	,,	11—16
SPECIALIST ARMAMENT OFFICERS	,,	17
OFFICIALS	,,	18—26
NON-COMMISSIONED OFFICERS AND OTHER RANKS	,,	27—28
CIVILIANS	,,	29—30
EMPLOYMENT OF WOMEN	,,	31—32
CONCLUSION	,,	33

PART 2

CHAPTER IV

SELECTION AND TRAINING OF GERMAN AIR FORCE PERSONNEL EMPLOYED IN SUPPLY AND TECHNICAL POSITIONS

INTRODUCTION.

1. In the German Air Force there were no officers equivalent to the R.A.F. Equipment and Technical Officers. The principle adopted was to train officers in flying duties and then to give them a broad experience in all aspects of the Air Force ancillary services. Thus, it was the flying personnel who were appointed to supply and technical positions. They were, however, seldom kept more than two years in such posts.

2. Officers interrogated in this subject considered the system to be workable in the junior appointments, but in the higher and more important positions there were no real experts who had sufficient grip of the subject to direct the supply and technical services vigorously. All personnel had a superficial knowledge only and specialisation was not encouraged. The consequence was that those at the top accepted the opinion of the mass without critical appreciation of the situation and direction suffered accordingly.

3. During the war there was a great shortage of Air Force officers suitable for appointment to high technical positions. This situation was tackled by the enlistment of engineers from industry and aeronautical research stations. Such people were given the normal officer operational training — though often in an abbreviated form — following which they would rapidly rise to fill important technical vacancies. The number of such officers was very small and amounted to a maximum of 200. These officers should not be confused with the Engineer Corps which is discussed in paragraph 23.

4. Another exception to the rule of non-specialisation was the Armament Officer. More will be said about this branch in the body of this Chapter.

5. It will be seen from the above review that, with the exception of a very small number of engineers and armament officers, there were no specialist supply and technical officers in the German Air Force. Furthermore, even the flying officers who filled these vacancies had little time in which to become thoroughly acquainted with the subject as they were nearly always posted to other duties after a mere two years. The lack of continuity and experience brought about by these conditions was to an extent balanced by the employment in large numbers of Wehrmachtbeamte (Armed Forces civil servants — officials). These officials specialised in certain subjects — supply, engineering and administration for example — and formed a reliable core of experience on which the officers depended very considerably.

SELECTION AND TRAINING OF OFFICERS

6. Young men who wished to be considered for commissioning in the Air Force would apply for employment at reception centres which existed

in every big town. The number of applications in peacetime was very large and a good selection was possible. In the war years, however, the Supreme Command of the Armed Forces made adjustments between the services partly prior to attestation but chiefly after basic military training. Seconding from the Army and Navy was also possible.

7. The candidates for commissions were required to have passed the Abitur examination at the High School (equivalent to having passed School Certificate), to satisfy a medical board, and to pass certain psychological tests. There was said to be no nepotism under the Nazi regime, though it seems that this rule was not always rigidly applied. Commissioning from the ranks was also possible.

8. Those selected as officer cadets were sent to training and reserve units where they were given basic military training for a period varying from 3 to 5 months. After this they proceeded with flying training for a further period of 9 to 12 months — the duration of this period was of course conditioned to some extent by the weather and the aircraft available. The cadet was categorised as fighter, bomber pilot or observer etc., during military basic training or at the latest during the flying training stage. Having completed successfully this 12 to 17 months training the officer cadet was promoted to "Oberfähnrich" (senior ensign) and was sent for a further course of instruction — lasting from one to two years — at the Kriegsschule (War School). There he was given training in air and ground tactics, history of war, armament, meteorology, technical and general education. Flying training was continued and physical development was encouraged by sport and drill. At the end of this course the cadet was promoted to full officer status, subject to having passed successfully the final examination. The above training was sometimes very much shortened to cope with increased demands for personnel — this applied particularly during the last years of the war. Total training in this case would amount to 18 months only so that the "Oberfähnrich" was posted to a unit 18 months after entering the service. After serving 6 months at a unit he would be promoted to officer status on the recommendation of his commanding officer.

9. On his reception at the squadron the young lieutenant (pilot officer) would be given a function, in addition to his flying duties, within the squadron organisation. He became the officer responsible for armament, the technical officer for airframe and engine maintenance and inspection, the squadron signals officer, or the adjutant. The young technical officers were given every opportunity to develop their elementary knowledge of these matters and from time to time they would be posted to short courses on technical and supply subjects. Such courses normally lasted from 8 to 14 days only. Technical courses were given at the G.A.F. Technical Schools (of which there were 6), at factories, or at experimental and research stations. Supply courses were arranged by the Director of Supply and took place generally at Main Depots but sometimes at airparks or even on occasion in Berlin.

10. As they became more experienced the better Squadron Technical Officers would be promoted to Group Technical Officers, Wing Technical Officers, and by the time they were senior captains or majors they might become the Quartermaster of a Fliegerkorps. Those officers who had a particularly pronounced flair for technical or supply work would be posted to appropriate positions as "Referenten" (Heads of branches of the staff) or appointments in the Flughafenbereich (ARC) Luftgau, and Storage Depots.

SELECTION OF OFFICERS FOR STAFF COLLEGE

11. It has already been stated that selected officers were posted to positions as "Referenten" etc. Those who proved their worth in such positions were recommended by their senior officers for training as general staff officers. Officers for the Staff College were selected by the Personnel Department of the Air Ministry and would be posted to the Luftkriegsakademie for a course of 4 to 6 months' duration (2 years in peace). The staff college training was designed to cover the whole field of Air Force activity and the relation with the other two services. The training did not aim at producing a ready made specialist but at turning out officers who were mentally adaptable and thoroughly trained both militarily and generally, and who could after experience during a brief period of probation be asked to cope with new and unaccustomed tasks. Within the General Staff there were specific trades in which the individual officers could to an extent specialise. In order to maintain the principle of versatility it was very exceptional that an officer should remain long in the same trade. The following trades may be distinguished in the General Staff:

(i) Ia Operational Service — Command and Employment of Units.
(ii) Ic Intelligence Service.
(iii) Quartermaster Service. Supply and Organisation.
(iv) Technical Service. This service was seriously neglected.
(v) Signals System — Staff Officer with Sigs. Branch.

12. The aim was to employ the young General Staff Officer first of all in a Quartermaster appointment in order to give him the necessary basis for subsequent service in the Ia department which was the favourite objective of most General Staff Officers. The career of a successful officer would then lead him from a Ia post to a Chief of Staff of a Fliegerkorps or a Luftflotte, which he would attempt to reach through the medium of an appointment as Chief Quartermaster. A constant change between the various types of appointment was aimed at — though there was a tendency to extensive specialisation in the Signals and Intelligence Staffs.

13. It is interesting to note that out of the 109 hours of instruction given at a Staff College course in October 1944, 12 were devoted to Quartermaster Services and 4 to Technology.

14. After passing successfully the leaving examination the aspirants to the General Staff were posted on the recommendation of the Staff College to an appointment in one of the services quoted. After serving a year's probation with acknowledged efficiency he would then be recommended by the head of the department to be a fully qualified General Staff Officer.

15. In the Director of Supply's Office at the Air Ministry there was no establishment for General Staff Officers and, therefore, no such officers could be posted to that office. This was unfortunate because it led to a regrettable lack of understanding about this particular sphere of activity on the part of all General Staff Officers.

16. In the Director General of Equipment's Department there were only two or three places for General Staff Officers. Furthermore, in the first two years of the war only very few first class G.S. officers had filled these positions. The result of this was that aircraft development was very little influenced by the competent military authorities. The gap between the technicians working in this department and the officers was emphasised by the cloak of secrecy with which these specialists surrounded

themselves — consequently, it proved that their labours were often of little military value. It was not until Milch took over the department that matters improved and technical development was more closely guided to war requirements. Even then the relationship between the Chief of the General Staff and Milch was strained.

SPECIALIST ARMAMENT OFFICERS

17.   Armament officers were the only really specialised officers serving in the supply and technical services in the Fliegertruppe of the Air Force. They were known as Waffenoffiziere and wore a distinguishing mark of "W" on their shoulders. The career was limited and the highest rank possible was that of Colonel. Although they had full officer status they were regarded in the mess rather as a tainted race. They handled armaments, explosives, ammunition and war gases but they were seldom found in front line units and were generally employed either in staff posts or in ammunition depots. They were nicknamed the "Einjährige" (those who had failed School Certificate).

OFFICIALS

18.   In the Introduction to this Chapter it was explained that the bulk of the work in the German Air Force was done by officials who specialised in many various subjects. These officials played such an important part in the Air Force organisation that it is necessary to study the system in some detail.

19.   The officials were German State officials and performed much the same function as British Civil Servants. The German State was administered by these individuals and they were found in State appointments from the highest ministerial positions to the lowest menial jobs. A special type of official, known as an Armed Forces Official, had provided the Army and Navy with administrative, professional and technical experts for three centuries and the Air Force, on its formation, somewhat naturally adopted this traditional institution. These Armed Forces Officials cannot be compared with the British civil servants for they were far more deeply integrated with services and, in accordance with the Geneva Convention, were classified as combatants. They expected to, and often did, take part in frontline defensive action. They were neither civilians nor truly soldiers.

20.   There were four categories into which all officials were classified:—
   (i)   "Simple Service". This was a grade approximately equivalent to junior N.C.O.s and Other Ranks and included officials performing such jobs as doormen, firemen and storekeepers. No particular educational requirements were needed to qualify for this grade.
   (ii)   "Middle Service". This was a grade approximately equivalent to Senior N.C.O. It covered officials in supervising positions which required some educational background.
   (iii) "Medium Higher Service". This grade was approximately equivalent to junior officers. Officials in this grade had to have qualifications that would enable them to assume a fair degree of responsibility. They had to have at least a High School education and to have passed the German equivalent of Matriculation.
   (iv)   "Higher Service". This grade was approximately equivalent to senior officers. This was the highest group in the hierarchy of officialdom and to enter it it was necessary to have had a university education or an equivalent degree from a military academy.

All professional and scientific officials belonged to the higher service.

Promotion from category to category was extremely difficult — except from "Simple" to "Middle" — and to reach "Higher Service" from "Medium Higher" usually required considerable qualifications including twenty years' service.

21. Every official regardless of importance had a title which usually described his employment and his rank. For example, Lagermeister (Supervisor of Stores), equivalent to Flight Sergeant; Oberstabsintendant (Chief Staff Administrator) equivalent to Squadron Leader; Oberstingenieur (Colonel Engineer) equivalent to Group Captain.

22. Within the German Air Force, by far the greater part of the technical work and organisation of the following services was in the hands of the officials:

(i)	General Administration:	"Verwaltungsdienst".
(ii)	Construction:	"Bautechnischen Dienst".
(iii)	Meteorology:	"Reichswetterdienst".
(iv)	Law:	"Justizdienst".
(v)	Supply:	"Nachschubwesen".
(vi)	Engineering:	"Ingenieurdienst".
(vii)	Munitions and Armament:	"Waffen- und Munitionsdienst".
(viii)	Aircraft Safety:	"Flugsicherungsdienst".
(ix)	Signals:	"Nachrichtenwesen".
(x)	Telecommunication:	"Fernmeldedienst".
(xi)	Medical Services (limited ext.):	"Sanitätsdienst".
(xii)	Motor Transport:	"Kraftfahrwesen".

23. Officials engaged in technical work would, as far as possible, be selected from people who had had previous experience in the appropriate subjects. In addition, they would be given courses on technical subjects in the Air Force Technical Schools and if it was considered necessary these courses would be supplemented by attaching officials to industrial concerns for short periods. The Engineer Corps, although classified as officials, were governed by regulations somewhat different to those applying to other branches. The Engineers were paid at a higher rate than officials but at a lower rate than officers. Furthermore, engineers could be put into the reserve at any time when there was no suitable employment for them. Officials, on the other hand, were employed for life — normally being pensioned off at the age of sixty-five. To be accepted into the Engineer Corps it was necessary to have a diploma in engineering or to have passed the final examination at a higher technical school and to have had three years' apprenticeship.

24. Officials possessed administrative authority over all those subordinated to them for duty but their military authority was limited to subordinate officials and civilian employees. This division of authority introduced a large degree of confusion and friction as to what constituted a purely military command reserved for officers and what was an administration sphere and, therefore, within the scope of officials.

25. Officials wore German Air Force uniform of a quality appropriate to their equivalent rank but without the insignia of military rank. Those officials who held ranks equivalent to officer status were accorded the privilege of salute from other ranks, they received the precedence of their rank at social but not at military ceremonies, and they were members of

officers' messes. Officers had a higher rate of pay and an improved rate of promotion which caused a certain amount of resentment amongst the officials.

26. The limitation of their command, combined with the lack of the advantages accorded to officers, developed in the minds of the officials a considerable feeling of inferiority. They claimed that because of their unfortunate status they were unable to discharge efficiently the duties with which they were entrusted. This situation developed to such a serious extent that it was realised by the highest authorities that drastic action would have to be taken to rectify the position. Consequently, it was decided in 1944 to form a Special Duties Branch (Truppensonderdienst) to which all officials of equivalent officer rank would be affiliated as officers — not officials — of the Special Duties Branch. At the same time improvements to pay and promotion of officials — or officers as they now were — were promulgated. Furthermore, the officials transferred to the new branch were given authority over all N.C.O.s and other ranks on duty under their direction but their disciplinary powers did not cover regular officers. However, by the end of the war very few officials had become "officers" and it is also doubtful whether the scheme would have been successful for, in spite of the better conditions, it did not really eliminate the feeling of inferiority because the officials were still without military training or command.

NON-COMMISSIONED OFFICERS AND OTHER RANKS

27. In contrast to the officers of the German Air Force, the non-commissioned officers and other ranks were trained as specialists in the various subjects. The trade of particular interest in a study of supply was that of Equipment Assistant and a syllabus of a course given to non-commissioned officers, in this subject, is attached as Appendix "A" to this Chapter.

28. The normal terms of service for non-commissioned officers and other ranks were two years for conscripts and four and a half or twelve years for volunteers. Non-commissioned officers who had been trained as specialists would often, on completion of their twelve years' service, become officials in the Middle Service.

CIVILIANS

29. Civilian employees recruited from German males who were too old or unfit for service, from females, from "voluntary" foreign workers, and from prisoners of war, were used by the German Air Force. Such civilians were governed by the same regulations as those which applied to regular soldiers. They were subject to military law as members attached to the Armed Forces. Furthermore, they carried certain identification of their combatant status.

30. Civilians were categorised in two classes:
   (i) Salaried Workers (Angestellte). These civilians were paid monthly and were employed as assistants to officials and, in some cases, would fill establishment vacancies for officials.
   (ii) Wage Earners (Lohnempfänger). These civilians were paid weekly and were usually employed on manual work.

EMPLOYMENT OF WOMEN

31. All women employed in the German Air Force came within the civilian category and there were no women officers or officials. Even during the war there was no real equivalent to the W.A.A.F. A women's auxiliary corps was organised in 1941 but the members of this corps (Luftwaffen-Helferinnenschaft) did not belong to the Armed Forces but to the civilian element. They were, however, subject to the provisions of the Military Penal Code and to military discipline. A uniform was authorised but it was usually not issued to office workers unless they were serving outside Germany. Grades were established for the Helferinnen which covered a range approximately from Aircraftswomen to Wing Officer but it is emphasised that these were not military ranks.

32. Women were not employed in the services to such a universal extent as they were in this country. Even in the last days of the war, for example, there were no women drivers in the service. Helferinnen were first employed in the Signals units where they were found to be very useful and efficient. It was not until after the second proclamation of total war by Goebbels in July 1944 that the employment of women began to any considerable extent. They were then employed at searchlight and barrage balloon units, and in greater numbers as clerks and typists. In August 1944 the employment of Helferinnen in the technical service was projected and training began in the Autumn but employment in such duties was never effected. A German Staff Officer interrogated in this subject rejected the idea of employing women on the maintenance of aircraft on the grounds of physical weakness and, furthermore, he condemned the employment of women at operational stations as, in his opinion, they undermined unintentionally the morale of the troops! He was, however, very impressed by the skill and dexterity of the W.A.A.F. drivers operating the Prison Camp vehicles.

CONCLUSION

33. The training of officers in the German Air Force was designed:
   (i) To train the officer as extensively as possible;
   (ii) To lead him back again and again to service in the line so that he should not lose contact with operational conditions.

The consequence of this training was that all Air Force officers had a very wide experience but their knowledge in all things was only superficial. A modern Air Force is so technically intricate that specialists are essential. In the German Air Force this specialisation was placed in the hands of "officials". The insertion of this system into the Air Force organisation proved to be exceedingly difficult to manage and although, individually, the officials were efficient, collectively they were a failure.

APPENDIX "A"
to Part. 2. Chap. IV.

TRAINING OF EQUIPMENT ASSISTANTS

1. The following information was obtained from a translation of a syllabus prepared for the training of N.C.O. Equipment Assistants. Similar courses, though in less detail, were given to other rank Equipment Assistants.

2. **Object of the Course**
    Further training of aircraft equipment assistants to enable them to supervise equipment in units, in air parks, and in Depots, and to take charge of stock records. After passing the course successfully they are promoted aircraft equipment Feldwebel.

3. **Duration of the course**
    2 months.

4. **Preliminary Conditions**
    Airmen should have completed prospective N.C.O.'s training and have had at least two years' service as aircraft equipment assistants.

5. **Practical Training**
    (Approx. 1/3 of the whole course.)
    The aim of the course is to give aircraft equipment assistants a comprehensive survey of equipment, replacement parts and consumable materials. Furthermore, to familiarise them with service regulations which concern them as N.C.O.s.
    Practical experience in the following subjects will be given during the course:
    >   Office organisation.
    >   Acceptance and Dispatch procedure.
    >   Accounts.
    >   Storage methods.
    >   Stock Recording.
    >   Function of Air Equipment Groups.

    Technical information will be taught by demonstrations in the instructional workshops.

6. **Theoretical Training**
    (Approx. 2/3 of whole course.)

    (i) **Technical Administration**

    (a) Organisation of the G.A.F.
    Organisation of G.A.F. with regard to supply (Airparks, Main Depots, Equipment Groups, Luftgau, Luftflotte. Directorate of Supply, ground and operational organisations).
    Time: approx. 8% of the theoretical training.

    (b) Equipment Procedures
    Technical administration of materials — regulations, equipment classification, equipment category numbers, indent reference numbers, Channels of supply. Branches of a Main Depot, Air Park and an Equipment Issuing Station.
    Establishments, stock records, material categories.
    Stocktaking of equipment and record of budgetary funds.
    Stock books, card index, reference card index, etc.
    Voucher numbers and supervision of stock records.
    Index inspection lists, index filing, index cards.
    Demand, supply, loan, etc.
    Documents, intake and exchange, etc.
    Taking on charge complete and incomplete sets.
    Examination and inspection.
    Demand through service supply channels, supply in open market.
    Repair circuit for aircraft equipment, fuselage and engine within and outside the station.
    Writing off equipment etc., "write off" permits in peace and war, repair and excess returns.
    Time: Approx. 18% of the theoretical training.

    (c) General Technical Administration
    Duties of the aircraft equipment assistant in different units.
    Duties of authorised deputy aircraft equipment assistants on G.A.F. stations (subordination, service duty, book-keeping).
    Types of documents according to L.Dv. 72 and appendix necessary for routine technical service. Purpose of and correct keeping of documents. Equipment of the Squadron, Gruppe and school, etc.
    Time: Approx. 8% of the theoretical training.

    (d) Financial Administration
    Funds, budgetary funds, cash supervision.
    Bookkeeping during wartime.
    Types of contracts.
    Compilation of accounts, account registers, State Accounts Office, inspection regulations.
    Collective vouchers.
    Time: Approx. 9% of the theoretical training.

(e) Acceptance and dispatch
Dispatch channels (safety, economy, speed, suitability for dispatch), delivery times, insurance.
Duties of transport commanders in war.
Packing, loading, etc.
Accompanying documents, rates.
Dispatch forms (transfer, packing chit, dispatch note, etc.).
Dispatch regulations of state railways, railways goods rates, railway traffic. Armed forces transport regulations.
Time: Approx. 8% of the theoretical training.

(f) Storing and maintenance
Store rooms, safety regulations, fire protection, accident prevention.
Storing and care of aircraft wings, tail units, airscrews, tyres, etc.
Drawing up stores plans.
Taking over engines, transport cases, storing, accessories, etc., inhibiting engines, engine replacement parts.
Storing and care of aircraft servicing equipment (heater, truck, engine pre-heater, starters, jacking equipment, tail wheel trolly, oxygen fillers).
Supervision of aircraft tools.
Storing and care of aircraft instruments.
Storing and treatment of fuels, oils and greases, fuelling installations, etc.
Storing of gases (safety precautions).
Storing of non-metallic materials.
Storing of metals and paints.
Time: Approx. 10% of the theoretical training.

(g) Correspondence and accounts
Regulations governing correspondence.
Unit filing system, types of correspondence, letter headings, secrecy, drafting of letters.
Drafts, duplicating, circulars, distribution lists, reports.
Service seals, stamps, documents, transactions, factual reports, keeping files, (unit filing system).
Personnel entitled to handle classified documents.
Practice in the four arithmetical tables, decimals fractions and percentages.
Length, area, volume and weight, mensuration.
Time: Approx. 12% of theoretical training.

(ii) **Theory of Technical Equipment**
Intensification of general knowledge in aircraft, engines, equipment and servicing equipment, tools, materials and fuels. Latest marks of aircraft engine and other equipment with modifications should be covered.

Theory of Aircraft
New aircraft types and parts with important modifications; fixed and retractable undercarriages, oleo legs and brakes, floats. Starting and landing aids, tail units, controls, rudder trimming. Schematic diagrams, trim regulations.

Theory of Engines
New engines and modifications.
Carburettors and injection pumps.
High altitude engines, boost pressure gauge and blower.
Types of starter, cold starting procedure.
Airscrew reduction gear, adjustable pitch airscrews.

Airframe equipment
Practical instruction in the aircraft instrument workshop on flying instruments, navigation and engine instruments, electrical system, armament, etc.
Time: Approx. 15% of the theoretical training.

(iii) **Theory of Materials and Fuels**
Intensification of general knowledge of tools and fuels.
Materials.
Meaning of standardisation.
Explanation of an alloy.
Characteristics and heat treatment of steels.
Testing procedure.
Corrosion protection of light metal alloys.
Eloxal process, plating.
Plywood and its use in a/c construction.
Glueing aircraft wood.
Fabrics and paints.
Safety glass and perspex.

Fuels
Demand and distribution.
Anti-knock and octane.
Storing qualities of petrols and oils.
Handling of incoming tank lorries, inspection, weighing and measurement.
Determination of density.
Careful handling of fuel.
Time: Approx. 12% of the theretical training.

7. **Examination**
The course terminates with a written and oral examination.

PART 2

CHAPTER V

MOVEMENT

INTRODUCTION	Paragraphs	1— 3
MOVEMENT BY RAIL	,,	4—13
Special Railway Transports	,,	9—13
SEA TRANSPORT	,,	14—17
INLAND WATERWAYS	,,	18
ROAD TRANSPORT	,,	19—24
AIR TRANSPORT	,,	25—39
Organisation of Air Transport in Peace	,,	29—31
Organisation of Air Transport in War	,,	32—34
Number of Air Transport Units	,,	35
Special Air Transport Tasks in the Various Theatres of Operations	,,	36
Types of Transport Aircraft	,,	37
Types of Transport Gliders	,,	38
Analysis of Loads Carried by Air 1939—1945	,,	39
RELATIONSHIP BETWEEN CIVIL AND MILITARY AVIATION	,,	40—44
PERSONNEL	,,	45
CONCLUSION	,,	46—49

PART 2

CHAPTER V

MOVEMENT

INTRODUCTION

1. The movement of equipment, supplies, and personnel to maintain an air force is essentially an "Equipment" matter and, therefore, consideration of the German system forms an integral part of this study of the supply organisation of the German Air Force.

2. The bulk of all movement in support of the German Air Force was effected by rail. Heavy Allied bombing of railway targets was delayed until the late stages of the war and, therefore, no serious setbacks were suffered generally by the Germans in this connection until the final phase. In the Russian campaign, however, difficulties arose continuously in view of the paucity of railway facilities and the fact that the normal communications system lay across and not parallel to the lines of the German advance (see Part 2, Chapter X — Campaign in Ukraine). The major German campaigns of the war were waged on the Continent of Europe and, therefore, sea transport was little used by the Air Force. Supplies for Africa, Norway, and the Greek islands, of course, necessitated the use of sea transport to an extent, but viewed generally shipping was a negligible factor — particularly in comparison with the British and American requirements. According to General Seibt — the Director of Supply — the average proportionate use of the various means of transportation was as follows:—

(i)	Railway:	80%
(ii)	Road:	10%
(iii)	Air:	7%
(iv)	Waterways:	3%

3. The German Air Ministry — the 4th Department of the Quartermaster General's department — controlled all movements matters for the Air Force. Movement by rail and by sea was centrally controlled by the Supreme Command of the Armed Forces (O.K.W.) to whom applications for space were made by the individual services. Road and Air movement (the latter until Spring 1945 only) were controlled by the 4th Department independently from the Supreme Command of the Armed Forces.

MOVEMENT BY RAIL

4. The railway transport system of the German Armed Forces was centrally directed by the Director of Armed Forces Transport at the Supreme Command of the Armed Forces. The Director of Armed Forces Transport exercised control through the following organisations:

    (i) **In Home Areas.** Through two directorates (Armed Forces Transport Directorates), Central at Berlin and South Eastern at Vienna.

    (ii) **In Operational Areas.** Through the General Officers Commanding Transport at the various Army Groups — Army Group North, Army Group West, Army Group Central, Army Group South, etc.

The territory of the directorates and of the Army Groups was divided into Transport Commands which matched the civil railway districts.

5. Railway movement for the Air Force was directed by Section III of the 4th Department. This Section exercised control through the Luftflotten (Chief Quartermaster, Section Qu. 3), the Luftgau (Quartermaster, Section Qu. 3), and through liaison officers. To ensure direct and informed collaboration with the various transport authorities Air Force liaison officers were attached to the Director of Armed Forces Transport (O.K.W.), to the Armed Forces Transport Directorates or G.O.C.'s Transport, and to the Transport Commands. These liaison officers were subordinated as follows:—

(i) **Liaison officer to Director of Armed Forces Transport.** Subordinated in every respect to the Air Ministry 4th Department.

(ii) **Liaison officer to Directorate of G.O.C.'s Transport.** Subordinated for operational purposes to the Air Ministry 4th Department and for discipline, rations, and pay to the territorially appropriate Luftflotte.

(iii) **Liaison officers to the Transport Commands.** Subordinated in every respect to the territorially appropriate Luftgau H.Q.

6. The 4th Department was responsible for calculating the Air Force requirements for railway trucks and it would submit the commitments to the Director of Armed Forces Transport. This authority then allotted to the Air Force a quota of trains for the following 14 days, and the 4th Department in turn allocated these to the appropriate users.

7. A distinction was made between the following types of transport, and the channels for notifying requirements varied according to the nature of the transport or consignments.

(i) **Troop Transports.** Troop transports existed in two categories — normal and priority. Priority troop transports could only be ordered by Air Ministry departments (Operations Staff and Specialist Air Officers — Waffengenerale) and application for the priority was made by the 4th Department either to the Director of Armed Forces Transport or to the Armed Forces Transport Directorates according to the general transport situation. For example, the order of Ia.Ops of Air Ministry General Staff to move a Parachute Division in a priority train would have been announced immediately it was received to the Director of Armed Forces Transport through the Air Force liaison officer who would authorise it. Meanwhile, the unit would have notified its requirements to the Luftgau Quartermaster (Qu. 3) who would have checked the requirements and then have informed the 4th Department of the precise needs. The 4th Department would then have placed this demand before the Director of Armed Forces Transport in completion of the previous notice.

(ii) **Supply Transports.** Supply transports existed in four categories:—
  (a) Normal — commonly known as LE trains.
  (b) Controlled transports — commonly known as LU trains. This was a slightly higher priority than normal. LU trains included the following: LU-F for Flak, Ammunition, LU-A for Bombs, LU-B for P.O.L., LU-N for general goods such as coal.
  (c) Transport of empty waggons required for immediate use. Similar priority to LU.

(d) Arrow trains. These trains had a very high priority which could only be granted by the Director of Armed Forces Transport.

The LU and arrow trains were checked through from stage to stage and progress reports were submitted to the Luftflotte Chief Quartermasters and to the 4th Department. The practice of running LU trains in place of ordinary LE trains increased enormously in the latter years of the war as shortages in every direction became more and more evident.

(iii) **Individual Supply Transports.**

All supply transports travelled in the form of complete trains. Before December 1944 a complete train consisted of a minimum of 21 waggons, after that date the minimum was raised to 30 waggons. Supply transports of less numbers than the minimum were despatched under the system known as individual supply transports. Special code-name supply transports also travelled by this method — e.g. "Ramme" for special ammunition and special fuel, and "Condor" for signals equipment in short supply. The individual supply transports were divided into two categories:—

(a) Transports in raid free areas. These were arranged between the applicant, the Luftgau, and the Transport Command, without reference to any higher authority.

(b) Transports in vulnerable areas. In this case the approval of the Air Force liaison officer to the Armed Forces Transport Directorates or G.O.C.'s Transport had to be given. Individual supply transports in vulnerable areas were organised on a quota basis and only a certain number of waggons per train were permitted.

8. A card index system was kept in the 4th Department to record the time of arrival empty, the departure, the contents, and the time of arrival at destination of every train ordered by the branch.

Special Railway Transports

9. It was the task of the Luftflotten to withdraw whatever units, supplies and installations had to be evacuated during retreats. The directions as to what should be evacuated, and in the case of installations, to what new location they were to be withdrawn, were issued by the 4th Department after consultation with the Operations Staff and the Director of Supply. The requirements for railway transport space were calculated by the 4th Department and were submitted to the Director of Armed Forces Transport who would sanction allocations in accordance with the space available after consideration had been given to the demands of the Army and civil authorities. If the quota received by the Air Force was less than its needs then the 4th Department had to establish the necessary priorities. In the case of retreats all trains were directed by the 4th Department.

10. Preparations were made to provide special transport trains in anticipation of invasion either in the North or West by the Allies. "Imminent Danger" was the code word for invasion and the special transports were known as Imminent Danger trains. Special time tables were arranged by the 4th Department to support the needs of the Air Force in countering such a situation.

11. In the early years of the war special mobile quartermaster reserves were set aside. These reserves consisted of truck loads of aviation fuel, bombs, and Flak ammunition made up into trains which were deployed in the East, West and South. Such trains were parked in sidings at small stations in the direction of these fronts to be used when unforeseen and urgent demands were made by units. These reserves were in addition to the allocations made regularly to the Luftflotten and could only be released on the authority of the 4th Department.

12. Aircraft fuel and lubricants for use by the Air Force were transported by rail in railway tank waggons which were the property of the Air Force. The employment of these waggons was directed by the 4th Department. Towards the end of the war the tank waggon space which was owned by the Air Force was transferred to railway authorities.

13. The 4th Department also controlled the command trains which were used as mobile headquarters for important staffs. Two such trains were used by "Robinson" (Air Ministry Advanced Headquarters) in the battle area — they were equipped with offices and sleeping quarters.

SEA TRANSPORT

14. It was explained in the Introduction to this Chapter that shipping played but a small part in the supply of the German Air Force. If the nature of the war fought by the Germans is considered this fact will be more readily appreciated. The only occupied territory that had to be almost continuously supplied by sea was Norway — and the Air Force commitments in that area were very small. In the Russian theatre the Black Sea was used to a small extent to support the Ukraine operation and in the North the Baltic was used to a somewhat larger degree, particularly in the final phases of the battles in Kurland (Latvia, Estonia and Lithuania) and East Russia. The largest use of sea transport was made during the African campaign. The majority of German battles were fought on the Continent of Europe and, therefore, the problem of moving material and personnel by sea was in no way comparable to our own problems.

15. All sea transport arrangements for the three Services were centrally controlled at the Supreme Command of the Armed Forces (O.K.W.) by a staff which was known as the O.K.W. Home Staff for Overseas, until the end of the African campaign, shortly after which it was renamed the O.K.W. Home Staff for Scandinavia. Under the latter title it performed the same duties as hitherto but in a more restricted area. The Headquarters of the O.K.W. Home Staff was near Berlin and it had branch offices to deal with local affairs in various appropriate areas such as Norway, Kurland, and Italy. The actual acquisition of shipping space was undertaken by a government office called the Commissioner for Shipping. This office was in Hamburg and was managed throughout the war by an individual known as Gauleiter Kaufmann. On instructions from the O.K.W. Home Staff Kaufman would requisition ships from the merchant navy and private firms and put them at the disposal of the Armed Forces. For the African campaign Italian shipping was used and this was arranged by Kaufman with the Italian Government.

16. All Air Force demands for shipping were put to the O.K.W. Home Staff by the 4th Department and Air Force liaison officers were posted as embarkation officers to all important ports when these were being used for the shipment of Air Force materials or personnel. The number of such

embarkation officers fluctuated, of course, with the necessity for this work. Shipping questions at Luftflotte and Luftgau levels were handled by the respective Qu. 3. sections.

17. In addition to shipping space obtained through the O.K.W. Home Staff organisation, the Air Force also owned its own ships. The types of ships owned by the Air Force were limited to a small number of tankers (about 30 of these varying between 250 and 700 tons capacity) for the movement of aviation fuel and small craft for air sea rescue. This shipping was controlled by the German Air Ministry and the departments concerned were the Inspector for Sea Matters and the 4th Department, both of whom worked together in close collaboration.

INLAND WATERWAYS

18. Movement of Air Force war materials by inland waterways was avoided as far as possible because of the extreme slowness of this method of transportation. When required, arrangements for transport by inland waterways were made by the railway transport authorities — Armed Forces Transport Directorates — to whom applications were made by the Qu. 3. section of Luftflotte and Luftgau without reference to the 4th Department.

ROAD TRANSPORT

19. In addition to unit establishments of motor transport the Air Force had at its disposal a number of Transport Columns. These columns were controlled by the 4th Department but were allocated to the Luftflotte. A small reserve was retained by the 4th Department — this reserve was attached to Luft III (Berlin) for employment after bombing attacks or for urgent allocation to Luftflotte to assist in particular emergencies. The columns allocated to a Luftflotte were entirely at the disposal of that command and the Luftflotte could deploy them as it wished — normally it allocated some to the Luftgau and some to the Airfield Regional Command. The 4th Department had the right — which it often exercised — to withdraw columns from one Luftflotte and transfer them to another where the need was greater. The Luftflotten were required to render a monthly report to the 4th Department showing how the columns were being employed and the state of serviceability of the vehicles. Within the Luftflotte area Transport Columns were controlled at Luftflotte and Luftgau by the respective Qu.Mot. sections and at Airfield Regional Command by 1.b.KOL.

20. At the beginning of the war the transport columns were employed mainly in the advanced areas but in the final phases they were moved more and more in the Reich territory to supplement railway traffic which had been dislocated by Allied bombing. At the peak period of German Air Force equipment strength (1944) the total lift by Transport Columns was approximately 30,000 tons and this represented about 10% of the total Air Force lift by motor transport.

21. The Transport Columns were of two functional types:—
   (i) **"Transport Columns"** which were chiefly engaged in carrying bombs, ammunition, rations and construction materials. These columns were generally made up of 20—40 vehicles each on the average with a capacity of 3 tons.
   (ii) **"Fuel Columns"** which were tank lorries for carrying aviation P.O.L. The size of such columns was normally 14 vehicles each with a capacity of 4,000 litres (= 880 gallons).

22. The composition of the Air Force Transport Columns varied in three ways — Air Force transport, N.S.K.K. transport and Speer transport.

   (i) **German Air Force Transport.**
These were Air Force owned vehicles which were driven by airmen.

   (ii) **N.S.K.K. Transport.**
The National Socialist Motor Transport Corps (National Socialist Kraftfahr Korps) was an organisation developed in peacetime to train a cadre of drivers and motor transport mechanics. Although ostensibly a civilian organisation it was developed on the leadership principle common to all Nazi movements and various ranks and leaders were appointed within the N.S.K.K. so that a graded institution was formed to resemble a military system. N.S.K.K. did not own large numbers of vehicles but sufficient to achieve its purpose, which was training. During wartime, regiments of this corps were attached to the armed forces to supplement the strength of drivers — a brigade of the N.S.K.K. was permanently attached to the Air Force throughout the war. It is emphasised, however, that the N.S.K.K. supplied only drivers and mechanics and had no vehicles of their own but drove and maintained service transport. The N.S.K.K. worked under its own leaders within the framework of the Air Force. There were two types of N.S.K.K. columns:

     (a) Pure N.S.K.K. Columns. These consisted of German personnel only and were used for special purposes — such as the transport by road of flying bombs.

     (b) Mixed Columns. These consisted of 20% key German personnel and 80% foreign "volunteers" (Flemings, Walloons, Frenchmen, Italians, etc.)

   (iii) **Speer Transport Columns.**
These columns were made up of vehicles belonging to the organisation Todt (construction organisation latterly subordinated to the Speer Ministry of Armaments and War Production) which were manned by civilians. Such columns were not permanently attached to the Air Force but loaned to assist in particularly difficult situations.

23. The military status of the N.S.K.K. and Speer Column drivers attached to the Air Forces was "Armed Forces Followers". As such they were governed by the regulations applying to regular soldiers, were subject to military law, were sworn in with the German oath of loyalty for soldiers and carried certain identifications of their combatant status.

24. The proportionate use of Air Force, N.S.K.K., and Speer Transport Columns was in the ratio of:—

        80% : 15% : 5%

AIR TRANSPORT

25. In peacetime the Air Force authorities considered the main object of air transport to be the movement and immediate support of Parachute Troops. A secondary object was to increase the mobility of flying units by using air transport to a limited degree. It was appreciated that airborne operations would only take place occasionally and that the demand for appropriate aircraft would fluctuate according to the presentation of suitable opportunities. Consequently, only a small cadre of transport aircraft were set aside for this particular purpose and these were to be supplemented by aircraft drawn from training establishments immediately prior to specific airborne operations. A small number of transport aircraft

was also allocated to the various Luftflotte and units within these commands for the movement of flying units.

26. The peacetime scheme was facilitated by the universal use of the Ju. 52 both for air transport and for training bomber pilots. The system was, however, designed for blitz operations of short duration and worked well in such short isolated campaigns as the annexation of Czechoslovakia and the invasions of Poland, France and Norway. But under the strain of ever increasing setbacks and the prolongation of the war the system gradually began to break down and the need for airborne operations was superceded by the urgency of air supply both to the Air Force and the Army. The small allocation of aircraft to the Luftflotte was insufficient for the unprecedented commitments that now arose. From late 1941 onwards, therefore, there were frequent organisational changes in the management of air transport — all directed to further its efficient employment and to concentrate control so that aircraft could be switched instantly to the most vital focal points. Although there were many changes of organisation, in the field, the supreme control was vested in the 4th Department until Spring 1945. At this time responsibility was transferred from the 4th Department to a newly-formed department called the Armed Forces Air Transport Directorate. This office had the status of an O.K.W. Department but it actually functioned as a part of the Air Ministry. The object of this new organisation was to give increased emphasis on the importance of air transport to services other than the Air Force and in this way it was hoped that greater assistance would be available for the retreating army. In the short life of this department no great improvements were noticed — probably because it was never truly severed from the Air Ministry.

27. It is interesting to note that approximately 700,000 tons of material and personnel were moved by air during the course of the war.

28. The following paragraphs will cover briefly the organisational changes referred to above, an outline of important special tasks undertaken by air transport, the types of aircraft used and their capacities, and the relationship between military and civil aviation during the war.

Organisation of Air Transport in Peace

29. The development of the newly established Parachute Corps made it necessary for the German Air Force to have at its disposal its own air transport facilities which could ferry parachute formations and bring them into action. In consequence, the first Air Transport Group was formed on 1st April 1938 at Fürstenwalde, Spree, under the name "Special Bomber Group 1". The new unit was an offshoot of No. IV Hindenburg Bomber Wing, 39 of whose Junker 52 aircraft it took over. The steady expansion of the Parachute Corps made necessary the formation of another Group at Brandenburg/Briest on 2nd August 1938 under the name "Special Bomber Group 2". In addition, and with a view to ultimate mobilisation, preparations were made to form further Ju. 52 formations for parachute and airborne operations. These formations, which were also to bear the name "Special Bomber Groups", were to draw their personnel and aircraft from the establishments of the training schools. These Special Bomber Groups were placed under the command of the 7th Fliegerdivision, together with the entire Parachute Corps.

30. The Special Bomber Groups were used at the time of the incorporation of Austria into the Reich and during the occupation of the

Sudetenland, practice parachute jumps and airborne landings being carried out at Freudenthal, Sudetenland. Parachute troops were again used during the occupation of Czechoslovakia, when airborne landings were made at Prague. The existing Special Bomber Groups were reinforced for this purpose by mobilizing further formations drawn from the Aircrew (Pilot) Training Schools. Shortly before the outbreak of the war No. 1 Special Bomber Wing was formed with four Groups. Groups I and II already existed in peacetime; Groups III and IV were newly formed from communications Squadrons and training schools. A further Special Bomber Wing was formed from the training schools on a wartime mobilisation basis. The strength of the Groups was increased to four Squadrons of 12 aircraft and a headquarters flight of 5 aircraft each — a total of 53 aircraft — so as to meet the requirements in terms of air transport of a parachutist or airborne Battalion.

31. The sole purpose envisaged was airborne or parachute landings, or alternatively the movement of troops to the combat area. No plans were made for the supplying of land forces by air; nor was it necessary to envisage the transport of flying units by air, as they disposed of transport facilities of their own.

Organisation of Air Transport in War

32. The whole of air transport came under the direct control of the 4th Department which directed the planning of operations or the temporary attachments of one unit to another according to requirements. The Special Bomber Groups were, to begin with, assigned to the 7th Fliegerdivision, which on account of the expansion of the parachute corps changed its name to the XI Fliegerkorps, while the units themselves came under the command of the A.O.C. XI Fliegerkorps. This command was concerned solely with parachute and airborne missions. Early in the war, however, transport of supplies and movement of entire units proved necessary and to a degree greater than had been anticipated in peacetime appreciations. For this special purpose, a separate Air Transport Command was set up at the beginning of 1940, which was also provided with Special Bomber Groups for the execution of its tasks. The name "Air Transport Command" was changed to "Air Transport Leader" in October 1941. For supply purposes the air transport units were attached to Luftflotten or Fliegerkorps as occasion demanded. The Air Transport Leader was in the first place concerned with the operational readiness and with the inspection of Special Bomber Groups, and was only temporarily charged with the directing of more important Air Supply operations which normally were controlled by the 4th Department.

33. In May 1943 the XIV Fliegerkorps came into existance. All transport units at home, as well as the liaison and air ambulance units, were subordinated to this Fliegerkorps. For operational purposes, units outside Reich territory continued to be under the command of the Luftflotten or Fliegerkorps in whose areas of command air transport forces under Air Transport Leader or Wing staffs were employed. At the same time the post of Air Officer for Transport Aircraft was created, the holder being at the same time A.O.C. XIV Fliegerkorps. Also, in May 1943, the Special Bomber Groups changed their names to Air Transport Groups and were reformed into Wings. In addition, airfield servicing companies were permanently attached and remained with the air transport units when these moved to new bases.

34. Through lack of personnel, a number of air transport units were disbanded in Summer, 1944. On 1st October 1944 the XIV Fliegerkorps and the Air Transport Leaders, and all Wing staffs, were disbanded and all units were again placed under the complete control of the various commands (Luftflotten, Fliegerkorps). In Spring 1945, the post of Armed Forces Air Transport Chief was created as a separate department of the Air Ministry to deal with all matters of air supply throughout the Armed Forces. The responsibilities of the department were:—
   (i) Supplying of ground forces by air.
   (ii) Issuing of directions in matters related to supply by air.
   (iii) Inspection of air transport formations.

Number of Air Transport Units

35. On 1st May, 1944 the total of Air Transport Units amounted to:—
   2 Air Transport Leader staffs.
   6 Wing staffs.
   24 Air Transport Groups, consisting of:—
      14 Groups (Ju. 52).
      4 Groups (SM. 82).
      1 Group (SM. 81).
      2 Groups (Me. 323).
      1 Group (He. 111).
      1 Group (Leo. 451).
      1 Composite reserve Group consisting of:—
         SM 79.   SM 81.
         SM 82.   Me 323
         Ar 232.   Fiat G 12.
   5 independent Squadrons, consisting of:—
      3 Squadrons (sea)   (Ju. 52).
      1 Squadron   (Fiat G. 12).
      1 Squadron   (Pi 108).

Special Air Transport Tasks in the Various Theatres of Operations

36. (i) **War against Poland and period up to 1st April 1940.**

The total of air transport amounted to 2 Wings of 4 Groups, which were under the command of 7th Fliegerdivision. Owing to the advantageous development of operations planned, parachute operations were not carried out. There were only some airborne operations against the Lodz area performed by the 22nd Infantry Division from bases in Silesia. On the Polish southern front it became necessary for the first time to supply tank spearheads, and some advanced flying units, by air transport. Movement of flying units took place on a minor scale only. At the end of the Polish war Groups mobilised from training schools were returned to these schools, but their organisation into Squadrons was retained so that they could be reformed at any time with a minimum of delay. No. 1 Special Bomber Wing consisting of Groups I and II remained as an operational formation. In December 1939, the III and IV Groups were also reassembled.

(ii) **Norwegian Campaign.**

All air transport units (about 10 to 12 Groups) were under the command of Chief of Air Transport-Land. Sudden occupation of key positions in Denmark and Southern Norway by parachute and airborne units took place, and subsequently transport of supplies to Southern

Norway and from there to Central and Northern Norway, where Narvik became a focal point of the air supply system. After 8 or 10 days the bulk of these units was withdrawn as a preparatory measure for a western campaign. Only one Special Bomber Group was left behind for current air transport from the Continent to Norway and from the south to the north of that country.

(iii) **Occupation of Holland, Belgium and Western Campaign.**

For the carrying out of parachute and airborne operations in order to occupy Holland and Eben-Emael between 10th and 14th May 1940, all units were attached to 7th Fliegerdivision: 3 Wings of 4 Groups each and 1 Group for towing transport gliders. The operations were carried out between 10th and 14th May 1940. From 15th May 1940 No. 1 Special Bomber Wing was attached to Luftflottes 2 and 3 for the transport of supplies to Belgium and France. At the same time most of the Special Bomber Groups were withdrawn to the Aircrew (Pilot) Schools.

(iv) **Balkan Campaign.**

All units under command of XI Fliegerkorps.

Important Missions:—

    Movement of 22nd Inf. Division (parts) from Vienna to Bulgaria and Rumania.
    Seizure of Corinth Isthmus by parachute units.
    Supply transports to Crete from 20th May to 15th June 1941, carried out by a total of 3 Wings with some 12 to 14 Groups.

(v) **Russia.**

Transport units subordinate to Luftflotten and Fliegerkorps.

Special missions:—

    Supply missions for Demjansk and Cholm pockets, in Winter 1941/42.
    Supply transports during advance to Stalingrad and Caucasus in Summer 1942.
    Supplying of Stalingrad fortress from 22nd November 1942 to 2nd February 1943.
    Supplying Kuban bridgehead from 5th February to 1st April 1943.
    Supplying Crimean peninsula from October 1943 to April 1944.
    Air supply of 6th and 8th Armies in Winter 43/44.
    Air supply of 1st Panzer Army and of Tarnopol from 26th March to 10th April 1944.
    Evacuation of the Crimean peninsula from 18th April to 12th May 1944.

(vi) **Campaign in Africa.**

Transport units attached to Luftflotten and Fliegerkorps. Missions carried out under the direction of Air Transport Leader—South:—
Supply transports to Africa.
Supply and evacuation of Tunisia in Spring 1943.

(vii) **Italy.**

Special Missions:—

    Reinforcement of own ground-fighting units in Sicily by parachutists, July 1944 (7 Groups).
    Evacuation of Sardinia and Corsica in September 1944.

(viii) **Balkans.**

Supply and evacuation of Crete and Aegean Isles and of the Balkans from July till November 1944.

(ix) **France.**

Supplying Atlantic and Channel fortresses from July 1944 to April 1945.

(x) **Defence of Reich Territory.**

Transport squadrons attached to Luftflotten and Fliegerkorps.

Chief engagements:—

    Air Supply Budapest.
    ,,   ,,   Breslau.
    ,,   ,,   Glogau.
    ,,   ,,   Graudenz.
    ,,   ,,   East Prussia.
    ,,   ,,   Schneidemühl.
    ,,   ,,   Posen.
    ,,   ,,   Berlin.
    ,,   ,,   Army Group B in the Ruhr.

Types of Transport Aircraft

37. (i) **Ju 52**

This aircraft became the most frequently used transport aircraft during the whole war. It fulfilled without essential changes in construction all demands of parachute and airborne operations, troop-carrying and supply transports and movements of flying units. Its advantages lay in its good flying qualities, its capacity for instrument flying, easy maintenance, and solid construction; its disadvantages were its lack of speed and armament. Since enemy fighter and anti-aircraft defence increased steadily, sorties could be carried out only under the cover of night, bad weather conditions or heavy fighter escort. Disposable load: 2 tons.

(ii) **Ju 252**

This was a development of the Ju. 52, all-metal aircraft, which on account of lack of raw material was not mass-produced. This type was especially suited for transport purposes because of the good loading facilities through the fuselage hatch. Disposable load: 3.5 tons — 4 tons.

(iii) **Ju 352**

This aircraft was of composite construction and was mass-produced on a small scale after 1944. Not reliable for flying with instruments. Disposable load: 3.5 tons — 4 tons.

(iv) **He 111**

Not often used for air transport, owing to small loading space. Chiefly used for dropping supplies. Disposable load: 1.5 tons — 2 tons commercial load.

(v) **Ar 232 and Ar 432**

Series production on small scale as an experiment. Well suited for air transport. Disposable load: 4 tons.

(vi) **Me 323**

A development of Me. 321 (transport glider). Suitable for transport because of large loading capacity, but lacking in solid construction and adequate defences. Not reliable in instrument flying. Disposable load: 10 to 12 tons.

(vii) **Fw 200, Ju 90, Ju 290**

Seldom used for transport missions, since required for other purposes.

(viii) **Italian Transport Aircraft**

These were only used because of lack of German transport aircraft. Not very serviceable except for the SM. 82, which could be used under some conditions. Available were:

SM. 82.
SM. 81.
SM. 79.
Fiat G. 12.
Piaggio 108.

Types of Transport Gliders

38. (i) **Dfs 230.** — disposable load 10 men or 1 ton.
Towing plane: Ju. 87; Do. 17; Ju. 52.
Used for airborne missions and supply transports.

(ii) **Go 242.** — disposable load 22 men or 2.2 tons.
Towing plane: He. 111.
Used for transport of supplies.

(iii) **Me 321.** — disposable load 8 to 10 tons.
Towing planes: He. 111 (towed 3 Me. 321's).

(iv) **He 110.** — Used for transport missions on small scale only.

Analysis of Loads Carried by Air: 1939—1945

39. Total load carried by transport units from outbreak of war until 31st March 1945 was as follows:—

(i) **Transports to front:**

341,648	missions.
289,030,566	kilometres flown.
71,591.4 tons	ammunition.
73,844,448 ltr.	petrol = 54,644.8 tons.
50,758.8 tons	aircraft equipment.
321,236.3 tons	other equipment.
34,497 tons	Army freight.
1,448,940	persons.

(ii) **Flights in evacuations and rearward movements**

657,740	wounded.
541,100	persons.
49,892.1 tons	war materials.

In performing the above missions 582,576,993 litres of petrol (= 432,238.2 tons) were consumed.

RELATIONSHIP BETWEEN CIVIL AND MILITARY AVIATION

40. In Germany all civil aviation was under the control of the Lufthansa Company which was a private commercial enterprise. Before the war the capital of this company amounted to 25 million Reichsmarks,

26 per cent of which was owned by the Reich and administered by the Air Ministry. The remaining 74 per cent was in the possession of municipalities, provinces, banks, traffic enterprises, etc. During the war, the increase of the share-capital of the German Lufthansa up to 50 million Reichsmarks, which had already been decided upon before the war, was carried through. By this action the share of the Reich was also increased. The German Lufthansa was exclusively responsible for all regular German air traffic. Before the beginning of any working-year the German Lufthansa had to submit a schedule of the proposed air lines to the German Air Ministry for approval. When putting up this schedule it had to consider as far as possible the wishes of all circles interested in communications and economic matters as well as of the German Ministries, i.e. German Ministry for Foreign Affairs, German Ministry for Economics, and above all the German Post Office. In view of the good co-operation carried on for many years between the Air Ministry and the German Lufthansa, difficulties in drawing up the air line schedules never arose. The submitted schedules were accepted almost in every case by the German Air Ministry without changes. On the basis of these schedules the German Lufthansa received the order to carry on air traffic on the proposed air lines. There was no direct supervision of the German Lufthansa by the Air Ministry or any other official authority, but there were officials of the Air Ministry on the Boards of Directors and on the financial sub-committee of the Lufthansa.

41. Before the war, the Lufthansa ran services connecting the traffic and economic centres of Germany with each other, with the capitals of the European continent and with the east coast of South America. The services to foreign countries were mostly flown on the basis of direct and independent pool agreements between the Lufthansa and the foreign air traffic companies concerned. They were, however, in principle based on the air traffic and air lines agreements, which were concluded between the German Air Ministry and the competent air authorities of the foreign governments.

42. As a consequence of the war, the air lines were considerably reduced and the lines to South America and to Western Europe had to be given up immediately. As a result of the necessary fuel economy, the requisitioning of equipment and the calling-up of flying personnel, the remaining continental air communications system had also to be limited to those air lines which were of the greatest political, economic and postal importance. The type of aircraft most generally employed on these continental lines was the Ju 52, but some FW 200s (Condor), DC. 3s (Douglas) and smaller types were also used. At the end of 1944 or early in 1945 the following lines were still regularly flown:—

    Berlin — Königsberg — Helsinki.
    Berlin — Stockholm.
    Berlin — Copenhagen — Oslo.
    Berlin — Stuttgart — Madrid — Lisbon.
    Berlin — Munich — Milan.
    Berlin — Prague — Vienna — Belgrade — Salonika — Athens.
    Vienna — Budapest — Bukarest.
    Vienna — Belgrade — Istanbul.
    Vienna — Agram.

The routes were mostly flown 6 times weekly. Later on, this figure was reduced to 4 times or 3 times or twice weekly.

43. The Army air mail lines set up in the East were military installations and were not subordinate to the civilian aviation authorities.

44. At the request of the Department or, later, of the Director of Air Transport of the Armed Forces, the German Lufthansa had to place personnel and material at the disposal of the air transport units to a considerable extent.

PERSONNEL

45. Personnel employed in "Movements" appointments were German Air Force officers usually of the older types. An endeavour was made to employ people who had had previous experience in transport work. Courses of about four weeks' duration were arranged by the Supreme Command of the Armed Forces (O.K.W.) to train personnel for "Movements" work.

CONCLUSION

46. The head of the 4th Department stated during an interrogation that the central control of rail and sea movements was efficient. His only criticism was that the departments of the Supreme Command of the Armed Forces were manned largely by Army officers and that this encouraged a lack of impartial treatment which did not help the Air Force.

47. Most of the movements of the Air Force war materials and personnel were effected by rail. The railway network — with the exception of that in the Russian theatre — was efficient and it was not until Summer 1944 that Allied bombing began to cause serious interruption. As the German forces retreated from all sides to the homeland so their lines of communication naturally grew shorter. This, however, was not an advantage because, at the same time, more concentrated targets were presented to the Allied bombers and, finally, the weight of bombardment from the air grew so great that by March 1945 rail movement was almost at a standstill.

48. Losses of motor vehicles and transport aircraft, coupled with serious shortages of petrol, coincided with the chaotic conditions of the railways and no considerable assistance could be given, therefore, by these forms of transport.

49. The breakdown of transportation in the last year of the war was brought about by the deterioration in the general war situation and cannot, therefore, be attributed to organisational weaknesses.

PART 2

CHAPTER VI

MOTOR TRANSPORT

INTRODUCTION	Paragraphs	1—2
MOTOR TRANSPORT ORGANISATION IN THE GERMAN AIR FORCE	,,	3—8
SUPPLY OF MOTOR TRANSPORT VEHICLES	,,	9—11
REPAIR AND SUPPLY OF SPARE PARTS	,,	12—13
SALVAGE OF MOTOR TRANSPORT VEHICLES	,,	14—15
MOTOR TRANSPORT FUEL	,,	16
MOTOR TRANSPORT TYRES	,,	17
CONCLUSION	,,	18—19

PART 2

CHAPTER VI

MOTOR TRANSPORT

INTRODUCTION

1. At the beginning of the war there was no control of Motor Transport by the Supreme Command of the Armed Forces (O.K.W.). The Army was the main user and, as such, provisioned Motor Transport vehicles for all three Services. During the course of the war the increasing shortage of vehicles and petrol made it necessary to establish a central committee to consider the problems thus created. This committee was formed under the authority of the Supreme Command and it was the nucleus around which the Directorate of Armed Forces Motor Transport was formed in April 1944 when it was decided to divorce joint control of Motor Transport from the War Office. The whole production of the German motor industry was then to the order of the military authorities and was controlled by the Supreme Command of the Armed Forces (O.K.W.) — the Director of Motor Transport. Allocation of vehicles, not only to the three services but also to para-military and civilian organisations, were made by this department — and in all cases the highest priority was given to the Army. Vehicles procured from Occupied Territories and captured from the enemy were also allocated in this fashion. The provisioning of spare parts and the control of major repair workshops for all organisations — both service and civilian — were handled by the Chief of Repair Services who was subordinated to the Director of Armed Forces Transport.

2. The object of concentrating in the Supreme Command the absolute authority for all motor transport matters was to ensure priority for the services, to prevent the three services competing against one another for production, to achieve a certain measure of standardization and to avoid duplication of staffs. It was also considered that, by removing the department concerned with Motor Transport from the War Office and establishing a Directorate of Motor Transport within the Supreme Command of the Armed Forces, a greater weight of authority would be exercised and a broader and more impartial view of the situation would be introduced.

MOTOR TRANSPORT ORGANISATION IN THE GERMAN AIR FORCE

3. The Directorate of Motor Transport of the German Air Force was set up in September 1943 as a department under the Quartermaster General. Its establishment came as the logical consequence of the need to centralise the control of Motor Transport under one authority within the Air Ministry. Three separate Air Ministry authorities had previously had a hand in the management of Motor Transport and the story of their unification under one chief and of the underlying reasons for the consequent changes falls into three sections:

(i) **From the beginning of the war until the end of the first Winter in Russia, 1941/42.** During this period the control of the supply of Motor Transport to the Luftflotten was exercised by the Supply Office of the Director General of Equipment. A second authority,

(ii) **From the Spring of 1942 till the establishment of the Directorate of Motor Transport in September 1943.** During this period the 6th Department of the General Staff assumed control of the allocation of vehicles to the Luftflotten, and the Supply Office of the Director General of Equipment, which in March 1943 had become Director of Supply and had been transferred to the authority of the Quartermaster General, carried out the instructions issued by this Department. Inspectorate 6 continued to exercise the functions outlined under sub-paragraph (i).

(iii) **From September 1943 until the end of the war.** Control during this period in respect of allocation and supply of vehicles, training and turning to account experiences relating to Motor Transport in the various theatres of war, passed to the new Directorate of Motor Transport. The 4th Department of the General Staff, which was responsible for the allocation of supplies, continued to allocate fuel and tyres. The 4th Department was also responsible for the allocation of Transport Columns to the Luftflotten.

4. The reasons for the changes set out above were as follows:— In the early years of the war up to the time of the first winter in Russia, Germany possessed ample vehicles for all purposes. The troops were well equipped, losses in campaigns were slight, and there were quiet periods of many month between the separate campaigns which permitted the accumulation of good stocks. In those days the flow of vehicles went forward from industry through the Supply Office of the Director General of Equipment to the Equipment Groups and Air Parks and on to units, without any important check by any department of the General Staff. On account of the heavy losses in the Winter of 1941/42 in Russia and the demand for new vehicles for replacement, and for initial equipment in the setting up of new units, it became necessary to control the allocation of Motor Transport more closely and to adjust supply to operational needs. At first the existing organisation was maintained, except that the allocation to Commands was taken over by the 6th Department while the Director of Supply carried out the orders of that department and managed the storage and delivery of stocks. During these two periods, training was supervised by Inspectorate 6.

5. There were then three separate departments in the Air Ministry handling Motor Transport, as follows:—

(i) Inspectorate 6.   subordinate to the Director for Air Affairs (under the Minister for Air).
(ii) Director of Supply.   ,,   ,, ,, Quartermaster General.
(iii) 6th Department.   ,,   ,, ,, Quartermaster General.

6. In the face of increasing difficulties in the Motor Transport situation, it became essential to bring these offices together under one head. In consequence the Directorate of Motor Transport was created and subordinated directly to the Quartermaster General. In this manner, the appropriate organisation was set up under a single authority to control Motor Transport according to operational needs in all its aspects as directed by the General Staff.

7. At the same time separate Motor Transport Stocks Depots were set up in the Luftgaus, and new posts at Luftgau Headquarters were created to control them. Prior to this stocks of vehicles, belonging to the Air Force, were held in Air Parks under the Equipment Groups and the Supply Office. With the creation of the new Stocks Depots, Air Parks no longer kept stocks of vehicles. Thus, the whole subject of Motor Transport supply, stocks and repairs was removed from Supply Office channels and diverted into Quartermaster channels, and the work of the Inspectorate was incorporated into the new organisation under a single head.

8. There was another important advantage gained by setting up one Directorate. In negotiations on behalf of the Air Force with the War Office and later with the Director of Motor Transport at the Supreme Command of the Armed Forces, a single representative of the Air Force was in a much stronger position in bargaining for his share of Motor Transport equipment than the three separate components had been.

SUPPLY OF MOTOR TRANSPORT VEHICLES

9. It was explained in the Introduction to this Chapter that the Director of Armed Forces Motor Transport was responsible for the procurement of motor vehicles from industry. The Air Force, therefore, had to submit their requirements to that Department and back up their requests with strong arguments to ensure that they received a fair allocation. The Director of Armed Forces Motor Transport was staffed almost entirely by Army officers and the Air Force was represented by a very small liaison staff — one Group Captain with one or or two assistants. Such a preponderance of Army officers tended to overwhelm the Air Force and to abort their efforts to obtain what they considered to be a reasonable proportion of the vehicles produced. The Army, according to Oberst Prillip, the Director of Motor Transport, in the Air Ministry, understood the Air Force to consist of a body of people who flew about in aeroplanes, and could never become reconciled to the fact that such a force had to be supported by motor transport. The Air Force bids to the Supreme Command were compiled from a review of losses coupled with an assessment of vehicles to fill establishments of newly formed or projected units. In preparing these figures the Director of Motor Transport would work closely with the Operations Staff, the Organisation Staff and the 4th and 6th Departments of the German Air Ministry, and would also take into account requirements submitted to him by the various Luftflotte Headquarters.

10. When the Air Force required special purpose vehicles — for example, flak waggons and signals trucks — the Director of Motor Transport would order only the chassis from the Director of Armed Forces Motor Transport. In conjunction with the appropriate Air Ministry specialist branch he would then contact the Director General of Equipment (later the Chief of Technical Armaments) who would arrange the development of suitable designs and pass the chassis to industry with instructions to them to embody coachwork to the Air Ministry specifications.

11. It is interesting to note that, at the beginning of the war, there were approximately 3,000,000 vehicles in Germany (including service vehicles) most of which were privately owned. At the end of the war German private economy had only 160,000 vehicles, and the services 750,000. The peak number of vehicles in the German Air Force was about 200,000 but this figure was considerably diminished by the end of the war. The peak strength of Royal Air Force vehicles was 204,000.

REPAIR AND SUPPLY OF SPARE PARTS

12.   Minor repairs to motor transport vehicles were undertaken within the Air Force organisation and major repairs were handled by the Army. The facilities available within the Air Force system were the repair shops of the Airfield Commands, the mobile workshops controlled by the Airfield Regional Commands and the static workshops controlled by the Luftgau Headquarters — small repairs were also effected by the Motor Transport Stocks Depots. Spare parts required by these various repair organisations were obtained from the Army Central Spares Depots which were located in all the larger towns. Normally, there would be an Air Force Liaison Office (say one N.C.O. and an assistant) at each Central Spares Depot to handle Air Force demands.

13.   Major repairs were undertaken by the Army through a system of Motor Transport Parks. These Parks were organised as follows:—

  (i)   A Headquarters and administrative office, together with a reception area in which vehicles requiring repair were stored.
  (ii) Requisitioned workshops and garages to which the vehicles were sent for repair.

The Park itself did not carry out repair work but was the authority in control of motor transport repair facilities in each area and it regulated the flow of vehicles from the reception area to the repair shops and garages under its command. At each Park there was normally a small Air Force liaison staff to handle Air Force requirements.

SALVAGE OF MOTOR TRANSPORT VEHICLES

14.   A standardized system for classification of the condition of motor vehicles was set up as follows:—

  (i)   Feldbrauchbar.   Fit for use in the field. Such vehicles had to meet the following requirements:—
    (a) To be not more than 5 years old.
    (b) To be fit for use under conditions of normal wear and tear.
    (c) To belong to the principal types manufactured and not need extensive repair after heavy usage.
  (ii) Heimatsverwendungsfaehig.   Fit for use only at home. Such vehicles included:—
    (a) Operationally safe vehicles, 5 years and older, regardless of type and make.
    (b) Vehicles which had been in use for five years or less, and which after complete overhaul could still not be regarded as fit for field use.
    (c) Vehicles of German and foreign make, for which spare parts were especially difficult to obtain.
    (d) Vehicles which, because of their construction, could not be used in the East, North, nor in Africa, e.g. 2 cylinder motor cars, vehicles with front wheel drive, sports vehicles, etc.
  (iii) Grundueberholungsbeduerftig.   In need of thorough overhaul.
    (a) Vehicles in which normal wear had advanced to such an extent that an overhaul of several components had become necessary.
    (b) Vehicles which were not safe, but which could be repaired by a general overhaul for use in the field or at home.
    (c) Vehicles which showed the total mileage from the time taken into service or since the last general overhaul as follows:—

PKW (Personnel vehicles)   50,000 km (31,250 miles) at least.
LKW (Lorries)   40,000 km (25,000 miles) at least.
ZGKW (Prime movers)   30,000 km (17,755 miles) at least.

(iv) Aussonderungsreif.   Ready to be scrapped.
  (a) Vehicles no longer safe, and which could not be made safe by a general overhaul.
  (b) Vehicles damaged by accident to such an extent that even a complete repair would not guarantee safety.
  (c) Types of vehicles no longer in production and in need of overhaul, and for which spare parts are not available.

15.   When vehicles had reached the stage when they were beyond repair for use by the Luftwaffe (Aussonderungsreif) they were disposed of by sale through the Salvage Office. The procedure was as follows: Twice a year, units had to send to the relevant Luftgau Headquarters a list of vehicles to be condemned, using a prescribed form which stated:—

  (i)   Description of the vehicle in detail.
  (ii) Mileage covered.
  (iii) Whether the vehicle is an obsolete type.
  (iv) Accidents and damage.
  (v)   Whether spare parts are difficult to obtain.
  (vi) Constructional defects.

This report was submitted to the Qu./Mot. at Luftgau Headquarters who had the vehicles surveyed. Reports were then sent to the Air Ministry for authority to act. Air Ministry passed disposal instructions to the Qu./Mo. at Luftgau Headquarters and arranged for replacement.

MOTOR TRANSPORT FUEL

16.   In the field the Air Force was supplied with Motor Transport fuel by the Army. At home, however, the Air Force received a quota of motor transport fuel from the Supreme Command of the Armed Forces. This quota was allocated to the various Luftgau by the 4th Department which, in this connection, worked in close conjunction with the Director of Motor Transport and the Operations Staff. Within their allocation the Luftgau received a number of Armed Forces coupons which could be used either for drawing fuel in bulk for storage in Air Force installations or for refuelling vehicles from fuel installations controlled by the Supreme Command of the Armed Forces. Approximately 10% of the Air Force vehicles were, at the end of the war, fitted with gas generators. The loss of power caused by the use of this apparatus was estimated to be as much as 30% and such vehicles could not be used over rough country.

MOTOR TRANSPORT TYRES

17.   All units of the Air Force were supplied with tyres out of a tyre quota which was placed by the Supreme Command of the Armed Forces at the disposal of the Air Force. This quota was allotted to the Luftgau by the Director of Motor Transport in the form of tyre coupons. The Luftgaus issued these coupons to the units requiring tyres, and such coupons authorised the holders to draw them at all tyre issuing stations (Reich Tyre Stores, O.K.W. Tyre Stores, and Tyre Sections at Army M/T Parks). The issue of tyres was usually contingent upon the return of old tyres.

CONCLUSION

18. In principle, the system of unified control of all Motor Transport which was vested in the Supreme Command of the Armed Forces was admirable and the provision of a combined repair organisation for all services was economical and efficient in design. In practice, however, the whole Motor Transport organisation was dominated by the Army to the considerable disadvantage of the other two services — particularly the Air Force which was, of course, more dependent on Motor Transport than the Navy. All German Air Force staff officers with whom this subject has been discussed agreed that the idea behind the system was excellent but that it could only be applied practically if all the staffs concerned were to perform their duties impartially. From experience, they considered that small Air Force liaison staffs were quite inadequate and that to ensure efficient and fair service it would be necessary to establish closely integrated staffs manned proportionately by the three services and commanded in turn by members of the different services.

19. In spite of the fact that central control of Motor Transport was established, the Supreme Command was unable to reduce the number of different types in use and, consequently, unnecessary difficulties arose from the multiplicity of spare parts that had to be provided.

PART 2

CHAPTER VII

FIELD INSTALLATIONS IN THE GERMAN AIR FORCE

SECTION 1:   EQUIPMENT INSTALLATIONS

INTRODUCTION	Paragraphs 1—10
AIR EQUIPMENT DEPOTS	,, 11—17
General	,, 11—16
Internal Organisation	,, 17
FLAK AND AIR SIGNALS EQUIPMENT DEPOTS	,, 18—28
General	,, 18—19
Flak Depots	,, 20—22
Air Signals Depots	,, 23—28
G.A.F. AIR PARKS	,, 29—36
General	,, 29—32
Functions	,, 33—35
Internal Organisation	,, 36
EQUIPMENT ISSUING STATIONS	,, 37—52
General	,, 37
Stationary Air Equipment Issuing Stations	,, 38—41
Mobile Air Equipment Issuing Stations	,, 42—49
Flak Equipment Issuing Stations	,, 50
Signals Equipment Issuing Stations	,, 51—52
AMMUNITION STORAGE INSTALLATIONS	,, 53—71
General	,, 53
Air Main Ammunition Depots	,, 54—67
Air Ammunition Depots	,, 68—69
Field Ammunitions Depots	,, 70
Issuing and Collecting Stations Ammunition	,, 71

SECTION 2:   MISCELLANEOUS SUPPLIES

NON-TECHNICAL SUPPLIES	,, 72—96
General	,, 72
Clothing	,, 73—81
Billet and Office Furniture	,, 82—84
Rations	,, 85—90
Canteens	,, 91—92
Coal, Wood and Heating Material	,, 93—94
Constructional and Building Materials	,, 95—96

SUPPLY AND STORAGE OF COMPRESSED GASES   Paragraphs 97—104
    General   ,,   97

General	,,	97
Oxygen	,,	98—101
Hydrogen	,,	102
Acetylene and Compressed Air	,,	103—104

SUPPLY AND STORAGE OF P.O.L.   ,,   105—129

General	,,	105—106
Sources of Supply	,,	107
Storage and Chain of Supply	,,	108—110
Protection and Dispersal	,,	111
Transportation	,,	112
Synthetic Oil Plants	,,	113—118
Effects of Bombing on Supply Organisation	,,	119
Provision of Fuel Oil for the Aircraft Industry	,,	120—121
Types of German Aviation Fuel	,,	122—125
Special Fuels for "V" Weapons, etc.	,,	126—128
Use of Substitute Fuels for Motor Vehicles	,,	129

ORIGIN OF W.I.F.O., AND DESCRIPTION OF STORAGE INSTALLATIONS   ,,   130—148

General	,,	130—133
Storage Installations	,,	134—135
Grossraumtanklagers (G.T.L.s)	,,	136—138
T.E.L. Blending	,,	139
Other Buildings	,,	140
Management and Staff	,,	141—142
Lufttanklagers (L.T.L.s)	,,	143
Locations	,,	144—145
Blending	,,	146
Other Buildings	,,	147
Management and Staff	,,	148

PART 2

CHAPTER VII

FIELD INSTALLATIONS IN THE GERMAN AIR FORCE

SECTION 1 — EQUIPMENT INSTALLATIONS

INTRODUCTION

1. In this Chapter an attempt is made to give a detailed explanation of the Field Supply System obtaining in the German Air Force up to the time when the Allied advances in 1944 and 1945 so completely disintegrated the administrative machine that equipment was, of necessity, obtained on a hand-to-mouth system by the few remaining units who were able, or who attempted to operate with anything resembling wartime efficiency. In the diagram "Basic Chain of Supply for 'Technical' Stores, Ammunition and 'Non-Technical' Stores in the G.A.F." (See appendix "A") the system may appear unnecessarily complex and unwieldy and would seem to compare unfavourably with that existing in the R.A.F. But, before any fair and reasonable comparison can be made, it is necessary to appreciate fully the basic differences in the operation and organisation of the two Air Forces.

2. In the German Air Forces there was no Equipment Branch, and an Equipment Section, such as we know on an R.A.F. Station, did not exist. Certain "officials" were admittedly highly trained in certain types of equipment such as Signals, Armament, Explosives, and weapons for Chemical Warfare, but there were no G.A.F. officers whose sole eployment was the supervision of equipment supplies. "Officials" or "Beampte", who were considered to be of Officer status but who were recognised as civilians, were employed on the more routine equipment duties and the nearest approach to a Station Equipment Officer in the R.A.F. sense would be the Technical Superintendent (with the equivalent rank of Major) who was responsible for demanding and storing all types of spares.

3. The fact that the G.A.F. Supply System broke down towards the end of the war is not necessarily a condemnation of the system itself. Supply administrations should be, admittedly, elastic but no system could hope to combine with efficiency the degree of elasticity required to adapt itself to the constantly changing and deteriorating situation which became apparent in the early part of 1944. An important point to remember is that, while the system worked, it worked well. In main principles there is little similarity between it and our own system, but in matters of detail there are some interesting points for comparison.

4. An example worthy of note is the "specialisation" of Air, Flak and Signals Equipment Depots in the G.A.F. Before the war all major ranges of R.A.F. equipment were stored in "specialist" depots. All clothing and M/T Spares, for example, were held at Kidbrook; all airframe spares at Milton; all Engines at Ruislip. The outbreak of hostilities accelerated the construction and operation of the "universal" depots and on the principle that vulnerability to air attack rendered it unwise to keep all our "eggs in one basket" a universal range of equipment became available at Nos. 3, 7, 14, 16, 35 and 61 Maintenance Units. Towards the end of the war shortage of spares in some of the Airframe ranges resulted, admittedly, in the intro-

duction of the "brigading" system, and certain depots undertook the almost exclusive responsibility for specific ranges; but, by that time, the danger of complete obliteration from the air was, to say the least, remote.

5. The German Air Force, on the other hand, encouraged specialisation to an extreme level. In the early days of the war Allied attacks on Germany were sporadic and slight. Objectives of a far more important nature than Equipment Installations commanded the attention of Bomber Command who rightly deemed the destruction of the enemy's industrial and production potential to be of greater importance than the destruction of accumulated reserves. It was not until the Allied air attacks reached a very high level that the inadequacy of the system became really apparent. A single raid might destroy the entire reserves, say, of Messerschmidt Airframe Spares — reserves accumulated at a time when production was sorely and continuously harassed. One or two bombers could wipe out, at an Air Equipment Depot, the "Bezirke" (Sektion) holding six months' reserve of photographic processing materials. There were, of course, duplicate ranges "in miniature" at the Air Parks and Air Equipment Issuing Stations, but these installations each held a bare three months' reserve with which to feed the Operational Units in their areas; and, at none of the other Air Equipment Depots, was any photographic processing material available.

6. In an attempt to minimise this danger the G.A.F. hastily began to disperse their Equipment Depots over a number of widely separated sites, but, in the end, the extent to which this dispersal was carried out became ludicrous. One equipment Depot would be dispersed into literally a hundred or more sites separated from each other by distances of up to 40 or 50 miles, and the problems of administration became more and more difficult. But even such dispersal, although a reasonable protection from air attack, was a useless precaution against actual territorial advances by the Allied armies and when the Depots at Kupper and Leignitz were overrun by the Russians in January 1945 the G.A.F. was deprived of its entire static reserves of Heinkel and Focke-Wulf spares. By this time production was hampered to such an extent that these aircraft were rendered virtually inoperative through the loss of two depots out of nine.

7. There existed, in the German Air Force, no organisation with precisely similar functions to the Master Provisioning Office under Maintenance Command of the Royal Air Force, although in certain respects the G.A.F. Equipment Groups (whose organisation and functions are described in detail in Part 1, Chapter V. paras. 22 to 34) had parallel activities. The basic difference is that a Royal Air Force M.P.O. is only required to deal with demands from units which the "parent" issuing depot is unable to meet, whereas the G.A.F. Equipment Groups received the initial request from the demanding units. As is explained in Chapter V. the Stock Records held by the Equipment Groups were far from up-to-date at all times, and it was partly to overcome the difficulties experienced in ascertaining stocks held in the various equipment installations that the "specialisation" of Main Equipment Depots was introduced. (See para. 12.) From all points of view it must be considered a retrograde step. Admittedly, the information required by the Director of Supply to enable him to plan production was more quickly forthcoming, but the disadvantages, even before the collapse, are evident. Not the least of these was the enormously increased transportation problem, for no matter where an Air Park was situated its spares for a particular type of aircraft could only be drawn from one Main Depot. This embarrassment was not felt initially by the Operational Units whose

source of supply was, directly or indirectly, the "universal" holding Air Park; but the Air Parks themselves were, in the later stages, quite unable to maintain stocks at the prescribed level due to the virtual non-existence of rail connections with, perhaps, five or six Main Equipment Depots located in five or six widely separated parts of Germany.

8. It is difficult to say whether the system operating in the German Air Force, to divorce the Operational Side (the Luftflotten) from the Administrative Side (the Luftgaus), was reflected either favourably or unfavourably in their Field Supply System. This complete separation was a fundamental point on which their Air Force differed from ours and the pros and cons of the system scarcely fall within the scope of this Chapter. Our own Equipment Officers in the R.A.F. are in some ways more divorced from operational experience than were the German Administrative Officers, since all G.A.F. Officers, whether employed in or subordinate to Luftflotte or Luftgau, were basically "operational" Officers, being merely seconded to administrative duties temporarily or, if permanently, on account of age or health. But, discounting any advantage which may have been derived from this fact, the situation arose when "G.D." officers, whose knowledge of war tactics and strategy may have been extensive, but who had received no thorough training in supply matters, were seated many miles behind the battlefronts endeavouring to cope with the formidable problems of supply administration. In the R.A.F. the Equipment Branch worked side by side with the General Duties branch in whatever area the latter operated.

9. In conformity with the German priciple that duties other than combat ones were essentially of a "non-Military" character and, therefore, unsuited for the employment of officers, a large proportion of the Administrative Staffs at Depots, Parks and Issuing Stations were civilian "Beampte". The majority of the employees were also civilians but, in this respect, although not an arbitrary rule, we have a parallel in five out of our own seven main R.A.F. Equipment Depots in the United Kingdom, and it seems a matter of opinion whether the efficiency of a unit is affected one way or the other by a predominance of civilian over service personnel.

10. No attempt is made in this paper to detail the advantages or disadvantages of the G.A.F. Depots as compared with our own, as there are no similar Equipment Installations in the two systems which can be made the subject of a fair comparison. From the point of view of the categories of equipment held, an Air Park could be compared with a Royal Air Force A.E.D. but the latter was, of course, considerably larger and carried far greater quantities of the items stored. We have no equivalent to the G.A.F. Air, Flak or Signals Equipment Depots, or to the "specialist" installations at a lower level in the form of the Air, Flak or Signals Equipment Issuing Stations. One can, of course, ask the purely hypothetial question "Would a system such as our own have been likely to afford better service to the operational units in Germany than that which existed?" The answer would appear to be that as soon as the tide of battle became on the turn it most certainly would.

AIR EQUIPMENT DEPOTS (LUFTZEUGAMTER)

General

11. The largest individual storage installations for equipment in the German Air Force were the Luftzeugämter or Air Equipment Depots, of which there were nine in existence until January 1945. These depots were located in various parts of Germany (see Appendix "B") on the outskirts

of a medium sized town, the selection of a site being influenced by the adequacy of existing railroad connections.

The function of the Air Equipment Depots was to supply all G.A.F. Air Parks, the chain of supply being Air Equipment Depot to Air Park, Air Park to Equipment Issuing Station, Equipment Issuing Station to the "Technische Verwaltung" (Technical Supply Office) of the individual Airfield or Unit. Only in the most exceptional circumstances was any "short circuiting" of this chain permitted. The overall strength of an Air Equipment Depot was anything from 1,000 to 1,400 persons, the Depot being commanded by an officer of the rank of Colonel but the vast majority of the staff being civilian employees.

12. Shortly after the outbreak of war the Air Equipment Depots departed from their original role of "Universal" equipment Depots and became responsible instead for particular and specific ranges. From that time they ceased, obviously, to supply G.A.F. Air Parks on a "Territorial" basis, and began instead to supply on a "Technical" basis. Each of the Air Equipment Depots would carry all the equipment required for a particular aircraft. For example, that at Küpper was entirely responsible for spares for Heinkel aircraft; that at Finaw for Junker aircraft. Spares for these aircraft would not be available at any other depot, and although the disadvantages of this system became instantly apparent when certain Depots (Kupper and Leignitz) were overrun by the Russians, the advantages in the early stages were immense. Each depot could place orders direct with industry for the range of spares for which it was responsible, whereas when they were run on a "Universal" basis it was necessary for the Director of Supply to obtain past consumption data and stock records from every depot before any order could be placed.

13. An immediate effect of the specialisation of the Air Equipment Depots was the need for a wide system of dispersal and with the increased violence of Allied air attacks an order was given by the Director of Supply that all equipment should be dispersed to at least four sites and that no one site should hold more than 30 % of total stocks. The original type of Depot consisting of perhaps a dozen large warehouses rapidly disappeared and as the intensity of air attacks increased the number of dispersed sites became out of all proportion with the original intention. At the time of the capitulation some Depots were dispersed over as many as 200 sites and were located over hundreds of miles of country. Brick kilns, inns, barns, breweries, empty factories, schools, farms, in fact any type of building of an inconspicuous nature with reasonable accommodation for storage was (latterly) utilised as a site.

14. An Air Equipment Depot was intended to hold a six months reserve stock of the items for which it was specifically responsible. The Air Parks were intended to hold a three months reserve stock of all items, i.e. the "Universal" range which would obviously have been demanded from various Air Equipment Depots. It was the responsibility of the Director of Supply and of the Officers commanding the various Depots and Parks to keep stocks at the levels prescribed but the policy ruling that these reserves should be kept was made by the General Staff.

15. To implement this policy, Air Equipment Depots dealt direct with industry and from their experience of consumption over past periods as well as on the basis of reports compiled periodically by Air Parks and Equipment Issuing Stations, they prescribed the quantities of equipment required to be produced for fixed periods in advance. The instructions to

industry were passed through Rings and Committees (Ringe und Ausschüsse) which although autonomous bodies, worked under the direction of the Speer Ministry.

16. As opposed to the method described above to maintain stocks at a prescribed level all initial and original orders for equipment were passed through the regular channel, i.e. from the Director of Supply to the Technical Office of the General T.L.R. (formerly Director General of Equipment) and thence to industry.

Internal Organisation

17. As will be seen from the Organisation Chart at Appendix "C" an Air Equipment Depot was divided into four or sometimes five main sections. These were:—

    (a) The Administration Gruppe.
    (b) Gruppe "A" — Flying equipment.
    (c) Gruppe "B" — General equipment.
    (d) Shipping and receiving section.
    (e) Weapon, aircraft or flak repair section.

A. **Administration Gruppe.** This section of an air equipment depot was usually located alongside the offices of the Commanding Officer and was normally under the control of a Beamte (official) whose relative rank was that of Major. Not unnaturally the internal organisation of this section was inclined to vary in accordance with the individual ideas of the official in charge, but it was customary for it to be subdivided into three main sections:—

    (i) **Registration and filing section:** This Section was responsible for the maintenance of all depot records other than those concerning stocks or consumption of equipment.

    (ii) **Personnel section:** This section was responsible for the engagement and dismissal of all workers in the depot and for their domestic administration. It would maintain records of the Party Membership, etc. of all employees and was also responsible for the administration of the frequently imported slave workers.

    (iii) **Book-keeping and Accounting section:** This section was responsible for the assessment of all wages paid to employees. The amount to be paid would be calculated from daily summaries received from all sections of the depot which would detail against every individual the hours worked, the number of days absent and so on. It took no part in the physical act of paying employees but would provide the necessary information to enable payment to be made by a central "Finance Office". This Finance Office was not actually part of the depot but was merely an agency constituted to undertake all financial transactions not only of the deport but of any other G.A.F. Organisation which was by chance in the same locality.

B. **Gruppe "A" — Flying Equipment:** A broad description of the work of this section of the depot would be to say that it handled all items of equipment which actually formed part of an aircraft. It was normally under the control of a member of the G.A.F. Corps of Engineers (Stabsingenieur) with the relative rank of major. This Group was sub-divided into three definite sections

("Bezirke") known as A. 1, A. 2 and A. 3. These Bezirke each handled separate and definite ranges and approximated to the various "sites" of an R.A.F. A.E.D. The ranges held by the various Bezirke were as follows:—

Bezirke A.1. Airframe spares.
Aircraft general spares.
Special airframe tools.

Bezirke A.2. Complete engines and power plants.
Engine spares.
Ignition spares and accessories.
Modification sets.
Propellors, propellor tools and spares.
Radiators.

Bezirke A.3. Guns and gun spares.
Rescue and safety equipment.
Instruments and spares.
Hydraulic equipment.

The stock control of Gruppe "A" equipment was undertaken by means of the Hollerith machine system, and the Stock Control Office was part of, or located alongside, the building in which the equipment was stored.

C. **Gruppe "B" — General Equipment.** Gruppe "B" contained all items of general stores and ground equipment and is estimated to have covered approximately 50,000 different items. This Gruppe was divided into nine different Bezirke, some of which were in their turn split up into sub-Bezirke. As a general rule one or two of these Bezirke were located at each Air Equipment Depot, which would then be the only depot carrying that range of equipment, but in exceptional instances (for instance, photographic equipment), stocks would be held at four or five different depots. Only one of these sections was a Bezirke in the real sense of the word, the others being sub-Bezirke. For example, one sub-Bezirke at one depot would store aerial cameras; at another depot another sub-Bezirke would store ground cameras; at a third depot, a sub-Bezirke would store projection and cine apparatus and at a fourth a sub-Bezirke would store processing materials.

As opposed to Gruppe "A" equipment, there was no Hollerith system for recording the stock position of Gruppe "B" equipment but a perpetual inventory was maintained by means of a card index system which recorded all items received from industry and issued to Air Parks. It was the intention eventually to install the Hollerith system for Gruppe "B" equipment but owing to war conditions, this scheme never materialised.

As far as can be ascertained, the equipment stored in the various Bezirke was as follows:—

Bezirke B.1. Flare path equipment.
Runway lights.
Searchlights (excluding searchlights for flak).

Bezirke B.2. Kitchen and messing equipment.
Hand and machine tools.
Special ground handling equipment.

Bezirke B.3. Small arms.
Ground and aerial machine guns.

Bezirke B.4. Signals equipment.

Bezirke B.5. Engineering (pioneer) equipment, entrenching tools, detonating fuzes, pontoons and bridging equipment.

Bezirke B.6. Raw materials and semi-finished products. Paints, dopes, oil, greases, cloth, leather, glue, glass, wire etc.

Bezirke B.7. Photographic equipment.

Bezirke B.8. Anti-gas equipment.

Bezirke B.9. Meteorological equipment.

D. **Shipping and receiving section:** This section, as its name implies, had functions parallel to those of the Transportation Section of a Royal Air Force A.E.D. All incoming stores were received by this section whose responsibility it was to re-distribute them to the appropriate Bezirke. In the same way all "outgoing" stores from the various Bezirke were received in this section and all consignments intended for a particular Air Park were assembled and despatched in one bulk consignment to ensure the greatest possible economy in transport.

E. **Weapon, aircraft or flak repair shops:**

(i) **Weapon repair shops:** A few Air Equipment Depots had weapon repair shops at which all types of repair, including complete overhauls could be undertaken. A valuable function of these shops was their ability to assemble complete weapons from spare parts in store in the event of an unexpected bottleneck or breakdown in production.

(ii) **Flak repair shops:** A few Air Equipment depots had flak repair shops at which all types of repair and overhaul to flak equipment could be undertaken.

(iii) **Aircraft repair shops:** Originally all depots were provided with an aircraft repair shop. This was operated entirely independently of the Werft. In both the Werft and the Aircraft Repair Depots all types of repair could be performed. The Werft was nominally the repair shop belonging to the airfield used by the depot but in the event of either it or the depot repair shop being hit by enemy action then whichever remained would immediately undertake the full range of repairs for both the depot and the airfield.

FLAK AND AIR SIGNAL EQUIPMENT DEPOTS
(FLAK UND NACHRICHTENZEUGÄMTER)

General

18.   In the first instance, G.A.F. Equipment and supplies were stored in Equipment Depots of three different types. They were the Air Equipment Depots, whose organisation has been described in the preceding paragraphs, and

(a) Flak Equipment Detpots, and
(b) Air Signal Equipment Depots.

19.   These depots were all under the direct control of the Director of Supply, and the stocks they held should properly be regarded as O.K.L. property, not yet distributed to the G.A.F. as such. In broad outline, the

Flak and Air Signals Equipment Depots were operated on the same lines as the Air Equipment Depots; that is, they specialised in certain ranges of equipment which would not be procurable elsewhere — they were subjected ultimately to the same intensive system of dispersal — they dealt directly with Industry via the Rings and Committees of the Speer Organisation. In internal organisation, however, they were necessarily somewhat different.

Flak Equipment Depots

20. The Flak Equipment Depots, of which there were 5 in number, operated under the supervision of the 4th Abteilung of the Directorate of G.A.F. Supply, and were responsible for all supplies of Flak Equipment to Luftparks, who in turn supplied the Flak Equipment Issuing Stations. These Flak Equipment Issuing Stations carried, of course, only Flak Equipment, whereas the Air Park's range was a universal one covering the equipment stored at Air, Flak and Signals Equipment Depots.

21. The five Flak Equipment Depots were located in the following places:—

F.E.D. 1/III	VELTEN	For Heavy Flak.
F.E.D. 1/VI	BRESLAU	For Light and Medium Flak.
F.E.D. 1/XI	ROTHENBURG	For Searchlights.
F.E.D. 1/VII	MUNICH-ERLANGEN	For Optical Equipment.
F.E.D.	STETTIN	For Special Equipment, Captured Equipment, Balloons and "V" Weapons.

22. As in the Air Equipment Depots, the Flak Depots were required to maintain a six months reserve stock of all items. The normal establishment of a depot was in the neighbourhood of 14 officers, or officials of officers status, about 12 N.C.O.s and 300 to 350 auxiliaries or employees. As the type of equipment varied at each of the depots, however, it is obvious that while the numerical strength of persons employed remained approximately the same at each, the t y p e s of personnel varied very widely.

Air Signals Equipment Depots

23. Originally there was only one Air Signal Equipment Depot, located at TELTOW, which worked in the closest of collaboration with the "Gruppe V" of the Director of Supply at O.K.L. With the enormous territorial gains achieved by the Wehrmacht in the early days of the war however, the need for additional depots became apparent, and several more were set up in occupied territory At the end of the war there were five Air Signals Depots, and their locations and details of the equipment carried by each were as follows:—

A.S.E.D. 1.	TELTOW	All ground and aerial radio equipment and spares.
A.S.E.D. 2.	WARSAW	Telephone installations and spares. This depot was subsequently evacuated to STOLPMUNDE.
A.S.E.D. 3.	BRUSSELS	Teleprinter equipment and spares. This depot was subsequently evacuated to HOF, Bavaria.
A.S.E.D. 4.	STRAUSSBERG	All Radar equipment.
A.S.E.D. 5.	GOLLNOW (Nr. STETTIN)	Secret and special equipment.

24. The chain of supply followed was the normal one, namely, Air-Signal Equipment Depot to Luftpark, Luftpark to Signal Equipment Issuing Station.

25. The internal organisation of an Air Signal Depot was very much the same as that of other depots. The two main sections were the Storage Section, which as is implied, took care of the physical storage of all equipment, and the Technical Section.

26. The Storage Section was sub-divided into various Bezirke, each of which carried certain categories of equipment.

27. The Technical Section undertook not only the repair and maintenance of all equipment damaged or returned from the actual battle area but was also responsible for the enormously important work of developing and designing all packing and crating methods and materials.

28. The establishment of an Air-Signal Equipment Depot was approximately the same as for a Flak Depot.

G.A.F. AIR PARKS

General

29. As has been explained, the Air Flak and Signals Equipment Depots constituted the largest individual storage units in the G.A.F., but their holding was essentially a "technical" rather than a "territorial" one and their stocks could rightly be considered as Director of Supply property prior to distribution to the Luftwaffe.

30. The Air Parks, on the other hand, represented the only G.A.F. Supply Installation responsible for supply on a "territorial" as opposed to a "technical" basis. They carried a "universal" range of equipment, their stocks being drawn from the Air, Flak and Signals Equipment Depots. It was the original intention to provide one Air Park to each Luftgau but, dependent upon the activity within the various Luftgaus, this intention was modified. An Air Park would sometimes service two Luftgaus, and on the other hand one Luftgau was sometimes serviced by two or more Air Parks.

31. An Air Park was nearly always located on an Airfield and operational units stationed on the same airfield were permitted to "short circuit" the normal chain of supply (i. e. Air, Flak or Signals Equipment Issuing Stations) and obtain their supplies direct from the Air Park. As a reciprocal measure, air transportation for items urgently required by Air, Flak or Signals Equipment Issuing Stations would be provided by the flying units on the airfield.

32. Towards the end of the war, the "dispersal" problem began to effect the Air Parks as well as the Equipment Depots, and by the middle of 1944 an order was issued by the Director of Supply that a maximum of only 15% of an Air Park's stocks was to be stored in the original location. All the remaining stocks were required to be stored in numerous "satellite" sites in the surrounding territory.

Functions

33. The Air Parks were required to hold a three months' reserve supply of the equipment likely to be required by all the units located within the Luftgau. Air Parks were directly subordinate to the Luftgau Commander, but directives and orders on purely equipment matters were

usually received from the Director of Supply. It was necessary, however, for the Air Park Commander to establish a close liaison with the Luftgau Quartermaster as it was from this source that he would receive information concerning the impending arrival of new units who might be equipped with a type of aircraft for which it had not previously been necessary to carry spares. Having received this advice the Air Park Commander would demand the appropriate range from whichever specialist Equipment Depot carried them.

34. At the same time as the Luftgau Quartermaster notified the Air Park Commander of the impending arrival, he (the Luftgau Quartermaster) would notify Abteilung 1 B of the Airfield Regional Command of the impending changes within the latter's territory. The A.R.C. would then inform the Equipment Issuing Stations who, in turn, would raise demands upon the Air Park in anticipation of future requirements.

35. In addition to the storage of equipment, Air Parks were expected to be able to undertake Repairs. They were invariably equipped with Aircraft Weapon and Flak Repair Shops, whereas it will be recalled that such shops were occasionally but not invariably to be found at Air Equipments Depots.

Internal Organisation

36. An Air Park was commanded by an Officer of the rank of Oberst (Colonel) and the personnel strength would be approximately 1000, made up of, say, 8 or 9 G.A.F. Officers, 100 G.A.F. N.C.O.s and "other ranks", 50 or 60 "officials" of Officer status and 700 to 800 "employees". It was divided up into four main departments which were:—

    (a) The Administrative section.
    (b) The Storage section.
    (c) The Technical section.
    (d) The Armament section.

(A) **Administrative Section**

This section consisted of the personal staff of the Commanding Officer — i.e. his Deputy Commander (a Major or Lt. Colonel), his Adjutant (a Captain), and various officers solely concerned in the unit administration. Also in this section was the small Flak detachment equipped with light ack-ack guns. On an airfield this Air Park Flak detachment was in addition to the normal detachment posted for the defence of the airfield so that an airfield at which an Air Park was located enjoyed double protection. The Administrative Section was responsible for the maintenance of all records, for the engagement and dismissal of staff, for book-keeping, accounting, etc., etc. The Head of this section was second in command of the Air Park.

(B) **The Storage Section**

This section was the largest and most important in the Air Park. It was, as its name implies, responsible for the physical storage of all equipment and was sub-divided for this purpose into Bezirke (sections) in which the different types of equipment were kept. In the preceding paragraphs dealing with Air Equipment Depots, the G.A.F. system of Gruppe "A" and Gruppe "B" equipment has been explained. These categorisations were constant in the G.A.F. at all levels, the Air Park being unique only in that (a) it maintained, as has already been explained, a supply of the universal range, and (b) it was responsible for Flak and

Balloon Equipment which it held as Gruppe "C". Even before the intensive dispersal began it quite frequently occurred that an Air Park was not big enough to accommodate the Gruppe "C" equipment. In such cases, the Flak and Balloon Equipment would be stored elsewhere — perhaps in a different town. This was merely a physical separation, however, and the Gruppe "C" remained, from all points of view, part of the main Air Park.

In an Air Park the Receiving and Despatching office came under the Storage Section. The Receiving and Despatching office was responsible for the recording and subsequent distribution to the dispersed sites of all incoming equipment, as well as for the administration of the Railhead and all railway matters affecting the despatch of items to the Air, Flak or Signals Equipment Issuing Stations.

(C) **The Technical Section**

The Technical Section of an Air Park was headed by a Beampte — a member of the G.A.F. Corps of Engineers with the relative rank of Major or Lt. Colonel. Although not second in command of the Park he had direct access to the Commanding Officer. His duties and responsibilities included the testing and examining of all items of equipment, whether assigned to the Park for storage or returned for repair. He was in charge of the Airframe, Engine and Instrument repair shops, and in the early days of the war was responsible for the completion of all airframe and engine modifications. (N.B. This work was later undertaken by a special organisation known as the Schreusen which operated under the jurisdiction of the Luftflotten.)

(D) **The Armament Section**

This section was responsible for the repair and maintenance of all armament equipment, including the Weapon Repair Shop and the Testing Ranges (located near the Air Park).

EQUIPMENT ISSUING STATIONS
(GAST = GERÄTEAUSGABESTELLE)

General

37. The smallest and final units storing equipment in the course of its flow from industry to consumer were the G.A.F. Equipment Issuing Stations. Equipment Issuing Stations, unlike the Air Parks, but in common with the Equipment Depots, were of three distinct kinds — Air Equipment Issuing Stations (for flying and general equipment), Flak Equipment Issuing Stations and Signal Equipment Issuing Stations. Air Equipment Issuing Stations were either mobile or stationary. Flak and Signal Equipment Issuing Stations, on the other hand, were invariably stationary. All stations could be identified as to origin of unit by the pair of numbers by which they were prefixed, the first of which was the serial number of the Issuing Station itself in Arabic, and the second the Luftgau number in Roman numerals. After the Luftgau number in Roman numerals was the suffix "mot" (mobile) or "O" (Ortsfest = stationary). For example, "Equipment Issuing Station 8/VII Mot" or "Equipment Issuing Station 5/XI. O".

Stationary Air Equipment Issuing Stations

38. The Air Equipment Issuing Station was responsible for supplying the requirements of all units within the area comprising an Airfield Regional Command (Flughafenbereich) in the same way as an Air Park

was responsible for supplying all requirements within the territory of a Luftgau. Dependant upon the size and operational activities of the A.R.C. was the number of Equipment Issuing Stations within its territory. As a general rule there would be one Issuing Station to one A.R.C., but cases have been known (a) where one Issuing Station would serve more than one A.R.C. and (b) where one A.R.C. would be served by more than one Issuing Station.

39. The immediate superior to the Officer in charge of an Equipment Issuing Station was the Commander of the A.R.C. The Equipment Issuing Station was responsible to the A.R.C. Commander for ensuring that stocks were maintained at the correct level — three months reserve — but Directives and Orders of a technical or specialist nature were conveyed to the Issuing Station direct from the Director of Supply through the normal channels.

40. It was the responsibility of the A.R.C. Commander to notify the Equipment Issuing Station well in advance of any impending changes of units or new arrivals which would necessitate a revision of the type of spares to be held. This work, to ensure that a unit arriving equipped with an unfamiliar aircraft in that particular area could be adequately serviced, was actually done in the 1B (Quartermaster) section of the A.R.C. The actual chain along which the information would be conveyed would be as follows. The proposed transfer of units from one theatre to another or from one section of a battle front to another, would be notified to the Luftgau Quartermaster by the Luftflotte Quartermaster. The Luftgau Quartermaster was responsible for advising the Officer Commanding the Air Park of the impending arrival of aircraft of a certain type in that area. It was then the duty of the Air Park Commander either to ensure that equipment and spares for these new units were already available, or alternatively to place demands upon the Air Equipment Depot holding these particular spares. At the same time, the Luftgau Quartermaster would notify the 1B of the A.R.C. of the impending changes within the latter's territory. Upon receipt of this advice from 1B of the A.R.C., the Equipment Issuing Station would raise demands on the Air Park.

41. Internally, the organisation of an Equipment Issuing Station was very similar to that of an Air Park or Air Equipment Depot; that is, the departmental breakdown into Bezirke, Gruppe "A" for Flying Equipment and Gruppe "B" for general and ground equipment. An important point to remember, however, is that whereas Air Equipment Depots would carry only one or two of the nine Bezirke of Gruppe "B" equipment, the Air Parks and Equipment Issuing Stations carried a range of spares from all nine Bezirke.

Mobile Air Equipment Issuing Stations

42. Mobile Air Equipment Issuing Stations were of three different types:—
    (a) Railroad trains.
    (b) Truck or Lorry Convoy.
    (c) Aircraft and towed glider, both containing equipment.

43. The advantages of Mobile Issuing Stations were, of course, particularly apparent during the rapid advances made by the Wehrmacht in the early stages of the war. In cases where units were transferred rapidly from one front to another or from one section of a front to another section, they were able to ensure continuous flow of equipment and spares

which would otherwise have been almost impossible. A Mobile Issuing Station would never carry spares for more than two or three types of aircraft and an Aircraft and Towed Glider type of Station would carry spares for one type of aircraft only.

44. Another occasion on which the Mobile Air Equipment Issuing Stations operated to great advantage was during the Airborne campaign in Crete, when the maintenance problems of the aircraft involved was very largely solved by the transfer of two (one Railroad and one Road Convoy) Mobile Issuing Stations to the territory where the flying units were stationed.

45. The allocation of Mobile Issuing Stations was made to individual Luftflotten by the 4th Abteilung of the General Staff, who in turn subordinated them either to a Luftgau or Airfield Regional Command.

46. During the latter part of the war, when the intensity of Allied attacks upon Railway Communications was at its peak, the Railroad Equipment Issuing Stations became originally a problem and eventually almost an embarrassment. Owing to the continued loss of territory, the necessity for mobile stations became obviously less and less, and an indication of the startling reductions made in a period of six months can be taken from the following figures:—

	On 20.7.44	On 1.1.45
Stationary Air Equipment Issuing Stations	34	19
Mobile Air Equipment Issuing Stations (Rail)	16	7
Mobile Air Equipment Issuing Stations (Motorised)	20	18

47. As will be seen, the attacks on rail communications is reflected by the great reduction in the number of Railroad Issuing Stations. The units least affected were, of course, the motorised stations, where the reduction, it will be observed, was the smallest.

48. The Railroad Issuing Stations had, of course, the advantage of being able to carry much larger components than the Motorised, and in consequence they were apt to be allocated to undertake the servicing of Bomber and Transport units. The Motorised Issuing Stations, on the other hand, would usually be allocated to Fighter Units, and would consist of about 20 large lorries or converted buses, each of which would carry a certain type of spares. Flying Equipment Issuing Stations consisted of one Aircraft — a J.U. 52 or H.E. 111, towing a large glider. The amount of spares which could be carried in this way was obviously limited, but they had the great advantage of being able rapidly to bring the essential spares to the very spot from which the flying unit was operating. During the latter part of the war, some 20 to 30 Flying Air Equipment Issuing Stations were in operation.

49. At Appendix "D" to this chapter is given a description of the contents of the various coaches of a typical Railroad Air Equipment Issuing Station.

Flak Equipment Issuing Stations

50. A Flak Equipment Issuing Station, invariably stationary, usually existed in every Luftgau supplying Flak Unit. Its functions were, of course,

very similar to those of the Air Equipment Issuing Stations, and the chain of supply from industry to consumer was Industry — Flak Equipment Depot — Air Park — Flak Equipment Issuing Station — consumer unit.

Signals Equipment Issuing Stations

51.   As in the case of Flak Issuing Stations, these were invariably stationary, serving one or more Luftgau, depending upon requirements in the area.

52.   The chain of supply was, of course, Industry — Signal Equipment Depots — Air Park — Signal Equipment Issuing Station — consumer unit.

AMMUNITION STORAGE INSTALLATIONS

General

53.   There were four different types of installation in the G.A.F. concerned with the storage and supply of ammunition. They were:—
    (a) Air Main Ammunition Depots (Lufthauptmunitionsanstalten).
    (b) Air Ammunition Depots (Luftmunitionsanstalten).
    (c) Field Ammunition Depots (Feldmunitionslager).
    (d) Ammunition Issuing and Collection Stations (Munitionsausgabe und Sammelstellen).

The functions of each of these installations were separate and distinct and are described in the following paragraphs.

Air Main Ammunition Depots

54.   These depots, which numbered 19 in all, were sub-divided into four different types:
    (i) "Flak" — for Flak Ammunition, of which there were 14.
    (ii) "M" — for Mines, of which there were 2.
    (iii) "T" — for Torpedoes, of which there was 1.
    (iv) "K" — for Gas Bombs ("Kampfstoff") of which there were 2.

55.   It was the responsibility of these Main Depots to supply the Air Ammunition Depots or (more generally) the Field Depots with their requirements, who in turn supplied the Issuing and Collecting Stations, who in turn supplied the consumer units. In these Main Depots were stored all metal parts and explosives separately for subsequent assembly into finished products as required by other G.A.F. Installations. This category included all Flak Ammunition larger than 3 cm., all mines, all torpedoes and all Gas Bombs. The assembly of the components as well as the subsequent storage was the responsibility of the Main Depots.

56.   Main Depots were located between 40 and 50 miles from a large city, and were required to comply with regulations concerning their proximity to smaller towns and villages. An important factor influencing the choice of a site was, of course, the opportunity available for natural camouflage, but an additional factor was the existence of railway connections within a reasonable distance from main-lines.

57.   Abandoned saltmines, particularly suitable due to constancy of temperature, were ideal sites, and sides of mountains with adjoining forests were also frequently used. Into the sides of mountains would be constructed shafts, 60 or 70 yards long and 40 or 50 yards apart, reinforced with concrete and heavy timber. In some shafts would be stored the

constituents required to make up the final product, and in others the finished products themselves.

58. Adjoining every depot was constructed a small marshalling yard to ensure the speedy and efficient despatch of items when required. In peace time, one or two loaded trains stood ready at all times in every main depot as a precaution against an "unexpected and unprovoked attack upon Germany by any of her neighbours!"

59. By far the most important task of these Main Depots was the actual fabrication of ammunition from the shell cases, explosives, etc. produced and delivered by Industry. In addition it was their responsibility to undertake the preparation, for re-use, of once used or damaged shell-cases. The Main Depots, it should be emphasised, were concerned only with Flak, Mines, Torpedoes and Gas Bombs, and were not concerned in the preparation or storage of small arms ammunition, signals ammunition, bombs or machine-gun ammunition.

60. The rate at which components were assembled in Main Depots was laid down by the Director of Supply, who in turn received a statement of requirements from the 4th Abteilung of the General Staff.

Administration and Organisation

61. The Commanding officer of an Air Main Ammunition Depot was an Explosives Specialist of the rank of Colonel. The strength of his depot was approximately 12 officers or officials of officer status, 70 to 100 N.C.O.s and "Other Ranks" and up to 1700 or 1800 civilian employees. Officers, Officials, and the majority of the G.A.F. "Other Ranks" would be weapon and ammunition specialists. The second in Command — a Major — was responsible for all administrative matters, as well as for Motor Transport and Repair Shops of all types.

62. As will be seen from the Organisation Chart at Appendix "E" to this Chapter, an Air Main Ammunition Depot was divided into four separate "Gruppe" — the Administration Gruppe, the Ammunition Administration Gruppe, the Ammunition Storage Gruppe, and the Ammunition Assembly Gruppe.

    (i) **Administration Gruppe.**
    This Gruppe was responsible for the procurement of all rations, billets, pay and wages, engagement and dismissal of personnel, fire-fighting, guards and security organisation, police, identification cards, etc. etc.

    (ii) **Ammunition Administration Gruppe.**
    This Gruppe was responsible for inventories of all components and finished products, and for the ordering of the materials, fuzes, powder, etc. required in the actual process of assembly. It was required to render reports on progress and/or difficulties to higher formations such as Luftgau H.Q., Director of Supply, etc.

    (iii) **Ammunition Storage Gruppe.**
    This Gruppe was responsible for the storage and custody of all assembled and finished items. It was divided into various "Bezirke" or sections, each of which undertook the storage of a certain type of ammunition. Subordinate to this Gruppe was the Shipping and Receiving Section, who were responsible for the loading and unloading of all trains, and for the operation of the marshalling yards and all other rail matters.

(iv) **Ammunition Assembly Gruppe.**
This Gruppe was responsible for the whole of the fabrication and assembly of the components and materials received from Industry into the complete item. Subordinate to this Gruppe were the various workshops engaged on the reconditioning of used shell-cases, shell-case cleaning, etc., etc.

Types of Air Main Ammunition Depots

63. The information given above under the heading "Administration and Organisation" was, of course, common to all Air Main Ammunition Depots whether Flak, "M", "T" or "K". Naturally in detail they varied in consequence of the specific nature of their activities.

Flak Depots

64. These were by far the most important and, as has been stated, represented 14 out of the 19 Depots in existence.

"M" Depots

65. The two "M" Depots were located one at Hosedorf, West of Hamburg, and one in the Bremen area. They were completely independent of those depots controlled by the German navy, and being G.A.F. Depots, were concerned, obviously, only with the types of mine dropped by aircraft.

"T" Depots

66. The one "T" Depot was located outside Madüsee near Stargard on the Baltic. It was, of course, concerned only with the type of Torpedo launched from an aircraft. Its work included not only the adjusting, calibrating and ranging of torpedoes, but also the test flights of every missile to ensure that it had the requisite speed and straightness of course. Every torpedo was tested, being subsequently recovered by divers, refilled and stored ready for actual use.

"K" Depots

67. The two "K" Depots were located, one at Mokrehna, near Leipzig and the other at Frankenberg, South-West of Kassel. These Depots undertook the filling of all liquid gas bombs, but bombs filled with smoke and choking gases were filled previously in the factories where they were made prior to delivery to the "K" Depots. In these bombs, however, the Depot installed the fuzes and prepared them for use. "K" Depots were manned by personnel specially trained in Chemical Warfare.

Air Ammunition Depots

68. As opposed to the assembling and fabricating activities of the Main Depots, Air Ammunition Depots were solely and entirely storage units. From a quantitive standpoint, as well as for the fact that they carried all types of ammunition, they were much larger and more important than the Main Depots. They were the direct recipients from Industry of bombs, small arms ammunition, signal ammunition, machine gun ammunition and Flak ammunition up to 3 cm. In all there were 64 Air Ammunition Depots in Germany, each with a storage capacity of approximately 5,000 tons. There were always one or two of these Depots in every Luftgau.

69. Obviously, being relieved of the work of assembly, an Air Ammunition Depot was able to operate with a much smaller establishment than a main Depot. The approximate strength, under a Major, was

4 Officers (or Officials of Officer status), 40/50 "Other Ranks" and up to 300 civilian employees. At Appendix "F" to this Chapter is a chart showing the organisation of an Air Ammunition Depot, from which it will be seen that, administratively, it was very similar to that of a Main Depot. (Appendix "E".)

Field Ammunition Depots

70.   These depots were responsible for the storage of ammunition on behalf of the Issuing and Collecting Stations, and for the collection of all used ammunition parts and empty cases. Storage accommodation was limited to approximately 1500 tons, in auxiliary buildings well camouflaged.

Ammunition Issuing and Collecting Stations.

71.   These represented the smallest type of Ammunition Supply Installation. They were responsible for supplying all units within their area, and for the collection of all used parts and cases. The amount of ammunition held was limited, the main supplies being drawn from Field and Air Ammunition Depots as and when required to maintain stocks at a prescribed level. This level was determined by the General Staff and varied among the various stations, in accordance with the amount of activity in the particular area concerned. The number of Issuing and Collecting Stations in each Luftgau varied considerably. In the Ruhr, for examble (Luftgau VI), in view of the heavy flak concentrations around the industrial area. there were 35 Issuing and Collecting Stations. Luftgau VIII (Silesia) which was comparatively immune from Allied attacks, had 3 Stations only.

SECTION 2 — MISCELLANEOUS SUPPLIES
NON-TECHNICAL SUPPLIES

General

72.   Technical and non-technical supplies in the German Air Force were the subject of two entirely separate and distinct systems and supply channels. "Technical" equipment was that equipment for which responsibility was assumed by the Director of Supply and the Quartermaster General, and covered the ranges held by Air, Flak and Signal Equipment Depots. "Non-Technical" equipment consisted of Clothing, Rations, Office Furniture and requisites, bedding, coal, wood etc. and came under the sole jurisdiction of the G.A.F. Administrative Office (Lw. Verwaltungsamt).

Clothing

73.   The G.A.F. Administrative Office was not only charged with the responsibility for the supply of clothing, rations, furniture, fuel etc., but also for planning and promulgation of policy affecting that supply. At the various Command levels, the Administrative Office at R.L.M. was represented by the Office of the Intendant. It was the responsibility of the General Staff to keep closely in touch with the Administrative Office and to keep them informed of the proposed formation of all new units and formations in order that the Administrative Office was enabled to translate the estimated requirements of clothing into terms of Raw Materials, and present its requirements to the Supreme Command of the Armed Forces.

74.   Periodically, a provisioning specialist in the Administrative Office would submit demands for raw materials to O.K.L. who would either

approve it or (more frequently) reduce it prior to approval. Clothing would then be produced from the quota of raw materials obtained, either by manufacture by the G.A.F. in their own Clothing Depots, or by placing a contract with industry. The majority of "common-user" items were covered by the Army on behalf of the Navy and the G.A.F. but the Army would only supply common-user items to the G.A.F. in proportion to the amount of raw materials previously turned over to them by the G.A.F. This system worked so well that towards the end of the war it had been planned to extend the "common-user" items to complete uniforms, the only difference between the services being a distinctive badge or insignia. The only exceptions proposed to this rule were to be Naval Crews.

75. Clothing held under the control of the Administrative Office — i.e., not yet distributed to command — was stored in Clothing Depots (Luftwaffen-Bekleidungsämter), and these Clothing Depots met the demands of the Clothing Stores (Bekleidungslager) operating on Luftgau level under the Luftgau Intendant. From the Clothing Stores supplies would be distributed to the Clothing Rooms of Airfields and units.

76. The Clothing Depots were responsible for the storage, fabrication and repairs of clothing. They had ample facilities for the production of garments, and their experience in actual manufacture put them in a very strong position when dealing with private contractors, who were also engaged on the manufacture of uniforms, etc. For example, the G.A.F. would know precisely how much raw material was required for a specified amount of clothing, and could asses with reasonable accuracy the number of man-hours needed to be expended on production. In some cases, the activities of private contractors would be restricted to the actual sewing together of parts of uniforms previously cut out by the Depots. This method had, at least, the advantage of ensuring "uniformity of uniforms".

77. All Clothing Stores at Luftgau level possessed certain facilities for repair, but anything considered beyond their capacity was returned to the Clothing Depots who, in view of the acute shortage of clothing and raw materials, would make every effort to effect satisfactory repairs. In sharp contrast to the smartness and adequacy of G.A.F. clothing in the early years of the war, the general condition in the later stages was extremely poor.

Clothing Supply at Luftgau Level

78. The responsibility for supply of clothing at Luftgau level was assumed by the Luftgau Intendant, and although subordinate in every respect to the Commanding General of the Luftgau, the Intendant received his orders, and directives of a technical character, direct from the Administrative Office of R.L.M.

79. Dependant upon the number of units and personnel to be served would depend the number of Clothing Stores within each Luftgau, but the number would vary between a minimum of two and a maximum of five. The Luftgau Clothing Stores were permitted and expected to hold reserve stocks of all clothing including flying clothing, amounting to 20% of the strength of the units they were responsible for serving.

80. As previously mentioned Clothing Stores were expected, in addition to storing clothing, to effect minor repairs. In certain Field Luftgaus, on the Eastern Front in particular, laundry and dry-cleaning sections were added due to the inadequacy (or frequently, non-existence) of captured civilian establishments. Clothing Stores, as well as Clothing Depots, were

required to provide the Administrative Office with Stock Inventories and past consumption data in order that future requirements could be assessed. An up-to-date record of stocks held in Clothing Stores also enabled the Administrative Office to order the transfer of stocks rapidly from one Clothing Store to another in the event of rapid and large scale troop movements from the territory of one Luftgau to another.

Clothing Supply on a Unit Level

81.   The last stage in the supply of clothing to G.A.F. personnel was the Clothing Room (Kleiderkammer) of either airfields or units. These Clothing Rooms actually issued the clothing to the individual personnel, and were normally controlled by a N.C.O. under the supervision of the Administrative section of the unit or airfield. The Clothing Rooms would, of course, draw their supplies from the Clothing Stores of their respective Luftgau, who in turn would draw from the Clothing Depots the quantities required to maintain their stocks at the prescribed level.

Billet and Office Furniture

82.   The rules, regulations and scales governing the issue of Billet and Office Furniture, including bedding, tents, etc., were again laid down by the Administrative Office, but most of the actual work was the responsibility of the various Luftgau Intendants, and included in their terms of reference was authority to make extensive purchases locally. Purchases involving very large sums, however, were required to be referred to and approved by the Administrative office in the first instance.

83.   In the same way, the Luftgau Intendants would frequently delegate authority to make local purchases to airfields, but although this obviously speeded up supplies it resulted in a complete departure from any standardised type of furniture and fittings.

84.   For the purpose of storing office and billet furniture, there existed in each Luftgau several large warehouses, which were subordinate to the Luftgau Intendant. These warehouses were entirely separate and independent from the Clothing Stores or Rations Stores and were, in fact, usually in different towns — a surprising fact as it cannot fail but to have resulted in a considerable wastage in transportation.

Rations

85.   The G.A.F. maintained no independent food or ration stores, the provision on their behalf being undertaken entirely by the Army. Only in exceptional instances, for example to cover the requirements of an outlying meteorological or Flak unit, where no Army unit was located, was a G.A.F. ration store installed for temporary use. Every G.A.F. unit was required to submit to the local Army Ration Store a daily strength return as a basis on which rations were issued, and in the event of a G.A.F. unit moving to another area it would be advised by the Luftgau Intendant of the new Army Ration Store from whom its supplies should be drawn. It was the responsibility of the Luftgau Intendant to keep his "opposite number" in the Army Rations Store advised of impending arrivals and departures of units, in order that food supplies could be properly planned.

86.   As is well known, during the war the German Armed Forces, contrary to the procedure of the Allies, lived "off the land". This procedure, although reasonably satisfactory (to the Germans) on the Western front, was the cause of extreme difficulties and dissatisfaction in parts of Eastern Europe, where practically no vegetables other than potatoes and a little

cabbage were available. Special kitchens, staffed by experts, were set up on the Russian front, and an endeavour was made to offset the effect of a monotonous daily diet of meat, potatoes and cabbage by presenting these available products in a great variety of forms. It was not unusual, for example, for cabbage and potatoes to be served in a single meal as soup, salad, vegetable and even as a sweet in the form of a pudding.

87. As a general rule, imported canned products would be issued by the Army Ration Stores in sufficient quantities to ensure a departure from meals composed of local products for at least one day in each week.

88. In addition to normal rations, members of flying crews were issued with special rations, but only on days when actual combat flights were to be undertaken, or before a normal flight of a minimum of four hours duration. Towards the end of the war, due to the increasing shortage of food, this period was increased to six hours. The rations consisted of:—

      1 pint fresh milk.
      1 egg.
      1 ounce butter.
      1 ounce oatmeal
      8 ounces white bread.
      $2^{1}/_{2}$ ounces roasted peanuts.

89. Aircrews were also issued with an "Aerial Ration" (Bordverpflegung) for consumption during a long flight or to be used in an emergency if an aircraft force-landed or was shot down. These Aerial Rations consisted of a small package containing highly concentrated foods, such as concentrated chocolate, dextrose tablets, biscuits, sweets, etc. Coffee was previously prepared and carried in a Thermos flask.

90. These "Special Rations", being peculiar to flying personnel, were kept in Special Ration Stores located on the various airfields, but such items as eggs, butter, white bread etc., were drawn from the Army Ration Stores. Again, since these rations were exclusively for flying personnel, the Special Ration Stores were subordinated to tactical rather than Administrative Headquarters, i.e., Luftflotte and Fliegerkorps rather than Luftgau Intendants, and if a Fliegerkorps was transferred from one area or country to another, it would take its Special Ration Store with it.

Canteens

91. Corresponding to the N.A.A.F.I. canteens in the R.A.F. were the German "Marketenderwaren" from which troops were permitted to purchase (in the early days) a fairly wide range of items. Canteens within the borders of Greater Germany were administered by, and were the sole responsibility of, the respective Airfield Commanders, and the task of operating the Canteen would be delegated to the Administrative Section (IVA) of each airfield. Supplies were obtained locally whenever possible and all canteen profits were used for the benefit of the canteen users. Items in short supply were rationed, and periodical checks were made by the Luftgau Intendant to ensure that there was no wide variation in prices for similar items in different areas.

92. As opposed to Canteens in Greater Germany, Canteens in the occupied countries were administered centrally from the Administrative Office, and the supervision of the Canteens to ensure equable distribution of available supplies was the responsibility of the Luftgau Intendant. Needless to say, on the Western front supplies were comparatively plentiful; on the Eastern front a continuous shortage existed.

Coal, Wood and Heating Materials

93. Coal, for use within Germany, was procured by the various units from local coal dealers, and payment was effected from the funds at the disposal of the various Luftgau Intendants. The amounts purchased varied in accordance with the quota allocated to the G.A.F. by O.K.W. which received its quota from the Reich Coal Commissioner. In Germany and the Western European countries, there were no important problems connected with the supply of coal other than the usual limiting factor of shortage of supply. But in the Russian and Italian theatres, an immense obstacle was the great distances between the battlefront and the coal mines. Special Coal Carrying Trains were placed at the disposal of the Administrative Office by the 4th Abteilung of the General Staff, and in these trains coal was carried directly from the producers to the various Luftgau. The Luftgau Intendant then allocated and arranged for the distribution of the coal to his subordinate units.

94. Wood for heating was procured locally whenever possible, in collaboration with and under the general direction of the Reich Forestry Sector.

Constructional and Building Materials

95. At the beginning of 1944, the whole of the G.A.F. Works Organisation was transferred (complete with a tremendous quantity of equipment and materials) to the TODT Organisation, which later, of course, became part of the Speer organisation. Prior to 1944, however, the whole Construction and Building organisation of the G.A.F. functioned very smoothly and efficiently under the Administrative Office. It constituted one of the major tasks in the Luftgau Intendant office, which was responsible for the engagement and dismissal of all workers, who numbered, at times, up to 100,000 men.

96. All types of constructional equipment, machines and building materials were stored in large depots (Bauhöfe) which were subordinated directly to the Administrative Office.

SUPPLY AND STORAGE OF COMPRESSED GASES

NOTE: The following paragraphs are not intended to deal with the Supply and Storage of Compressed Gases from a scientific or technical aspect, but solely to indicate the means by which G.A.F. units obtained their supplies. Those desirous of acquainting themselves with technical detail are recommended to visit the Aviation Medical Institute, Farnborough, and the Compressed Gases Section of the R.A.E., Farnborough, where samples of G.A.F. equipment are held. Reference should also be made to the translations of German Technical Handbooks held by R.T.P./M.A.P.

General

97. Oxygen, Hydrogen and Compressed Air were used by the German Air Force for a variety of purposes.

    Oxygen — for aircraft breathing systems, and for autogenic welding and cutting.

    Hydrogen — for barrage balloon filling.

Compressed Air — for starting aircraft engines, for boring and rivetting tools, for pneumatic trigger and loading devices of automatic weapons, and for the recoil mechanism of heavy flak guns.

Oxygen

98.   The Oxygen used by the G.A.F. was produced by civilian Oxygen plants of which there were a large number throughout Germany. It was collected from the producing plants in special Oxygen Tank lorries of which there were four or five to each Luftgau. These lorries were, in effect, giant "Thermos" flasks, and carried the oxygen in liquid form thereby adding considerably to the amount of Oxygen that could be transported at one time.

99.   The Lorries conveyed the Oxygen only to the Main Airfield in each A.R.C. (The LEITHORSTE) where it was transferred, still in liquid form, to a smaller static container known as the Pufferbatterie.

100.   The Tank Lorries were sent out to deliver the Oxygen on carefully mapped-out routes designed to begin and end at Oxygen producing plants. For example, in the Luftgau XI area the lorry would start from the Producing plant at Lubeck and, after visiting all Main Airfields in the district of Schleswig, would be refilled at Odense and proceed to supply airfields in Denmark. Another lorry, beginning its journey at Lubeck would supply the airfields of Mecklenburg, refill at Borsigwalde, and proceed with the supply of Oxygen to airfields in the Hanover area.

101.   The Main Airfield (Leithorste) was responsible for supplying oxygen to all other airfields in the A.R.C. Every airfield was equipped with a Mobile Oxygen Refilling Apparatus, which was an assembly of 18 to 20 Cylinders each with a capacity of 50 litres, mounted on a lorry. These lorries collected the Oxygen from the Pufferbatterie which, in the course of transfer to the cylinders, converted the Oxygen from liquid to gaseous form. On arrival at the airfields the gas would be transferred from the Mobile Refilling Apparatus to the normal cylinders for storage prior to use.

Hydrogen.

102.   The main source of supply for Hydrogen in the German Air Force was the Luftwaffe Hydrogen Plant at Oranienbaum, near Dessau. Contracts for the supply of Hydrogen were also made with various civilian establishments. Hydrogen was delivered direct to all consumer units from the producing plants or from a Cylinder Storage Unit of which one or two were located in each Luftgau. No technical vehicles were employed in its distribution, the gas being delivered ready for use in Cylinders, which were exchanged for empty Cylinders held by the units. Stringent safety regulations were imposed on those responsible for distribution. Full gas cylinders were permitted to be piled one above the other up to five cylinders. They were required to be piled at right angles to the direction in which the vehicle was travelling to avoid sliding. If they were loaded into closed railway trucks, the air outlets of the trucks were required to be opened so that any escaping gases could effuse freely. The transportation of full cylinders in open railwagons or lorries was permitted only if they were protected by canvas covers from the influence of sunshine.

Acetylene Gas and Compressed Air

103.   Compressed Acetylene Gas was produced by two civilian plants in Germany — the Vereinigte Sauerstoff Werke at Borsigwalde, near Berlin, and the firm of Rommenholler in Altona. Compressed Air was produced by Luftwaffe Compressor plants which were available on each airfield and at the storage installations at all levels. Special store rooms were constructed at every unit in which the gases were stored in steel cylinders, adequate precautions being taken to ensure protection from excessive heat, oil or petrol vapours and sunshine.

104.   As a precautionary measure and to facilitate immediate identification, the caps of all gas cylinders were painted in the following distinguishing colours:—

Hydrogen	:	Red Caps
Oxygen	:	Blue Caps
Compressed Air	:	White Caps
Acetylene	:	Green Caps

SUPPLY AND STORAGE OF P.O.L.

General

105.   All branches of the German Oil Industry were controlled centrally by the Zentralbüro für Mineralöl, whose head offices were in Berlin. Operating under the control of the Zentralbüro were three main concerns:

   (i)   Kontinental-Oel G.m.b.H. — concerned with crude oil production in S.E. Europe.

   (ii) Mineralöbau G.m.b.H. — concerned with production within Greater Germany.

   (iii) Wirtschaftliche Forschungs G.m.b.H. concerned with storage, distribution and transport.

106.   The Wirtschaftliche Forschungs (WIFO) operated the higher levels of storage and transport for all branches of the armed forces. At lower levels responsibility was assumed by the individual arms of the services.

Sources of Supply.

107.   Up to the period immediately before the outbreak of the war, the greater portion of Germany's supply of Fuel Oil was imported from foreign countries. The commercial undertakings Rhenaniaossag, D.A.P.G., and D.P. Olex, imported a monthly average of 20,000 tons, whilst in addition a smaller quantity was imported from Rumania. This, by reason of its poor quality, was utilised for storage purposes. The quantity imported from Rumania seldom exceeded 1500 to 2000 tons per month. It was of a vastly inferior quality to that obtained from other sources, particularly as regards octane and residual tests, seldom reaching the required 72 octane. Importation was continued, however, in view of the urgent need of accumulating large reserves but it was only used for aviation purposes when blended with German synthetic fuel.

Storage and Chain of Supply

108.   Initially, imports surplus to requirements were stored by the Commercial companies but, as the construction of the G.T.L.s (Großraumtanklager) by WIFO progressed, the stocks were transferred to them. These stocks were classified as "National Reserve" and were not, at that stage, earmarked specifically for any particular branch of the Wehrmacht.

The G.T.L.s each had a storage capacity of up to 200,000 tons. These were underground depots, carefully camouflaged and thickly covered with earth and concrete.

109. Luftwaffe suplies were obtained in the following manner. Each Luftflotte was required to submit a daily report of its consumption and of stocks held to the 4th Abteilung of the General Staff by teleprinter or in code by telephone. This information was interpreted by the 4th Abteilung in the light of anticipated operational activity, and formed the basis on which the requirements of each Luftflotte was assessed. Instructions were then issued to the Director of Supply to draw from the WIFO G.T.L.s the required amount of fuel, for storage in the G.A.F. Fuel Depots, known as Luftwaffentanklager (L.T.L.). These were smaller surface storage installations built for the exclusive use of the G.A.F., each with a capacity of up to 15,000 tons. Stocks in these depots, however, seldom exceeded 5000 tons. There was at least one, and occasionally two, L.T.L.s in each Luftgau.

110. From the L.T.L. the fuel was drawn in accordance with the requirements of the flying units, by the G.A.F. P.O.L. Issuing Stations which operated at A.R.C. level. These Issuing Stations were usually in the form of Barrel Dumps with a capacity of 500 to 1000 tons. At Appendix "G" to this Chapter is a diagrammatic indication of the chain of supply from Industry to consumer.

Protection and Dispersal

111. Wherever possible (for example at Issuing Stations) fuel stocks were dispersed over a wide area. All surface tanks were protected by brick walls, concrete structures, or earth mounds. Railway sidings in fuel depots were subjected to extensive camouflage and rail wagons, if left in sidings, were required to be well spaced-out.

Transportation

112. Transportation of fuel oil in the G.A.F. was by four methods: Rail, Road, Water and Air.

Rail. Special wagons with capacities of either 15, 22 or 46 tons were employed. An average fuel train would comprise up to 30 wagons and would have a capacity of 350—450 tons. Normal wagons would also transport fuel oil in barrels, each of a capacity of 200 litres (44 gallons) or 300 litres. (66 gallons.) Empty or non-inflammable wagons were usually interspersed between fuel wagons with a view to minimising risks from air attack.

Road. A medium fuel column would consist of 8—10 tank lorries each with a capacity of $2^{1}/_{2}$—$3^{1}/_{2}$ tons, making a total of 25 to 35 tons. A small fuel column would consist of 8—10 ordinary lorries and trailers carrying barrels, and would convey up to 25 tons.

Water. Fuel barges and lighters were used on the inland waterway system to replenish Issuing Stations and Airfields.

Air. This method was for emergency use only. It was seldom used in Germany and only occassionally in the occupied territories where transportation facilities were poor.

Synthetic Oil Plants.

113. The tense political situation early in 1939 brought all imports of oil to a standstill with the exception of those from Russia and Rumania, and neither the Russian nor Rumanian products were of a sufficiently high standard to be used for aviation purposes without blending. At the outbreak of the war supplies from Rumania ceased altogether and, as far as the Luftwaffe was concerned, did not recommence until early in 1942.

114. The solution, therefore, was to turn these synthetic plants already in production over to aviation spirit and to delve into the accumulated reserves at G.T.L.s.

115. At the outbreak of hostilities, all synthetic plants already in production received their "orders for the duration" (Mob. Auflagen). Due to insufficient experience of large-scale hydration, as well as to variation in origin and quality of ingredients used, considerable difficulties were experienced initially in attaining a quality up to the technical requirements set, and in some cases it was as long as six months before the synthetic product was acceptable to the G.A.F.

116. The products of the synthetic plants were never, in any circumstances, transported direct to consumer units as they were first required to be blended and ethylised. This was done either at the WIFO, G.T.L.s, or at certain of the L.T.L.s, which were specially equipped with laboratory units in order to test and bring into use captured fuels as quickly as possible.

117. It is of interest to note the production output of synthetic fuel plants which, between the middle of 1942 and April 1944 (when the Allied attacks were at their peak) was beween 150,000 and 180,000 tons monthly. In May 1944, however, the Allied bombing of Leuna, Gelsenberg and Peolitz resulted in the immediate loss of 50% of the monthly production. Against a planned monthly production of 200,000 tons, the actual production of synthetic fuel had dropped to 10,000 tons per month in January 1945, 6000 tons in March and by April was at a virtual standstill.

118. In April 1945, in spite of the severest restriction in the Luftwaffe and the aircraft industry, in spite of the complete suspension of transport flying, in spite of reductions in the quality of the fuel and the use of pure iso-octane, all stocks were exhausted. The operational activity of the Luftwaffe was ended.

Effects of Bombing on Supply Organisation

119. The catastrophic fuel situation existing in Germany at the end of 1944 placed an immense burden on the supply organisation of the Luftwaffe. Quotas to individual units had to be adjusted at short notice, blending regulations were constantly being changed in accordance with the varying qualities of fuel available, and after the attacks upon and destruction of the synthetic plants, the main petrol dumps themselves were the objects of constant and severe attacks by Allied bombers. Although only small quantities of fuel were destroyed by these attacks, pumps, pipe lines and rail facilities in storage installations were, to a large extent, paralysed for long periods and supplies to units were constantly held up.

Provision of Fuel Oil for the Aircraft Industry

120. Aviation fuel required by Repair Organisations and the Aircraft Industry was supplied by auxiliary Luftwaffe Fuel Depots known as Hilfslufttanklager, or H.L.T.L.s. These H.L.T.L.s were storage installations which had originally belonged to Commercial undertakings and which had been requisitioned by the Luftwaffe for the war period. They remained

the properties of the private companies and the employees, who were exempt from military Service, received their pay from the commercial firms. Their supplies were drawn from the L.T.L.s and represented part of the quota allocated to the Luftwaffe by the 4th Abteilung.

121. In 1944, owing to increasing transport difficulties, the Aircraft Industry was permitted to draw supplies direct from L.T.L.s or even from a G.T.L. of WIFO, providing such a source was more favourably situated than the nearest H.L.T.L. If drawn from a G.T.L., however, it counted against the Luftwaffe quota.

Types of German Aviation Fuel

122. The three main German Aviation Fuels in order of their importance, were known as Green Fuel C. 3., Blue Fuels B. 4 and A. 3, and Starter Fuel (Anlaßkraftstoff).

123. C. 3 was a high grade product chiefly used for fighter aircraft. Its Octane number was 96.

124. B. 4 and A. 3 may conveniently be treated together, the main difference between them being the T.E.L. content. The octane number of B. 4 was 90 and that of A. 3, 80.

125. The Anlaßkraftstoff was a mixture of Ethyl Ether, lubricating oil and petrol, and was merely employed for quick starting of aircraft, a small auxiliary tank of about one litre being fitted to most aircraft for this purpose.

Special Fuels for "V" Weapons and Motivation of Rockets and Rocket Propelled Aaircraft

126. Special fuels were used for the above purpose, known as T-Stoff and Z-Stoff. These fuels were stored in a special depot at Giebelstadt, and small storage dumps were erected near the runways from which Flying Bombs were launched or from which Rocket Propelled weapons were operated.

127. **"T"-Stoff.** This fuel was 80% Hydrogen peroxide and was stored in alumiinum containers in a cool place. It was required to be handled with extreme care, as materials of an organic nature, such as wood and clothing, would burst into flames on contact. Contact with the skin produced painful and sometimes serious blisters. The liquid was transported in special aluminium tank lorries, and was stored in airfields in 10 or 20 gallon aluminium containers.

128. **"Z"-Stoff.** This fuel was concentrated aqueous solution of calcium or sodium permanganate. It could be handled without any particular precautions and was stored in steel drums. Care was required to be taken to avoid spilling in transit, as contact with organic materials was liable to cause fire. Providing adequate precautions were taken it could be transported without restriction. At airfields and units it was stored in steel drums of 10 or 20 gallon capacity.

Use of Substitute Fuels for Motor Vehicles

129. Large-scale conversion of all Motor vehicles to Substitute Fuels began in Germany in 1941 and, by the middle of 1942, the vast majority of commercial vehicles had been converted. In 1943 instructions were issued for the conversion of private cars. The following four methods were adopted throughout Germany:—

(i) Producer Gas — obtained from Wood, Charcoal, Peat, Anthracite, Coke or Lignite.
(ii) Normal "Town Gas" or methane.
(iii) Liquid Gas (Treibgas) — a mixture of propane and butane which liquifies at low pressure.
(iv) Acetylene gas, obtained from Calcium Carbide.

NOTES ON THE ORIGIN OF W.I.F.O. AND BRIEF DESCRIPTION OF STORAGE INSTALLATIONS

General

130. The Wirtschaftlich Forschungsgesellschaft m. b. H. was founded in 1934, with a capital jointly subscribed by the Government (four parts) and the firm of I.G. Farben (one part) of RM. 100,000. The intention was to undertake bulk storage of petroleum products and to manufacture nitric acid. Within a few months of its formation, the capital of W.I.F.O. was increased to the startling figure of RM. 100,000,000, all subscribed by the German Government, and its objects were stated to be responsibility for the storage of all military and economic reserves, both for the Wehrmacht and Industry.

131. The management of W.I.F.O. was controlled by a Board of Directors, and its activities were divided into five main spheres:—
   (a) General Administration.
   (b) Mineral Oil Storage.
   (c) Transportation.
   (d) Construction.
   (e) Factories.

132. Before the war, W.I.F.O. was mainly concerned in negotiating the imports of petroleum products for reserve storage. In 1935 and 1936 large quantities were purchased from the U.S.A., these products being transported to Germany by tankers, and subsequently transferred to barges on the rivers Weser and Elbe and shipped to the W.I.F.O. Großraumtanklager.

133. Inside Germany, W.I.F.O. purchased supplies from the Zentral Büro für Meneralöl, which was a syndicate of all German oil undertakings (Shell, Standard, D.P. Olex, etc.) handling motor fuels and lubricants for German Industry. As the war progressed, however, W.I.F.O. tended to by-pass the Z.B. and purchases were made direct from refineries, synthetic producers, and coal tar manufacturers.

Storage Installations

134. Oil storage and blending installations were divided into four main classes:—

(i) Großraumtanklager: Large installations designed and constructed for the storage of bulk reserves. (N.B.. With these installations may be grouped the slightly smaller plants sometimes referred to as Hauptlager.)

(ii) Lufttanklager:
(iii) Heerestanklager:
(iv) Marinelager:
   These installations, as their names imply, were concerned specifically with storage for the Air Force, Army and Navy, respectively.

135. Shortly after the outbreak of the war, the G.A.F. took over the Lufttanklager from W.I.F.O. and operated them independently as G.A.F. units.

Großraumtanklagers (G.T.L.s)

136. These depots, somewhat naturally, varied in detail and the description given below is of a typical and not particular installation.

137. The G.T.L.s were normally located in well-wooded parts of Germany and would be flanked wherever possible by a river or inland waterway system. Good rail and road connections were also essential. The total storage for petrol would consist of approximately 30 underground tanks each with a capacity of 3,000 to 4,000 cubic metres, giving a total of approximately 100,000 cubic metres. Each tank was self-contained. They were constructed of 10 mm. iron plate and were laid horizontally with a slightly inclined axis to ensure complete emptying. A small pump-house was erected for each tank which could be employed either for pumping petrol to other locations or for the circulation of the contents.

138. Oil storage consisted of a large number (50 to 80) of individual underground tanks each with a capacitiy of 500 to 600 cubic metres, giving a total capacity of approximately 50,000 cubic metres. The construction of the tanks was in general principle similar to that of the petrol tanks, each having its own small pump house for the purpose of circulation, pumping to other locations, removal of residues, sludge, water, etc.

T.E.L. Blending

139. Tetra Ethyl Lead blending was normally undertaken by special mobile W.I.F.O. units who would visit a site as and when gasolene was required to be leaded, and conduct the operation of blending through the man-hole of the tank.

Other Buildings

140. In addition to the main plant there were the usual office buildings workshops, stores, and a fair-sized laboratory well but not elaborately equipped.

Management and Staff

141. The management of all W.I.F.O. depots was nominally in the hands of General Director Baurat Wehling operating from Berlin. In actual practice, each depot was under the control of three managers — a Works Manager, a Commercial Manager, and a Technical Manager, and any one of these would be appointed by Wehling to be responsible for the smooth and efficient running of the Depot, and for its general safety. In general, the man selected would be the one considered as "most reliable" from the political aspect!

142. A typical staff at a W.I.F.O. G.T.L. would be:—

```
           Works Manager
           Commercial Manager
           Technical Manager
                                              3.
           Technical and Skilled Employees:  70.
           Semi- and Non-skilled employees: 110.
           Guards and Foresters:             50.
           Clerical Employees:               30.
           Chemists:                         10.
                              Total Staff:  273.
```

In addition a Luftwaffe Liaison Officer was normally located on the Depot.

Lufttanklagers (L.T.L.s)

143. The L.T.L.s were constructed by W.I.F.O. and were taken over by the G.A.F. shortly after the outbreak of the war. They were, of course, much smaller than the G.T.L.s and were surface as opposed to underground installations.

Locations

144. L.T.L.s were frequently constructed in or adjacent to small woods to facilitate camouflage. Their location was also influenced by the adequacy of existing rail facilities. Connection with main lines was provided by marshalling yards and sidings within the depot.

145. The total capacity of an L.T.L. was anything between 5,000 and 15,000 tons. The tanks were protected by concrete structures, brick walls and earth mounds, and netting was used extensively to prevent observation from the air.

Blending

146. Some, but not all, L.T.L.s were equipped with laboratory units which could undertake blending operations.

Other Buildings

147. Apart from the main storage tanks, there existed the usual office buildings, workshops, stores and a laboratory.

Management and Staff

148. An L.T.L. was commanded by an officer of the rank of Lieutenant Colonel. The total staff engaged would usually number approximately 180 to 200, made up as follows:—

Commanding Officer:	1.
2nd in Command (Major): and i/c Administration:	1.
G.A.F. Personnel as Guards:	30.
Technical and Skilled Civilian Employees:	50.
Semi- and Non-skilled Employees:	80.
Clerical Employees:	20.
Chemists and Trainees:	6.
Total Staff:	188.

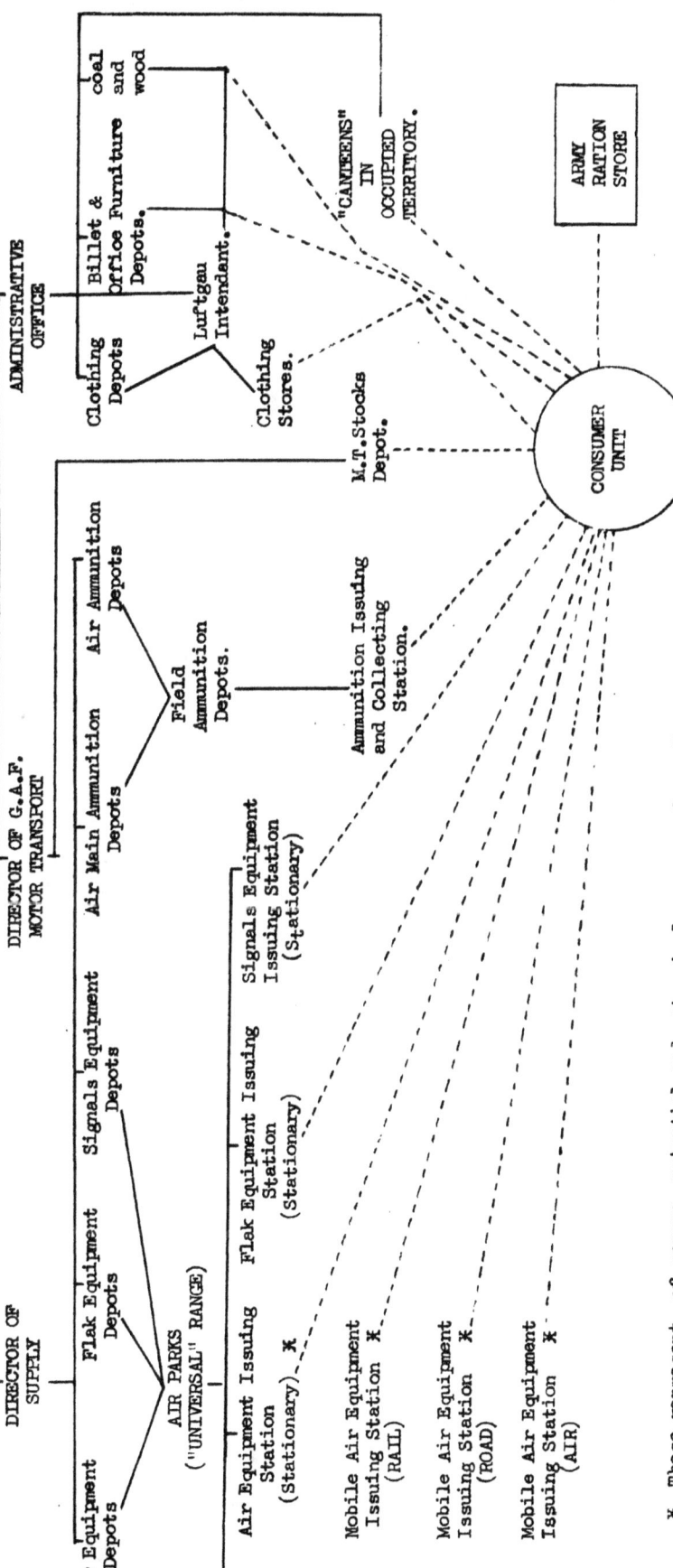

APPENDIX "B"
to Part 2. Chap. VII.

Air Equipment Depots in Germany as at 31st December 1944
In January 1945 the Depots at Küpper and Liegnitz were overrun by the Russian forces

Depot No.	Location	Equipment held
A.E.D. 1/III.	FINOW	Gruppe "A" equipment — Junkers aircraft
		No Gruppe "B" equipment held
A.E.D. 1/IV.	KÖLLEDA	Gruppe "A" equipment — Dornier aircraft.
		Gruppe "B" equipment — Bezirke B.1
		,, B.2
		,, B.3
		,, B.6
		,, B.7
A.E.D. 1/VI.	KÜPPER	Gruppe "A" equipment — Heinkel aircraft
		Gruppe "B" equipment — Bezirke B.1
		,, B.7
A.E.D. 3/VI.	GÖTTINGEN	Gruppe "A" equipment — All French and Italian Aircraft in use
		Gruppe "B" equipment — Bezirke B.7
A.E.D. 1/VII.	ERDING	Gruppe "A" equipment — Messerschmitt and Klemm aircraft
		Gruppe "B" equipment — Bezirke B.1
		,, B.2
		,, B.7
A.E.D. 1/XI.	SCHWERIN	Gruppe "A" equipment — Arado, Bücker and Blohm and Voss aircraft
		Gruppe "B" equipment — Bezirke B.2
		,, B.5
		,, B.7
		,, B.9
A.E.D. 2/XI.	TRAVEMÜNDE-PÖTENITZ	Gruppe "A" equipment — All sea planes
		Gruppe "B" equipment — Bezirke B.2
		,, B.7
A.E.D. 3/XI.	LIEGNITZ	Gruppe "A" equipment — Focke-Wulf aircraft
		Gruppe "B" equipment — Bezirke B.7
		,, B.8
A.E.D. 1/XVII.	PRÖSSNITZ	Gruppe "A" equipment — Siebel aircraft.
		Gruppe "B" equipment — Instructional equipment

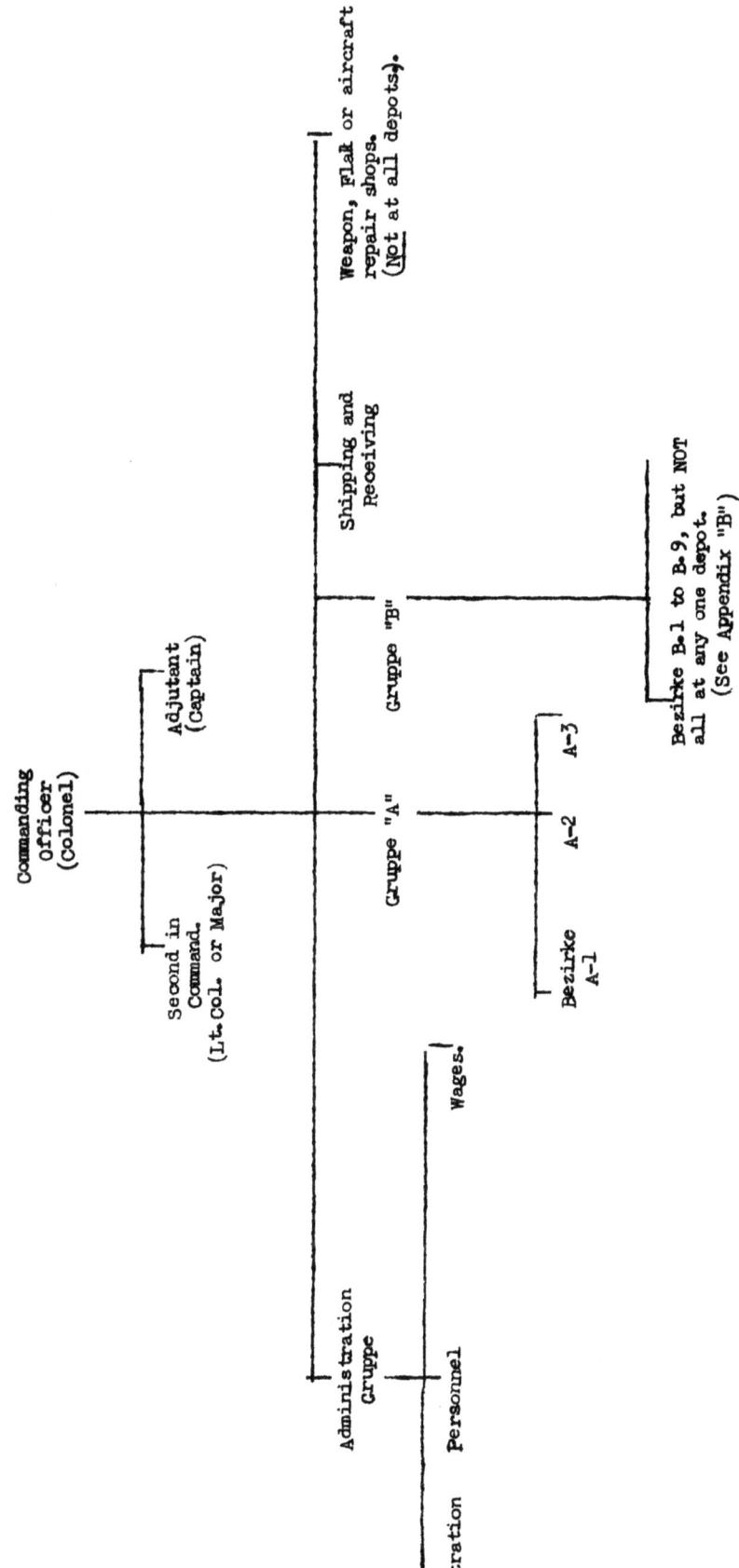

APPENDIX "D"
to Part 2. Chap. VII,

The following is a description of the contents of the various coaches which would make up a typical Rail Equipment Issuing Station. Telephonic communication would exist between all cars.

No. 1. This would be an open Luggage Van, with specially constructed Machine Gun position. It would carry a motor-cycle and sidecar, one barrel of petrol, one of oil, and one of crude oil. Drinking Water and a portable toilet.

No. 2. A normal railway coach, reconstructed to form a sleeping car with accommodation for 18 persons, bunks being arranged in tiers of three. Its equipment would include a stove, wash basins, wardrobe, toilet etc.

No. 3. A coach converted for use as Kitchens, Office and Rest-room for personnel. Its equipment would include a field telephone exchange linking all coaches, office equipment (portable typewriter etc.) messing equipment, stove etc.

No. 4. Workshop coach. Equipment to include a lathe, welding apparatus, various machine and hand-tool sets.

No. 5. Power Installation Car. Electric power would be produced here by two Junkers Diesel Engines. Facilities would also be available for charging of batteries.

No. 6. Storage for Air-frame spares. This coach would be fitted with built-in shelves, tables, cabinets etc. to facilitate the storage and handling of equipment.

No. 7. Same as Coach No. 6.

No. 8. Storage for Engine spares and components, tool etc. The equipment in this coach would include a moveable overhead crane for the handling of a complete engine.

No. 9. Storage for complete engines.

No. 10. Storage for machine guns and spares, entrenching tools, workshop and tradesmens' tools and equipment.

No. 11. Storage for wireless equipment, first aid and gas-defence equipment.

No. 12. Storage for oxygen, oxygen bottles, searchlights, M/T repair equipment and two complete bicycles.

No. 13. Storage for fire-fighting equipment, special fuels and oils, cleaning materials and works materials.

No. 14. Storage for airframe major components and propellors.

No. 15. An open luggage van as for No. 1. again with special Machine Gun position. It would also carry special loading and unloading ramp.

APPENDIX "E".
to Part 2. Chap. VII.

ORGANISATION OF AN AIR MAIN AMMUNITION DEPOT (FLAK, "M", "T" OR "K").

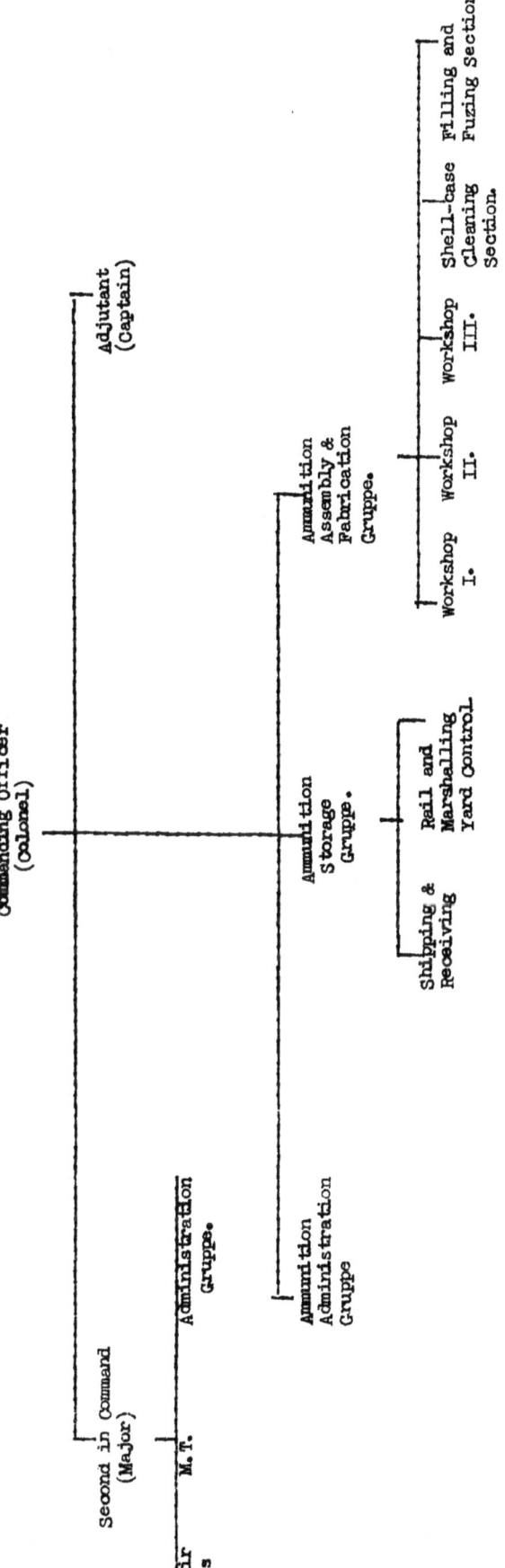

APPENDIX "F".
to Part 2. Chap. VII.

ORGANISATION OF AN AIR AMMUNITION DEPOT.

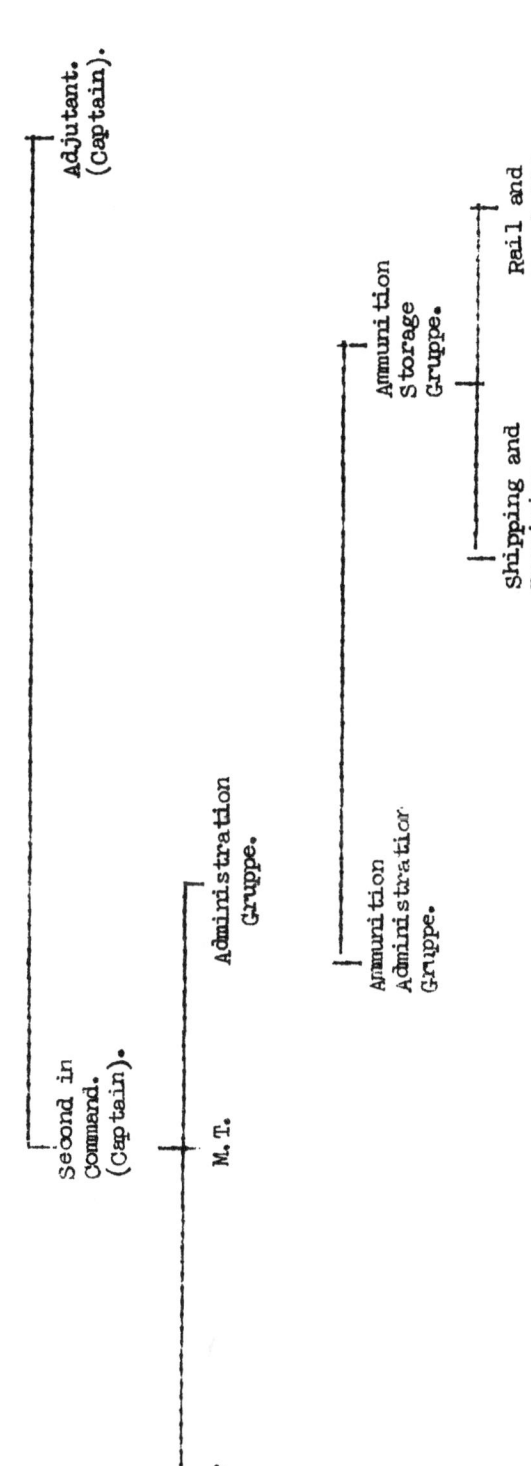

APPENDIX "G".
to Part 2. Chap. VII.

CHAIN OF SUPPLY FOR P.O.L. IN THE G.A.F.

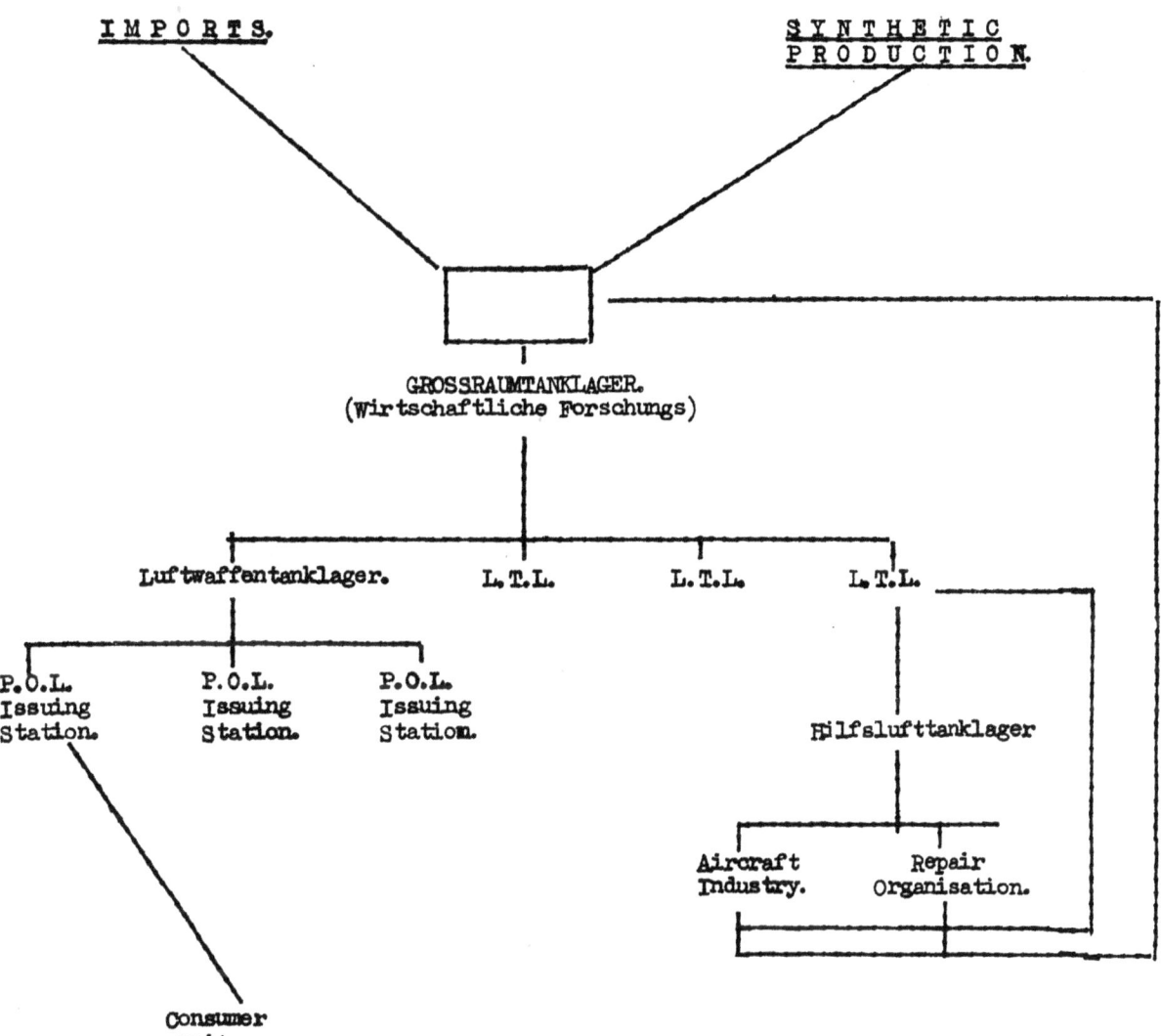

PART 2

CHAPTER VIII

REPAIR AND SALVAGE

INTRODUCTION	Paragraphs 1—4
CLASSIFICATION OF EQUIPMENT	,, 5—7
REPAIR UNITS	,, 8—18
Repair of Air Equipment	,, 9—15
Repair of Signals Equipment	,, 16—17
Repair of Intendant Equipment	,, 18
CONTROL OF REPAIR UNITS	,, 19—23
SUPPLY OF EQUIPMENT AND SPARES	,, 24—28
Station Equipment Sections	,, 25
Predetermined Supply Kits	,, 26
Front Repair Units	,, 27
Motor Transport Spares	,, 28
REPAIR CIRCUITS	,, 29—33
Air Equipment	,, 30—31
Signals Equipment	,, 32
Intendant Equipment	,, 33
MODIFICATIONS	,, 34—37
SALVAGE	,, 38
CONCLUSION	,, 39—40

PART 2

CHAPTER VIII

REPAIR AND SALVAGE

INTRODUCTION

1.   In the execution of their functions the Repair and Maintenance services of an Air Force consume large quantities of equipment and spare parts. The efficiency of such services is dependent, therefore, to a large degree on satisfactory support from the supply organisation. The aim of this Chapter is to examine the organisation that existed for the repair and maintenance of German Air Force equipment and to consider the connection between the repair and maintenance units and the supply installations.

2.   According to a number of German officers who were interrogated on the subject of repair and maintenance, a high standard of serviceability of German Air Force equipment was maintained throughout the war and the supply of equipment and spares for this purpose was good. Unfortunately, it has not been possible to obtain any statistics showing the number of aircraft that were rendered unserviceable through lack of spares or for how long such aircraft remained unserviceable. All such statistics were destroyed in the last days of the war.

3.   Salvage is a subject closely allied to that of repair and maintenance and an account of the German Air Force salvage organisation is included in this Chapter.

4.   The technical aspects of repair and salvage are not considered in this publication as such matters are outside the present terms of reference.

CLASSIFICATION OF EQUIPMENT

5.   All German Air Force equipment was classified in the five following categories of condition: —
   (i)   Standard   I: Newly manufactured equipment.
   (ii) Standard   II: Used but fully serviceable equipment.
   (iii) Standard   III: Unserviceable equipment that was worth repairing. After repair such equipment was classified in Standard II.
   (iv) Standard   IV: Unserviceable equipment that was not worth repairing (scrap).
   (v)   Standard   IV L: Unserviceable equipment that was not worth repairing but which was required for the construction of instructional models.

6.   To guide units in categorizing equipment into the above Standards basic instructions were issued from time to time by the Air Ministry (Director of Supply). These instructions were prepared for the various types of equipment and laid down for each the degrees of damage that were to be repaired and the degrees that were beyond economical repair. The Director of Supply prepared such instructions in consultation with the 6th Department of the General Staff, the Director General of Signals,

the Director General of Equipment (later Chief of Technical Air Armaments) and the Main Committees of the appropriate industries. Factors such as the probable time the repairs would take, the value and operational importance of the equipment in question, the stock holdings of the equipment, and the raw materials and repair capacity available, were taken into account at these conferences.

7.   The Technical Officials in charge of station workshops were responsible for determining whether, within the terms of the basic instructions previously mentioned, unserviceable equipment should be repaired or not. They were also responsible for deciding where such equipment should be repaired and in this matter they were guided by the following formula. Equipment damaged to the extent of 20% of its cash value was to be repaired by the Air Force repair organisation; from 20% to 60% by industry; and above 60% was to be scrapped. This formula was, of course, subject to alteration by over-riding clauses in the basic instructions.

REPAIR UNITS

8.   Procedure for the repair of German Air Force equipment differed for four main groups of materials and the repair units associated with these groups must, therefore, be considered in the following separate classes:

  (i)   **Repair of Air Equipment.** Air Equipment included all aircraft and airborne equipment and spares, armament, ground technical equipment and Motor transport.
  (ii) **Repair of Signals Equipment.** Signals equipment, included ground and airborne signals equipment, radar and Flak radar equipment.
  (iii) **Repair of Intendant Equipment.** Intendant equipment included clothing and barrack equipment.
  (iv) **Repair of Flak Equipment.** Flak equipment included all anti-aircraft guns, equipment and searchlights. The repair of such items will not be considered in this Chapter as it has already been covered in a publication prepared by the British Army and is at present of no direct interest to the Royal Air Force.

Repair of Air Equipment

9.   The following were the most important formations connected with the maintenance and repair of Air Equipment and will be described briefly in the following paragraphs.

  (i)   Airfield Servicing Companies.
  (ii) Static Workshops.
  (iii) Field Workshops (Mobile).
  (iv) Ground Technical Equipment Workshops.
  (v)   Industrial Repair Shops.
  (vi) Motor Transport Repair Shops.

10.   **Airfield Servicing Companies.** At the beginning of the war maintenance of aircraft and minor repairs that would not take longer than two days were undertaken by technical personnel attached to the flying formations. In the case of very mobile flying formations (fighter, ground attack, and dive bomber units) the technical personnel were organised into Headquarters Companies permanently attached to the Wings. All other flying formations were served by technical personnel organised into Air-

field Servicing Companies which were attached when required to appropriate Wing Headquarters. It was intended originally that Airfield Servicing Companies should be attached only to formations which were operating from airfields which had no other workshops. In contrast to the Headquarters Companies the Airfield Servicing Companies were to be independent of flying formations, and it was intended that they should operate only within a given area, viz., the Airfield Regional Commands, and not be moved over any great distances. It was soon apparent, however, that this system would not function as planned. The principal cause of this was the diversity of aircraft types in existence and neither the training nor the equipment of the Airfield Servicing Companies was sufficiently universal to deal with the situation. Airfield Servicing Companies were, therefore, reorganized to cope with specific aircraft types; they were permanently attached to flying formations and subordinated to them in every respect. It was found in practice that this subordination also had its disadvantages. In the case of a transfer of a flying formation to another airfield the Servicing Company arrived at the destination much later than the flying elements. Alternatively, the Airfield Servicing Companies had to be transferred long in advance, leaving the formation without its maintenance services. To overcome this difficulty Airfield Servicing Companies (Qu) were formed and were subordinated as a "pool" to the Quartermaster General and were only temporarily attached to the flying formations to which they were allocated. This system and also the Headquarters Company system worked reasonably well until the lack of transport aircraft, fuel and motor transport made itself felt. Both Airfield Servicing Companies and Headquarters Companies found it increasingly difficult to catch up with the flying formations to which they were allocated At the end of 1944 it was decided, therefore, that both the Airfield Servicing Companies and the Headquarters Companies should be abolished. They were replaced by maintenance companies which were independent of particular flying formations. Although the Airfield Servicing Companies had proved the impracticability of such an organisation at the beginning of the war it was now considered to be more feasible in view of the reduction in types of aircraft which had now taken place. The new organization took the form of Aircraft Maintenance Companies which were subordinated to the Station Commands and their task was the maintenance of aircraft landing on the particular airfield to which they were subordinated. By the end of the war, however, this reorganization had not been completely effected.

11. **Static Workshops.** All German Air Force stations designed to peacetime standards were equipped with static workshops. Such workshops were able to undertake repairs or modifications of Air Equipment that could be completed in ten days or under. These workshops were originally designed in such a manner that they were unsuitable for removal. Experience gathered early in the war led to a redesigned workshop which was more easily dismantled, loaded and transported — such workshops were referred to as transferable. Until 1944 static and later transferable workshops were subordinated for discipline and administration to the Station Commands. Technical direction and technical instructions came from the Luftgau Engineer who issued orders through the Airfield Regional Commands and the Station Commands to the workshops. Normally a workshop would only move if the Station Command was moved, but in 1944 the workshops were classified as independent units which could be moved by the Luftgau Headquarters from station to station

as the situation demanded. It is emphasised that these workshops were responsible not only for aircraft and aircraft equipment repair but also armament, ground technical equipment (until 1944) and minor motor transport repairs.

12. **Field Workshops (Mobile).** At the beginning of the war there were no workshops which could follow the advancing flying formations. Fully motorised workshops which required no buildings and which were supplied with independent sources of power were, therefore, hastily improvised and became permanent German Air Force formations. They were controlled by Field Workshop Groups of which there was one in each Luftflotte subordinated directly to the Luftflotte Chief Engineer. The duties of a Field Workshop did not differ from those of a static or transferable workshop though, in consequence of its motorisation and its independence from buildings or power services, the Field Workshop could be brought far closer to the front than the other types of workshop.

13. **Ground Technical Equipment Workshops.** Prior to 1944 the repair workshops responsible for Ground Technical Equipment formed a section of the Static Workshops referred to in paragraph 11. When the static workshops were reclassified as independent units which could be switched from place to place by the Luftgau the Ground Technical Equipment Workshops remained as static units subordinated to the Station Commands. Ground technical equipment included such items as engine starters, oxygen refilling apparatus, bomb trolleys, engine heaters, etc.

14. **Industrial Repair Shops.** Repairs requiring an average time of more than ten days were undertaken by the appropriate industrial firms. When the Air Force advanced a considerable distance away from the homeland as, for example, was the case in the Russian campaign, the lines of communication became overloaded and serious delays in transit resulted. This meant that large quantities of valuable equipment were frozen in pipelines to and from the industrial repair shops at home. The problem was resolved by establishing, in the occupied territories, "out stations" of the various home industries. These "out stations" were called Front Repair Units. In the majority of cases the Front Repair Units specialised in particular types of aircraft or Air Equipment. The units were manned by German civilian specialists who were assisted by foreign "volunteer" workers. The units were subordinated in every respect to their parent firms.

15. **Motor Transport Repair Shops.** Minor repairs to Motor Transport vehicles were undertaken within the Air Force organisation and major repairs were handled by the Army. Facilities available within the Air Force were small sections of the static workshops and a number of mobile workshops which were controlled by the Airfield Regional Command Headquarters. Owing to the inefficient handling by the Army of Air Force motor transport repairs the Air Force was forced to set up a number of large static repair shops. These were not offically recognised and were found mainly in the Russian theatre. Major repairs undertaken by the Army were effected through a system of Motor Transport Parks. These Parks were organised as follows:—

(i) A Headquarters and administrative office, together with a reception area in which vehicles requiring repair were stored.

(ii) Requisitioned workshops and garages to which the vehicles were sent for repair.

The Park itself did not carry out the repair work but was the authority in control of motor transport repair facilities in each area and it regulated the flow of vehicles from the reception area to the repair shops and garages under its command. At each Park there was normally a small Air Force Liaison Staff to handle Air Force requirements.

Repair of Signals Equipment

16. Small repairs of airborne signals equipment were undertaken by the static workshops referred to in paragraph 11. Small repairs of ground signals equipment were effected by the technical signals personnel of the unit to which the equipment belonged. When such personnel were not available or when the repairs were of such magnitude that such personnel (or in the case of air signals equipment — the static workshops) could not manage the tasks involved, repairs were undertaken by Air Signals Repair Shops. These repair shops were allocated by the Luftgau Headquarters to the various Airfield Regional Commands. Air Signals Repair Shops were not available at all Station Commands but a total of approximately 100 existed.

17. Air Signals Repair Shops were not specialised but handled repairs to all signals and radar equipment both for the Air, Ground and Flak units. These repair shops were not subordinated to the Signals officer but to the Technical Superintendent of the Station Command to which were allocated. Work that could not be done by the Air Signals Repair Shops was sent to the appropriate firms in the radio industry or in occupied countries to the representative sections of the firms in the Front Repair Units.

Repair of Intendant Equipment

18. Repairs to Intendant materials were handled quite separately from any of the materials previously discussed. Supply of clothing and barrack equipment was controlled by the Intendants at the various command levels and at Station Command level by the Administrative Officer. Repairs of such materials were handled through the same channels and the facilities available for repairs were as follows:—

(i) **Clothing:** Minor repairs were effected by small staffs in the Station Command Clothing Rooms. Other repairs were undertaken by the Luftgau Clothing Stores and the Air Ministry Clothing Depots. Both the latter types of unit were responsible for making up Air Force clothing and also had considerable facilities for repair work at their disposal.

(ii) **Barrack Equipment.** Minor repairs of this type of equipment were effected by Station Command staff working under the orders of the Administrative Officer. Other repairs were arranged by local contracts with suitable civilian firms.

CONTROL OF REPAIR UNITS

19. The control of the repair units for clothing and barrack equipment was in the hands of the Intendants and Administrative Officers and has been discussed in paragraph 18. The control of repair units concerned with air equipment and signals equipment needs further explanation.

20. The Air Force repair units for air equipment and signals equipment were based on Station Command airfields and were controlled by the Technical Superintendent. For disciplinary and administrative matters they were subordinated to the Station Commander. Technical direction of all repair units was exercised by the Air Ministry Chief Engineer who issued instructions through the Luftflotte Chief Engineers, the Luftgau

Engineers and the Airfield Regional Command Engineers. Basic instructions giving rules for equipment classification and outlining the amount of repair work considered economical were, however, issued by the Director of Supply as explained in paragraphs 5 to 7.

21. It should be noted at this stage that all Engineer Staffs were subordinated to the Quartermasters at the various levels of command and that the Quartermaster General of the Air Ministry commanded both the Director of Supply and the Chief Air Force Engineer. The supply and technical staffs were, therefore, under the same command and closely allied to each other. The Engineer staffs were, however, in a somewhat weaker position as they were entirely manned by officials, whereas the Supply staffs possessed a proportion of officers.

22. All maintenance publications, technical manuals and spare parts lists were prepared by the manufacturers of the equipment concerned. The original drafts of such publications were submitted to the Air Ministry for approval and editing before authority to publish was given. The Air Ministry Departments concerned were the Director General of Equipment (later Chief of Technical Air Armaments), the Director General of Signals and the Chief Engineer.

23. The Front Repair Units were subordinated to their parent firms. The Air Force was, however, responsible for providing any administrative facilities required. Technical directions from the Air Force to such units were issued by the Director General of Equipment and later by the Chief of Technical Air Armaments through the Special Commission for Repairs in the Main Committee for Aircraft Production.

SUPPLY OF EQUIPMENT AND SPARES

24. In the Introduction to this Chapter the importance of an efficient supply of equipment and spares to Repair units was stressed and the following paragraphs will be devoted to an assessment of the most important features of the German methods used in this connection.

Station Equipment Sections

25. In contrast to the system used on Royal Air Force airfields, there were no central Equipment Sections on German airfields from which the various flights and sections demanded whatever materials they required. Each repair and maintenance unit had, however, within its own organisation a small equipment store (though larger than an R.A.F. flight lock-up) which contained reserves of its own particular requirements. Each repair unit also had a small equipment staff to maintain this store: for example, a static workshop had a staff of 11 such personnel and a Ground Technical Equipment Repair Shop had a staff of 10 for a similar purpose. All equipment required by repair units was demanded through the Technical Superintendent who placed demands on the appropriate Issuing Stations or Parks which served the particular area.

Predetermined Supply Kits

26. It is interesting to note that predetermined supply kits were issued to the repair and maintenance units. These kits or pack-ups existed in two forms. The first was known as a T-1 kit and was issued to the maintenance formations — Headquarters Companies and Airfield Servicing Companies. Such kits contained parts and materials that it was anticipated would be needed for maintaining a squadron of aircraft for 30 days. T-2 kits contained a supply of repair parts normally required for 30 days. Spares

in these sets necessarily included larger and more bulky items than the T-1 sets. T-2 sets were issued to static and field workshops. The quantities and types of spares stocked in these sets were decided by the Chief Engineer in consultation with the Director of Supply. The repair units obtained replenishments through the Technical Superintendents who demanded on the appropriate Issuing Stations or Parks.

Front Repair Units

27.   Front Repair Units normally received supplies of spare parts directly from their parent firms. They were, however, permitted to place demands on Air Force stocks if they desired.

Motor Transport Spares

28.   The Technical Superintendents demanded motor transport spares from the Army Central Stocks Depots.

REPAIR CIRCUITS

29.   The methods used for despatching unserviceable equipment to the various repair units and receiving the repaired items back into service use must be examined under three headings, viz:—

        (i)   Air Equipment.
        (ii)   Signals Equipment.
        (iii) Intendant Equipment.

Air Equipment

30.   The usual channels followed for air equipment were:—
  (i)   For equipment repaired in the unit area the procedure was for the holding unit to pass the equipment to the Station Command; the Station Command passed it to the workshop or field workshop. The equipment when repaired was then passed back to the original holder through the same circuit.
  (ii) For equipment which could not be repaired in the unit area the procedure was for the holding unit to pass the equipment to the Station Command, the Station Command to a Supply Installation and the Supply Installation to a Front Repair Unit or Factory. (Sometimes the equipment was passed directly from the Station Command to a Front Repair Unit or Factory.) The repaired equipment was returned to the original holding unit through the same channels.

31.   It was not always possible to keep rigidly to the above procedure. In some instances the holding unit would have to demand a new item to replace the unserviceable equipment instead of waiting for the unserviceable item to be returned. Furthermore, it would not always be in a position to return the unserviceable equipment immediately, for such reasons as shortage of transport, a lack of repair facilities or storage space at repair units. It was the responsibility of the Technical Superintendents and the Airfield Regional Commands and the Luftgau Quartermasters to ensure that all such unserviceable equipment was eventually repaired. The equipment was generally sent to the nearest supply installation where it would be held pending disposal instructions.

Signals Equipment

32.   A special feature which applied to signals equipment and Flak equipment only was that the holding unit returned signals equipment that

it was unable to repair with its own facilities to the appropriate Signals Equipment Park or Issuing Station. **It received immediately a serviceable item in exchange** and the Park passed on the unserviceable equipment to the Air Signals Repair Shop in industry. When the equipment was repaired it was returned to the Park from which it was re-issued to the original holder **in exchange for the item loaned.** Although judged by standard R.A.F. practice this is an extraordinary procedure, the information is obtained from a German lecture on Supply in the German Air Force.

Indendant Equipment

33.   The repair circuits for Intendant materials were based on the same principles as those for Air Equipment.

MODIFICATIONS

34.   Modifications were broadly divided into two classes, those required for operational or safety reasons and those required for production purposes. The German Air Ministry instituted a committee to supervise proposed modifications of equivalent terms of reference to the British Airframe Modifications Committee, and this Committee classified each approved modification under one of four classifications:—

(i) **Class A:** A safety modification which had to be incorporated before the next flight. Aircraft were grounded until embodiment.

(ii) **Class B:** Modifications which had to be embodied before any aircraft left the firm. Flight tests by the firm's pilots only were authorised prior to the incorporation of such a modification.

(iii) **Class C:** A non-retrospective class to be introduced at an agreed state of production (e.g. 761st aircraft).

(iv) **Class D:** To be introduced only when a new Series was to be started in production. It was a non-retrospective class.

35.   In the cases of Classes A and B, retrospective action was taken by the parent firm producing the modification kits which were issued to either the squadrons or to the "Schleusen" — "Modification Centres" or "Locks". Modification kits were not used whenever it was possible to issue a complete component embodying the modification. For example, if a carburettor or an oleo leg of an aircraft were to be modified every effort was made to place the complete new component at the disposal of the units or repair shops charged with the modification. Modification kits were used only when this policy proved impracticable or inadvisable. Small modifications were embodied at the aerodrome by squadron personnel under the guidance and instruction of firm's representatives. For larger modifications the aircraft were returned from the front line to the "Schleusen" or "Locks" where the modifications were embodied. These "Locks" were organised on a Luftflotte basis — that is to say there were so many "Locks" in each Luftflotte and they were directed by the Chief Engineer of the Luftflotte. They were manned by the German Air Force personnel but later were handed over to Herr Frydag in his post as personal controller of the aircraft industry under Speer. For Class A and B modifications, aircraft from the production line which were delivered without the modification embodied had to go direct to the "Lock" and were then treated as front line aircraft.

36.   The flying formations were not allowed officially to embody modifications of their own in their aeroplanes. It was done, however, and at first a certain amount of latitude was permitted. At a later stage this

had to be stopped owing to the fact this introduced to great a measure of non-standardisation amongst aeroplanes in the same squadron. Thereafter, unit proposals had to be submitted to the Air Ministry General Staff and then to the Modifications Committee which represented six different departments of the Air Ministry. Responsibility for such authorised modifications, both for design and production, was then transferred to the parent firm and in due course was issued to the daughter firms.

37. Modifications to facilitate production could be put up by daughter firms to the parent firm who would decided whether or not they should be applied generally or permitted as an alternative for local use to suit special plant etc., of the daughter firm. Emphasis in all cases was laid on inter-changeability; for example, if the designing firm produced a built up section member and a daughter firm wished to replace this by a pressing, they would be accepted as alternatives providing that either the pressing or the built up component could be used in any aircraft as a spare.

SALVAGE

38. The Salvage organisation was centrally controlled at the Air Ministry by the Director of Supply and later the responsibility was transferred to the Chief Air Force Engineer. At each Luftflotte Headquarters there was a very small section which supervised the salvage organisation throughout the Luftflotte area. At the Luftgau there was a small salvage staff which was a section of the Luftgau Engineer's Office. This office had at its disposal within the Luftgau area a Salvage Battalion, a Booty Park, a Cannabilisation Centre, and Dismantling Establishment.

(i) **Salvage Battalion.** This consisted of a Battalion Headquarters (3 officers and 15 O.R.s) and four companies. In each company there was a Headquarters platoon (2 officers and 13 O.R.s) and from 5 to 9 other platoons (1 senior N.C.O. and 15 O.R.s). The Platoons were manned by two technical N.C.O.s, a mechanic, an electrician, a carpenter, 4 drivers, and 4 labourers. Typical equipment for a platoon was 1 passenger car, a motor cycle or cross-country vehicle, a derrick car with a winch or a tractor with a winch, 1 heavy lorry (5 tons), 1 flat trailer and 1 trailer which carried provisions, tents, tools, and a tripod, and a bladder. (The latter item was placed under heavy equipment and inflated, thus raising the object).

(ii) **Booty Park.** Each Luftgau operating in an active theatre of operations set up a Booty Park to which all captured or salvaged enemy material was despatched — if practicable. Here the various types of equipment would be sorted out and examined — new items or items of particular interest would be reported to Air Ministry, useful equipment would be issued to the fighting troops (particularly petrol) and redundant equipment would be returned to Germany as scrap. Booty Parks were manned by a specialist platoon of the Salvage Battalion.

(iii) **Cannabilisation Centres.** In addition to the Booty Parks, Cannabilisation Centres were set up in the Luftgaus to handle crashed German Aircraft. Aircraft classified as total losses would be transported to these centres where they were stripped of all equipment that could be of use to the fighting units. The remains were then despatched to the Dismantling Establishments in Germany where they were reduced to scrap. These Cannabilisation Centres received disposal instructions from the Air Ministry (Director of Supply) which indicated the action to be taken with surplus parts and materials collected.

(iv) **Dismantling Centres.** Certain centres specialising in the various types of aircraft were set up in the homeland for the purpose of dismantling aircraft and despatching the resultant scrap metal to appropriate melting plants. The centres were usually divided into two sections — one for enemy aircraft and one for allied aircraft. In the homeland the Dismantling Centres were generally located in the vicinity of melting plants.

CONCLUSION

39. Little attention was given in peacetime to the organisation for repair of German Air Force equipment. Experience in the early campaigns of the war quickly proved to the General Staff the need for developing an efficient system for undertaking work of this nature. The system that was established has been described in the preceding paragraphs but whether it was efficient or not it is difficult to ascertain without studying the appropriate statistics — none of which are now available as they were destroyed wilfully by the General Staff in the final days of the war. It is known, however, that high standards of maintenance and mechanical efficiency were demanded and according to interrogations of German officers it appears that such standards were indeed attained. It would seem, therefore, that the system was satisfactory.

40. A noteworthy feature from an "Equipment" viewpoint was the integration within a unit of the Equipment and the Repair Sections. This ensured the closest collaboration between the supplier and the user and eliminated many of the causes of the friction that sometimes arises between such people.

PART 2

CHAPTER IX

INSPECTION

INTRODUCTION	Paragraphs	1—4
The Inspector General of the German Air Force	,,	3—4
INSPECTORATES	,,	5—18
Influence of Inspectors on Supply	,,	13
Changes to Inspectorates during the War	,,	14
"Waffengenerale" (Specialist Air Officers)	,,	15—17
Summary of Changes in Inspectorates	,,	18
OTHER GERMAN AIR FORCE INSPECTION AUTHORITIES	,,	19—24
Fuel Inspection	,,	22—23
Factory Inspection	,,	24
INSPECTION OF AIRCRAFT TECHNICAL EQUIPMENT	,,	25—26
CONCLUSION	,,	27

PART 2

CHAPTER IX

INSPECTION

INTRODUCTION

1. Although Field Marshal Milch held the title of Inspector General, there was no central department in the German Air Ministry that was solely occupied with the task of general service inspection. Inspection in this sense was carried out by the Commanders in Chief of the Luftflotten themselves and by their staffs. They were ultimately responsible for the efficiency of all units and staffs within their sphere of command and, consequently, it was necessary for them to convince themselves by inspection that their orders were being carried out efficiently and accurately.

2. In contrast to the R.A.F. functional Commands — for example, Bomber Command — the German Air Force was organised on a territorial basis, the Commanders in Chief of the Luftflotten being directly responsible to Göring and exercising supreme authority over all units in their area. In view of the fact that each Luftflotte contained units with very different functions — for example bomber, fighter, and reconnaissance units — it became necessary, in order to achieve a uniformity in the employment of these arms, to establish central control by means of Inspectorates set up in the German Air Ministry. These Inspectorates had powers of inspection in all the units within their sphere of influence, but inspection was only one of their many duties as will be explained in the following paragraphs.

The Inspector General of the German Air Force

3. In addition to the Inspectorates there was in the German Air Force an Inspector General, an appointment which was held by Field Marshal Milch from 1938 until the end of the war. Milch was an exceedingly busy man for, in addition to this appointment, he was Secretary of State for Air and Director General of Equipment. It is not, therefore, surprising to learn that he had little time to carry out the duties of Inspector General which became nothing more than a courtesy title.

4. The Inspectorates — except for a brief period at the beginning of their existence, were never under the direct control of the Inspector General. Shortly after they were established the Inspectorates were all subordinated to Director of Training who was at first directly under the Inspector General but, by February 1939, was only subordinate to Milch through the Director of Air Defence. During the course of the war all Inspectorates and Specialist Air Officers (Waffengenerale) because subordinated to the Chief of General Staff.

INSPECTORATES

5. At the beginning of the war there were fourteen Inspectorates:
   (i) Air Force Inspectorate Number (1): Reconnaissance.
   (ii) „ „ „ „ (2): Bombers and Dive Bombers.

(iii) Air Force Inspectorate Number (3): Fighters and Ground Attack Aircraft.
(iv) ,, ,, ,, ,, (4): Flak.
(v) ,, ,, ,, ,, (5): Aircraft Safety and Technical Equipment.
(vi) ,, ,, ,, ,, (6): Motor Transport.
(vii) ,, ,, ,, ,, (7): Signals.
(viii) ,, ,, ,, ,, (8): Coastal Aircraft.
(ix) ,, ,, ,, ,, (9): Aircraft Pilot Schools.
(x) ,, ,, ,, ,, (10): Education and Training.
(xi) ,, ,, ,, ,, (11): Air Landing and Parachute Troops.
(xii) ,, ,, ,, ,, (12): Air Navigation.
(xiii) ,, ,, ,, ,, (13): Passive Air Defence.
(xiv) ,, ,, ,, ,, (14): Medical Service.

6. The head of each of these Inspectorates had the title of Inspector (Inspekteur). The work of these Inspectors is described in the following paragraphs.

7. The chief responsibility of Inspectors was the care of all units and schools falling within their specialist sphere. Their work endeavoured to ensure the attainment by their particular branch of a maximum standard of performance within its special sphere and to guarantee unified training throughout the individual branches of the Air Force. In accordance with the instructions of the Air Officer for Training, Inspectors prepared training directions for units and the instructional publications required for the normal course of duties and training within their particular branch or sphere of responsibility. Publications drawn up in this way were subject to the counter-check of the Chief of Air Staff as a means of harmonizing the conflicting tactical view-points of the several Air Force branches. Inspectors were responsible for:—

(i) Advising on the planning and equipment of units.
(ii) Drawing up instructional material for units in accordance with the instructions of the Director of Training and in co-operation with the Air Staff.
(iii) The supervision of all units and schools falling within their specialist sphere in order to obtain maximum efficiency and unified training.
(iv) Acquainting themselves with experiences gained by units in the field of specialist training, organisation and equipment, and imparting this information to the appropriate departments of the Air Ministry. Fixing requirements which equipment had to meet to satisfy unit needs.

8. Inspectors had the responsibility and right:—
(i) To be present during the normal course of the duties of any unit by agreement with the superior authority concerned.
(ii) To carry out inspections of schools and units by agreement with the appropriate superior authority.
(iii) In the case of schools not within their responsibility but whose curriculum fell within their special sphere of duty, to be present during the course of regular duty and to attend passing-out inspections and examinations.

9. Where, in the instances quoted above, it proved necessary to modify or suspend current orders, regulations, etc., concerned with training,

a proposal was submitted to the Air Officer for Training. Inspectors were not entitled to issue orders, regulations or directives of a general nature during their sojourns with units.

10. Proposed duty tours had to be reported in good time by Inspectors to their appropriate superior authority and before embarking on such journey they had to contact any other Inspectors concerned. Also, agreement had to be reached well in advance with the appropriate Commander in Chief Luftflotte, etc., in respect of proposed inspections, or in the case of schools and units with the competent senior commanding officer for training, so that these commanders could make any adjustments required to harmonise the proposed visit or inspection with unit duties.

11. When important facts were established, Inspectors had to make a personal report on the matter to the appropriate C. in C. Luftflotte, etc., on the completion of their tour. Furthermore, a copy of the Inspector's report on his tour of inspection was sent to the appropriate Luftflotte commands and higher Training Commands, etc., irrespective of whether a personal report was made or not.

12. During their tour of duty Inspectors were ordered to conduct their conferences so as to make it quite clear that they were speaking in the name of and by order of the Reichs Minister for Air and Commander in Chief of the German Air Force.

Influence of Inspectors on Supply

13. From their close relationship with units in the field, inspectors would frequently reveal subjects of interest to the supply and technical department. The reports and recommendations of the various inspectors would, therefore, be forwarded to the appropriate Air Ministry authorities for any action that was deemed necessary.

Changes to Inspectorates during the War

14. By the end of the war so many changes had taken place that, of the fourteen Inspectorates, not one of them was still known by its original name. Some were amalgamated with other authorities, some were dissolved, and some new ones were formed (see paragraph 18). The most important change, however, was that certain Inspectorates became "Waffengenerale". (Specialist Air Officers.)

"Waffengenerale" (Specialist Air Officers)

15. The effect of this change was that Inspectorates Numbers 2 and 3, for example, became "Waffengenerale Bombers" and 'Waffengenerale Fighters" and the heads of the Inspectorates changed their titles from Inspectors to Air Officers for Bombers, Fighters, etc. (This indicated that the Officers were of General rank and were responsible for a particular arm of the German Air Force.) The most exact translation of "Waffengenerale" is Specialist Air Officers.

16. The change to Specialist Air Officers was brought about as the result of an attempt by Göring to set up authorities in the German Air Force that would correspond to the British Bomber, Fighter and Coastal Commands, etc., as he had been impressed by these organisations ever since the Battle of Britain. He made no effort to alter the basic regional organisation of the German Air Force, however, and merely hoped that the idea of an "Air Officer" for each operational branch of the Air Force would be good for the morale of the units coming within its sphere of influence.

17. The change from Inspectorates to Specialist Air Officers did not alter fundamentally the role of these departments but did to an extent broaden their terms of reference in various aspects, the chief of which were:—

   (i) The Air Officers were made personally responsible to the Supreme Commander of the Air Force:

   (ii) The Air Officers were permitted to make direct proposals to the Operations Staff regarding the allocation and organisation of units.

Summary of Changes in Inspectorates

18. The following table shows the various changes that occurred during the war:—

   (i) Luftwaffe Inspectorate 1, Reconnaissance, became the "Air Officer for Reconnaissance".

   (ii) Luftwaffe Inspectorate 2, Bombers and Dive Bombers, became the "Air Officer for Bombers".

   (iii) Luftwaffe Inspectorate 3, Ground Attack and Fighters, was divided into two "Waffengenerale": the "Air Officer for Ground Attack" and the "Air Officer for Fighters". The "Air Officer for Fighters" had under him two inspectors, one for Day Fighters and one for Night Fighters.

   (iv) Luftwaffe Inspectorate 4, Flak and Flak Training, was divided into two "Waffengenerale": the "Air Officer for Flak" and the "Air Officer for Flak Training".

   (v) Luftwaffe Inspectorate 5, Technical Equipment and Aircraft Safety, was divided into two departments: one the "Air Officer for Aircraft Safety" and the other the "Inspector of Aircraft Technical Services".

   (vi) Luftwaffe Inspectorate 6, Motor Transport, was absorbed by the Directorate of Motor Transport.

   (vii) Luftwaffe Inspectorate 7, Signals, was taken over by the Director General of Signals.

   (viii) Luftwaffe Inspectorate 8, Coastal, became the "Air Officer for Sea Matters".

   (ix) Luftwaffe Inspectorate 9, Pilots' Schools, became the "High Command of Flying Schools".

   (x) Luftwaffe Inspectorate 10, Education and Training, was divided into two "Waffengenerale": The "Air Officer for Military Education" and the "Air Officer for Flying Training".

   (xi) Luftwaffe Inspectorate 11, Air Landing and Parachute Troops, was taken over first by the Fliegerdivision 7, then by Fliegerkorps XI, and, finally, by the Parachute Army.

   (xii) Luftwaffe Inspectorate 12, Air Navigation, was absorbed by the Air Officer for Bombers.

   (xiii) Luftwaffe Inspectorate 13, Passive Air Defence, was taken over by the Director of Air Defence.

   (xiv) Luftwaffe Inspectorate 14, Medical Services, was absorbed by the Director of Medical Services.

   (xv) Luftwaffe Inspectorate 15, Air Defence Zones, was created and dissolved during the war.

   (xvi) Luftwaffe Inspectorate 16, Sea Rescue, was created during the war and was absorbed by the Air Officer for Sea Matters.

- (xvii) Luftwaffe Inspectorate 17, Works Services, was created during the war and remained in being until the end although part of its functions was taken over by the Director of Works.
- (xviii) An Air Officer for Personnel was established during the war.
- (xix) An Inspector of Eastern Personnel was established during the war.
- (xx) An Inspector of Female Auxiliaries was established during the war.

OTHER GERMAN AIR FORCE INSPECTION AUTHORITIES

19. It has now been shown that although Inspectors had powers of inspection this task was only part of their duties. There were, however, other inspectors in the German Air Force whose duties were entirely devoted to technical inspection. Such people were known as "Inspizienten" in contrast to the "Inspekteuren". To preserve this distingtion they will be called by their German names in the following paragraphs.

20. The Inspizienten were employed by heads of Air Ministry departments who had powers of inspection but, in view of their other duties, were not able to perform physical inspections themselves. Inspizienten employed at various times through the war were:—

- (i) Inspizient for Signals, subordinated to Director General of Signals
- (ii) Inspizient for Supply, subordinated to the Director of Supply.
- (iii) Inspizient for Clothing, subordinated to the Administrative Office.
- (iv) Inspizient for Aircraft Mines, subordinated to the Air Officer for Bombers.
- (v) Inspizient for Flak Equipment and Ammunition, subordinated to the Air Officer for Flak.
- (vi) Inspizient for Meteorology, subordinated to the Director of Meteorology.

21. Each of these Inspizienten had a small staff of approximately six people who travelled with him on tours of inspection. Inspection in this case was limited to technical inspection within the scope of the subject covered by the particular Air Ministry department of which the Inspizient was a member.

Fuel Inspection

22. The Director General of Equipment, and later the Chief of Technical Armaments, controlled a section called the "Fuel Inspectorate" which was an authority responsible for inspecting the quality of aviation fuel in the Air Force storage installations. The section was also responsible for testing the quality of captured enemy stocks of aviation fuel. In the performance of these duties the Fuel Inspectorate employed a number of airborne and motorised laboratories.

23. It is interesting to note that constant inspection of German Air Force fuel installations was necessary because the bulk of aviation spirit used was synthetic and inclined to precipitate some of the constituent chemicals during prolonged storage.

Factory Inspection

24. The Director General of Equipment and later the Chief of Technical Armaments, also controlled the officials responsible for quality control at factories producing material for the German Air Force. These officials were commonly known as B.A.L., an abbreviation of Bauaufsichten des Luftfahrtministeriums. Details of their organisation and duties are given in Part 2, Chapter II.

INSPECTION OF AIRCRAFT TECHNICAL EQUIPMENT

25.   The Inspector of Aircraft Technical Equipment was the only Inspectorate under the control of the Quartermaster General and warrants, therefore, some explanation. Actually, the Inspectorate was subordinated to the Chief Engineer of the Luftwaffe who, in turn, came directly under the Quartermaster General.

26.   The Inspector of Aircraft Technical Services was responsible for:—
   (i) The inspection and co-ordination of policy in all technical ground services throughout the Air Force;
   (ii) Supervising the training of technical personnel;
   (iii) Superintending the establishment and disbandment of technical units;
   (iv) Making recommendations for maintaining and raising the standard of the performance and serviceability of technical services both in respect of personnel and equipment;
   (v) Assessing the results of practical experience gained during the war in his sphere of activity;
   (vi) Making recommendations in regard to the development and improvement of the technical efficiency of equipment.

CONCLUSION

27.   It is apparent from the above survey that, although Commanders in Chief of Luftflottes were responsible for general service inspection within their command areas, the Air Ministry also had considerable powers of inspection. This was extremely advantageous as it meant that units could be inspected objectively and, furthermore, that uniformity throughout the Air Force could be attained. It must be remembered, however, that without such inspection agencies there was no other way in which to ensure standardization in an air force that was organised regionally.

PART 2

CHAPTER X

CAMPAIGN IN THE UKRAINE

INTRODUCTION	Paragraphs 1—15
Climate	,, 5—7
Communications	,, 8—11
The War of Movement	,, 12
The Loss of Initiative	,, 13
Official Secrecy	,, 14
Manpower	,, 15
ORGANISATION OF SUPPLY	,, 17—32
Supply for Mobile Flying Units	,, 19—22
The Role of the Airfield Regional Commands	,, 23
The Luftflotte H.Q. Assumes Certain Responsibilities for Detailed Supply	,, 24—26
Dissolution of the Equipment Groups	,, 27
The Importance of the Airfield Regional Command is Increased	,, 28—29
Supply Staffs	,, 30—31
Conclusion to Supply Organisation	,, 32
SUPPLY INSTALLATIONS	,, 34—38
Main Depots	,, 34
Air Parks	,, 35—37
Equipment Issuing Stations	,, 38
AVIATION FUEL	,, 39—40
MOTOR TRANSPORT FUEL	,, 41
OXYGEN	,, 42
TRANSPORT	,, 43—47
Sea Transport	,, 43
Rail Transport	,, 44
Motor Transport	,, 45—46
Air Transport	,, 47
ALLOCATION OF AIRCRAFT	,, 48—50
GROUND ORGANISATION	,, 51—56
AIRCRAFT REPAIR	,, 57—65
Maintenance of Close Combat Squadrons	,, 60
Reporting	,, 61
Specialization by Types	,, 62
Transport Difficulties	,, 63
Front Repair Services	,, 64
Supply of Spares	,, 65
SALVAGE	,, 66—67
REPAIR OF MOTOR TRANSPORT VEHICLES	,, 68—69

PART 2

CHAPTER X

CAMPAIGN IN THE UKRAINE

INTRODUCTION

1.   The following Chapter has been compiled from the experiences of General Schultz, who was Chief Quartermaster and later Chief of General Staff at the Headquarters of Luftflotte 4 — the German Air Force Command which operated in the Ukraine theatre. The opinions expressed in the following paragraphs are those of General Schultz who is a man of some considerable ability and who has had a great deal of military experience. His views can, therefore, be regarded as useful and sound.

2.   The supply of the Air Force in the Ukraine was one of the most difficult tasks undertaken by the Germans during the war. It is, therefore, of value to study the experiences in that theatre because it is only under strain that the real weaknesses of a System are revealed.

3.   Supply in the Ukraine must be considered in the light of two particularly important factors — one, the main reason that caused the problems and the other the methods by which such problems were solved. The greatest problems arose from the nature of the theatre itself and the constant movement — first forwards and then backwards — of the battle. Goebbels once said "The chief problem in this war goes by the name of Movement", and above all this applied to the battle of the Ukraine. The solution to many such problems was resolved largely by Field Marshal von Richthofen who was the Commander in Chief of Luftflotte 4 from August 1942 to June 1943. Richthofen was a man of remarkable personality and held very violent views which he forced into practical application. He trained his staff to work on his theories and they became convinced of his opinions and endeavoured to their utmost to perform their duties in accordance with his directives. The supply problems in the Ukraine were tackled, therefore, by the staff of Luftflotte 4, who, infected by Richthofen's personality and enthusiasm, arrived at practical but sometimes impetuous and unorthodox solutions. The Air Ministry often disapproved of these methods and pronounced them unsuitable, but the important point is that they were effective and efficient and no other alternatives were ever proposed by the Air Ministry. Throughout this study, therefore, one must remember the importance of movement and the influence of Richthofen on the consequent supply difficulties.

4.   As an introduction to the particular problems and answers, General Schultz considered that note should be taken of six main points which will be developed in the following paragraphs:—

        (i)   Climate.
        (ii)   Communications.
        (iii)   The War of Movement.
        (iv)   Loss of Initiative.
        (v)   Official Secrecy.
        (vi)   Manpower.

Climate

5. In the Ukraine the change between winter and summer takes place very rapidly and with little warning — just a short transitional period with very frequent but local showers which were sufficient to cause a temporary stoppage on parts of the roads. The summer proper is distinguished by beautifully dry weather with high temperatures. The roads, also the majority of the airfields, become on that account very dusty. The complications caused by the dust were in many areas extraordinary and often resulted in an interference with traffic as well as preventing take-offs and landings on the airfields. Breakdowns of engines and bearings increased even when carefully protected by filters and the ground often became so hard that it was necessary to fit points on skids and to increase holdings of spares for undercarriages. Lack of water, particularly germ-free drinking water, was noticed even in the early summer.

6. There is a muddy period which lasts from 3 to 4 weeks, commencing in mid September, and which introduces the Autumn and Winter. The mud is caused by prolonged periods of rain in the intervals between which the short periods of weak sunlight are not sufficient to dry up the quantity of rain which has fallen. In short, all roads and paths and even the airfields, where they are not reinforced, become impassable. Low lying terrain is swamped at times, so that insufficient precautions (e.g. in the choice of flak sites, equipment and supply stores) may entail the loss of equipment and even personnel. Autumn, which begins after the muddy period, soon brings, in spite of warm days, night frosts. Temperatures with 5 degrees of frost necessitate preparations for winter. The Winter follows very quickly, often surprisingly so. It is distinguished by fairly frequent falls of snow, in the South 4 to 6 inches deep, in the North up to 20 inches deep, and by average temperatures of $-20°$ C. interrupted suddenly by peak temperatures of $-45°$ C. There are also frequent and powerful winds and generally fine, clear weather. Weather conditions bringing mists and low lying clouds occur temporarily in the first and last months of Winter for short periods of 8 to 10 days only. The strong cold winds, with a consequent fall in temperature, provided the greatest difficulties to men and equipment and the snowdrifts caused thereby, because of their suddenness and depth (up to 6 yards) interfered considerably with flying and traffic. In the L. of C. areas (Poland, Rumania and Hungary) the damp atmospheric conditions arising on the mountain ranges of the Carpathians, the Vertesgebirge and the Alps, produce mist and low lying clouds which last for weeks and even for months and prevent all flying carried out without blind flying equipment. Flying between the Ukraine and Rumania was, therefore, frequently interrupted for long periods.

7. Just as there is a muddy period in the transition from Summer to Autumn, so there is a similar muddy period in the transition from Winter to Spring. This is caused by the extensive thaws which, because of the heavily frozen ground, cannot seep away but can only flow off slowly southwards or evaporate. It is similar in its effects (becoming worse from the South to the North) to the Autumn muddy period. It lasts somewhat longer and is correspondingly more unpleasant as the hard frozen ground lies under a layer of mud. Even long after the surface has dried up heavy vehicles and aircraft break through into the layers of underneath mud and remain stuck fast and may freeze up after a quick frost. On airfields where continuation of flying has been unavoidable irreparable damage may occur by cutting up the humus layer.

Communications

8.　The vast area of the Ukraine combined with its low density of population and its agricultural nature was undoubtedly disadvantageous for military traffic. The few railway lines which ran across the country were mostly from North to South — that is they ran obliquely to the German line of advance. Furthermore, they were not very useful on account of their light structure (which meant slow speeds and light loads), the lack of sufficient shunting points and sidings and the inadequacy of the few railway stations, which were rarely provided with platforms and loading installations. During the German advance considerable time and effort was devoted to rendering the railway system more adequate. Track had to be relaid to European gauge, station installations were erected, bridges which had been blown had to be reconstructed, additional water tanks were installed because the Russian refilling points were set up at distances too great to cope with German tank capacities, water softening apparatus had to be installed and the whole railway signalling system had to be redesigned to conform with the German regulations on transport security. In spite of all the efforts made to increase the efficiency of the railways, they remained, even much later, insufficient for the proper support of the war and the economy of the occupied territory. This was particularly the case in winter, when the greater sensitivity to cold of the German locomotives, the lack of spares and of sufficient repair shops, the increasing difficulties in water supply through freezing of refilling plants, and lack of softening devices, added to the obstacles. The increasing interruptions of railway traffic, as the war lengthened, by partisan activity far behind the German lines, was also a factor which should not be overlooked.

9.　The Russian road system was just as inadequate as the railway network. The number of reinforced roads was small and in the centre and east of the Ukraine they were almost completely absent. The majority of roads consisted of broad highways without any support or reinforcement. They were rolled in peacetime and were serviced in a corresponding manner during the occupation. During the muddy periods vehicles became stuck fast but generally the roads were quite practicable. They became, however, after every heavy rainfall or thaw, impassable and had then to be closed to all traffic so that, by reason of the deep tracks made by the traffic, they did not remain useless when they dried up or again became frozen. In addition, during the Winter there were frequent snowdrifts, as neither the roads nor the railways were properly protected against them. In spite of numerous road repair and maintenance services and above all because of insufficient safety patrols against increasing partisan interference, traffic on the road had to be confined to a few highways and was greatly hindered by the frequent interruptions and the limitation of journeys to daytime.

10.　Signals communications left by the Russians in the Ukraine were also poor. The network was limited and the material inferior — weak poles, glass insulations and iron wire. The whole system had to be revised and new materials had to be imported to produce communications of a sufficiently high standard to support the German war machine.

11.　The whole area of the Ukraine presented a picture of a deserted territory — there were few railways, roads of only a limited capacity and poor signals communication. In addition, there were very few large towns and even those that existed contained very limited numbers of buildings that were suitable for the accommodation of the large masses of men and materials that had to be brought forward.

The War of Movement

12. The inadequacy of the system of communications was a particular disadvantage because the war on the Eastern front was, in contrast with all the other fronts, always, at least as far as Luftflotte 4 was concerned, a war of movement. Up to the winter of 1942/43 the German advance went as far as the Caucasus Mountains and the suburbs of Stalingrad. From then on, with the exception of a few weeks of defence and quiet in Spring and early Summer 1943, and also in Spring and early Summer of 1944, the front was continually being pressed back by the Red Army into Germany itself. The areas won and lost in this war of movement were large in comparison with the territorial changes during the operations in Europe. This demanded great mobility of all units and installations, which, with the increasing scarcity of vehicles and fuel and the continual overloading of the railway transport, became progressively more difficult to maintain. On the other hand, the operations themselves on the Eastern front were, in contrast to the home and other fronts, almost exclusively limited to the front proper, as the Russians carried out only single and unimportant air raids on the rear areas. This meant that at least the lines of communication were free from harassing air attacks. The situation changed, however, in 1944 and in Rumania and Hungary there were repeated Russian night attacks although they were not very effective. Furthermore, the operations of the Anglo-American formations from Italy, though not continuous, still had a nuisance value.

The Loss of Initiative

13. In the Winter of 1942/43 there was a fundamental change in the war situation on the Eastern Front — the initiative which up to then had been unquestionably on the German side, went over to the Red Army. There, with a few local exceptions, such as the attack leading to the capture of Kursk in Summer 1943 and the attack which won back the Danube in March 1945, the initiative remained until the cessation of hostilities. The loss of initiative affected the supply services in that it brought an end to forward planning for definite offensive operations and introduced a multitude of imponderable factors. Instead of building up reserves to back known operations the supply services had to disperse stocks to meet any possible enemy attacks that might develop from many different directions. Then, when the direction of the enemy attack was known, hasty concentrations of war materials had to be formed at appropriate focal points. This constant movement of reserves not only caused a great deal of extra work for the supply staffs and added strain to the transport services but was also not at all economical. Furthermore, the loss of initiative coincided with the beginning of the period in which shortages of certain war materials became more and more acute. For it was in the Winter of 1942/43 that signs of scarcity appeared for the first time and demands from the front for supplies of arms, equipment, aircraft, motor vehicles and reinforcements, could not be fully met. At first only isolated cases of shortages occurred — particularly, with reference to supplies of aviation and motor spirit. Later, however, they extended to deliveries of spares for motor vehicles and, finally, the difficulties extended to all aspects of supply except clothing, rations, and bombs. In the late Winter of 1942/43 the Luftwaffe experienced its first manpower difficulties when the first demands came for men for the Army. This led to drastic

thinning out of all staffs and the complete cessation of all replacements with the exception of aircrew. The scarcity of aviation fuel became very serious in the Summer of 1944 and grew worse continually from then on until March 1945, when flying almost ceased. Thus, at a time when, from an economical point of view, concentration was most essential, enemy tactics demanded dispersal. It may be clearly seen, therefore, that the loss of initiative in battle aggravated considerably the supply position. This was particularly disastrous as the General Staff had envisaged neither a war of attrition nor battles of German retreat.

Official Secrecy

14. In the first year of the war (1939) the German Supreme Command of the Armed Forces observed a very considerable lack of security within the fighting services and on many occasions they had reason to believe that through such carelessness important orders had become available to the Allies. This weakness of security continued in spite of precautions and even during the German campaign in Russia strategical plans were compromised. Finally, the situation became so bad that the Supreme Command initiated very drastic measures by which they hoped to maintain a real degree of secrecy. Security now became so strict that the strain on the machinery of the command was greatly increased — the circle of people in possession of secret information was so limited and the responsibility placed on key officers was so increased that very often important details were forgotten. Gradually the supply services became less and less aware of the intentions of the operations staff and, consequently, were unable to perform their duties in accordance with the real needs of the situation.

Manpower

15. There was never a separate branch of the German Air Force that concerned itself solely with supply matters and, consequently, at the beginning of the war there was no reserve of suitably trained officers. The supply services were manned by old officers of the first world war and who had little or no knowledge of the manner in which an air force should be maintained and by officials who had an insufficient understanding of military affairs. This situation was considered by General Schultz to be a very great handicap to the efficiency of supply in the German Air Force. During the course of the war efforts were made to encourage younger and more active officers to take an interest in this aspect of the German Air Force but without very notable success. Furthermore, as the war progressed more and more unfavourably for the Germans, so manpower had to be directed from all directions to strengthen the Army. Manpower given by the Air Force to the Army was drawn mainly from ground services and so the standard which was never high declined still further.

ORGANISATION OF SUPPLY

16. A brief picture has been given of the conditions that prevailed in the Ukraine at the time of the German campaign and it should now be possible to visualise the nature of the battles and some of the difficulties that beset those who had to support the fighting men with supplies. It is now appropriate to examine the supply organisation that was available to the German Air Force and to see how this organisation was modified and adapted to actual battle conditions.

17. Even in the pre-war days the subject of supply for the German Air Force was considered to be so complex, on account of the multiplicity of weapons and equipment and their constant modification, that it appeared inexpedient to deal with such an intricate matter through a single channel. Supply, therefore, was divided into two parts, "Supply Control" (Versorgungsführung) and "Supply Operations and Administration" (Versorgungsdurchführung und Verwaltung). The first task was to control supplies, that is to issue orders for the provision of the necessary war materials and for the allocation of such materials in accordance with the plans of the operational staffs. The staffs controlling supply were:—

(i) The Quartermaster General at Air Ministry.
(ii) The Chief Quartermasters of the Luftflottes.
(iii) The Quartermasters of the Luftgaus, Flieger- and Flakkorps.

18. The execution of supply orders and the administration of supplies was effected through the channel known as "Supply Operations and Administration". The functions of this channel were to store, issue, replenish and transport war material to the units in accordance with the orders of "Supply Control", and to safeguard and repair the items supplied (insofar as this last function was not handled by the unit itself). The staffs handling this aspect of supply were:—

(i) The Supply Office, later Directorate of Supply at Air Ministry.
(ii) The Air Equipment Groups at the Luftgau Headquarters.

Originally, all the units forming part of "Supply Operations" — Air Parks, Equipment Issuing Stations, Munition Depots, Munition Issuing Stations, Aircraft Fuel Depots, Aircraft Fuel Issuing Stations, Transport Columns and Repair Services, etc. — came under the Air Equipment Group. Later, when the Equipment Groups were dissolved, responsibility was transferred to the Quartermaster Staff at Luftgau.

Supply for Mobile Flying Units

19. For the supply of the mobile Fliegerkorps, Special Luftgau Staffs (Luftgaustäbe z.b.V.) under the Luftgaus were created. Working directly with the Fliegerkorps, and following close behind the advancing units, these special staffs became responsible for setting up the ground organisation and organising supply to the squadrons. The Luftgau, through the Air Equipment Group and the installations under the Air Equipment Group, was responsible for supply up to the advanced supply bases and from there the Special Luftgau Staffs took the supplies up to the forward flying units.

20. The control of the Special Duties Luftgau Staffs by the Luftgau, to whom they were subordinated, was only a loose one and the formers' connection to the Fliegerkorps was considerably closer. Hence the Air Ministry agreed to the demand of the Fliegerkorps VIII (whose Commanding Officer was at that time von Richthofen) for the Special Luftgau Staffs with their dependent services to be placed directly under the Fliegerkorps in this particular case — the Special Luftgau Staff becoming known as Supply Controller. However, no general ruling covering all Fliegerkorps was given, not even for all close support Fliegerkorps. In the Autumn of 1942 in the Luftflotte 4 area only the Fliegerkorps VIII was supplied by a Special Luftgau Staff and in taking over command of the Luftflotte Richthofen pressed for a uniform solution to this question, at least in the area of his command. Opposition arose from the Luftgau who foresaw in the creation of a Fliegerkorps Supply Controller an

unwelcome limitation to their powers and expected difficulties to arise from divided control in supply operations. The Air Ministry also had considerable doubts. A concession was granted, however, and Fliegerkorps IV was also given a Supply Controller and at the same time the Fliegertruppe Equipment Issuing Stations were subordinated to the Supply Controllers.

21.   The following arrangements for supplying the flying units in the Luftflotte 4 area were employed. When the front was not stable, that is to say in an advance or retreat, it was the duty of the Luftgau with its Air Equipment Group, in accordance with the orders of the Luftflotte or the wishes of the Fliegerkorps, to see that supplies got up to the advanced supply bases and then the Fliegerkorps, through its Supply Controller, brought the supplies up to the frontline airfields operated by its own ground services. When the front was stable, however, and a passive defensive situation existed, the Supply Controllers with their auxiliary services came under the Luftgau which in this case assumed responsibility for carrying out supply operations and for the thorough and systematic development of the ground organisation. The Luftgau was not allowed to make changes in the organisation of the Supply Controller's services without the agreement of the Fliegerkorps.

22.   The ruling was never tested out in practice because it was made during a period of static warfare, and had given way to a new ruling before another phase of the war of movement began. With the growing shortage of men and materials, which made it more difficult than it already was to divide supply problems between the Luftgau and the Supply Controllers of the Fliegerkorps, and the change in command of the Chief of the General Staff at the Air Ministry, as well as the Commanding Officer of Luftflotte 4 (Richthofen went to Luftflotte 2 in Italy), the Supply Controllers of the Fliegerkorps were abolished and the supply services, with the exception of the Air Equipment Issuing Stations, were again placed under the control of the Luftgau. The deciding factor for the Air Ministry was that this special arrangement in two Fliegerkorps made them somewhat unwieldy and they were also harder to move into other Luftflotte areas where this system had not been introduced and was not in some cases agreed in principle.

The Role of the Airfield Regional Commands

23.   For the area of Luftflotte 4 the following revised decision was made. The Luftgaukommando was made responsible for overall supply operations. The Luftgau's Airfield Regional Command, in whose area the bulk of the squadrons of the Fliegerkorps were situated, was instructed to co-operate as closely as possible with the Fliegerkorps, and to carry out the wishes of the Fliegerkorps in all matters of ground organisation and supply. It should be noted that the Fliegertruppe Equipment Issuing Stations were at this stage subordinated to the Airfield Regional Command. In addition, Luftflotte and Luftgau were able to ensure that the Airfield Regional Command areas corresponded with the Fliegerkorps areas. It was decided not to place the Airfield Regional Command under the Fliegerkorps, because only the Luftgau, situated as it was in a rear area, was in a position to do the necessary detailed administrative work. Only in special cases or in isolated areas — for example the Crimea — did an Airfield Regional Command come under the temporary operational control of a Fliegerkorps.

The Luftflotte H.Q. Assumes Certain Responsibilities for Detailed Supply

24. Before and during the first phase of the war it was customary in supply control matters for the higher commands (Air Ministry and Luftflotte) to initiate supply measures through general directives and leave the Luftgau, Flieger- and Flakkorps to give the orders. In this way these latter were largely left free in their choice of methods and in execution of the details. With the appearance of shortages, transport difficulties and greater need for security and flexible control, the Luftflotte was forced to supervise supply measures more and more closely down to small details, and also on occasion to take a hand in supply operations. Above all, this applied to fuel and munition supply, allocation of aircraft, aircraft spares in which there was a bottleneck, motor vehicles and later even of anti-aircraft guns.

25. Instead of ordering the Luftgau, as formerly, to provide such and such supplies in such and such areas, the Luftflotte took on this job itself in all items in which there were bottlenecks. With daily reports on the supply position of such items coming in it was able to direct war materials to the individual Airfield Regional Commands in accordance with day to day needs and the plans of the Higher Command. Working closely with the Fliegerkorps the Airfield Regional Commands distributed the items to the individual airfields, or notified the Flieger- or Flak-korps, that the supplies were to be collected. In special cases the Luftflotte itself used air transport to collect the bottleneck items (for example special anti-tank ammunition), direct from the factories in Germany and bring them to the flying units. As a result of this the important functions of the Luftgau came to be more and more those of undertaking supply operations, personnel administration, specialist supervision of supply services, and the development of ground organisation, rather than that of supply control.

26. This development caused considerable friction between the Luftflotte and the Luftgau. The Luftgau would not admit it was a matter of operational necessity and felt that the strict control exercised by the Luftflotte kept the Luftgau in an unduly subordinate position and insinuated a lack of confidence. The development was also not welcomed by the Luftflotte as it drew that Headquarters far too much into details and blurred the hitherto clear division of duties.

Dissolution of the Equipment Groups

27. Parallel with the development previously mentioned and partly because of it, serious doubt arose as to whether the further existence of the Air Equipment Groups was justified. The important task of providing supplies and doing all the detailed administrative work was essential and had to be continued but, in the matter of supplying flying units, one thing — in spite of the frequent changes in procedure — had become clear: the Air Equipment Groups were not suited to getting supplies right up to the frontline flying units in a war of movement. In an advance and to a lesser extent in a retreat those responsible for supplying a Fliegerkorps had to meet so many detailed and specialised demands, that the task could only be satisfactorily accomplished by a body that was constantly in the closest touch with the Fliegerkorps and was able to concentrate all its energies on this task. The Air Equipment Group could not do this, because it had a large area and a multiplicity of jobs on its hands. In addition, there were the following reasons for abolishing the Air Equipment Groups:

(i) The Air Equipment Group had a large staff and on the Eastern front could hardly ever be accommodated with or near the Luftgaukommando. They could not handle the day to day development of the situation in common and thereby assure the timely preparation and carrying through of supply measures. Things were made more difficult by the added security regulations, the constantly stricter control by the Luftflotte and the extension of its operations in supply matters.

(ii) The Air Equipment Group, with its specialised duties, had come to be a little world of its own, both as regards its personnel and its duties — it was cut off from the Higher Command and out of touch with the units.

(iii) An ever more noticeable shortage of manpower, as a result of which the Air Ministry decided to wind up the Air Equipment Groups, first in the Luftflotte 4 area, later on the whole Eastern front and, finally, throughout the Air Force. The job of supply operations and administration was given to the Luftgau Quartermaster whose staff was increased by the corresponding specialists from the Air Equipment Group.

The Importance of the Airfield Regional Command is Increased

28. The supply services and installations which had formerly come under the operational and administrative control of the Air Equipment Group were, in the Luftflotte 4 area, subordinated to the Airfield Regional Commands in whose areas they were operating at the time. This was a development which corresponded with what had already been in the minds of the Luftflotte Commanders, namely the extension of the Airfield Regional Command's field of activity. Originally they were only responsible for such matters as the organisation, defence and development of airfields, signals communications, and control of transport, and now they directed all the supply operations services and installations in their area and were thereby responsible for executing the wishes of the Fliegerkorps in supply matters. All Air Force units in their area now came under them, except for those belonging to a Fliegerkorps or a Flakkorps.

29. The duties of the Airfield Regional Commands were considerably extended, in that they took over tasks which had formerly been dealt with centrally at the Luftgau — especially in the sphere of administration. In the Luftflotte 4 area the staff post of Intendant was created at the Airfield Regional Commands. This Intendant was allocated small clothing depots with repair facilities and aircrew ration stores, so that he could provide clothing replacements and exchanges (summer and winter) as well as special aircraft rations without calling on outside sources. In addition, he was given powers of decision in minor administrative matters. This arrangement considerably speeded up the solution of many administrative questions, for postal and signals communications with the Luftgaus were often very difficult. It proved especially satisfactory in retreat and the Intendants managed to save considerable quantities of clothing and rations that would otherwise have been lost. In spite of this and for reasons unknown to General Schultz they were never approved by Air Ministry and were not introduced in the rest of the Air Force. The creation of Airfield Regional Command medical officers and meteorologists was also planned, and did occur in some cases. These also helped to meet the pressing need for decentralisation of the Luftgau's duties.

Supply Staffs

30. One principle was clearly established — that in every staff anything that dealt with supplies to the front line troops should come

under the Quartermaster. Therefore, at Luftflotte the Chief Engineer was subordinated to the Chief Quartermaster. Hitherto the Engineer had been technical adviser to the Commanding Officer and to the Chief of the General Staff, had supervised technical matters throughout the Command area, and had advised the Chief Quartermaster in the control of technical supplies. He was thus above all a critic without personal responsibility. Friction was, therefore, unavoidable, especially as the technical control of supplies at the Quartermaster level was in the hands of "officers and not specialists". With his subordination to the Chief Quartermaster the Chief Engineer was given definite responsibilities which included the control and supervision of all technical services, the planning, control and supervision of the whole technical supply and repair of aircraft, the allocation of aircraft and equipment and the planning, control and supervision of special winter equipment. This was in addition to his advisory capacity with the Commanding Officer and the control of the engineer personnel in the Command area. In order also to obtain the best use from the other technical services (radar, arms, flak equipment and M/T repairs) the Chief Engineers of the Luftflotte and Luftgau, were made responsible for the technical work of all repair services. As such they had the duty of supervising continually the methods of procedure and increasing full utilisation of the technical services, also in regulating adjustments in their employment, in technical personnel and workshop equipment.

31. The subordination of the Intendant and the Medical Officer to the Chief Quartermaster did not take place because their chief duties — administration and medicine — were very specialised and lay outside the ambit of supplies. Furthermore, these posts were occupied mostly by older and senior officers and officials whose subordination to the very considerably younger Quartermasters appeared unsuitable. They were, however, directed in all questions which concerned supplies (medical supply installations, clothing stores, ration stores and transport) to discuss matters with the Quartermaster. Certain administrative duties such as rations, clothing, billeting equipment and office materials for general use should, in General Schultz' opinion, have been combined with other supplies and have been included with the other responsibilities of the Quartermaster. Custom decreed, however, that they should come under the Intendant and this was usual throughout the Armed Forces. A change in organisation would have been practicable only if carried out simultaneously by all branches of the Armed Forces but would have met with strong restistance from the officials.

Conclusion of Supply Organisation

32. In all problems of supply it should be observed that the Air Ministry only interfered generally in such matters of organisation as affected the basic structure of the Air Force (the creation or dissolution of staffs, etc.). Otherwise, it left the methods of procedure to the judgment of the field commanders and the latter were given the opportunity to make generous allowances for local conditions. In the opinion of General Schultz the following priciples should be adhered to when considering the most suitable organisation for supplies:

(i) There should be a division of duties between the control of supplies and the operations and administration.

(ii) The Luftflotte should attend only to the broad aspects of supply and leave the responsibility for the details of supply control and

GERMAN AIR FORCE, 1935—1945

the whole task of supply operations and administration to the Luftgau Headquarters. The Luftgau Headquarters would in this way be given freedom to choose the means and method of effecting their tasks.

(iii) To enable the Luftgau Headquarters to discharge its responsibility for the details of supply control and the operations and administration of supplies, the Quartermaster of the Luftgau and the Air Equipment Group should form one staff at the Luftgau Headquarters.

(iv) Luftgau Headquarters should delegate the day to day work on the details of operations and administration of supply to Airfield Regional Commands and the supply services and installations required for these purposes should be subordinated to those Commands.

(v) There should be very close co-operation between those responsible for the issue of operational orders to flying units, those responsible for the issue of complementary supply directives, and those responsible for the execution of the directives and administration of supplies. A more frequent interchange of specialists between the different staffs and between the staffs and the frontline formations would create a basis for mutual appreciation.

(vi) In special conditions it might be convenient to allot temporarily a Supply Staff with all the necessary supply services to a Fliegerkorps. As a fixed regulation this is not practical as it makes the Fliegerkorps very cumbersome and thereby reduces mobility for extensive operations. In addition it is fraught with the following dangers:—
 (a) The Commander would be distracted from his own duties by having to undertake responsibility for delivery of his own supplies.
 (b) The division of responsibility for the delivery of supplies between Fliegerkorps and Luftgau would lead to overlapping and thence to friction.

33. After survey of the supply organisation in the Ukraine General Schultz considered the following subjects to be worthy of additional comment:—

(i) Supply installations.
(ii) Aviation Fuel.
(iii) Motor Transport Fuel.
(iv) Oxygen.
(v) Transport.
(vi) Allocation of Aircraft.
(vii) Ground organisation (Airfield Construction).
(viii) Aircraft Repairs.
(ix) Salvage.
(x) Motor Transport Repairs.

SUPPLY INSTALLATIONS

Main Depots

34. In order to bridge the distance between the front and home territory, the Director of Supply and the Administration Office established Signals Main Equipment Depots and Clothing Main Depots in occupied

territory. The Luftflotte had no operational authority over these depots and could not influence the amount of stocks held. The advancement of the Equipment Depots certainly served to speed up the execution of supply orders but the Luftflotte should have had a say in the locations of the depots and the extent of the stocks they held, since they alone could judge requirements and supervise transport. At the beginning of the general retreat the Luftflotte was made responsible for the evacuation of these depots and the requirements of this large and unexpected task caused great difficulties.

Air Parks

35. It proved advisable not to store too much equipment in the Air Parks. The accumulation of stocks of a large Air Park presented serious transport problems when they had to be transferred. It proved advisable, therefore, that the stocks in advanced Air Parks should be limited to a month's requirements, even though that meant a hand to mouth existence. The presence of two Air Parks in the Luftflotte area was very useful, since, during periods of movements either forwards or backwards, one Air Park could carry on while the other was in process of transfer. In the Spring of 1943 when, taking a long view, it appeared unsafe to hold the position Mius-Donetz, the Air Park supplies at Saporoshje were reduced in such a manner that it became, practically speaking, only a large Equipment Issuing Station. It was useful to retain it as an Air Park, however, so that the right to make direct demands on the Main Equipment Stations, and thus ensure speedy supplies, remained.

36. The Air Equipment Parks stocked a universal range of equipment. The bulk of this equipment was controlled by the Director of Supply but operationally important equipment was controlled by the 6th Department and the Director General of Signals in the Air Ministry. This meant that the Park Commanders received orders from three different sources. The result of this was that there was no co-ordinated control of all equipment and conflicting orders would frequently be given.

37. A further complication was caused by the fact that office equipment was also held in the various sections of the Parks. Such equipment was controlled by the Intendant, which meant that the Park Commander had to deal with yet another outside authority.

Equipment Issuing Stations

38. Motorised Equipment Issuing Stations were the type mostly used on the Eastern front. Railway Equipment Issuing Stations, once they had reached their base, were very useful as they contained large stocks of equipment and were technically independent — that is to say they had sources of light and power. Their mobility was, however, on account of the difficulties attendant on rail travel, very questionable. During retreats they were particularly vulnerable, as on the tracks which ran parallel to the front there was danger of being cut off by the enemy. They had, therefore, always to be withdrawn very early even when they were urgently needed at the front. The Flying Equipment Issuing Stations (loaded into Ju 52's or freight gliders) were not large enough and, therefore, in spite of their great mobility were not very practical.

AVIATION FUEL

39. No great problems arose in supplying aviation fuel apart from the scarcity inside the area of the Luftflotte. The different supplies of

aviation fuel B. 4 (80 octane) or C. 3 (100 octane) for the various types of aircraft proved easier than was first thought, especially as C. 3 was chiefly required for close combat formations which had a relatively lighter consumption. Supplies of one kind of aviation fuel only would naturally have been much simpler.

40.   The careless treatment of aviation fuel drums on the airfields particularly during removals, showed, in spite of all Luftflotte instruction, little improvement. It was repeatedly necessary to erect large and expensive collecting depots where complete trains of empty drums from the home territory were discharged.

MOTOR TRANSPORT FUEL

41.   Complete dependence on the Army was disadvantageous to the German Air Force. In view of the prevailing shortage Air Force interests were always given second place, particularly when units had to move outside the Army area of supplies. In emergency aviation fuel was mixed with the motor transport fuel to eke out the latter but the consequent damage to engines was severe. Repeated requests by the Luftflotte to make the Air Force independent in matters of Motor Transport fuel supply were not heeded by the Air Ministry.

OXYGEN

42.   Special problems did not arise in this respect as quantities used were not very great, for most flying was at low altitudes. The consumption inside the Luftflotten was almost always covered without difficulty. A producing plant was set up in the Luftflotte area for manufacturing oxygen which was delivered in a liquid condition to the airfields in specially equipped JU. 52's. Attempts to take oxygen from Germany by rail broke down because of evaporation en route. Filling up on airfields was done by means of motor driven pumps.

TRANSPORT

Sea Transport

43.   For large scale transport the Luftflotte used railways and ships. Transport by sea, however, was limited for the following reasons:—
  (i)   Transport facilities for conveying supplies from the coast to the interior were poor.
  (ii) Scarcity of supplies often did not permit protracted sea journeys.
  (iii) Harbours were only available after the capture of the Crimea and then they were often frozen.
  (iv) Only a limited shipping tonnage, particularly for tankers, was available in the Black Sea.

Transport by sea was, therefore, only used to supply the rear coastal areas and the Crimea with unwieldy and large scale supplies (coal, cement, huts and, where possible, fuel).

Rail Transport

44.   The bulk of large scale transport was done by the railway. The railway lines on the Eastern front had only a very limited capacity and this had to be shared with the Services and other users. The allocation was made by the OKW/Director of Transport to whom the Air Force requirements were submitted by the Air Ministry. The Army caused much

friction by continually trying to reduce the already small Air Force quota which scarcely satisfied the most pressing supply requirements. Furthermore, the OKW. were frequently inclined to grant preference to Army demands as the Director of Transport's Office was staffed preponderantly by Army officers. As soon, therefore, as the conduct of operations was threatened by lack of transport the Luftflotte Operations Department had to press vigorously for recognition of Air Force requirements and in this way Army obstruction was often overcome. Supply trains to the limit of the quota were brought up on Quartermaster General instructions to the boundary stations of the Luftflotte L. of C. areas. In periods of great transport difficulty (e.g. at Stalingrad) it proved necessary to let the Luftflotte denote which trains were most important. When the frontier had been crossed the Luftflotte itself took over the control of the trains. The area was divided into several reporting sections in which there were at each large station German Air Force reporting centres which reported the trains. All these gave the Luftflotte daily the exact movements of each train. It was thus possible to keep in constant touch with the transport situation and to manipulate the train schedules according tho the supply position. The Luftflotte took the trains into the airfield region and handed them over to the Airfield Regional Command which then forwarded them to the consignee railway station in close co-operation with the Fliegerkorps and the relevant Army Transport authority.

Motor Transport

45. The Luftflotte had only sufficient Motor Transport for local movements. Motor Transport movement on a large scale was carried out only once. For this purpose all available Motor Transport from all Air Force units in the command (ground organisation, Flak and Signals M/T) was assembled together with the necessary repair services. This procedure had, however, to be suspended as vehicles had to be returned to the units and the wear and tear was found to be excessive. The Transport Columns available for the Luftflotte were originally controlled by an O.C. Transport Column on the staff of the Luftflotte. As, however, these columns were divided up among the separate Airfield Regional Commands this organisation proved superfluous and the post at the Luftflotte was disestablished. There was also a column Commander at the Luftgau H.Q. who controlled the columns in the various Airfield Regional Commands and watched the interests of all users. He was also dimissed, this time for reasons of manpower economy and the columns were placed entirely under the control of the Airfield Regional Commands.

46. The numerous vehicles possessed by close support units were only fully used during movements and a proposal was made, therefore, to take them away from the units and form a pool. The plan was to form a pool of transport regiments under their Fliegerkorps or under the relevant Airfield Regional Command. The general need for vehicles was, however, always greatest during the retreats and it was then that the flying units themselves were also on the move and needed their vehicles. It was essential to ensure the utmost mobility of close support units in order to avoid serious losses of valuable equipment and it was finally agreed, therefore, to leave vehicles with the units in spite of the fact that they were not fully employed.

Air Transport

47. Air transport was only available to the Luftflotte on a limited scale, apart from the large air transport undertakings (Stalingrad, Kuban

bridgehead, Crimea, etc.). Each Fliegerkorps had a few squadrons of transport aircraft for use in fetching urgently required items and for maintaining a courier service inside the area of the Fliegerkorps. The Luftflotte also possessed on the average from 1 to 2 transport Gruppen (54 aircraft per Gruppe) which it used to fly equipment between Equipment Issuing Stations and Parks and the airfields on which the units were stationed. These aircraft were a very useful standby which enabled the Chief Quartermaster to adjust quickly any serious local scarcities. They were controlled centrally under the Luftflotte and this was very wise in view of the fuel position and the strict control necessary over supplies in all areas. In addition the Quartermaster General (Air Ministry) controlled a regular air service with large transport aircraft from home territory to the front areas. This proved particularly useful in relieving the Luftflotte of transport duties for the Army, which often required transport of "bottle-neck" equipment over large distances outside the command area. The state of aviation fuel supplies and the general air situation entailed the suspension of the Quartermaster General's air service and limited considerably all air transports.

ALLOCATION OF AIRCRAFT

48. The allocation of aircraft replacements to the operational units of the Command was made by the Chief Engineer according to operational activity, the crew situation, and the intentions of the High Command. To avoid withdrawl of operational crews from formations for the purpose of collecting aircraft, the aircraft were flown to the front by "feeder" crews. On arrival in the forward areas it was necessary to overhaul the aircraft and make them ready for the front line and also to install the additional fittings and armament deemed necessary for the respective units. So-called "Schleusen" (sluices), that is airfields particularly well laid-out and provided with corresponding testing and repair services, were set up for the overhaul and preparation of replacement aircraft. New aircraft were flown from the assembly airfields by the Director of Supply's ferry pilots to the "Luftflotten Schleusen" in the forward areas where they were taken on charge by the Luftflotte. They were then brought forward temporarily to special "Schleusen" where they were inspected and fitted out for the front. These special "Schleusen" were, where possible, connected with the front repair services and main workshops for their particular type. The aircraft ready for the front were taken away by the formation crews from the specialist "Schleusen". Only during particularly hard fighting, when demands for squadrons and crews were very great, was a feeder service to the operational airfields set up. For this purpose as well as for ferrying aircraft inside the "Schleusen", a ferrying Geschwader, composed of crews not suitable for operations at the front, was at the disposal of the Luftflotte. The squadrons often complained about these crews and accused them of treating the aircraft with insufficient care. Losses through lack of adequate flying ability were not infrequent. In spite of this the system had to continue, as operational demands did not permit crews to be withdrawn from operations to ferry aircraft from the rear.

49. Due to long spells of bad weather during the winter in the feeder places in Roumania, Hungary and north of the Carpathians, it was not possible to fly aircraft without blind flying equipment and so railway transport up to the L. of C. areas was provided. Although these measures were taken very late in both winters (1941/42 and 1942/43), they proved of value. The previous considerable losses occasioned by ferrying and

the complete lack of certainty in arrival of the planes no longer occurred. Although somewhat delayed the aircraft could be distributed intact and in larger numbers to the formations and at a previously determined time.

50. Some "bottleneck" equipment — radio, bomb sights, armament — was no longer built into new aircraft but was kept in sufficient quantities as H.Q. equipment on the operational airfields. When, for any particular reason, an aircraft was withdrawn from a squadron the equipment was taken out again and kept back by the formation. Considerable loss of time occurred in removing it and also the parts were often damaged. In consequence, all the H.Q. equipment belonging to the formations in the area of Luftflotte 4 was concentrated in their special "Schleusen" and the equipment was built- in regardless of who owned it and according to the demand and supply of aircraft. The necessary adjustments were made by book entries.

GROUND ORGANISATION

51. Ground organisation — that is development and construction of installations for the Air Force — was originally controlled by the Administrative Office in the German Air Ministry and by the Intendant staffs at other command levels. This organisation developed in peacetime when the dealings with contractors and the complicated nature of estate laws made it advisable to put control of such work in the hands of the Administrative Office, who were experts in the management of regulations. This, therefore, was the system that was transferred to the Eastern front. At the front, however, the work became entirely military in character and dealings with civilian authorities did not occur. Labour was provided by German Air Force works units, P.O.W.s, native labour, and to a very small degree, by the Todt organisation. Materials were as far as possible obtained from local sources. Consequently, it became more and more desirable to transfer control of ground organisation from the Administration to a military department and eventually this was done and the Chief Quartermaster of the Luftflotte assumed the responsibility. At the same time, of course, control was transferred at the lower command levels.

52. For a war of movement which demanded the employment of close combat formations from improvised airfields, special Motorised Works Companies were set up and placed under the Airfield Regional Command or the O.C. Supplies of the Fliegerkorps. These Works Companies, in contrast to the majority of the companies which were very strongly diluted with P.O.W.s, consisted only of young German front line troops. As well as constructional tasks, these companies undertook the defence of airfields and also assisted the flying formations by transporting fuel and bombs and by servicing, fuelling and loading aircraft.

53. The Works Units that were manned by P.O.W.s and native labour worked usually at base installations. The Organisation Todt was divided into two Groups:—

(i) The group which was responsible for the reconstruction of bridges and roads during the advance. These squads accompanied the advancing ground troops.

(ii) The group which was responsible for the reconstruction of bridges, roads and large buildings (factories and fortifications) in the L. of C. areas.

Attempts by the Luftflotte to use this second group for the construction of airfields failed except in a few cases. The arguments against this were lack of personnel, the fact that the Army exercised a very strong influence on the employment of the Organisation Todt for their projects, and that the organisation itself was particularly interested in confining its work as far as possible to independent constructional tasks of great magnitude.

54. The static rear ground organisation was set up according to the orders of the Luftflotte. These orders, which fixed the total works programme for each airfield, were based on the proposals of the Luftgau, wishes of the Fliegerkorps, Luftflotte plans, and the available works material and personnel. Broad principles were determined by the Luftflotte as to how the work should be carried out; for instance, which airfields were to be permanent winter airfields and which only emergency ones. In the western and centre parts of the Ukraine a large number of Russian airfields with runways, mostly under construction, were found. They were not all useful as the runways were usually too small and too lightly built, moreover, on many of them there was a lack of any kind of hangar and billeting arrangements and railway access. Because of lack of raw material there were no temporary devices — such as steel grids or mats — for erecting runways and the construction units had to use cement, road metal and cinders. The question of transport from the home territory was, therefore, of great importance in the building programme. The aim was to erect in the front line areas 5 or 6 airfields with runways and reinforced taxiways, parking places protected from shrapnel and reinforced roads to the railhead, also at least one temporary hangar where important work on at least one aircraft could be carried out without being affected by the weather. The number and position of the runway airfields were, where possible, fixed in such a manner that every part of the front line could be reached from a runway airfield by a close combat formation.

55. The taking-over, late in the war, of the whole of the Air Force works by the Organisation Todt, caused no basic change in the Luftflotte on the Eastern front. The Organisation Todt was accustomed to construction work on a large scale and was unsuited to serve the needs of the Air Force. Above all, in continually planning building programmes for the retreat and continually improvising, the Organisation Todt experienced special difficulties. The erection of close combat airfields was, therefore, undertaken by the units themselves and the Motorised Construction Companies were renamed the Pioneer Companies and placed under the Fliegerkorps. However, no change was made in the work they did. By the closest co-operation with the local Organisation Todt Chief (the former works specialists with the Quartermaster were now liaison officials to the Organisation Todt), the Air Force succeeded in persuading him that the previous procedure was the right one. So even in the L. of C. areas practically no change took place. In certain ways the taking over by the Organisation Todt led to an increase in building capacity as it brought in additional building material, machines and personnel.

56. Finally, mention must be made of the valuable help given to the works undertakings by the large number of local workers. Without them, since suitable machinery was lacking (bull-dozers, light railways, etc.) a large number of jobs — especially moving earth, clearing snow, repairing roads, etc. — would not have been practicable. The population was very willing to work and pay was the only difficulty. As there was too much money and too few goods the Air Force resorted to barter. The workers received food and, where possible, shoes and articles for use (salt, paraffin oil, sewing neddles, buttons, etc.). Procuring these articles caused con-

siderable difficulty because of the scarcity all over Germany. Local industries were planned but did not come into operation because of the loss of territory.

AIRCRAFT REPAIR

57. An account of a supply system would not be complete without some reference to the repair organisation and General Schultz, therefore, supplied the following information on this subject.

58. Workshop facilities were only provided on German Air Force Main or Permanent Stations and, therefore, it was necessary to provide minor repair and maintenance facilities for squadrons which had to operate from operational airfields (temporary or semi-permanent) or landing grounds. The mobility of flying formations had to be assured and, therefore, maintenance organisations for bomber and heavy fighter squadrons were provided by attaching to each Gruppe (Wing) independent formations known as Airfield Servicing Companies. Close combat Gruppen had their own maintenance organisation which formed an integral part of their establishment. These minor repair and maintenance organisations executed work that took no longer than three days. Repairs or modifications requiring from three to ten days were executed at home by static workshops on the Main Airfields and at the front by field workshops units which were fully motorised.

59. The extent of the territory in the Ukraine ruled out more and more the possibility of allotting Airfield Servicing Companies to all appropriate airfields. In fact, there were fewer companies available than there were Gruppe, with the result that certain airfields could only be supplied with a skeleton service although they were located in an operational area.

Maintenance of Close Combat Squadrons

60. The mobility of the maintenance services for close combat formations was sufficient during an advance but not for swift movements over long distances paralled to the front, as were repeatedly necessary on the Eastern front, particularly around Stalingrad. The state of the Motor Transport and the small fuel quota militated against the conveyance of the ground services over such large distance. The flying units, therefore, carried the first section of the maintenance personnel along with them by air, while the second followed by rail. This railway transport was so protracted that ground personnel were often held inactive for weeks in the trains. Help was procured by collecting temporarily, in the area of operations, maintenance personnel from Airfield Servicing Companies, Field Workshop Units, etc., which serviced the formations in a simple manner and with a great decrease in technical efficiency. Proposals were put forward by the Luftflotte to the Air Ministry suggesting that maintenance personnel should be withdrawn from the close combat squadrons and placed in a common pool under the control of the Luftflotte. Maintenance services would then have been distributed in accordance with the pitch of the battle and key personnel would have been available for distribution by air to focal points. Although the Air Ministry did not accept these proposals the suggestion was, in fact, put into practive in Luftflotte 4.

Reporting

61. Each formation had to give daily a complete report showing the number of crews and serviceable aircraft, the probable time necessary to

repair unserviceable aircraft and information as to the damage. Special details, such as lack of particular spares (tools, etc.) had also to be given. By means of this report the Luftflotte and the Chief Engineer had a complete synopsis of the technical situation on all formations. He could appreciate existing and future difficulties in procuring replacements, be warned of the particular liability to damage of certain aircraft parts, and supervise generally the employment of the repair system.

Specialization by Types

62. The station workshops in the area of Luftflotte 4, in contrast with those in Reich territory, each specialized in certain types of aircraft. This simplified the supply of spares and increased the capacity of the workshops. This specialization proved successful and it was intended to introduce it throughout the Air Force but for some reason unknown this was not done. Such specialization also had the result that each workshop became a main workshop to those formations equipped with the aircraft in which the workshop was specializing. It was found that in this way a better technical connection was established between flying unit and workshop than under the previous system when the workshop was dealing with a greater variety of equipment. The revised system could not be maintained, however, as the size of the area, the frequent movement of formations — even into the areas of other Flotten — over large distances required a frequent changing of main workshops. The production of the workshops was supervised by the Chief Engineer with the help of the daily reports which enabled him to control the distribution of repaired aircraft, the allocation of spares in short supply and also, if necessary, the allocation of additional personnel and machinery.

63. Special difficulties attended the timely delivery of engine spares. These, which were transported in separate wagons and frequently held up by other important supplies or by troops, arrived very irregularly and in small quantities. Transport by lorry was not economical over such large distances served only by bad roads. Transport by air, although very suitable, had to be dispensed with because of the great distance from the Reich to the front and the large quantity of engines and spares required. With the subordination of the Chief Engineer to the Chief Quartermaster a definite improvement was observed. In Luftflotte 4 the Chief Engineer had encroached somewhat on the Chief Quartermaster's responsibility in that he exercised considerable influence on the supply of aircraft and engine spares to the theatre. Since, however, he was not in control of transport services he was in continual difficulties to achieve the distribution of spares. It was, therefore, not until the Chief Quartermaster had properly reasserted his control of the supply of spares, through the subordination to him of the Chief Engineer, that supply and transportation fell into singlehanded control with a consequent improvement in efficiency.

"Front Repair Services"

64. The great transport difficulties mentioned above made the transfer of engine repairs from the home territory to the front appear advisable but there were not enough Field Workshops available for such work. An answer to the problem was provided by establishing in the Command area outstations of the aircraft industry. These were called "Front Repair Services". They were equipped with machinery from the home territory or from industry in the occupied areas and, employing more and more

trained natives, these services soon provided a sufficient engine pool reserve to satisfy the total requirements of all formations in the area. These front repair sevices belonged to firms (for example, Junker) and received their raw materials and spares from the trade. They were billeted and rationed by the Luftgau and represented on the German administrative units. As far as their methods of working were concerned they were supervised and directed by the Chief Engineer of the Luftgau or Luftflotte. In view of the good results obtained this method was later applied also to airframes and equipment (armament, radio). At the same time an attempt was made to take over the manufacture of spares in the area itself and thus be as independent as possible of home production. When drawing up plans to utilise the raw material, workshops and manpower of the occupied territories for German economy, it was intended to manufacture also arms or parts of armament and ammunition as well as aircraft under licence and to make demands on home industry only for special equipment which could not be made on the Eastern front. This was only partly carried out (skid forks for H.e. 111, shields for flak guns, huts, billeting equipment, nails, being a few typical examples) as the losses of territory brought this system swiftly to an end. The Front Repair Services were set up in such a manner that work on various parts of one type of aircraft was, as far as possible located in the same area (e.g. at Saporoshje: servicing Junkers engines, airframes for Ju. 88/87, repairing armament and radio for Ju. 88/87). Therefore, one type of aircraft could be repaired in all of its parts in one place. The Russian workers, both men and women, proved very eager to learn skilled work and so apprentice workshops were attached to all plants in order to free more and more German workers for employment at other places.

Supply of Spares

65. In the supply of spares, which had hitherto arrived in the quantities required, bottlenecks occurred frequently from the beginning of 1942 and, by keeping to the normal supply channels, these bottlenecks would have kept the aircraft unserviceable for long periods. To help in overcoming these shortages an emergency classification D. I was created. This was a degree of priority applied to those spares the procurement of which was vital to the repair of aircraft. A special express demand channel in the supply system and a special express transport to the front were established. The Luftflotte procured the D. I parts already ordered by telephone, from one of the Main Equipment Depots or from the relevant Chief Committee of the industry and they were delivered either by air, using all aircraft available in the Flotten area, or by road courier. This very effective step led to a considerable acceleration in repais. The scheme was opposed by the Supply Directorate and, after a short while, was suspended. The reporting organisation allied to this procedure inside the Flotten area remained in force and proved of value. It should be explained that this procedure was an unofficial arrangement made by the Chief Quartermaster of Luftflotte 4 and was rightly opposed by the Director of Supply because it meant that this particular Luftflotte was obtaining priority of treatment to the detriment of others.

SALVAGE

66. At the beginning of the Russian campaign there were motorised platoons for salvage and captured material in the Luftflotten area. They were directed by the Air Ministry (D.G.E.) and were only loosely connected

with the Luftflotte. Their duties were to obtain and salvage enemy aircraft equipment and fuel and also to salvage German aircraft which crashed outside airfields. As time passed, the latter task came more and more into prominence and control of salvage eventually passed to the Quartermaster where it was handled by the Chief Engineer and Salvage Platoons were attached to the various Airfield Regional Commands.

67. The salvage of "bottleneck" items from crashed aircraft at the front was of great value and salvage units were given every available facility to ensure the efficient execution of this important task.

REPAIR OF MOTOR TRANSPORT VEHICLES

68. The Army was responsible for repairing vehicles for the three Services, the result of which was that continual difficulties were created by the unjustified preference that was given to Army work and even the appointment of Air Force liaison officers at the Army repair shops (Central Spares Stores and Army Vehicle Parks) did not enable the Air Force to obtain fair treatment.

69. The Air Force was more mobile than the Army and, before an air force formation, newly transferred to the area of a particular Army, had become accustomed to the local procedure, it often had to move away again. The Air Force further suffered from protracted delays in deliveries by the Army, lengthy channels, and lack of interest. Spares were always in short supply due to the multiplicity of types and, in spite of all attempts to remedy matters, the shortages increased progressively. Quotas were fixed at 15% for the Air Force in the delivery of spares and in repair facilities. The Army, however, when fixing the capacity, deducted as a matter of course the large transport requirements of the Quartermaster General of the Army and allocated to the Air Force 15% of the remainder — only a fraction of the total capacity! In view of such treatment, the Air Force had to look for ways in which it could make itself independent of the Army and repair its own vehicles. Attempts were made to procure machine tools from home territory to train and employ inhabitants of the country as assistants and also to purchase independently spare parts from home industries. In this way independent air force repair shops were established and, as the Air Force moved forward, they left behind, where possible, a permanent and gradually increasing vehicle repair service operated by the local inhabitants. Finally, the Luftflotte erected its own front repair services for vehicle repairs, called K-services, with the help of the material from home territory and by utilising the resources of the country. The attempts of the Army to seize these services failed. The Luftflotte by means of so-called "workshop mirrors" (weekly performance reports) supervised the production and full employment of the separate repair services at the different subordinate H.Q.s (Luftgau, Fliegerkorps, Flakkorps, High Signals C.O.) and ascertained where it was necessary to make adjustments and where to concentrate. They succeeded, therefore, in spite of continually increasing difficulties (heavy demands on old and overstressed vehicles made by the bad roads, insufficient new parts and limited delivery of spares) in maintaining the required mobility.

PART 2.

CHAPTER XI

IDENTIFICATION AND CLASSIFICATION OF G.A.F. EQUIPMENT

General	Paragraph	1
Material Categories	Paragraphs	2—4
Reference Numbers	,,	5
Classification Letters	,,	6—10
Airframe and Engine Spares	,,	11—16
Airframe and Engine Accessories	,,	17
Equipment Markings	,,	18—21
Conclusion	,,	22—24

PART 2

CHAPTER XI

IDENTIFICATION AND CLASSIFICATION OF G.A.F. EQUIPMENT

General

1. Considerable difficulties have been experienced in determining the exact methods employed in the German Air Force to identify and classify equipment. Their system was decidedly more complex than our own and, although in some instances it provided "double-checks" against errors in typing or transmission faults in signals, it must be considered unnecessarily cumbersome when compared with the straightforward system of "Vocabulary section plus reference number" used in the R.A.F. No captured publication is available explaining their system satisfactorily in detail and the non-existence of any Equipment Specialists in the G.A.F. has resulted in our information being obtained by the interrogation of Engineer Beampte, Depot employees or Administrative Officers, whose knowledge of the subject was, as they were quick to admit, incomplete. The following facts, however, have been obtained from a variety of sources and may be considered as being sufficiently reliable to enable a reasonably clear picture of the German system to be obtained. In a few instances only logical supposition has been made by the G.A.F. personnel supplying the information.

Material Categories

2. All classes of equipment fell, in the first instance, within a Material Category and were grouped under a Material Category Number. (Stoffgliederungsziffern.) **To a limited extent** it is permissible to compare these numbers with the R.A.F. vocabulary sections, in that as "Section 1" or "Section 3" immediately indicates to an R.A.F. Equipment Officer "Hand Tools" and "Machine Tools" respectively, so in the G.A.F. did "Material Category 18" indicate "Bomb Release Gear" and "Material Category 38" — "Anti-Gas Equipment". The Material Categories were allotted by the Chief T.L.R. in O.K.L. and were (as is implied) solely a G.A.F. means of categorisation. It seems evident, however that the German Army and Navy had similar systems, as reference is made in a captured German publication (D. Luft 3051/1 "Handbook on the Administration of Equipment") to the use of three figure Material Category numbers in certain cases "...... to distinguish the items of equipment of the individual Arms of the Service...." For example:

Small Arms.   Material Category No. 1. =
Small Arms (Army).   ,,   ,,   ,, 001. =
Small Arms (G.A.F.)   ,,   ,,   ,, 101. =
Small Arms (Navy)   ,,   ,,   ,, 301. =

The list of Material Categories shown at the Appendix to this Chapter should be considered as covering solely G.A.F. Equipment, however, and if certain of the categories appear at first sight to cover items more appropriate to Army Units (e.g. Pioneer and Entrenching Tools) it should be remembered that for a long period of the war the Administrative Office was responsible for the entire Constructional and Building Organisation of the G.A.F., only relinquishing control to the Organisation Todt in January 1944.

3. Material Category numbers had no **essential** connection with the normal indenting procedure adopted by units although in certain instances they were quoted by the units for reasons which will be explained later. They were essentially a "catalogue" of **Industrial** production and were invariably quoted by the G.A.F. on their indents to Industry. It has not been possible to discover whether these material Categories were allotted arbitrarily or on a systematic basis.

4. The various "categories" of equipment were stored in the Equipment Depots in various Bezirke (Sections) and in consequence a unit initiating a demand was required to raise a separate demend form for items in different categories, in the same way as in the R.A.F. it is necessary to raise a separate Form 600, 674 or 1368 for items in different vocabulary sections. At Appendix "A" to this Chapter is a list of the various Material Categories. Cross reference to Part 2. Chapter VII Para. 17 (c) will provide an indication of the Bezirke in which they were stored, whilst reference to Appendix "B" to Part 2. Chap VII. will indicate the physical "location" of the various Bezirke.

Reference Numbers

5. A "block" of reference numbers was allotted to each Material Category Number (see Appendix "A") and the reference numbers in themselves were, therefore, an indication of the nature of the equipment. For example, any reference number between 33,000 and 33,999 **must** be associated with Category 1 equipment — Small Arms. Any reference number falling between 54,000 and 55,999 was associated with Category 21 — M.T. Equipment. Apart from the disadvantage of using long and unwieldy numbers, it is obvious that this provided a valuable insurance against clerical errors. In the R.A.F., of course, reference numbers may very frequently be repeated but 1B/1234 will be as unlike 7B/1234 as is chalk from cheese.

Classification Letters

6. At this point, it is necesary to explain that the G.A.F. adopted separate and distinct identification systems for (a) Airframe and Engine Spares, and (b) other equipment. The Airframe and Engine Spares system will be explained later but the "other equipment" was divided up into Groups and given "Classification" letters as follows:—

        F.L.   Aircraft and Ground Equipment.
        T.M.   Torpedoes and Mines Equipment.
        L.   Flak Equipment.
        L.N.   Signals Equipment.
        L.K.   M.T. Equipment.
        L.Ch.   Chemical Warfare Equipment.
        F.W.   Armaments and Bombs.
        F.B.   Photographic Equipment.
        L.F.   Special Parachute and Airborne Equipment.
        L.B.   Clothing and Personal Effects.
        L.W.   Meteorological Equipment.

7. These equipment Class Letters were also used by the German Army, and "common user" items between the two services retained the same

letters, although the reference numbers would n o t be the same. The Luftwaffe merely added the letter "L" before the Army letter, as indicated below:

Army Signals Equipment	— N.
G.A.F. Signals Equipment	— L.N.
Army Clothing	— B.
G.A.F. Clothing	— L.B.
Army M./T.	— K.
G.A.F. M./T.	— L.K.
Army Chemical Warfare Equipment	— Ch.
G.A.F. Chemical Warfare Equipment	— L.Ch.

8. The combination of letters used ensured that there were no duplications in lettering between items of solely G.A.F. or Army equipment.

9. **For all equipment other than airframe and engine spares it was the Class Letters, plus the reference number, that was used by units when demanding equipment through the normal chain. For example:**

F.B.   38742.

10. The above item is immediately known to be an item of photographic equipment; (a) because of its "Class Letters" and (b) because the reference number falls within the block allocated to Material Category 35. This number (F.B. 38742) is known as the "Anforderungs-Zeichen" number, or "Demand Reference Number".

Airframe and Engine Spares

11. The method adopted for referencing airframe and engines spares differed from that for other items of equipment and was itself sub-divided into two methods, i.e.

(i) Components.
(ii) Accessories.

The sense in which the G.A.F. employed the word "accessories" is somewhat obscure but an Engineer Beampte has described it as covering "items of airframe and engine spares common to several types of aircraft or engines". Further questioning of this official indicated that what they describe as "accessories" would probably cover the majority of our Aircraft General Spares in R.A.F. Vocabulary Section 28, and a fair number of the non "special to type" items in R.A.F. Sections 27 and 37.

12. To deal first with the "Components". These were divided up into a number of "Construction Groups" (Konstruktionsgruppe) which were arbitrarily decided upon by the aircraft or engine manufacturer. The following example of Construction Groups applies to a Ju 52. Generally speaking, groups 1 to 5 are the same for all aircraft, but obviously different types of aircraft will more readily lend themselves for division into certain set "groups" than others.

Construction Group.	**German.**	**English.**
1.	Rumpfwerk	Fuselage
2.	Fahrwerk	Undercarriage
3.	Leitwerk	Control Surfaces
4.	Steuerwerk	Flying Controls
5.	Tragwerk	Mainplanes
6.	Triebwerksgerüst	Power Unit Mounting
7.	Triebwerksanlage	Power Unit Installation
8.	Triebwerksbehälter	Fuel Tanks
9.	Ausrüstung	Aircraft Equipment

13. These nine groups were further divided into Main Assemblies (Baugruppen) which were sub-divided into Sub-Assemblies (Baureihe) which were sub-sub-divided into individual Components and/or parts. Each "division" and "sub-division" had a seperate identification number which began with the main construction group number as shown above.

14. To illustrate this system it is simpler to analyse a particular example and work backwards. Thus:—

        8 — 108B — 501 0315 is part of a rib in the port mainplane of an ME 108B aircraft, because:—

    8 = Material Category No. — (Airframes).
  108B = Type of Aircraft — (ME 108B).
    5 = Construction Group — Mainplanes.
   01 = A Port Mainplane.
   03 = A Rib in the Port Mainplane.
   15 = Part of a Rib in the Port Mainplane.

15. In actual practice it frequently occurred that the Material Category number was omitted and the item would be demanded as "108B — 501 — 0315".

16. The system for demanding engine spares (other than those vaguely described as "accessories") was identical with that described above for airframes. The engine was divided up into construction groups, but these obviously would vary according to the type of engine concerned. For example, the "Construction" groups for a small air-cooled radial engine would obviously differ from those for a 12 or 24 cylinder "in line" liquid cooled supercharged engine. But the basis on which the reference numbers was compiled was the same; i.e. first the material category number, which for engines was 9, followed by the construction group number, followed by whatever numbers represented the break-down of that group into assemblies, sub-assemblies, and parts. A typical (and quite imaginary) engine spare reference number, therefore, might be:

        9 — 801 — 415 — 1406.

In the above example:

    9 = Material Category Number (Engines).
  801 = Type of Engine (B.M.W. 801).
    4 = Construction Group — (say, lubrication system).
   15 = say, Scavenge Pump Assembly.
   14 = say, Piston in Pump Assembly.
   06 = say, Shackle or Bolt (peculiar to type) in Piston in Pump Assembly.

Airframe and Engine Accessories

17. Airframe and Engine accessories were demanded in a similar manner to the items of equipment "other than airframe and engine spares" except that the Material Category number was used in place of the "Class Letters" -- the reference numbers being taken from the blocks allocated to Material Categories 8 (aircraft) and 9 (Engines). For example:

        8 — 19437 or 9 — 18642.

Equipment Markings

18. Unless an item of equipment was of too delicate a nature, it was marked with the Anforderungs Zeichen number prior to delivery into the

Equipment Depots. In addition to this number, there appeared, usually but not invariably, other numbers which were without significance to G.A.F. demanding units, but which corresponded to some extent to the manufacturer's part numbers quoted on items of R.A.F. equipment. These numbers were:—

    (a) The "Gerat" or "Sach" number.
    (b) The "Werke" number.

19.   The literal translation of "Gerat" number is "Apparatus" number, and the difference between it and a "Sach" number (only one of which ever appeared) has been for a long time obscure. An explanation given by Oberstabsingenieur Keil, a Beampte employed in the Chief T.L.R. office of O.K.L., is that a "Gerat" number was so-called when the item of equipment was a purely "service" one, whereas, a "Sach" number was allotted to an item of equipment in the service but of purely commercial origin. The "Gerat" (or "Sach") number consisted of the Material Category (which was, as previously mentioned, essentially a link between O.K.L. and Industry rather than units and O.K.L.) followed by a three, four or five figure number. The first digit of this last number represented the "series" (or, as we would say "mark") of the equipment and the remaining digits the manufacturer's part number. Thus:— 2 — 1640 indicates that the item is in material category No. 2 (Machine Guns), it is the first series (Mark I), and the manufacturer's part number (to be used when O.K.L. places an order on Industry) is 640. It is an interesting point to note that the Anforderungs-Zeichen number (say F.W. 45674) remained the same irrespective of the "series" (or "mark") of the item, and the unit demanding F.W. 45674 would automatically receive 2 — 2640 or 2 — 3640, whichever was the latest item without so specifying in their demand.

20.   A certain amount of confusion has been caused to Allied investigators by the occasional discovery of an item of equipment which had a "Gerat" number consisting of an initial group of three figures instead of one or two. Thus:—

    102 — 1457 or 124 — 2371.

An explanation of this has been given by a Herr Hans Baudach, a civilian administrative employee in O.K.L. and is as follows:—

Towards the end of the war the number of "material categories" was increased from 95 to 108 or 109, and numbers **up to 109** still represent the normal Material Category number. The number 124, however, is unique. Material Category 24 covered the whole range of G.A.F. signals equipment. This range was so immense that it became necessary to allot a distinctive Material Category number to "Spares" as opposed to "main sets". Material Category 24, therefore, became "Main sets" only and all components and spares became Material Category 124.

21.   The other number, occasionally found on items of equipment, was the Werke (or Works) number. This number merely indicated the actual quantity of an item produced by Industry and proved very useful to the Allies in checking enemy production figures when enemy war material was captured. For identification and recording purposes it could be ignored.

Conclusion

22.   Basically, it would seem that the German system had little to commend it when compared with our own, and the slight "advantage" of a "double check" against clerical error (i.e. the "Class Letters" corresponding with the block of reference numbers in a particular Material

Category) is more than discounted by the long and unwieldy series of numbers and the fact that for an enormous proportion of the range (airframe and engine spares) the double check did not exist. The "construction group" system gave, it is claimed by G.A.F. personnel, an immediate indication of the "identity" of an item whereas, in the R.A.F., 36DD/4500 tells us nothing more than that it is a Rolls Royce engine spare — whether for Kestrel or Merlin, whether crankshaft or gudgeon pin, we cannot tell. On the other hand it must be remembered that the "construction groups" for different makes of engines varied so that, unless one were familiar with, say, a BMW. 801 engine, the inclusion in a reference number of "construction group 4" would not indicate whether the item was in the lubrication system, cooling system, or ignition system.

23. The construction groups for Airframes were, admittedly, more "constant" and numbers 1 to 5 could usually be relied upon to be the same for all aircraft. These "major components", however, are readily identified in the R.A.F. system by their segregation in Vocabulary Section 24, whilst the suffix letters provide an immediate indication of the aircraft type.

24. The G.A.F. method whereby the various "marks" or "series" of an item retained the same Demand Reference number is, perhaps, one respect in which, from the unit's point of view, their system may be better than our own. In other respects it would seem that there are no refinements which could be superimposed on the R.A.F. system.

APPENDIX "A"
to Part 2. Chap XI

LIST OF G.A.F. MATERIAL CATEGORIES

Material Category No.	Type of Equipment	Reference Numbers where known
1.	Small Arms, spares and accessories	33,000 — 33,999
2.	Machine Guns, spares and accessories	45,000 — 49,999 and 200,000 — 224,999
3.	Mortars, spares and accessories	Not known
4.	Close combat detonating and fuze **apparatus** — (see Mat.Cat.No.14).	73,200 — 73,499
5.	Guns, spares and accessories	Not known
6.	Aircraft Cannons	Not known
7.	Gun Mountings	Not known
8.	Airframes, spares and accessories	19,000 — 19,999 and 37,000 — 37,999 and 75,000 — 75,499
9.	Aero-Engines, propellers, spares and accessories	18,000 — 18,999
10.	Parachutes, aircraft rescue and safety equipment, Oxygen Equipment	29,600 — 30,699
11.	Sea rescue equipment for aircraft	36,000 — 36,999
12.	Marine craft, spares and accessories	85,000 — 85,999
13.	All kinds of ammunition	53,000 — 53,999 EXCEPT: 53,100 — 53,199) See 53,300 — 53,399) Mat. 53,416 — 53,429) Cats. 53,800 — 53,809) 57 & 18
14.	Close combat detonating and fuze **materials.** — (see Mat.Cat.No.4).	86,000 — 86,499
15.	Chemical Warfare materials	Not known
16—17.	No record of use	
18.	Bomb Release Gear	50,000 — 50,999 and 72,000 — 72,999 and 53,416 — 53,429
19.	Hydraulic, pneumatic and heating equipment in aircraft	21,000 — 21,999 and 32,000 — 32,999 and 34,000 — 34,999
20.	Horse-drawn vehicles and handcarts	Not known
21.	All M/T equipment	54,000 — 55,999
22.	General Tele-communications Equipment	Not known
23.	Bicycles and accessories	85,000 — 85,499
24.	All W/T and R/T Equipment	26,000 — 28,999
25.	Searchlight Equipment	Not known
26.	Electrical Equipment	56,000 — 56,999 and 32,000 — 32,999 and 34,000 — 34,999
27.	Observation and Survey Equipment	52,000 — 52,999
28.	Bridge Construction Equipment	Not known
29.	Pioneer and Entrenching Tools	58,000 — 58,999
30.	Engineering Tools	59,000 — 59,499
31.	No record of use	

32.	Camouflage material	59,500 — 60,999
33.	Fire-fighting Equipment	61,000 — 61,999
34.	Armoury Equipment	62,000 — 62,999
35.	Photographic Equipment	38,000 — 42,999 and 75,500 — 75,999
36.	Medical Equipment	Not known
37.	Veterinary Equipment	Not known
38.	Anti-gas Equipment	64,000 — 64,999
39.	Sundry Departmental Equipment	30,700 — 30,999
40.	Workshop and Tradesmen's Equipment	68,000 — 69,999
41.	Airmen's Clothing	Not known
42.	No record of use	
43.	Printed publications	80,000 — 80,499
44.	Drawing and Office Equipment	51,000 — 51,999
45.	Rations	Not known
46.	Saddlery and Harness gear	Not known
47.	P.O.L. and cleaning materials	43,000 — 44,999
48.	Works and buildings materials	70,000 — 71,999
49.	P.T. and Sport Gear	Not known
50.	Dog Equipment	Not known
51.	No record of use	20,000 — 20,999 and 22,000 — 22,999
52.	Aircraft instruments	20,000 — 20,999 and 22,000 — 22,999
53.	Balloon apparatus	Not known
54.	Meteorological Equipment	76,000 — 76,999
55.	Balloon Barrage Equipment	Not known
56.	Railway rolling stock and construction Equipment	Not known
57.	Aircraft Servicing Equipment	65,000 — 66,999 and 53,100 — 53,199 and 53,300 — 53,339 and 53,800 — 53,809
58.	Tent Equipment	67,000 — 67,999
59.	Barrack Equipment	Not known
60—70.	No record of use	
71.	Predictor and computing Equipment	Not known
72—74.	No record of use	
75.	Navigational Equipment, excluding wireless	23,000 — 23,999
76—79.	No record of use	
80.	Torpedoes	Not known
81—92.	No record of use	
93.	Instructional and practice Equipment	Not known
94.	Target Recognition Material	Not known

www.ingramcontent.com/pod-product-compliance
Lightning Source LLC
Chambersburg PA
CBHW080357170426
43193CB00016B/2746